ON THE RECEPTION OF THE HETERODOX INTO THE ORTHODOX CHURCH

THE PATRISTIC CONSENSUS AND CRITERIA

Left front center: Saint Auxentios of Mount Katirli (+1757), spiritual father of Patriarch Cyril V (+1775) of Constantinople blessing the Council of Three Patriarchs (Constantinople, Jerusalem, and Alexandria) in 1755 and the adoption of its Encyclical whose policy Antioch also later accepted. Right front center: Saint Hermogenes the Patriarch of Moscow and all Russia (+1612) blessing the convening of the 1620 Moscow Council under his successor and disciple Patriarch Philaret of Moscow (+1633). Artwork by Joseph Kulits.

ON THE RECEPTION OF THE HETERODOX INTO THE ORTHODOX CHURCH

The Patristic Consensus and Criteria

An Orthodox Ethos Publication

Uncut Mountain Press

ON THE RECEPTION OF THE HETERODOX
INTO THE ORTHODOX CHURCH:
The Patristic Consensus and Criteria
© 2023
Uncut Mountain Press

uncutmountainpress.com

Cover Artwork: George Weis

Interior Artwork: Joseph Kulits, Iconography from Uncut Mountain Supply or public domain, unless otherwise stated.

Scriptural quotations are primarily taken from the New King James Version. The authors have emended some quotations to better reflect the original Greek text.

An Orthodox Ethos Publication.
https://www.orthodoxethos.com/about

On the Reception of the Heterodox into the Orthodox Church: The Patristic Consensus and Criteria.—1st ed.

ISBN (Hardcover): 978-1-63941-027-9
ISBN (Softcover): 978-1-63941-028-6

I. Orthodox Christian Ecclesiology
II. Orthodox Christian Sacraments
III. Orthodox Christian History

Go therefore and make disciples of all the nations, baptizing them in the name of the Father and of the Son and of the Holy Spirit, teaching them to observe all things that I have commanded you; and lo, I am with you always, even to the end of the age.

— The Lord
(Matthew 28:19-20)

Christ the Vine

CONTENTS

* indicates first appearance of a glossary term.

LIST OF ILLUSTRATIONS

PREFACE

What is the patristic* consensus vis-a-vis the rites of the heterodox? What are the criteria by which the Holy Fathers determined the application of economy in the reception of converts? Which are the presuppositions that must be met before a temporary, pastoral diversion from evangelical precision can be implemented in a salvific way—without overturning Orthodox dogma and undermining the Orthodox *phronema*?

These are some of the most important and pressing questions facing the Church's mission today, with answers urgently needed most especially in missionary lands. These questions must be answered collectively and decisively by today's Orthodox Church, in the tried-and-true Orthodox conciliar manner, based upon the patristic consensus and criteria. The extensive and unprecedented examination of this subject that you now hold in your hands will prove to be of immense value in this process for the Church catholic.

Conversions to Orthodoxy worldwide are at the highest levels since the first millennium. We have, in terms of mission, returned to a pre-Constantine status quo in much of the western world, where the Church is largely made up of adult converts who are passing through the catechumenate. Thus, for the good estate of the Church, especially in missionary lands, proper catechism and reception of the Holy Mysteries in the process of initiation is of the greatest importance. The immediate establishment and future growth of the House of God largely depends upon the expert craftsmanship of the builders as they lay the foundation stones, sealing and uniting each one, one at a time. If the Lord's workmen are operating on the basis of a mistaken method of construction, one which does not take into proper consideration expert specifications and essential presuppositions, the consequences may, sooner or later, be catastrophic. It is not a question of if, but when, an earthquake will strike and thus expose the ignorance of the engineers' design and the shoddiness of the builders' workmanship.

The significance of this book for the Church at this time can be likened to the necessity of both following the chief engineers' designs and the master builders' methods in the construction of one's home. Without these, the builders largely labor in vain and for vanity's sake. So, too, following the evangelical and patristic designs for initiation into, and dwelling within, the House of God is absolutely essential if the inhabitants are to "put on Christ" and the Church is to be built up. Each one of us must "take heed how [we] build" up the Church, "for other foundation can no man lay than that [which] is laid, which is Jesus Christ" (1 Cor. 3: 10-11).

A mindful observer today, however, notes that there is confusion among many who have been charged with the task of the mystagogue— the initiator into the Mystery of Christ and the Mysteries of the Body of Christ. Some pastors are unknowingly—and unevenly—implementing decisions which are expressing an ecclesiological* outlook which they themselves otherwise reject. Even as they are proclaiming to the world "the best kept secret"—that *the One Church* founded on Pentecost is the Orthodox Church—they are carrying out pastoral decisions of the greatest import in the lives of their faithful which essentially deny this proclamation. But, just as "every house divided against itself shall not stand" (Matt 12:25), so too continuing in such inner confusion brings ever greater degrees of instability.

At stake here is not only the proper ecclesiastical approach and the necessary prerequisites of pastoral economy, but also the very identity of the Body of Christ and the integrity of the dogma of the Church. These two—dogma and ethos, ecclesiology and pastoral economy—are inseparable and interdependent. This unity points us to the essential and perennial interpretative key of the Church's practice in the reception of converts—the twofold governance of *akrivia* and *oikonomia*, by which the managers of the household of Faith, the "economists of the Spirit," regulate the spiritual affairs of those being saved. These two "wings" of the Dove's pastoral management are so important that, whether one fails to grasp the wisdom of this "key" or rejects it altogether as the "key" which opens the door of understanding the patristic approach, his misfortune is the same: an inevitable fall from the Orthodox dogma of the Church.

This failure is often reached due to another failure: not following the hierarchy of things. For, if, as is often the case today, one who seeks to apprehend the identity of the Church and boundaries of the Body begins at the end with the outcome of the Church's pastoral management and economic regulation in the sea of history, he has the order of things backwards and is ignoring the proper hierarchy. It is essential that we begin with Revelation, with the Incarnation and its continuation, the Church—Her nature, identity, boundaries—and *only then* examine Her journey through history and Her shepherds' pastoral management of the flock. Christ and His Body, the Church, are the same *yesterday, and today, and forever* (Heb. 13:8), even if His appearance may change from that of an infant to that of one crucified and buried, resurrected and ascended, or come to judge the world, or from a small house-Church in Jerusalem to the Hospital of the Empire and once again to a Church in the catacombs.

We must respect the order of things and begin with the identity once delivered before we set out to interpret the implications of economical exceptions in history. Thus, for example, before we enter behind the veil of the Mysteries we must encounter the Face of Christ in the *kerygma* (preaching). Again, before we can speak authoritatively, from experience, of the inner workings of the Body, we must be initiated properly and fully into the Life and Way of that Body. Only from within the experience of the Body of Christ, of the Mysteries in the Mystery of the Incarnation, can we understand the working-out of the Economy of Salvation which is guided directly by the free and all-wise hand of Christ. And only when we are well grounded in the *faith* in the Church *once delivered* (a "given" that, like all dogma, does not develop or change) are we able to understand the patristic and canonical* wisdom surrounding the occasional, exceptional economic reception of the heterodox into the Church.

God is not only over all His created works with mercy (Ps. 144:9) but even over His work of salvation and even over His own commandments. He is not "under" them, bound or limited by them. Therefore, just as the order of nature was overcome, but not undone, in His divine *kenosis* (self-emptying), the God of all being conceived in the womb of a Virgin, so too, if and when *He* so wills, He Himself may set aside, for a time, according to need, the *akrivia* of His own divine order of salvation for the sake of some special *oikonomia-philanthropia*. The thief on the cross, who was not born of water and the Spirit (Jn. 3:5) and yet nevertheless entered Paradise on the strength of his confession of Christ's divinity, is such a unique instance of *oikonomia*, which, however, did not thereby overturn in the least the commandment to baptize. Thus, such exceptional "economizing" can never become the rule or be done when it in any way undermines or compromises the identity and nature of the Church or Her Mysteries.

As an erudite observer wrote nearly 100 years ago, "The Church is fully *tamiouchos* [treasurer], possessed of stewardship in her own household, and in her exercise of *oikonomia*, *philanthropia* must relax *akrivia* for the good of human souls and for her own cause, whenever need demands and the condescension is possible."[1] And as St. Theophylact of Bulgaria writes, he who does anything "by economy, does not do so…because it is a good thing in and of itself, but because it is needful to do so in this particular circumstance."[2]

It is clear then that while *oikonomia* is an irremovable component of the Body in the hands of the shepherds, it is also governed by presuppositions, such as the existence of a particular and pressing need, never impairing the well-being of the Church, never undermining Her identity and boundaries, and always serving the salvation of the members of the Body. Contrary to contemporary claims of the unlimited authority of the overseer, there is nothing arbitrary or purely subjective about the exercise of *oikonomia*. "*Philanthropia* can justify *oikonomia* only so long as it does not produce *anomia* [lawlessness]."[3] The undermining of the boundaries and blurring of the identity of the Body so prevalent today in ecumenical circles is a contemporary example of such lawlessness.

This short review of the *akrivia* - *oikonomia* interpretative key is necessary as a preparation to reading this book, for without it, it is not only both impossible to properly understand the Church's pastoral practice in the reception of the heterodox but also impossible to remain faithful to the Church's identity, boundaries and mission. It is these which are not only the casualty of negligence or ignorance but also the target of those today who are carried off by the demonically inspired heresy* of syncretistic ecumenism.[4]

It is not surprising that the crucial matter of the proper reception of the heterodox into the Church is found at the epicenter of both the mission and the dogma of the Church, and in both the challenge of strange doctrines and destructive practices. Distortion is not limited to theology and church administration. In many parishes much distortion

---

1   Canon J.A. Douglas, "The Orthodox Principle of Economy, and Its Exercise," *The Christian East*, 1932, 13:3, 4; pp. 91-98.

2   Theophylact, *The Explanation of The Epistle of Saint Paul to the Galatians*, pp. 69-70.

3   Douglas, ibid.

4   According to the respected professor emeritus of Dogmatic Theology at the University of Thessaloniki, Demetrios Tselengides, Saint Ephraim of Katounakia famously said that, after fervent prayer, Christ indicated to him that contemporary ecumenism has a spirit of wickedness and is dominated by unclean spirits.

and confusion exists today as to the boundaries and identity of the Church. There is no coherent or consistent consideration of heterodox rites, often even within the same parish or diocese. It is commonplace to hear of a catechumen who entreats to be baptized to be flatly denied on account of a diocesan policy which indiscriminately, even without need, implements economy. It is also possible to hear of catechumens who are not baptized because their heterodox baptism is considered to be "the one baptism" (even if they were never triply immersed) but are nevertheless subsequently joined in the Mystery of Matrimony (by the same priest) because "there are no sacraments outside the Church."

In addition to a general confusion there are ecclesiological theories being advanced which consider the heterodox and the Orthodox to be in partial or incomplete communion[5] and, thus, there is no more talk of return but only of "reconciliation." Therefore, the thinking goes, those turning to the Church from Catholicism, for example, are not *now* being initiated *into the Body* but simply being "reconciled" to the Orthodox Church. Such a category is, of course, not commemorated anywhere in the canonical or patristic literature, such as St. Basil the Great's three-fold classification of those returning to the Church.

The implication of this stance is that fundamental differences in faith no longer prevent us from effecting a *de facto* union with the heterodox. There is implicitly a new confession of faith being posited, one which says that the "one baptism" is every baptism, whether it be performed within the Church or outside thereof, by an Orthodox Christian or by the heterodox, according to apostolic form or not. Furthermore, this new confession of faith also holds that, since we share the "one baptism" with the heterodox and enjoy so-called partial union with them, they too are *members of the Church*—even if perhaps "ecclesiastically lacking" in some way. The attempted implementation of such a theory and practice of reception of the heterodox in the near future, which is rumored to be on the horizon, would certainly conclusively confirm the timeliness and need of this study.

In light of these and other innovative theories which "reshape" the Face of Christ and His Body, the authors of this present work redoubled their efforts to strictly follow the Holy Fathers and be successors in every way of the recently glorified Saints of the Church. Both in their writings

---

5   One hears sentiments such as the Orthodox and the heterodox "are united by baptism in the Trinity and participate in the ecumenical movement as baptized Christians but are in a state of division because they can't express one faith."

and in our own personal encounters with them or their disciples and those directly guided by them with regard to reception into the Church, we have found great clarity and consistency with the patristic consensus. St. Paisios of Mt. Athos and his disciples, St. Iakovos of Evia and his spiritual children, and Elder* Ephraim of Arizona and his spiritual children, to name just three of the Church's recent holy ones, all confirmed and implemented the teachings and practice of the whole host of saints and canons commemorated in this book. We were greatly aided and encouraged seeing this oneness of mind and practice among the saints of our day[6]—a sure sign of the continued presence and inspiration of the Holy Spirit.

It is perhaps this struggle to be faithful to the Holy Fathers of this and every age that makes this present study immensely valuable for every pious Orthodox Christian, whether clergyman or layman. The scope and depth of this study likewise makes it unprecedented in any language, as does the angle from which it has been written—from within the context of mission among the heterodox.

All of this and more makes this present work essential reading for all who would acquire the patristic mind on the matter and implement it with discernment in their parishes and lives.

Holy and Great Wednesday 2023

6   See chapter 17.

Holy Trinity (Andrei Rublev, 15th century)

INTRODUCTION

The teaching concerning the reception of the heterodox[7] into the Orthodox Church continues to be a topic of debate and even controversy, particularly among Orthodox Christians in the West where patristic commentaries on the canons and the testimonies of God-bearing saints and elders are not well known. While there are good patristic writings on this subject, new articles on this topic have continued to appear which have received considerable attention and which criticize the practice of receiving into the Church by baptism those who have been "baptized" in a heterodox group in the name of the Holy Trinity.[8, 9, 10] Such articles may contain quotes from saints, canons, and councils of the Church but arrive at mistaken conclusions about ecclesiology[11] and the reception of converts due to misquoting, misinterpreting, inaccurately translating, and taking texts out of context (whether intentionally or unintentionally). Some of these articles contain claims and content that have not been thoroughly addressed in a single text. When saints, canons, and councils are misquoted and misinterpreted in this manner, the

---

7   The term "heterodox" and "heretic" are synonymous. In the context of reception into the Church, these terms are used interchangeably to refer to those who identify themselves as Christians but who are not part of the Orthodox Church. "Heterodox" is often used in place of "heretic" due to the abrasive connotation that has developed around the term "heretic" in the West.

8   Yakovlev, *Sacramental Rigourism: Tradition or Modern Phenomenon?*

9   Cabe, *Rebaptism: Patristic Consensus or Innovation?*

10   Justinianeus, *Why I Don't Support Re-Baptism.*

11   Ecclesiology has to do with what is meant dogmatically by "the Church."

impression can be given that an author is "following the Fathers" while arriving at conclusions contrary to the teachings of the Fathers, resulting in further confusion among the faithful. False and misleading teachings about ecclesiology and the reception of converts are unfortunately not only found in a few articles on the Internet but are even repeated by some Orthodox priests, bishops, and seminary professors. The purpose of this book is to present the teachings of the Holy Fathers and Ecumenical Councils on the boundaries of the Church and the reception of converts, and to explain why and how critics of the patristic teaching on this topic arrive at their mistaken conclusions.

A few of the common criticisms one finds against the patristic teaching on the reception of the heterodox include the following: The Apostolic Canons are no longer relevant; the teaching of St. Cyprian of Carthage that there is no grace* in the mysteries of schismatics and heretics is not accepted by the Orthodox Church; the Orthodox Church instead accepts that there is "ecclesiality" and the "presence of the Holy Spirit" in the mysteries of heretics and schismatics; those who are baptized by heretics in the name of the Holy Trinity have a "valid" baptism; those who receive "valid" baptisms outside of the Orthodox Church must not be received into the Orthodox Church by baptism; St. Nikodemos the Hagiorite and others who have agreed with St. Cyprian of Carthage do not represent Orthodox tradition; and that distinctions made by St. Nikodemos about exactitude (akriveia) and economy (oikonomia)[12] in the reception of heretics constitute a "novel" teaching invented by St. Nikodemos in the 18th century. This book will demonstrate how these assertions are based on a misunderstanding of Church history, mistranslations of canons, misunderstandings regarding the teachings of the Fathers, a lack of awareness of what constitutes authoritative teaching in the Church, and a reliance on the writings of a few recent saints who were unfortunately influenced by the

---

12 Economy or *Oikonomia* means "the management of the house." It is an exercise of stewardship by the Church in allowing deviations from the exactitude of the standard (*akriveia*) when necessary for particular circumstances and for the salvation of the many. *Oikonomia* cannot become *akriveia* but is temporary, circumstantial, and driven by necessity as this text will discuss further. See also Chapter 8.

heterodox ecclesiology of the post-Schism Latin Scholastics. The problematic approach to the canons and Fathers found in such writings often leads to a heretical ecclesiology (reminiscent of Vatican II) which separates Christ from His body (the Church) and reduces the Mystery of Baptism to a magical formula that transmits the grace of the Holy Spirit regardless of whether the person administering the baptism is an organic member of the Orthodox Church, which is the body of Christ.

This book will also demonstrate that the ecclesiology of St. Cyprian of Carthage is the ecclesiology of the Apostles and of the Orthodox Church despite the fact that some councils and canons historically allowed for the reception into the Church of certain heterodox groups by chrismation with certain presuppositions. It will also be shown that when the Church has received heterodox by chrismation this was never accompanied by an acknowledgement of the presence of grace in heterodox mysteries but was allowed by economy due to particular needs of the Church and was permitted only if the convert had received the apostolic form of baptism from the heterodox (three full immersions in the name of the Holy Trinity). We will also show that those baptized by the heterodox without the apostolic form (three immersions in the name of the Trinity) were historically required to be received into the Orthodox Church by baptism. Latins around the time of the Schism who began to baptize with a single immersion, as well as Orthodox who were influenced by the Latins to deviate from the apostolic form of baptism, have historically been considered as unbaptized and in need of baptism in three immersions according to the apostolic requirement.

This book will examine the sources of the patristic teaching on the reception of heterodox into the Orthodox Church, discuss and examine various criticisms raised against this teaching, and present the patristic consensus and criteria regarding the reception of the heterodox into the Church.

St. Cyprian of Carthage (+258)
Feast Day: August 31

CHAPTER 1

"Ecclesiality" and the Presence of the Holy Spirit in Rites of the Heterodox

Critics of patristic ecclesiology often assert that by allowing some heterodox to be received by chrismation, the Orthodox Church has historically acknowledged the "presence of the Holy Spirit" in the mysteries of the heterodox. While many who have advocated for the reception of Latins, Protestants, and other heterodox by chrismation have taught that the mysteries of the heterodox do not have grace, and that the empty forms of heterodox mysteries are filled with grace only when the convert is received into the Orthodox Church; there have been increasing efforts to claim that the reception of the heterodox by chrismation proves that the Orthodox Church acknowledges the presence of the Holy Spirit and "ecclesiality" in heterodox mysteries. This view implies that the heterodox are in some way already part of the Church while not being in communion with the Orthodox Church and while not confessing the Orthodox faith. Such assertions about "ecclesiality" in heterodox groups and the presence of the Holy Spirit in heterodox mysteries are a dangerous departure from Orthodox ecclesiology and can lead to the embrace of the pan-heresy of Ecumenism[13] which pursues

---

13 St. Justin Popovich and other modern saints have referred to Ecumenism as a "pan-heresy," meaning that the Ecumenical Movement strives to create unity among "Christians" regardless of dogmatic truth. When external unity is pursued without unity of Faith, such a unity becomes a "pan-heresy" in that it is a uniting of all heresies.

external unity with various heretical bodies without unity of faith. The concern that receiving the heterodox by a means other than baptism can lead to a heretical ecclesiology was expressed by St. Cyprian of Carthage:

> For if [the heretics] shall see that it is determined and decreed by our judgment and sentence, that the baptism wherewith they are there baptized is considered just and legitimate, they will think that they are justly and legitimately in possession of the Church also, and the other gifts of the Church; nor will there be any reason for their coming to us, when, as they have baptism, they seem also to have the rest. But further, when they know that there is no baptism without, and that no remission of sins can be given outside the Church, they more eagerly and readily hasten to us, and implore the gifts and benefits of the Church our Mother, assured that they can in no wise attain to the true promise of divine grace unless they first come to the truth of the Church.[14]

Objecting to the ecclesiology of St. Cyprian which states that there are no true mysteries outside of the Church, one critic asserts:

> On the contrary, my position, and that of the majority of the Church today and historically, is that there is a degree of validity to the sacramental practice of heterodox confessions which find their origin in the Orthodox Church (Roman Catholics, Oriental Orthodox, Old Calendarist schismatics, etc.) This is demonstrated by the three methods of reception employed by our Church in the reception of converts: baptism, chrismation, confession. Apart from baptism, each method assumes the ontological, and not merely formal presence of the former method. To chrismate assumes the presence of a baptism, to receive by confession assumes the presence of the previous two, and to receive a clergyman by

---

14   Cyprian of Carthage, *Epistle LXXII* to Jubaianus (ANF 5:385).

confession assumes the same of his ordination (and therefore ecclesiality).[15]

[The] onus is on the rigourist[16] to demonstrate that the position of St. Cyprian is the historic, normative position of the Church to the degree that universalizing statements are justified. Indeed, they must demonstrate that the logic articulated in economic theory is not merely a post facto phenomenon, but was the logic inherent to the ruling of the ancient Church... This article will demonstrate that each of these premises is faulty. First that St. Cyprian's view is universal and normative in the Church, and second that the economic theory is the fundamental and valid way of interpreting any instance where the Church prescriptively receives individuals by any method other than baptism... If the economic theory is not valid, this implies that sacraments are not merely present in valid 'form' but have an ontological presence by the movement of the Holy Spirit.[17]

The above quotes are representative of those who attempt to promote a false ecclesiology by asserting that there is grace and ecclesiality in mysteries performed outside of the Orthodox Church. These authors also display an alien spirit from the Fathers concerning the reception of the heterodox when using language such as "normative" (which, importantly, is a criteria the Fathers never use) and "economic theory."[18] The various canons, councils, and quotes from saints which have been used by likeminded critics of patristic ecclesiology to arrive at such false conclusions will be examined further in the following chapters.

---

15 Yakovlev, op. cit.

16 The author doesn't define what a "rigourist" is but uses the term pejoratively to criticize those who believe there is no grace in the mysteries of heretics and that heretics should be received by baptism.

17 Ibid.

18 The "economic theory" refers pejoratively to the teaching of St. Nikodemos the Hagiorite (but in reality repeating the Fathers) that all heretics should be received into the Church by baptism according to the exactitude (*akriveia*) of the canons, and those canons that allow for the reception of heretics by chrismation do so only by economy (*oikonomia*), which is a temporary deviation from the standard due to necessity.

Baptism of the Ethiopian Eunuch (Russian)

CHAPTER 2

The Holy Scriptures on Baptism and the Church

The Lord, God and Savior Jesus Christ, during His earthly ministry, said to the Pharisee Nicodemus, "Most assuredly, I say to you, unless one is born of water and the Spirit, he cannot enter the kingdom of God."[19] Prior to His crucifixion, the Lord promised His disciples that He would send down the "Spirit of truth" Who "will guide you into all truth."[20] After the Lord's glorious Resurrection,

---

19 John 3:5. The phrases "kingdom of God" or "kingdom of heaven" need to be understood in an Orthodox and patristic manner as they are often misunderstood by the heterodox (and sadly even many Orthodox today held captive by some heterodox ideas), leading to confusion regarding teachings of the Lord and of the Fathers with respect to baptism. As Fr. John Romanides explains, "the phrase 'kingdom of God' which makes it a creation of God instead of the uncreated ruling power of God. What is amazing is that the term 'kingdom of God' appears not once in the original Greek of the New Testament. Not knowing that the 'rule' or 'reign of God' is the correct translation of the Greek 'Basileia tou Theou,' Vaticanians, Protestants and even many Orthodox today, do not see that the promise of Christ to his apostles in Mt.16:28, Lk. 9:27 and Mk. 9:1, i.e. that they will see God's ruling power, was fulfilled during the Transfiguration which immediately follows in the above three gospels. Here Peter, James and John see Christ as the Lord of Glory i.e. as the source of God's uncreated 'glory' and 'basileia' i.e. uncreated ruling power, denoted by the uncreated cloud or glory which appeared and covered the three of them during the Lord of Glory's Transfiguration. It was by means of His power of Glory that Christ, as the pre-incarnate Lord (Yahweh) of Glory, had delivered Israel from Its Egyptian slavery and lead It to freedom and the land of promise. The Greek text does not speak about the 'Basileion (kingdom) of God,' but about the 'Basileia (rule or reign) of God,' by means of His uncreated glory and power" (Romanides, *The Cure of the Neurobiological Sickness of Religion*, Part 1, Section 5.).

20 John 16:13

He confirmed His promise to His disciples saying, "Behold, I send the Promise of My Father upon you; but tarry in the city of Jerusalem until you are endued with power from on high."[21] Before His glorious Ascension, the Lord said to His disciples, "All authority has been given to Me in heaven and on earth. Go therefore and make disciples of all the nations, baptizing them in the name of the Father and of the Son and of the Holy Spirit, teaching them to observe all things that I have commanded you; and lo, I am with you always, even to the end of the age."[22] This promise of the Lord was fulfilled on the day of Pentecost when the Holy Spirit fell upon the Apostles in the form of "divided tongues, as of fire" and "they were all filled with the Holy Spirit."[23] After receiving the Holy Spirit, the Apostles travelled to the ends of the earth preaching the gospel, baptizing, and ordaining bishops and priests as leaders of local churches.

When Saul persecuted the Apostolic Church, Christ appeared to him and revealed that He is the Church, saying, "Saul, Saul, why are you persecuting Me?"[24] Through baptism and the laying on of hands, the Apostles bestowed the Holy Spirit on others,[25] granting "remission of sins"[26] unto salvation,[27] transforming man into a "new creation."[28] Those baptized by the Apostles and their successors were "buried with Him through baptism into death... just as Christ was raised from the dead by the glory of the Father."[29] For "by one Spirit we were all baptized into one body."[30]

The Church established by Christ through the Apostles is guided by the "Spirit of truth"[31] and the Church is the "pillar and

---

21   Luke 24:49
22   Matt. 28:18-20
23   Acts 2:3-4
24   Acts 9:4
25   Acts 8:17
26   Acts 2:38
27   1 Peter 3:21
28   2 Cor. 5:17
29   Rom. 6:4, Col 2:2
30   1 Cor. 12:13
31   John 16:13

ground of the truth."[32] In the Church there is "one Lord, one faith, one baptism."[33] The Lord Jesus Christ has "one body,"[34], Christ is "the head of the body,"[35] and the "one body" of Christ is united by a common faith.[36] The Lord said, "I am the vine, you are the branches. He who abides in Me, and I in him, bears much fruit; for without Me you can do nothing."[37] To abide in Christ is to remain in the unity of His "one body" and in spiritual communion with Him through keeping "His commandments."[38] The Lord said that he "who eats My flesh and drinks my blood abides in Me, and I in him."[39] The Holy Mysteries cannot be separated from Christ and Christ cannot be separated from His Church. The Mysteries by which man is purified* and becomes a "partaker of the divine nature"[40] can only exist in Christ's "one body."

Those who preach heresy, a teaching not handed down by the Apostles, are accursed.

> But even if we, or an angel from heaven, preach any other gospel to you than what we have preached to you, let him be accursed. As we have said before, so now I say again, if anyone preaches any other gospel to you than what you have received, let him be accursed.[41]

Those who teach something contrary to that which has been received from the Apostles preach "another Christ." Those who cause "divisions and offenses, contrary to the doctrine which you learned," we are to "turn away from them."[42] Those who cause

---

32   1 Tim. 3:15
33   Eph. 4:5-6
34   1 Cor. 12:12
35   Col. 1:18
36   Eph. 4:5-6
37   John 15:5
38   1 John 5:2
39   John 6:56
40   2 Peter 1:4
41   Gal. 1:8-9
42   Rom. 16:17

schisms "don't have the Spirit."[43] If we follow into schism those who preach "another gospel" we are following those who are "accursed" and who preach "another Christ" and who "don't have the Spirit."

The Church has authority from Christ to "bind and loose,"[44] and when the Church declares "anathema"* against a heresy, those in the Church who continue to believe the anathematized heresy, and those who break off from the Church to persist in heresy, are condemned unless they repent of their heresy and remain united in the unity of the faith of the one Church. The Lord said:

> Moreover if thy brother shall trespass against thee, go and tell him his fault between thee and him alone: if he shall hear thee, thou hast gained thy brother. But if he will not hear thee, then take with thee one or two more, that in the mouth of two or three witnesses every word may be established. And if he shall neglect to hear them, tell it unto the church: but if he neglect to hear the church, let him be unto thee as an heathen man and a publican. Verily I say unto you, Whatsoever ye shall bind on earth shall be bound in heaven: and whatsoever ye shall loose on earth shall be loosed in heaven. Again I say unto you, That if two of you shall agree on earth as touching any thing that they shall ask, it shall be done for them of my Father which is in heaven. For where two or three are gathered together in my name, there am I in the midst of them.[45]

Blessed Theophylact (+1108), in his patristic commentary on the Holy Scriptures, states:

> ... the wrongdoer is considered as a publican or a Gentile, that is, a sinner or an unbeliever.... If you, He [the Lord] says, who have been wronged deem the wrongdoer a publican and a Gentile, he shall be so in heaven as well.

---

43 Jude 1:19
44 Matt 17:18
45 Matt 18:15–20

And if you loose, that is, forgive him, he shall be forgiven in heaven as well.[46]

The claim that the charismatic boundaries of the Church are broader than the canonical boundaries of the Church (and that the Holy Spirit works through sacraments outside of the unity of the one Church) contradicts the Lord's teaching that what is bound on earth by the Apostles (and their true successors) remains bound in Heaven.[47] The decisions of the Church on earth remain in force in eternity, as Christ is the Church.[48]

The Lord says also in the Gospel according to St. John:

I am the vine, ye are the branches: He that abideth in me, and I in him, the same bringeth forth much fruit: for without me ye can do nothing.[49]

To abide in the Church is to abide in Christ. Without abiding in Christ and the Church through obedience to Christ and reception of the Holy Mysteries, a person cannot bear spiritual fruit.

In the book of Acts, St. Philip preached the gospel in Samaria and baptized those who believed, yet those baptized did not receive the Holy Spirit. The Apostles Peter and John had to go to Samaria and lay hands on those who were baptized that they might then receive the Holy Spirit.[50] As St. Bede the Venerable explains, those in Samaria did not receive the Holy Spirit because Philip was one of the seven deacons and deacons did not have the authority to bestow the Holy Spirit on others through baptism. Only the Apostles had

---

46   Theophylact, *The Explanation of the Holy Gospel According to St. Matthew*, 156-157.

47   While the charismatic boundaries of the Church do not extend beyond the canonical boundaries of the Church, one could say that within the canonical boundaries of the Church the Holy Spirit does not work within each person to the same degree, but only to the extent to which a person is struggling against the sinful passions* and is living the ascetical life of the Church so that he may truly become a living temple of the Holy Spirit. See Vlachos, *Empirical Dogmatics, Volume 2*, pp. 250-252 and Novoselov, "Understanding the Important Distinction between Church-Organism vs. Church-Organization."

48   Acts 9:4

49   John 15:5

50   Acts 8:5, 14-17

the authority to bestow the Holy Spirit on others, and they granted this authority only to bishops and priests.[51] While some have claimed that those in Samaria did not receive the Holy Spirit when St. Philip baptized them because they "had only been baptized in the name of the Lord Jesus,"[52] this wording is used elsewhere in the Holy Scripture in cases where the Holy Spirit was received at the time of baptism when such baptisms were done by St. Paul or another of the Apostles who had the authority to bestow the Holy Spirit on others.[53] Being baptized "in the name of the Lord Jesus" was used as another way of saying that they were baptized in the name of the Holy Trinity. St. Bede the Venerable here agrees with the interpretation of St. Cyprian of Carthage, that while St. Philip baptized those in Samaria correctly, those in Samaria did not receive the Holy Spirit until the Apostles laid hands on them since St. Philip was a deacon and did not have the authority to bestow the Holy Spirit on others through baptism.[54]

St. Nikodemos the Hagiorite, in his commentary on Canon 49 of the Holy Apostles, also agrees with this interpretation of St. Bede and St. Cyprian when he says:

> Note... that all the Canons of the Apostles that relate to and speak of baptism mention only Bishops and Priests. For they alone have permission to baptize, and deacons and other clergymen have not.[55]

While the Lord established the rule (canon) that man must be baptized to receive the Holy Spirit and enter the kingdom of heaven, the Lord and His Church, through the Holy Spirit, have nevertheless made exceptions by economy. The Lord said to the thief on the cross, who had not received baptism by water, "today you will be with me in Paradise."[56] When St. Peter doubted as to

---

51   The Venerable Bede, *Commentary on the Acts of the Apostles*, 79-80.
52   Acts 8:16
53   Acts 2:38, 19:5
54   Cyprian of Carthage, Epistle LXXII to Jubaianus (ANF 5:381).
55   Agapios and Nicodemus, *The Rudder (Pedalion)*, The 85 Canons of the Holy and Renowned Apostles, Canon 49.
56   Luke 23:43

whether he should baptize the Gentile centurion Cornelius, the Lord sent down the Holy Spirit on Cornelius and his family as a sign that St. Peter must baptize them.[57] Likewise, as a person who is baptized by water is baptized into the death and resurrection of Christ, the Church has acknowledged those who have died by martyrdom without water baptism as being "baptized by blood," as entering into the Mystery of baptism through their death for Him who died for all (provided they died in defense of the truth and not in defense of heresy).

Nevertheless, such exceptions by economy do not nullify the rule, or canon, established by the Lord that the Apostles and their successors are to receive people into the Church by baptism with three immersions in the name of the Holy Trinity, whereby remission of sins is granted and the Holy Spirit is bestowed. Exceptions to this rule have been made by Christ and the Church out of economy for man's salvation but these exceptions are never intended to become a new rule or new canon. That such exceptions are permitted in specific circumstances does not imply that exceptions are permitted in every circumstance. The Lord's words to the thief on the cross, and the Holy Spirit descending on Cornelius and his household who were unbaptized, do not render baptism as unnecessary for the reception of the Holy Spirit and for salvation. On the contrary, far from considering the need for baptism superfluous, St. Peter baptized Cornelius and his household even after they received the Holy Spirit and thus fulfilled the command of the Lord to baptize all.

---

57   Acts 10: 44-48

The Twelve Apostles
Feast Day: June 30 (Synaxis of the Holy Apostles)

CHAPTER 3

Apostolic Canons and Constitutions on the Rites of Heretics

The Second Canon of the Fifth-Sixth Ecumenical Council in Trullo in AD 692 accepted the authority of the Apostolic Canons and the Apostolic Constitutions as expressing the teaching and tradition handed down by the Apostles. The canon acknowledges that the Constitutions of the Apostles had become corrupted by heretics at some point prior to the Council, but such corruptions were removed from later editions. The following words from the Constitutions are reflected also in the Apostolic Canons and "contain nothing improper or spurious,"[58] according to St. Nikodemos the Hagiorite:

> Be ye likewise contented with one baptism alone, that which is into the death of the Lord; not that which is conferred by wicked heretics, but that which is conferred by unblameable priests, "in the name of the Father, and of the Son, and of the Holy Spirit:" and let not that which comes from the ungodly be received by you, nor let that which is done by the godly be disannulled by a second. For as there is one God, one Christ, and one Comforter, and one death of the Lord in the body, so let that baptism which is unto Him be but one. But those that receive polluted baptism from

---

58 Agapios and Nicodemus, op. cit. Quinisext Council, Canon 2.

the ungodly will become partners in their opinions. For they are not priests. For God says to them: "Because thou hast rejected knowledge, I will also reject thee from the office of a priest to me." Nor indeed are those that are baptized by them initiated, but are polluted, not receiving the remission of sins, but the bond of impiety... Nay, he that, out of contempt, will not be baptized, shall be condemned as an unbeliever, and shall be reproached as ungrateful and foolish. For the Lord says: "Except a man be baptized of water and of the Spirit, he shall by no means enter into the kingdom of heaven." And again: "He that believeth and is baptized shall be saved; but he that believeth not shall be damned."[59, 60]

The Constitutions of the Apostles clearly state that there is no priesthood among heretics, and that the baptism of heretics is a "pollution" that does not grant remission of sins. Regarding the Apostolic Canons, the Fifth-Sixth Ecumenical Council in Trullo states:

This too has appeared best to this holy Council, as well as most important, that the 85 Canons handed down to us in the name of the holy and glorious Apostles, and as a matter of fact accepted and validated by the holy and blissful Fathers preceding us, be henceforth retained and left firm and secure for the care of souls and the cure of diseases... and no one shall be permitted to countermand or set aside the Canons previously laid down, or to recognize and accept any Canons, other than the ones herein specified... If, nevertheless, anyone be caught innovating with regard to any of the said Canons, or attempting to subvert it, he shall be responsible in respect of that Canon and shall receive the penance which it prescribes and be chastised by that Canon which he has offended.[61]

---

59   Mark 16:16
60   *Constitutions of the Holy Apostles*, Book VI:III:XV (ANF 7:456-457).
61   Agapios and Nicodemus, op. cit. Quinisext Council, Canon 2.

Similarly, the Seventh Ecumenical Council declared in its first Canon:

Fathers of the Seventh Ecumenical Council

For those who have been allotted a sacerdotal dignity, the representations of canonical ordinances amount to testimonies and directions. Gladly accepting these, we sing to the Lord God with David, the spokesman of God, the following words: "I have delighted in the way of thy testimonies as much as in all wealth," and "thy testimonies which thou hast commanded witness righteousness... Thy testimonies are righteousness forever: give me understanding, and I shall live."[62] And if forever the prophetic voice commands us to keep the testimonies of God, and to live in them, it is plain that they remain unwavering and unshakeable. For Moses, too, the beholder of God, says so in the following words: "To them there is nothing to add, and from them there is nothing to remove."[63] And the divine Apostle Peter, exulting in them, cries: "which things the angels would like to peep into."[64] And Paul says: "Though we, or an angel from heaven, should preach to you any gospel besides that which ye have received, let him be anathema."[65] Seeing that these things are so and are attested to us, and rejoicing at

---

62   Ps. 118:14, 138 and 144
63   Deut. 12:32
64   1 Pet. 1:12
65   Gal. 1:8

them "as one that findeth great spoil,"[66] we welcome and embrace the divine Canons, and we corroborate their decrees entire and unmovable,[67] as set forth by the renowned Apostles, who were and are trumpets of the Spirit, and those both of the six holy Ecumenical Councils and of the ones assembled regionally for the purpose of setting forth such edicts, and of those of our holy Fathers. For all those men, having been guided by the light dawning out of the same Spirit, prescribed rules that are to our best interest. Accordingly, we too anathematize whomsoever they consign to anathema; and we too depose whomsoever they consign to deposition; and we too excommunicate whomsoever they consign to excommunication; and we likewise subject to a penance anyone whom they make liable to a penance. For "Let your conduct be free from avarice; being content with such things as are at hand,"[68] explicitly cries the divine apostle Paul, who ascended into the third heaven and heard unspeakable words.[69, 70]

The Canons of the Holy Apostles, therefore, are established by the Fifth-Sixth Ecumenical Council in Trullo and the Seventh Ecumenical Council as divinely inspired and of apostolic authority. Those who teach contrary to these canons are considered "anathema" and as preaching "another gospel."

The Serbian canonist Bishop Nikodim (Milas)[71] rightly states regarding the Apostolic Canons:

---

66   Ps. 118:162
67   English translation slightly clarified from the Greek.
68   Hebrews 13:5
69   2 Cor. 12:2-4
70   Agapios and Nicodemus, op. cit. The Seventh Ecumenical Council, Canon 1.
71   Bishop Nikodim was glorified in 2012 by the Diocese of Dalmatia of the Serbian Orthodox Church but has not yet been glorified by the Serbian Patriarchate nor by any other local Orthodox Church. Since he is universally known as "Bishop Nikodim (Milas)" rather than "St. Nikodim," and we are not familiar with accounts of his sanctity, we have referred to him in this text as "Bishop Nikodim (Milas)."

That these rules deserve in the full sense the authoritative name of the Holy Apostles and the respect that the universal Church recognizes for them, and that they serve as an exact expression of what the Apostles set forth in writing and handed over to their first successors orally - the proof is the full agreement of these rules in their main thoughts with the teaching that is contained in the canonical books of the New Testament Holy Scripture; further evidence is that they strictly correspond to church practice presented to us in the writings of the apostolic men and their immediate successors, and finally, the apostolic authority is recognized for them by the councils and the fathers of the first centuries of the Church.[72]

Regarding the apostolic authority of the canons, St. Nikodemos the Hagiorite states:

All the 85 Apostolic Canons are confirmed by Canon II of the 6th Ecumenical Synod and by Canon I of the 7th, and Justinian Novels 6 and 137 also confirm them...

They are also confirmed by the following exegetes of the Canons: Zonaras, Balsamon, Alexios Aristeros, Symeon the Magister and Logothete, Matthew Blastaris the hieromonk, Joseph the Egyptian, and Photios. John Damascene also confirms them by saying: "The 85 Canons of the Holy Apostles through Clement" (Book. IV, Chapter 18, concerning Orthodoxy). John the Antiochian also calls them Canons of the Holy Apostles in Title L; and John Scholasticos, the patriarch of Constantinople, in his preamble to the collection of the Canons, speaks thus: "The holy disciples and Apostles of the Lord promulgated 85 Canons through Clement." I am leaving out of this account the perfectly obvious fact that the twenty-five Canons of the synod held at Antioch are not only consonant with the

---

72   Milas, *Rules of the Holy Apostles and Ecumenical Councils with Interpretations* (In Russian).

Apostolic [canons] in respect of sense, but even contain whole sentences taken from this but not verbatim.[73]

St. Nikodemos also states:

> St. Meletius (Sermon on Unleavened Wafers), adducing the Apostolical Canon concerning unleavened wafers in evidence, says that Clement wrote the Apostolical Canons at the command of Peter and Paul. Of course, that the same phrase of the Apostolical Injunctions [or Constitutions] is preserved also in the Apostolical Canons, is a fact which every critic will concur in acknowledging when he simply but reads them. But it is also to be noted that George Sougdouris, too, says that in the times of Peter and Paul, after meeting and uniting in Antioch, Peter and Paul made these Apostolical Canons. And Clement himself writes his own name in Apostolic Canon 85.[74]

The canons of the Holy Apostles that are most relevant to the subjects of ecclesiology and the reception of the heterodox are Canons 46, 47, and 50. Canon 46 states that the mysteries of heretics cannot be accepted as having grace or efficacy for salvation; Canon 47 refers to the baptism of heretics as a pollution rather than as a Mystery that transmits grace and requires that heretics be received by baptism; and Canon 50 requires that baptism be performed with three immersions in the name of the Holy Trinity.

APOSTOLIC CANONS 46 AND 47:
HERETICS MUST BE RECEIVED BY BAPTISM

Apostolic Canons 46 and 47 threaten with deposition any priest or bishop who accepts the mysteries of heretics as true Mysteries, or who fails to receive a heretic into the Church by baptism, or

---

73 Agapios and Nicodemus, op. cit. Prologue Concerning the Canons of the Holy Apostles.
74 Ibid. Footnote 2.

who baptizes a second time a person already baptized in the one Church.

> CANON 46: We order any Bishop or Priest, that has accepted any heretic's baptism or sacrifice be deposed; for "what consonance has Christ with Belial? Or what part has the believer with an unbeliever?"

> CANON 47: If a Bishop or Priest baptize anew anyone that has had a true baptism, or fail to baptize anyone that has been polluted by the impious, let him be deposed, on the ground that he is mocking the Cross and Death of the Lord and for failing to distinguish priests from pseudo-priests.[75]

Regarding Apostolic Canon 46, the canonist Bishop Gregory (Grabbe) says:

> This rule is, as it were, [also] directed against modern ecumenists, who recognize behind all heretics a baptism performed even by extreme Protestants...

In the same sense, this rule is commented on by [the canonist] Bp. John of Smolensk. Mentioning the existence of various ranks for the acceptance of heretics, he writes: "In general, the Apostolic canons indicate one important reason for the rejection of heretical rites: that in heresy there is not and cannot be a true priesthood, but only false priesthood. This is because with the separation of those who think differently from the Church, the Apostolic succession of the hierarchy, one and true, is interrupted for them, and at the same time, the succession of the grace-filled gifts of the Holy Spirit in the sacrament of the priesthood is also cut short; and next, the ministers of heresy, just as they do not have grace on themselves, so they cannot give it to others, and just as they themselves do not receive the legal right to priesthood, they cannot make the rites they perform true and saving..." From this principle, the Church proceeds in

---

75   Agapios and Nicodemus, op. cit. The 85 Canons of the Holy Apostles.

the practice of accepting heretics, however, modifying the latter in accordance with the need for the salvation of souls coming from error, which will be discussed when judging other relevant canons.[76]

On Canon 46 of the Holy Apostles, St. Justin (Popovich) (+1979) says:

It is obvious even to those who have no eyes that this decree specifically orders us not to recognize any of the heretics' holy mysteries, to consider them invalid and devoid of grace.[77]

Relying on Bishop Nikodim (Milas), some have recently claimed that Apostolic Canon 46 "Applies only to heretics who existed in Apostolic times" since "there are corresponding prescriptions of other rules of councils and holy fathers." While it would be correct to say Canon 46 applied to the heretics that existed in apostolic times, it would not be correct to say that the canon applies only to these heretics. The Apostolic Canons did not name specific heretics nor describe the type of heresies that these canons applied to, but rather spoke of "heretics" in general. St. Justin (Popovich), a contemporary Holy Father, understood the reference to "heretics" in Apostolic Canon 46 as applicable to Latins, Protestants, and anyone else who is not in communion with the Orthodox Church and who has a different faith than the Orthodox faith.

St. Raphael of Brooklyn (+1915) quoted Apostolic Canon 46 in his 1912 letter to the Orthodox flock in America who had inquired about whether Orthodox Christians could seek baptism and other mysteries from Anglican (Episcopalian) clergy if no Orthodox clergy were available. At the time, Anglican clergy in America were encouraging the Orthodox to receive mysteries from them, claiming that St. Raphael considered their mysteries to be "valid." St. Raphael wrote his flock to clarify the matter, stating that Orthodox Christians could not receive mysteries from Anglicans according to

---

76   Grabbe, *Canons of the Orthodox Church* (In Russian).
77   Popovic, *The Orthodox Church and Ecumenism*, p. 158.

Apostolic Canon 46, indicating that he understood the canon referring to "heretics" as applicable to Anglicans and other non-Orthodox:

SAINT RAPHAEL OF BROOKLYN

St. Raphael of Brooklyn (+1915)
Feast Day: Saturday before the
Synaxis of the Bodiless Powers of Heaven
(Antiochians) or February 27 (OCA)

I, therefore, felt bound by all the circumstances to make a thorough study of the Anglican Church's faith and orders, as well as of her discipline and ritual...I am convinced that the doctrinal teaching and practices, as well as the discipline, of the whole Anglican Church are unacceptable to the Holy Orthodox Church... The Orthodox Church differs absolutely with the Anglican Communion in reference to the number of Sacraments and in reference to the doctrinal explanation of the same...

I direct all Orthodox people residing in any community not to seek or to accept the ministrations of the Sacraments and rites from any clergy excepting those of the Holy Orthodox Catholic and Apostolic Church, for the Apostolic command that the Orthodox should not commune in ecclesiastical matters with those who are not of the same household of faith (Gal. 6:10), is clear:

"Any bishop, or presbyter or deacon who will pray with heretics, let him be anathematized; and if he allows them as clergymen to perform any service, let him be deposed."(Apostolic Canon 45) "Any bishop, or presbyter who accepts Baptism or the Holy Sacrifice from heretics, we order such to be deposed, for what concord hath Christ with Belial, or what part hath he that believeth with an infidel?"(Apostolic Canon 46)

As to members of the Holy Orthodox Church living in areas beyond the reach of Orthodox clergy, I direct that the ancient custom of our Holy Church be observed, namely, in cases of extreme necessity, that is, danger of death, children may be baptized by some pious Orthodox layman, or even by the parent of the child, by immersion three times in the names of the (Persons of the) Holy Trinity, and in case of death such baptism is valid.[78]

On the applicability of the Apostolic Canons to heretics of later centuries, the Fifth-Sixth Ecumenical Council in AD 692 and the Seventh Ecumenical Council in AD 787 ratified these canons and declared them to be God-inspired with no qualifications limiting their applicability in time. Furthermore, when later canons (Canon 7 of the Second Ecumenical Council and Canon 95 of the Fifth-Sixth Ecumenical Council in Trullo) allowed for some named heretics to be received by economy, these canons stated that those coming from "all the other heresies" should be baptized, again affirming that baptism is the standard for receiving the heterodox into the Church. The Lord's instructions to His disciples to "go and baptize," and the Apostolic Canons which require heretics to be received by baptism, establish the rule and *akriveia* for receiving the heterodox. If some heretics have been permitted afterwards for specific reasons to be received instead by economy, such decisions do not establish a "new standard" nor somehow "abrogate" or replace the authority of the Lord and the Apostolic Canons, but rather have to be understood as temporary deviations from the standard for the good of the Church and the salvation of many.

---

78   Kohanik, *The Most Useful Knowledge for the Orthodox Russian-American Young People.*

APOSTOLIC CANON 50:
BAPTISM MUST BE PERFORMED WITH THREE IMMERSIONS

Apostolic Canon 50 requires baptism to be performed with three immersions and threatens with deposition priests and bishops who fail to do so.

> CANON 50: If any Bishop or Priest does not perform three immersions (baptisms) in making one baptism, but only a single immersion (baptism), that given into the death of the Lord, let him be deposed. For the Lord did not say, "Baptize into my death," but, "Go ye and make disciples of all nations, baptizing them in the name of the Father, and of the Son, and of the Holy Spirit."[79, 80]

St. Basil the Great (+379) states:

> Whether a man have departed this life without baptism, or have received a baptism lacking in some of the requirements of the tradition, his loss is equal.[81]

Some have claimed that Apostolic Canon 50 is not necessarily objecting to deviations from the practice of baptism in three immersions but only objects to those who practice baptism by a single immersion "into the death of the Lord." The words, "into the death of the Lord," however, are from Romans 6:3:

> Or don't you know that all of us who were baptized into Christ Jesus were baptized into his death? We were therefore buried with him through baptism into death in order that, just as Christ was raised from the dead through the glory of the Father, we too may live a new life.[82]

---

79   Matt 28:19
80   Agapios and Nicodemus, op. cit., The 85 Canons of the Holy Apostles.
81   Basil the Great, *On the Spirit*, 10:26 (NPNF 2/8:17).
82   Rom 6:3-4

St. John of Damascus (+749) in *An Exact Exposition of the Orthodox Faith*, says concerning the words, "into the death of the Lord":

> For although the divine Apostle says: "Into Christ and into His death were we baptized" (Romans 6:3), he does not mean that the invocation of baptism must be in these words, but that baptism is an image of the death of Christ. For by the three immersions, baptism signifies the three days of our Lord's entombment.[83]

Apostolic Canon 50 was not written to oppose those who believed that Christ died but was not resurrected, nor was there a practice at that time of baptizing with an invocation "into the death of the Lord." Rather, baptism in a single immersion was rejected by the Church as failing to represent Christ's death and three days in the tomb prior to His Resurrection. If baptism by a single immersion fails to represent Christ's three-day burial, baptism by pouring or sprinkling fails even more to represent the mystery of Christ's three-day burial.

St. Cyril of Jerusalem (+386) explains that the three immersions in baptism represent the three-day burial of the Lord before His Resurrection:

> ...[Y]ou were led to the holy pool of Divine Baptism, as Christ was carried from the Cross to the Sepulchre which is before our eyes. And each of you was asked, whether he believed in the name of the Father, and of the Son, and of the Holy Spirit, and you made that saving confession, and descended three times into the water, and ascended again; here also hinting by a symbol at the three days burial of Christ. For as our Saviour passed three days and three nights in the heart of the earth, so you also in your first ascent out of the water, represented the first day of Christ in the earth, and by your descent, the night; for as he who is in the night, no longer sees, but he who is in the day, remains in the light, so in the descent, as in the night, you saw nothing,

---

83   John of Damascus, *An Exact Exposition of the Orthodox Faith*, Book IV: 9 (NPNF/9:78).

but in ascending again you were as in the day. And at the self-same moment you were both dying and being born; and that Water of salvation was at once your grave and your mother.[84]

St. Basil the Great also affirms that baptism is to be done in three immersions:

> In three immersions, then, and with three invocations, the great Mystery of baptism is performed, to the end that the type of death may be fully figured, and that by the tradition of the divine knowledge the baptized may have their souls enlightened.[85]

In the West, St. Ambrose of Milan also spoke of baptism as a triple immersion, or plunging, in water with a triple confession of faith through which man is buried with Christ and resurrected with Him.[86]

Pope St. Leo the Great (+461) also spoke of baptism as a threefold immersion representing the Lord's three days in the tomb:

> …[I]n the baptismal office death ensues through the slaying of sin, and threefold immersion imitates the lying in the tomb three days, and the raising out of the water is like Him that rose again from the tomb.[87]

Aside from the Apostolic Canons, one of the earliest witnesses to triple immersion baptism is found in the writings of Tertullian (155–220 AD). In *De Corona*, Tertullian says that triple immersion baptism is one of the many traditions handed down by the Apostles that was not recorded in the Scriptures. Describing this tradition, he says:

---

84   Cyril of Jerusalem, *Catechetical Homilies*, pp. 352-353.
85   Basil the Great, op. cit. 15.35 (NPNF 2/08:22).
86   Ferguson, *Baptism in the Early Church: History, Theology, and Liturgy in the First Five Centuries*, p. 638.
87   Leo the Great, Letter XVI:IV (NPNF 2/12:28).

When we are going to enter the water, but a little before, in the presence of the congregation and under the hand of the president, we solemnly profess that we disown the devil, and his pomp, and his angels. Hereupon we are thrice immersed, making a somewhat ampler pledge than the Lord has appointed in the Gospel.[88]

Another translation reads:

We are thrice immersed, while we answer interrogations rather more extensive than our Lord has prescribed in the gospel.[89]

In his writings *Against Praxeas*, Tertullian speaks of the connection between triple immersion baptism and a Trinitarian confession of faith:

Christ commanded that his disciples immerse [*tinguerent*] into the Father, Son, and Holy Spirit [Matt. 28:19], not into one; and indeed it is not once only, but three times, that we are immersed [*tinguimur*] into each individual person at each individual name.[90]

The extant Latin writings of St. Hippolytus of Rome (170-235 AD) also attest to baptism being performed through triple immersion and that baptism was linked with confession of faith.[91]

Prior to the departure of the Latins from the Orthodox Church in the 11th century, all local councils of the East and West, all Ecumenical Councils, and all rubrics of the East and West affirmed that baptism must be done with three full immersions.[92] Among the Monophysites, and particularly the Syrians and Maronites, the innovation developed of partially immersing and then splashing or pouring water over the person being baptized[93], which also violates

---

88   Tertullian, *The Chaplet, or De Corona*, Ch. 3 (ANF 3:94).
89   Ferguson, p. 341.
90   Ibid., p. 342.
91   Ibid., p. 331.
92   Crystal, *A History of the Modes of Christian Baptism*, pp. 133-136.
93   Ibid. p. 137.

the apostolic command to fully immerse which was observed by the entire Church.

St. Gregory Palamas (+1359) further explains the significance of baptism in three immersions in the context of the Feast of Theophany which commemorates the Baptism of the Lord and the revelation of the Holy Trinity:

> Man is the only creature who, in the image of the tri-hypostatic Being, has a mind, reason, and a spirit which gives life to his body, inasmuch as he also has a body which needs to be infused with life. When our nature was re-made in the Jordan, the most sublime and all-accomplishing Trinity was made manifest, as the archetype of the image in our soul. Therefore those who receive Christian baptism after Christ are baptized with three immersions, whereas John baptized with one immersion in the Jordan.[94]

St. Kosmas Aitolos (+1779) taught that spiritual problems can result if a person is not immersed three times fully at the time of baptism.

> You, holy priests, should baptize the children of your parish according to the teaching and purpose of our holy Eastern and Apostolic Church. Immerse them in the holy font. Have plenty of water and immerse them and lift them up thrice, saying the names of [the persons of] the Holy Trinity.[95]

St. Kosmas Aitolos
(+1779)
Feast Day: August 24

> Holy priests, you must have large baptismal fonts in your churches so that the entire child can be immersed. The child should be able to swim in it so that not even an area as large as a tick's eye remains dry. Because it is from there (the dry area) that the devil advances, and this is why your children

---

94   Palamas, *The Homilies*, p. 495.
95   Vaporis, *Father Kosmas The Apostle of the Poor*, p. 61.

become epileptics, are possessed by demons, have fear, suffer misfortune; they haven't been baptized properly.[96]

In the 1848 Encyclical of the Eastern Patriarchs to Pope Pius IX, the Patriarchs of Constantinople, Alexandria, Antioch, and Jerusalem, along with many bishops, criticize the Latins for falling away from the apostolic form of baptism in three immersions:

> Our bounteous LORD and God, who hath redeemed us by his own Blood, requires nothing else of us but the devotion of our whole soul and heart to the blameless, holy faith of our fathers, and love and affection to the Orthodox Church, which has regenerated us not with a novel sprinkling, but with the divine washing of Apostolic Baptism.[97]

St. Philaret of Moscow (+1867) taught in his Longer Catechism that three immersions are "essential" in performing baptism:

> Question: What is most essential in the administration of Baptism?

> Answer: Trine [triple] immersion in water, in the name of the Father, and of the Son, and of the Holy Spirit.[98]

St. Raphael of Brooklyn (+1915), writing to his flock in America to explain how the Orthodox understanding and performance of the Mysteries differs from the Anglican teaching and practice, says:

> In the case of the administration of Holy Baptism it is the absolute rule of the Orthodox Church that the candidate must be immersed three times (once in the name of each Person of the Holy Trinity). Immersion is only permissory in the Anglican Communion, and pouring or sprinkling is the general custom.[99]

---

96   Ibid., p. 77.
97   *Encyclical of the Eastern Patriarchs, 1848.*
98   St. Philaret of Moscow, *The Longer Catechism of the Eastern Orthodox Church*, p. 125.
99   Kohanik, op. cit.

The Serbian St. Sebastian (Dabovich) of Jackson and San Francisco (+1940) wrote that baptism must be done with three immersions and if a person is not baptized in three immersions then what took place was not a baptism and those "baptized" need to be baptized correctly afterwards.

> [For a] Priesthood to be lawful must administer the Sacraments orderly, according to the rules of the Holy Church Catholic, not changing essential actions, as there are acts and conditions in the rites of Mysteries that are essential, without which a certain Sacrament may not be valid. Should a sacred minister violate an essential rule he is subject to degradation [deposition], if the violation has been intentional, or at least the Mystery is void of power. The [50th rule] of the Apostolic Canon enjoins, 'Should anyone, bishop or presbyter, administer not three immersions in Baptism in commemoration of the death of the Lord, but one, let him be cast out.' And those who were baptized by one immersion, it was ordered that they should be rebaptized.[100]

St. Luke the Surgeon, Archbishop of Simferopol and Crimea (+1961), was greatly grieved by the laxity he observed in many of the priests under him and wrote several decrees on the absolute necessity of priests performing baptism in three immersions according to Apostolic Canon 50, the historic practice of the Church, and the testimony of the saints and Fathers. Exceptions to this rule were only to be permitted in times of dire emergency where baptism in three full immersions was not possible:

> To my deep chagrin, I learn that until now, despite my repeated instructions, the Sacrament of Baptism is performed by some priests through pouring, and by many others, out of laziness and negligence, completely intolerable reductions in the rite of baptism set forth in the trebnik are allowed. Canon 50 of the Holy Apostles threatens to

---

100 Dabovich, *The True Church of Christ*, p. 186.

deprive a bishop or priest of their rank for performing baptism without three immersions. From the history of the Church we know that already in apostolic times baptism was performed by threefold immersion in the name of the Father and the Son and the Holy Spirit. In the Acts of the Apostles we read that for the baptism of the nobleman of the Ethiopian queen, the Apostle Philip went down with him into the water, which, of course, was necessary for immersing the person being baptized into the water. The holy fathers of the Church wrote a lot about baptism by triple immersion in water as an absolutely obligatory form of baptism: Cyril of Jerusalem, Basil the Great, John Chrysostom, Simeon the New Theologian, Dionysius. The Orthodox Eastern Church allowed baptism by pouring only in the most exceptional cases, such as, for example, in a serious illness of the baptized, whose immersion is impossible, or over martyrs who are imprisoned, where one could have only very little water.[101]

St. Luke was so adamant that baptism be done in three immersions that he sent another decree to his clergy in June of 1952 threatening to suspend from liturgizing for six months any of his priests that "baptize" by pouring or sprinkling:

The mystery of baptism should be performed canonically. In other words the whole person should enter into the water in the font; the priest should not just sprinkle his head. If I learn that the mystery is being done in another manner and not canonically, I will forbid those clergy from liturgizing for six months.[102, 103]

---

101 Luke of Simferopol and Crimea. "Decrees of St. Luke Voyno-Yasenetsky". Decree dated January 12, 1955.

102 Marushchak, *The Blessed Surgeon: The Life of Saint Luke Archbishop of Simferopol*, p. 107.

103 St. Luke also issued in his Decree No. 63 on September 17, 1954, that the priest John Osipov was suspended for six months for not following a number of his directives, and this instruction on the form of baptism is listed first and foremost. He mentions two other priests who were undergoing discipline for this in a decree from June 28, 1950. From Luke of Simferopol and Crimea, op. cit.

In his *Catechetical Talks*, the martyred Russian Priest Daniel Sysoev (+2009) also taught that baptism must be done in three immersions and those who were not fully immersed three times may fall into confusion and wonder if their baptism resulted in spiritual rebirth.

One of the most painful and gross violations in performing the sacrament of baptism is baptizing by effusion (pouring), or even by sprinkling, for no apparent reason. Due to this distortion many hundreds of Christians are confused as to whether their spiritual birth was indeed valid. Many commune unto judgment and condemnation because of this. Dozens of schisms profit by this distortion, claiming that many Christians, even bishops, are not actually baptized.[104] The priest's criminal laziness and indifference give rise to conflicts between local churches. The churches of Greece and Mount Sinai and Holy Mount Athos doubt the validity of baptism by effusion (to say nothing of baptism by sprinkling), yet our censer-swingers cannot be troubled to furnish their churches with a simple barrel! And this despite the fact that His Holiness the Patriarch (along with many other bishops) has demanded each year for over 15 years that baptism be performed exclusively by immersion! But the "effusionists" brazenly claim that it makes no difference how they baptize, that this is mere "ritualism," and has absolutely nothing to do with the essence of the sacrament. They care nothing for the opinion and the words of God, the tradition of the Church, and the dictates of their own hierarchs...

Baptism by triple immersion is expressly required by the Word of God. Our Lord Jesus Christ received baptism through total immersion in the waters of the Jordan. It is no accident that the Gospel says: *And straightway coming up out of the water,*

---

104 Perhaps Fr. Daniel is referring to the many Old Believer groups in Russia. The error of "baptizing" using pouring or sprinkling resulted from Latin influence in Russia in the 17th century, around the same time as the Old Believer schism, and this error was used by Old Believers to claim that the Russian Orthodox Church had fallen into heresy and many of its clergy and bishops were actually unbaptized.

He saw the heavens opened, and the Spirit like a dove descending upon Him (Mk. 1:10; Mt. 3:16). The very word "baptism" used in the Gospel (Gr. βάπτισμ – "immersion into water") literally means "immersion." Hence, the statement "the immersion was performed by effusion" sound an absurdity. We know that the holy apostles, having received the commandment to baptize all nations (Mt. 28:19), performed the sacrament specifically through immersion...

It is no accident that it is this means of baptism that the canons decree canonical. The 50th canon of the Holy Apostles states: "If anyone, bishop or presbyter, does not perform three immersions in a single sacramental rite, but performs only one immersion, into the death of the Lord, let him be deposed."[105]

Counter to this requirement of the Apostolic Canons and the universal practice of the Orthodox Church throughout time, the claim is sometimes made that baptism by pouring or sprinkling is permitted according to the following words in *The Didache* (The Teaching of the Twelve Apostles):

> And concerning baptism, baptize this way: Having first said all these things, baptize into the name of the Father, and of the Son, and of the Holy Spirit (Matthew 28:19), in living water. But if you have not living water, baptize into other water; and if you cannot in cold, in warm. But if you have not either, pour out water thrice upon the head into the name of Father and Son and Holy Spirit. But before the baptism let the baptizer fast, and the baptized, and whatever others can; but you shall order the baptized to fast one or two days before.[106]

These words from *The Didache* have been understood in the Orthodox Church as applicable only to emergencies where baptism by immersion is not possible and a person is at risk of dying without

---

105 Sysoev, Fr. Daniel, *Catechetical Talks*, pp. 328-330.
106 *The Teaching of the Twelve Apostles* (Didache), (ANF 07:379).

baptism. Then, only under such a condition, and by economy, it is better to baptize by pouring, or even in the air, than not at all.

St. Kosmas (Aitolos) states regarding emergency baptisms:

> And if by chance a child is about to die and the priest hasn't baptized it yet, let anyone baptize it, father, mother, brother, neighbor, and especially the midwife. Take a lot of water and oil, make the sign of the Cross over the child, and baptize it, saying: "The servant of God is baptized in the name of the Father, and of the Son, and of the Holy Spirit. Amen." If the child lives, the priest will complete the service. If it happens that you have no water, take three handfuls of sand and spill it over the child's head and repeat as I have said. If again you happen to have no sand, baptize it in the air and repeat the same.[107]

If in such an emergency, when a layman conducts the baptism and the person baptized survives, a priest is to afterwards baptize the person.[108] Regarding such deviations from the apostolic requirement of baptism in three immersions, Fr. Daniel Sysoev explains:

> And so it turns out that one who distorts the apostolic form of the sacrament [triple immersion baptism] disrupts the symbol of rebirth. But for us this symbol is by no means meaningless. It is participation in the reality of the Lord's death and Resurrection! How then can one believe the form of baptism to be irrelevant to salvation?
>
> As we have said, effusion or sprinkling may be occasioned only by highly extraordinary circumstances. Yes, both in church history and in the lives of the saints we see examples of God-pleasing baptisms performed in this way, but all of them were occasioned by illness or severe persecution. Yes, according to ancient tradition the apostle Peter baptized those who believed in the Mamertine Prison in a spring which

---

107 Vaporis, op. cit., pp. 76-77.
108 See Canon 1 of St. Basil where he states that those baptized by a layman must afterwards be baptized.

he caused to flow from the cliff, and St. Laurence baptized prisoners by effusion. Baptism by effusion was practiced in the desert, and also in times of illness. But how can this be compared to the practice of baptizing by sprinkling without undressing, without even removing the person's stockings (and hence without anointing the feet with holy chrism), in Russia with its abundant water sources, where a large barrel (or even a beautiful font) can be purchased for a paltry sum?

It is my firm conviction that baptism by effusion is permissible only for the gravely ill, whose mobility is restricted, or for prisoners, soldiers fighting in arid regions, desert dwellers, if there are no large water sources, or in the tundra at subzero temperatures, when no suitable heated facility is available.

Baptism by sprinkling is permissible only for patients in intensive care, who cannot have water poured over them completely (for instance, a dying infant in an incubator). But every effort should still be made to moisten as much of the body as possible with holy water.[109]

According to Apostolic Canon 50, priests who do not baptize in three immersions should be deposed unless this is done due to dire emergency where a person may repose before it is possible to baptize them in three full immersions (in which case baptism by pouring may be done out of economy). While a priest who does not baptize correctly in three immersions will ultimately have to answer to God for this failure, the saints quoted above show that the person received without a baptism in three full immersions may also suffer spiritual harm as a result. The requirement for priests and bishops to perform baptism in three immersions is not merely for the priest's or bishop's sake, but for the sake of the person being baptized. For baptism to be true and salvific, it must be performed by a priest of the Church in the manner in which the Lord commanded through His Apostles.

---

109 Sysoev, op. cit., pp. 334-335.

THE CANONICAL COMMENTARIES OF SAINT NIKODEMOS THE HAGIORITE AND BISHOP NIKODIM (MILAS)

As some critics have relied on the canonical commentary of Bishop Nikodim (Milas) over the commentaries of St. Nikodemos the Hagiorite in support of their views on the boundaries of the Church and the reception of converts, and since Bishop Nikodim and St. Nikodemos have both authored lengthy commentaries on the canons, it is fitting to say a word here about each of them and the authority and reliability of their commentaries.

St. Nikodemos the Hagiorite (+1809)
Feast Day: July 14

etsy.com/listing/779135458/saint-nikodimos-orthodox-icon-saint

St. Nikodemos the Hagiorite (+1809) is a universally venerated saint and Holy Father who was at the heart of the revival of hesychasm* during the difficult years of the Turkish Yoke. St. Nikodemos not only wrote extensive commentaries on the canons but compiled the Great Synaxaristes (Lives of Saints), the *Theotokaria*, and wrote commentaries on the Holy Scriptures. He was instrumental in compiling and publishing some of the most important spiritual texts in the Orthodox Church, including the *Philokalia, Evergetinos, Concerning Frequent Communion*, and the *Exomologetarion* (Handbook of Confession). He was not only well educated with a very keen memory, but he embodied the patristic teachings that he published and was himself a skilled spiritual father and guide to many along the way of salvation. As St. Nikodemos contributed to the flourishing of hesychasm and spiritual fatherhood in the Greek world, his contemporary who preceded him on Mt. Athos, the Russian St. Paisios Velichkovsky, revived hesychasm and spiritual eldership in the Slavic world, including in Russia through St. Seraphim of Sarov and the Optina Elders.[110]

The *Rudder*, or *Pedalion*, that contains the canons and extensive commentary of St. Nikodemos is the only comprehensive commentary that has been produced by a major saint of the Church. The *Rudder* was reviewed and approved by St. Makarios of Corinth and St. Athanasios Parios before being approved and authorized by the Holy Synod of the Ecumenical Patriarchate.[111] The Ecumenical Patriarch insisted that the *Rudder* be translated and distributed throughout the Orthodox Church. The *Rudder* remains the most authoritative book of canons in the Orthodox Church and is not simply the work of academic research but the spiritual fruit of an erudite holy saint that was inspired by the Holy Spirit, a skilled spiritual father whose fragrant skull is treasured on Mt. Athos and venerated by all.[112] St. Nikodemos not only compiled and disseminated the teachings of the Holy Fathers, but also shared the same experience of illumination and theosis* as the Holy Fathers who composed the canons of the Ecumenical Councils.

Bishop Nikodim (Milas) (+1915) was a Serbian bishop in Dalmatia who lived about 100 years after St. Nikodemos. In his youth, Bishop Nikodim "completed his primary school run by Franciscans and secondary school in Zadar which was run by the Jesuit order at the time."[113] He later studied at the Kievan Theological Academy, which was known for the influence of post-Schism Latin Scholastic teachings which influenced his own views (this was the same school attended by St. Paisius Velichkovsky in the 18th century, from which he fled to Mt. Athos after being "repelled by the secular tone of the teaching"[114]).

Bishop Nikodim provides good patristic commentary on the canons in some places, but his commentary is also plagued by heterodox ideas and troubling contradictions. Compared with the

---

110 Cavarnos, *St. Nicodemus the Hagiorite*, p. 14.

111 Holy Apostles Convent, *The Great Synaxaristes of the Orthodox Church*. July, 630.

112 Ibid, p. 638.

113 "Nikodim Milas – bishop." Serb National Council.

114 Ware, *The Orthodox Church*, p. 117.

commentaries of St. Nikodemos; the latter's commentaries are full of quotes demonstrating the patristic basis of his explanations; whereas Bishop Nikodim, at least in his commentaries on canons relevant to this topic, may provide Orthodox teaching that agrees with St. Nikodemos at the beginning of his commentary on a given canon, only to contradict himself and introduce heterodox teachings by the end of the same commentary. In the introduction to his commentary on the canons, he mentions utilizing post-Schism Latin and Anglican commentaries in addition to Orthodox sources. The way some of his commentaries read, he seems to start with Orthodox sources and end with Post-Schism Latin Scholastic or Latinized Russian sources, and unable to resolve the contradictions, he just allows his commentary to remain in contradiction.

An example of Bishop Nikodim's conflicting comments includes the following regarding Apostolic Canons 46 and 47:

> According to the teaching of the Church, every heretic is outside the Church, and outside the Church there can be neither true Christian baptism nor true Christian sacrifice, and, in general, no true Holy Mysteries. The present Apostolic canon expresses this teaching of the Church with reference to Holy Scripture, and permits no communion between one who confesses the Orthodox faith and one who teaches against it. We also read this in the Apostolic Constitutions (IV, 15), and the fathers and teachers of the Church have taught this from the very beginning.[115]

On Canon 47 of the Apostles, Bishop Nikodim states:

> Baptism... is an essential condition for entry into the Church and for becoming a true member thereof. It must be celebrated according to the Church's teaching (Apostolic Canons 49-50) and only such baptism is called true according to this canon... From true baptism the canon distinguishes false baptism which has not been performed

---

115 Milas. Quoted in Grabbe. *Strictness and Economy: Resolution of the ROCA Synod of Bishops on the Reception of Converts.*

by an Orthodox priest according to the Church's teaching, and which not only does not cleanse a man from sin but, on the contrary, defiles him.[116]

These comments are correct. But then, in Bishop Nikodim's commentary on Canon 7 of the Second Ecumenical Council, he states:

> But if there are other Christian groups who are outside the Orthodox Church and who have conscientious intention to bring a newly-baptized person into the Church of Christ (that is, they intend to impart divine grace to him through baptism, that by the power of the Holy Spirit he will become a true member of the Body of Christ and a reborn child of God), then the baptism received in such a group will be considered valid insofar as it has been performed on the basis of a faith in the Holy Trinity, in the name of the Father and of the Son and of the Holy Spirit; for when baptism is given and received with faith, it must be effective to impart grace and Christ's help will not fail to be made manifest. Any group with a distorted teaching on God which does not recognize the Trinity of Persons in the Godhead, cannot perform a valid baptism, and any baptism which is performed by them is not a baptism because it is outside Christianity. On this account, the Orthodox Church recognizes as valid and salvific the baptism of any Christian group which is outside her confines, whether heretical or schismatic, but whose baptism is truly performed in the name of the Father and of the Son and of the Holy Spirit.[117]

> Arians, Macedonians and Apollinarians, although they preached against Orthodox teaching, performed baptism in the correct form, namely, they performed it in the name of the Holy Trinity, which they did not deny, although they understood it somewhat distortedly. It was enough that their

---

116 Ibid.
117 Ibid.

baptism was recognized as correct, because according to the teaching of the Orthodox Church, it is and was that every baptism performed in the name of the Holy Trinity is considered correct and valid, no matter who performed it. Anyone who performs baptism is only an instrument that Christ chooses to win a person into His kingdom. This instrument performs the rite, but grace descends from God. Only thanks to this view, the Church could and did recognize the baptism of such heretics as the Arians and Macedonians.[118]

On such contradictions, Fr. George Grabbe (later Bishop Gregory), the canonist of the Russian Orthodox Church Outside of Russia (ROCOR), says:

Undoubtedly, Bishop Nikodim's reasoning is here in accord with the present teaching of Roman Catholics and with arguments often encountered among intellectuals who have no theological education. However, it is decidedly unworthy of an Orthodox theologian and in no way accords with Bishop Nikodim's own opinions which we cited above. Primarily, there is no basic logic in what he says here. In what way can a group, which does not belong to the Orthodox Church, "have a conscientious intention to bring a newly-baptized person to the Church of Christ and impart grace to him" by baptism and make him a true member of the Body of Christ? Only a person who belongs to the Church can be such a member. By receiving baptism in a heretical group, a man unites himself to that group and not to the Church. Can a priest or a pastor who himself does not belong to the Church bring someone to her? On the other hand, as we have seen, Bishop Nikodim himself has recognized this as impossible. How can a person who has joined a heretical or schismatic group, which is outside the confines of the Church, be within the true Church by receiving baptism from that group? Baptism is not a magical act with an important

---

118 Milas, op. cit.

formula of incantation which takes effect independently of the position of the person pronouncing it and of the faith of the person being baptized. Nowhere in the Orthodox Church can we find a faith of this sort in a parallel church, in a salvific Christian group which does not belong to her. On the contrary, the Apostle writes: "One Lord, one faith, one baptism."[119, 120]

Bishop Nikodim in his commentary on Apostolic Canon 47 initially states that baptisms performed contrary to Apostolic Canons 49 and 50, without three immersions, are false baptisms:

> Regarding which baptism was considered false at the time of the publication of the Apostolic Canons, it is said in the 49th and 50th Apostolic Canons. Such a false baptism was considered invalid, i.e. the one who received it, as it were, was not baptized.[121]

However, by the end of his commentary on Canon 47, Bishop Nikodim again contradicts himself by introducing the idea of "valid priesthood" outside of the Church, claiming that heretics, indeed without the apostolic faith, nonetheless have apostolic succession, and those heretics who have maintained the external form of apostolic succession have genuine and effective mysteries:

> Further, it must be considered whether a given religious society regards the priesthood as a divine institution and hierarchical authority as an authority derived from divine right, or whether it regards the priesthood as a service, received like any other worldly service without the participation of divine grace and necessary only in order to maintain a certain order in the performance of any religious duties. In the latter case, there is no true priesthood, and therefore it cannot be recognized by the Church. Finally, since the basis of the legitimate priesthood is the continuous succession

---

119 Ephesians 4:5
120 Grabbe, op. cit.
121 Milas, op. cit.

of hierarchical authority from the Apostles to the present day, then when judging about a heterodox priesthood, it is necessary to pay special attention to whether this apostolic succession has been preserved in a given religious society or not. The priesthoods of the religious societies which have preserved this unbroken succession are considered, in spite of their differing opinions, to be canonically correct, unless otherwise they affect the very foundations of the Christian faith, and the essence and power of the sacraments.[122]

Such teachings constitute a truly bizarre innovation unheard of in the writings of the Fathers, and completely contradict his previous comments that baptisms performed outside of the Orthodox Church are "false baptisms."

In his commentary on Apostolic Canon 50, that baptism must be performed by three immersions, Bishop Nikodim states:

This prescription is justified by the practice of the Church of all ages. It is strictly forbidden to use aspersion instead of immersion at baptism, except in cases of illness. Churches strictly made sure that baptism in ordinary cases was performed only through immersion, and not through pouring, so that she even forbade the admission to the clergy of persons who were not baptized, due to any exceptional circumstances, through immersion[123]... In the interpretation of the 47th Apostolic Canon, we have seen that, due to some historical reasons in the 17th and 18th centuries, the Greek and Russian churches were ordered to rebaptize Roman Catholics who converted to the Orthodox Church. These instructions were motivated, among other things, by the fact that Roman Catholics were baptized by pouring rather than by immersion, as a result of which their baptism was considered heretical and, therefore, invalid.[124]

---

122   Ibid..
123   Agapios and Nicodemus, op. cit., Canon 12 of the Council of Neocaesarea.
124   Bishop Nikodim Milas, op. cit. Canon 50.

However, in his commentary on Canon 47 of the Apostles, he states:

> Among the current non-Orthodox denominations that we have to deal with, the most important is the Roman Catholic. None of the conciliar canons with generally binding significance proclaimed the invalidity of baptism performed according to the prescriptions of this denomination, as a result of which those who pass from this denomination to the Orthodox Church...their baptism is recognized and, therefore, they are not baptized again.[125]

This despite the fact that Canon 50 of the Holy Apostles requires that baptism to be done with three immersions!

In discussing these matters, Bishop Nikodim speaks of the Church "recognizing" mysteries outside of the Church, which is a term not found in the canons of the Ecumenical Councils or in the teachings of the Fathers dealing with the reception of heretics into the Church and is a phrase that leads to considerable confusion as will be discussed further in this text.

Many of Bishop Nikodim's comments on the canons are helpful when they agree with the teachings of the Fathers, but when his views diverge from patristic teaching, we should overlook what is in disagreement with the Fathers rather than rely on such views as of greater value than the teachings of the Fathers. Many saints, including St. Justin (Popovich), a Serbian saint who came after Bishop Nikodim and who is universally venerated, have clearly understood the Apostolic Canons regarding heretics as being applicable to Latins, Protestants, and other heretics of our times.

The commentaries of St. Nikodemos the Hagiorite, by contrast, are full of patristic quotes and are not plagued by the contradictions and inconsistencies found in Bishop Nikodim's commentaries. Regarding the spurious claim that St. Nikodemos did not believe what he wrote in the *Rudder* concerning the reception of Latins and other heretics into the Church, the extensive published correspondence between the Kollyvades Fathers* and Fr. Dorotheos Voulismas has

---

125 Ibid.

shown this claim to be utterly false.[126, 127] While academics have tried to find fault with the *Rudder* in order to discard the teachings of St. Nikodemos in support of a more ecumenistic ecclesiology, the *Rudder* nevertheless continues to be the most authoritative commentary on the canons in the Orthodox Church and has been upheld as such by innumerable holy saints and elders up to our own time.

---

126 See in Greek *Οι Κολλυβάδες και ο Δωρόθεος Βουλησμάς. Το ζήτημα της "ανακρίσεως" του Πηδαλίου και του Κανονικού* (Ιερά Μονή Παναγίας Χρυσοποδαριτίσσης Νεζερών). *The Kollyvades and Dorotheos Voulismas. The Case of the Examination of the Pedalion and the Canonikon (Holy Monastery of Panagia Chrysopodaritissa of Nezeron).*

127 See also Heers, "St. Nikodemos, the Rudder and the Reception of Converts into the Orthodox Church: A Look at the Correspondence Between the Kollyvades Fathers & Dorotheos Voulismas."

St. Symeon the New Theologian (+1022)
Feast Day: October 12

CHAPTER 4

The Patristic Consensus and
Errors in the Writings of the Saints

Before examining the rulings of the Ecumenical Councils and the teachings of the saints and Holy Fathers on the reception of the heterodox, we must understand the manner in which Orthodox interpret them, the Orthodox hermeneutics (so to speak) of Patristics and Ecumenical Councils.

The Church has glorified among its saints Prophets, Apostles, Martyrs, Confessors, Fathers, and Ascetics. These categories are not necessarily exclusive, as the Fathers were also ascetics and most of the apostles died as martyrs. Some who reposed as martyrs were glorified by the Church for the ultimate sacrifice they made for their love of Christ, but their glorification is not necessarily the Church's endorsement of all that the martyrs did and taught prior to their martyrdom. All saints, however, are glorified for their faithfulness to the Lord and His Holy Apostles in their lives and/or by the manner of their repose. Martyrs are glorified for their martyrdom, confessors by their confession, monastics for being full of the Holy Spirit and healing those around them. The Church recognizes their sanctity and glorifies them for specific reasons.

When seeking to understand the teaching of the Orthodox Church on a given subject, it is not merely to the writings of all of the saints that we should turn indiscriminately, trying to determine how many saints said one thing and how many said another. Above all, we must turn to the teaching, decrees, and canons that have been adopted and ratified by the Ecumenical Councils as God-inspired. If the Ecumenical Councils clearly addressed a given subject, we must follow the teachings of the saints and Fathers to the extent that their teachings agree with that which has been firmly established by the Ecumenical Councils.

However, saints glorified for their teachings on the Trinity, the Person of Christ, or the Church; and who struggled in defense of the Faith in these areas, we recognize as authorities over those saints who make passing comments about such teachings. When such saints who made a clear defense of the Church's teaching in a given area are afterwards viewed as authorities by the saints who came after them, the authority of their teachings become firmly established in the Church. When we speak of the "patristic consensus" on a particular topic, then we do not simply mean a numerical and quantifiable majority, but the teachings of saints who are testified as the most authoritative on a given topic and the consensus among the authoritative saints and Fathers.

To follow the Church is to follow the Holy Fathers, and to follow the Holy Fathers of ancient times is to follow the Holy Fathers of our own times who share in the same experience of purification, illumination, and deification as the Holy Fathers before them. If we are not connected with the saints of our time, then we must seek guidance from the faithful disciples of these saints. While even the words of holy people must be examined in the light of the consensus of the Councils and Holy Fathers, it is necessary to become a faithful disciple of a spiritual father who understands and embodies the patristic way of life and teaching in order to help ensure that we correctly understand and remain faithful to what has been handed down, and are not just compiling and misunderstanding quotes and texts from previous centuries in a merely academic intellectual exercise. We can only understand texts inspired by the Holy Spirit to the extent to which we are filled with the same Spirit, and to become temples of the Holy Spirit we must seek out those among us who are filled with the Holy Spirit and seek guidance from them.

St. Symeon the New Theologian speaks of the necessity of being in living contact with the "golden chain" of saints in this way:

> The Saints — those who appear from generation to generation, from time to time, following the Saints who preceded them — become linked with their predecessors through obedience to the divine commandments, and endowed with divine grace, become filled with the same light. In such a sequence all of them together form a kind of golden chain, each Saint being a separate link in this chain, joined to the first by faith, right actions and love; a chain which has its strength in God and can hardly be broken. A man who does not express a desire to link himself to the latest of the saints (in time) in all love and humility owing to a certain distrust in himself, will never be linked to the preceding saints and will not be admitted to their succession, even though he thinks he possesses all possible faith and love for God and for all His saints. He will be cast out of their midst, as one who refused to take humbly the place allotted to him by God before all time, and to link himself to that latest saint (in time) as God had disposed.[128]

The saints of our times have the same mind as the Councils and Fathers that came before, particularly when they are assured in prayer and revelation how to interpret and understand patristic teaching. We especially turn to them, in humility, for guidance and illumination. We do not trust in our own opinions and mental abilities since the thoughts are the battlegrounds against demons.

As one reads the writings of holy people, it is possible to encounter areas where saints and Fathers spoke incorrectly on a given topic, and to some the discovery of such errors can cause shock and confusion. St. Barsanuphius of Gaza was asked how it is possible for holy people to speak in error. His answer provides us with another interpretive key when reading the Fathers. The saint's words are necessary for a proper understanding of how to follow the Holy Fathers and how to interpret their writings.

---

128 Kadloubowsky, *Writings from the Philokalia: On the Prayer of the Heart*, p. 135.

Sts. Barsanuphius and John of Gaza (6th century)
Feast Day: February 6

Question... Father, tell us why such a person does not speak correctly, as befits a holy person who has been counted worthy of speaking for the Holy Spirit...

[St. Barsanuphius]: ...May all the fathers who have pleased God, the saints and the righteous and genuine servants of God pray for me. Do not think that, because they were saints, they were able actually to comprehend all the depths of God. For the Apostle says: "We know only in part." (Cor. 13:9) And again: "To one is given through the Spirit such and such, and not all of these gifts to one and the same person; but to one person it was given in this way, to another in that way, and all of these gifts are activated by one in the same Spirit" (cf. 1 Cor. 12:4-11). Knowing then, that the [mysteries] of God are incomprehensible, the Apostles cried out: "O the depths of the riches and wisdom and knowledge of God! How unsearchable are His judgments, and how inscrutable His ways! For who has known the mind of the Lord? Or who has been His counselor?" (Rom. 11:33-34), and so forth. Applying themselves, therefore, to becoming teachers of their own accord, or else obliged by others to come to this point, they achieved great progress, sometimes even surpassing their own teachers. Moreover, they were assured about the truth in developing new doctrines, while at the same time remaining faithful to the traditions of their teachers.

In this way, there are also some [brothers] here who have received certain doctrines from their teachers, which are not, however, correct. For after achieving progress and themselves becoming spiritual teachers, nevertheless, they did not pray to God about their teachers, in order to learn whether what they said was spoken through the Holy Spirit. Rather, trusting that their teachers possessed wisdom and knowledge, they did not in fact bother to discern their teachings. And so the teachings of their teachers became mingled with their own teachings, and they spoke sometimes from the doctrines learned from their masters, while at other times from the brilliance of their own intellect. Thus, even the words of their teachers were ascribed to their name. For while they received these words from others, they progressed and improved more than their teachers, and they spoke through the Holy Spirit; that is to say, they were assured by the Spirit and spoke from the doctrines of their teachers who proceeded them, but they did not actually examine these words in order to discern whether they needed to be assured by God through supplication and prayer in regard to their truth. So the teachings [of the two] were mingled together. Thus, since it was they who spoke the words, it was to their names that they were ultimately ascribed. Therefore, when you hear that one of them received from the Holy Spirit whatever he speaks, then this is clear assurance that we ought to trust him. When, however, this person speaks on those matters, it does not seem that he refers to the same kind of assurance, but rather to the teachings and tradition of those who preceded him. In this way, while paying attention to their knowledge and wisdom, nonetheless, they did not ask God about these matters, as to whether or not they are true.[129]

These words are absolutely necessary to understand what happened in the development of policies regarding the reception of the heterodox in the history of the Church. Where the infallible Ecumenical Councils have addressed a particular teaching in its God-inspired canons and decrees, we can only accept the teachings of other saints and Fathers to the extent that their teachings remained faithful to the teachings adopted by the Ecumenical Councils. Even among those who have been purified of the passions, illumined by the Holy Spirit, and have attained theosis, they may possibly fall into an error if they simply accepted what they had been taught and did not pray to God to reveal the truth about a specific teaching. At various times and places in the history of the Church, false teachings have even crept into theological texts that have been endorsed by local synods, and even saints may have assumed that such errors were Orthodox because the error was endorsed by their local hierarchs and theological institutions, even inserted into their service books, and such teachings were assumed to be true.

We can also find saints and Holy Fathers even of our times who had the same experience of purification, illumination, and theosis as the Holy Fathers of the past and who remained faithful to the consensus of the Holy Fathers. But we may also find some errors in the writings of these saints where they may have accepted what they were taught by their teachers without careful examination and fervent prayer for God's enlightenment about a particular topic. With this view, we should embrace all of the teachings of the saints that agree with the canons and decrees of the Ecumenical Councils, in context of the saintly dogmatic authorities who interpret them for the faithful.

---

129 Barsanuphius and John, *Letters*, Vol 2., pp. 186-187.

At the same time, we must resist the temptation to become scandalized when some saints unknowingly may have adopted a teaching foreign to that which has been established by the Councils. When a saint embraces an error accidentally, we should overlook this mistake while venerating the saint for the truth that he did teach and for the holiness, virtue, and other characteristics for which God glorified him. We, like Noah's good sons Shem and Japheth, "cover the nakedness"[130] of our fathers with excuses rather than

Shem and Japheth covering their father's (Noah) nakedness (Mosaic)

exposing their errors to bring them dishonor.[131] If a saint or Father even says something which contradicts the Ecumenical Councils, we should neither fall into the extreme of denouncing such saints as heretics for making a mistake, nor should we consciously embrace their errors with the mistaken notion that we too can become saints and attain salvation by holding such incorrect beliefs. While God has glorified saints despite some unintentional mistakes, we cannot be assured that we will likewise find mercy before God if we knowingly embrace the same errors.

Without the aforementioned principles, and the interpretive key of *oikonomia* (economy) and *akriveia* (exactitude), it becomes impossible to reconcile apparent contradictions in the canons, councils, and writings of the saints. Without these principles, one often is left to pick and choose what teachings from the canons, councils, and saints agree with their own thinking, rather than being led to the truth. The most authoritative teachings on the reception of the heterodox into the Church are those adopted and ratified as

---

130 Genesis 9:23
131 See Photios the Great, *The Mystagogy of the Holy Spirit*, p. 93.

divinely inspired by Canon 2 of the Fifth-Sixth Ecumenical Council in Trullo and Canon 1 of the Seventh Ecumenical Council. These divinely inspired canons include Canon 7 of the Second Ecumenical Council, Canon 14 of the Fourth Ecumenical Council, Canon 84 and 95 of the Fifth-Sixth Ecumenical Council in Trullo, Apostolic Canons 46, 47, and 50; Canons 1 and 47 of St. Basil the Great, the Canon adopted by the Council of Carthage under St. Cyprian, and Canons 66 and 80 of the Council of Carthage that convened in AD 419.

All Saints
Feast Day: First Sunday after Pentecost

St. Basil the Great (+379)
Feast Day: January 1

CHAPTER 5

The Ecumenical Councils and the Reception of the Heterodox

The teaching of the Ecumenical Councils on ecclesiology and the reception of converts is the God-inspired and infallible teaching of the Orthodox Church. As St. Sophrony of Essex stated:

> The definitive form of expression of the Church's teaching at the Ecumenical Councils cannot be subject to any change. All future academic work must obligatorily concur with what was given in divine revelation and in the teaching of the Ecumenical Councils of the Church.[132]

Canon 2 of the Fifth-Sixth Ecumenical Council in Trullo (AD 692) commemorates and ratifies the canons and councils that the Church accepts as divinely inspired.

> This too has appeared best to the holy Council, as well as most important, that the 85 Canons handed down to us in the name of the holy and glorious Apostles, and as a matter of fact accepted and validated by the holy and blissful Fathers preceding us, be henceforth retained and left firm and secure for the care of souls and the cure of diseases...
> [We] ratify all the rest of the sacred Canons promulgated by

---

132 Sakharov, *Striving for Knowledge of God,* p. 146.

our holy and blissful Fathers, to wit: the three hundred and eighteen foregathered in Nicaea, those convened in Ancyra, and furthermore also those who met in Neocaesarea, likewise those who attended the meeting in Gangra, but in addition to these also those who convened in Antioch, Syria, and furthermore also those who held a Council in Laodicea; further, again, the one hundred and fifty who convened in this God-guarded and imperial capital city, and the two hundred who assembled at an earlier time in the metropolis of Ephesus, and the six hundred and thirty holy and blissful Fathers who met in Chalcedon. Likewise, those who convened in Sardica; furthermore those in Carthage. Further, and in addition to all these those now again convened in this God-guarded and imperial capital city in the time of Nectarius the president of this imperial capital city, and of Theophilus who became Archbishop of Alexandria. Furthermore also of Dionysius who became Archbishop of the great city of Alexandria, and of Peter who became Archbishop of Alexandria and a Martyr withal, and of Gregory the Thaumaturgus (or Miracle-worker) who became Bishop of Neocaesarea, of Athanasius the Archbishop of Alexandria, of Basil the Archbishop of Caesarea in Cappadocia, of Gregory of Nyssa, of Gregory the Theologian, of Amphilochius the Archbishop of Iconium, Timothy a former Archbishop of the great city of Alexandria, of Theophilus an Archbishop of the great city of the Alexandrians, of Cyril an Archbishop of Alexandria, and of Gennadius who became a Patriarch of this God-guarded imperial capital city. Furthermore, the Canon promulgated by Cyprian who became an Archbishop of the country of Africa and a martyr, and by the Council supporting him, which alone held sway in the places of the aforesaid presidents, in accordance with the custom handed down to them; and no one shall be permitted to countermand or set aside the Canons previously laid down, or to recognize and accept any Canons, other than the ones herein specified, that have been composed under a false inscription by certain persons who have taken in hand to barter the truth. If, nevertheless, anyone be caught innovating with regard to any of the said Canons, or attempting to subvert it, he shall be responsible in respect of that Canon and shall receive the penance which it prescribes and be chastised by that Canon which he has offended.[133]

Canon 1 of the Seventh Ecumenical Council[134] accepted the canons of the Fifth-Sixth Ecumenical Council and the others mentioned above as "the testimonies of God" that "remain unwavering and unshakeable," as "divine canons" written by those who were "guided by the light dawning out of the same Spirit," and declared that those who preach against such canons preach another gospel and are "anathema."

On the necessity of following the Holy Canons, Metropolitan Hierotheos (Vlachos) of Nafpaktos and Agios Vlasios says:

> Those who do not accept the spirit and essence of the sacred Canons do not actually have the mind of the Church. They do not accept the sanctified pastoral theology of the holy Fathers of the Church and are unable to experience God's purifying, illuminating and deifying energy, which is the aim of the spiritual and monastic life.[135]

With such words in mind, we must approach the canons ratified by the Ecumenical Councils with reverence and fear, lest by contradicting and opposing them we oppose the Holy Spirit and become liable to condemnation (anathema). We will discuss the canons most relevant to the subject of the reception of heretics into the Orthodox Church in their chronological order starting with the Canon of the Regional Council of Carthage under St. Cyprian, the canons of St. Basil the Great, the Seventh Canon of the Second Ecumenical Council, the Council in Carthage in AD

---

133 Agapios and Nicodemus, op. cit. Canon 2 of the Quinisext Council.
134 The canon is quoted in Chapter 3.
135 Vlachos, *Orthodox Monasticism as the Way of Life of Prophets, Apostles and Martyrs*, p. 456.

419, Canon 95 of the Fifth-Sixth Ecumenical Council in Trullo, and finally the decree of the Seventh Ecumenical Council regarding the Iconoclasts.

The Local Council of Carthage under St. Cyprian (AD 258)

Canon 2 of the Fifth-Sixth Ecumenical Council ratifies and upholds the canon issued by the Council of Carthage in AD 258 under St. Cyprian. Some have claimed that St. Cyprian's canon was "abrogated" by the Council of Carthage in AD 419 and the Fifth-Sixth Ecumenical Council in Trullo. This claim is based on a corrupted Latin translation of the AD 419 Council and ignores the wording of Canon 2 of the Fifth-Sixth Ecumenical Council which specifically "ratifies" the canon of St. Cyprian's council and elevates it from local to Ecumenical authority. The relevant wording from Canon 2 of the Fifth-Sixth Ecumenical Council regarding St. Cyprian's canon says:

> This too has appeared best to this holy Council, as well as most important... as a matter of fact accepted and validated by the holy and blissful Fathers preceding us, be henceforth retained and left firm and secure for the care of souls and the cure of diseases... we ratify all the rest of the sacred Canons promulgated by our holy and blissful Fathers, to wit... the Canon promulgated by Cyprian who became an Archbishop of the country of Africa and a martyr, and by the Council supporting him, which alone held sway in the places of the aforesaid presidents, in accordance with the custom handed down to them.[136]

The Council held under St. Cyprian of Carthage issued one canon which, on the subject of the reception of converts and the boundaries of the Church, stated:

---

136 Agapios and Nicodemus, op. cit.

[I]nasmuch as you are of the same communion with us and wished to inquire about this matter on account of a mutual love, we are moved to give you, and conjoin in doing so, not any recent opinion, nor one that has been only recently established, but, on the contrary, one which has been tried and tested with all accuracy and diligence of old by our predecessors, and which has been observed by us.

Ordaining this also now, which we have been strongly and securely holding throughout time, we declare that no one can be baptized outside of the catholic Church, there being but one baptism, and this being existent only in the catholic Church...

For this reason anyone joining the Church ought to become renewed [by baptism], in order that within, through the holy elements, he become sanctified...

For to sympathize with persons who have been baptized by heretics is tantamount to approving the baptism administered by heretics. Or one cannot conquer in part or vanquish anyone partially. If he was able to baptize, he succeeded also in imparting the Holy Spirit. If he was unable, because being outside, he had no Holy Spirit, he cannot baptize the next person. There being but one baptism, and there being but one Holy Spirit, there is also but one Church, founded by Christ our Lord... And for this reason whatever they do is false and empty and vain, everything being counterfeit and unauthorized... And to those who from error and crookedness come for knowledge of the true and ecclesiastic faith we ought to give freely the mystery of divine power, of unity as well as of faith, and of truth.[137]

The canon of this Council which was adopted by the Fifth-Sixth Ecumenical Council in Trullo affirms that there is only one Church and that it is not possible to acknowledge the presence of the Holy

---

137 Agapios and Nicodemus, op. cit. The Canon of the Third Holy Council Held in Carthage in the Time of Cyprian.

Spirit in baptisms performed outside of the unity of the Church. The Fifth-Sixth Ecumenical Council also affirms that the canon promulgated by the Council of Carthage was the tradition that had been received in Carthage at that time and was not a new teaching or innovation. The Council of Carthage was said to have "held sway" only in Carthage since it was a local council at that time with only local authority, prior to being ratified by the Ecumenical Council.

According to the Council of Carthage, all heretics should be received by baptism unless they were already baptized in the Church prior to falling away in schism and heresy. As St. Cyprian states in his Epistle to Pompey:

> Therefore, dearest brother, having explored and seen the truth; it is observed and held by us, that all who are converted from any heresy whatever to the Church must be baptized by the only and lawful baptism of the Church, with the exception of those who had previously been baptized in the Church, and so had passed over to the heretics. For it behooves these, when they return, having repented, to be received by the imposition of hands only, and to be restored by the shepherd to the sheep-fold whence they had strayed.[138]

The teaching of St. Cyprian, which was adopted by the Council of Carthage in AD 258 and ratified by the Fifth-Sixth Ecumenical Council in Trullo, is consistent with the ecclesiology expressed in Apostolic Canons 46 and 47. Some who have claimed that the Holy Spirit is present in the mysteries of heretics, or that the Orthodox Church has historically recognized grace or "ecclesiality" among heretical groups, have said that the decisions of the Council of Carthage under St. Cyprian were "abrogated" by the Council of Carthage in AD 419 and were "rejected" by the Second and Fifth-Sixth Ecumenical Councils since these later councils allowed for some specific heretics to be received into the Church by chrismation. These arguments present a number of problems, chief among them being that the Fifth-Sixth and Seventh Ecumenical Councils

---

138 Cyprian of Carthage, *Epistle LXXIII:12 to Pompey* (ANF 5: 389-390).

did not reject the Council of Carthage under St. Cyprian rather it did "ratify" its canon. The grammar of Canon 2 that mentions Cyprian's canon rests on "ratify." The exact verb translated as "ratify" is, in Greek, "ἐπισφραγίζομεν" meaning the Holy Fathers have "stamped" Cyprian's canon or put their seal on it. Many local councils occurred in the Church prior to the Fifth-Sixth Ecumenical Council which were not ratified as God-inspired, so this Council was not simply listing all previous councils as if all local councils had equal authority. The fact that the Council of Carthage in 258 under St. Cyprian was ratified by name by the Fifth-Sixth Ecumenical Council elevates the authority of the local Council in Carthage to Ecumenical authority (authoritative for the whole Church), and the *akriveia* of St. Cyprian's canon was accepted as divinely inspired.[139]

ST. BASIL THE GREAT AND HIS CANONS 1 AND 47

The Ecumenical Councils were guided by the Holy Fathers who were purified and filled with the Holy Spirit. Selections from the writings of many Holy Fathers that were understood as inspired by God and useful for addressing the challenges faced by the Church were codified into canons and ratified by the Ecumenical Councils. Among the Holy Fathers whose writings were used for the formulation of Holy Canons, more canons were derived from the writings of St. Basil the Great than from any other Church Father.

Of the canons of the Holy Fathers that were adopted by the Ecumenical Councils, St. Basil's canons 1 and 47 most directly deal with the boundaries of the Church and the rites of the heterodox. Canon 1 of St. Basil discusses the distinctions between heresy and schism, explains that when priests and bishops depart from the unity of the Church they lose the grace of the Holy Spirit and cannot bestow the Holy Spirit on others through baptism or ordination, acknowledges that some bishops in his time received heretics into the Church without baptizing them, and says that it is best to "serve the canons with exactitude" and receive all heterodox by baptism

---

139 Metallinos, *I Confess One Baptism*, p. 36.

as St. Cyprian and St. Firmilian taught. The relevant sections of this lengthy canon are as follows:

St. Basil the Great

> Hence [the older authorities] have called some of them heresies, and others schisms, and others again parasynagogues (i.e., unlawful assemblies). Heresies is the name applied to those who have broken entirely and have become alienated from the faith itself. Schisms is the name applied to those who on account of ecclesiastical causes and remediable questions have developed a quarrel amongst themselves. Parasynagogues is the name applied to gatherings held by insubordinate presbyters or bishops, and those held by uneducated laities. As, for instance, when one has been arraigned for a misdemeanor held aloof from liturgy and refused to submit to the Canons, but laid claim to the presidency and liturgy for himself, and some other persons departed with him, leaving the catholic Church — that is a parasynagogue. … Heresies… are such as those… involving a difference of faith in God itself. So, it seemed good to the ancient [Fathers] to reject the baptism of heretics altogether, but to accept [the baptism] of those who have gone into schism with the understanding that they formerly belonged to the Church;[140] as for those, on the other hand, who were in parasynagogues, if they have been improved by considerable repentance and are willing to return, they are to be admitted again into the Church, so that often

---

140 Note the corrected translation which is explained following the text of the canon.

even those who departed in orders with the insubordinates, provided that they manifest regret, may be admitted again to the same rank.... As for the Cathari, they too are to be classed as schismatics. Nevertheless, it seemed best to the ancient authorities — those, I mean, who form the party of Cyprian and our own Firmilian — to class them all under one head, including Cathari and Encratites and Aquarians and Apotactites; because the beginning, true enough, of the separation resulted through a schism, but those who seceded from the Church had not the grace of the Holy Spirit upon them; for the impartation thereof ceased with the interruption of the service. For although the ones who were the first to depart had been ordained by the Fathers and with the imposition of their hands they had obtained the gracious gift of the Spirit, yet after breaking away they became laymen, and had no authority either to baptize or to ordain anyone, nor could they impart the grace of the Spirit to others, after they themselves had forfeited it. Wherefore they bade that those baptized by them should be regarded as baptized by laymen, and that when they came to join the Church they should have to be repurified by the true baptism as prescribed by the Church. Inasmuch, however, as it has seemed best to some of those in the regions of Asia, out of economy for the many, to accept their baptism, let it be accepted. As for the case of the Encratites, however, it behooves us to look upon it as a crime, since as though to make themselves unacceptable to the Church they have attempted to anticipate the situation by advocating a baptism of their own; hence they themselves have run counter to their own custom. I deem, therefore, that since there is nothing definitely prescribed as regards them, it was fitting that we should set their baptism aside, and if any of them appears to have left them, he shall be baptized upon joining the Church. If, however, this is to become an obstacle in the general economy (of the Church), we must again adopt the custom and follow the Fathers who economically regulated the affairs of our Church. For I am inclined to suspect that we may by the severity of the proposition actually prevent men from being saved because of their being too indolent in regard to baptism. But if they keep our baptism, let this not deter us. For we are not obliged to return thanks to them, but to serve the Canons with exactitude. But let it be formally stated with every reason that those who join on top of their baptism must at all events be anointed by the faithful, that is to say, and thus be admitted to the Mysteries.[141]

The critical phrase, from an ecclesiological point of view, in this excerpt from the canon is "ὡς ἔτι ἐκ τῆς Ἐκκλησίας ὄντων," which some interpret as "because they [the schismatics] still belong to the Church."[142] This error is nearly universal among English renderings of the canon. Yet the aforementioned rendering is not only in direct opposition to the general teaching of St. Basil the Great, who considers the heretics and the schismatics, and even those who are in unlawful congregations (parasynagogues), as being outside of the Church, but also to the ancient text itself. Moreover, this interpretation does not stand from a syntactic point of view, either: the isolation of the phrase "ὡς ἔτι ἐκ τῆς Ἐκκλησίας ὄντων" from the verbal "ἀποσχισάντων," from which it depends, creates the mistaken impression that the dependent participial phrase "ὡς ἔτι ἐκ τῆς Ἐκκλησίας ὄντων" is in the present tense. In fact, the main verbal ("ἀποσχισάντων") is what determines the tense of the dependent participial phrase "ὡς (...) ὄντων." In other words, the participle ("ὡς (...) ὄντων") is in the past tense, because the "ἀποσχισάντων" from which it depends is itself also in the past tense. Consequently, an acceptable English rendition would be "with the understanding that they [then] formerly belonged to the Church" (the introductory conjunction "ὡς" is rendered by the phrase "with

---

141 Agapios and Nicodemus, op. cit. We have amended the translation in certain areas to better reflect the original Greek text, as noted and explained above.

142 See: Prodromos I. Akanthopoulos, *Κώδιχας Ἱερῶν Κανόνων*, 3rd ed., Vanias: Thessaloniki 2006, pp. 450-455. See also the following examples of online sources which utilize this mistaken translation: Letter 188 of St. Basil of Caesarea, New Advent Encyclopedia; St. Basil the Great, Canon 1, Holy Trinity Mission.

the understanding that" or "that supposedly/purportedly," since it expresses the subjective reasoning of the speaker). With this in mind, the aforementioned passage from the first canon of St. Basil the Great can be rendered into English with precision as follows: "So it seemed good to the ancient [Fathers] to reject the baptism of heretics altogether, but to accept [the baptism] of those who have gone into schism with the understanding that they formerly belonged to the Church." This hermeneutical approach is in complete agreement with the immediately following phrase of the canon, according to which even those in unlawful congregations are outside of the Church and only once they have been corrected after considerable repentance are they united again with the Church ("συνάπτεσθαι πάλιν τῇ 'Εκκλησίᾳ"). This means that before the repentance, while they are in their state of unlawful assemblage, they were not united with the Church. If, according to Basil the Great, those in unlawful assemblies are outside of the Church, how much more so the schismatics! This same understanding is shared by St. Hilarion (Troitsky).[143]

Bishop Nikodim (Milas) summarizes the commentary of Zonaras on this canon as follows:

Referring to this rule of St. Basil, Zonaras expressed this in more detail, saying: "heretics are all who think not in accordance with the Orthodox faith (παρά τήν ὀρθόδοξον πίστιν δοξάζοντας), even if long ago, even if recently they were excommunicated from the church, even if they were ancient, at least they held on to new heresies." This teaching, which is contrary to the Orthodox faith, should not, however, necessarily concern the foundations of the Orthodox dogma, in order for a given person to be considered a heretic - it is enough that he erred in at least one dogma, and because of this he is already a heretic. "By the name of heretics, we mean those who accept our sacrament (μυστήριον), but in some parts of the teaching they err and disagree with the Orthodox" (διαφερομένους

143 Troitsky, *Unity of the Church*, pp. 43-44.

τοῖς ορθόδοζοις), says Zonaras... In general, according to the canonical teaching of the Orthodox Church, whoever is not Orthodox is a heretic: αἱρετικός εστί πᾶς μή ορθόδοζος.[144]

In this canon, St. Basil agrees with the ecclesiology expressed by St. Cyprian of Carthage, St. Firmilian, and the Apostolic Canons that there are no true Mysteries outside of the one Church. St. Basil makes the distinction between parasynagogues (unlawful assemblies), schismatics who "formerly belonged to the Church" and who disputed over "ecclesiastical causes" and "remediable questions," and heretics who have broken off entirely from the Church and disagree regarding "faith in God itself." Significantly, while parasynagogues or unlawful assemblies are considered to be not yet in schism or heresy, St. Basil nevertheless refers to those who join them as "leaving the catholic Church" and speaks of them being "admitted again into the Church" when they repent and "return."

St. Basil also says in Canon 1 that St. Cyprian and St. Firmilian classified heretics and schismatics "under one head," requiring all to be received into the Church by baptism. St. Basil then says that even if the Encratites received Orthodox into their fold by a method other than baptism, this should not influence how the Orthodox receive the Encratites, as the Orthodox are obliged to "serve the Canons with exactitude"[145] and receive heretics by baptism.[146]

While St. Basil says that the Encratites should be received by baptism, he acknowledges that "some of those in the regions of Asia" did not require schismatics to be received by baptism "out of economy," and that if insisting on their reception by baptism

---

144 Milas, *Rules of the Holy Fathers of the Orthodox Church with Interpretations* (in Russian).

145 The Church of Caesarea, if not Asia Minor generally, clearly continued in the tradition and teaching of the Councils of Iconium, Synnada and Carthage which decreed that heretics should be received by baptism. It was likely to these councils that St. Basil was referring when he said that he was obliged "to serve the canons with exactitude."

146 These words remind us of words spoken by St. Cyprian regarding Pope Stephen's citing the practice of heretics as reason for not baptizing them: "To this point of evil has the Church of God and spouse of Christ been developed, that she follows the examples of heretics" (Letter 73.4.1, To Pompey).

prevented them from returning to the Orthodox Church, he would rather follow the "Fathers who economically regulated the affairs of our Church" by allowing them to be received by chrismation than for them to remain completely outside of the Church.

The Encratite sect, led initially by Tatian, the former disciple of St. Justin Martyr, and later by a certain Severus, held heretical views on marriage, the eating of meat and drinking of wine, and used water instead of wine in the Eucharist.[147] Eusebius quotes St. Irenaeus' *Against Heresies* on Tatian and this sect, describing him as an "apostate" from the Church but adding nothing in the way of Trinitarian heresy. St. Epiphanius in his *Panarion* also makes no mention of them holding heretical views regarding the Trinity.[148] St. Basil, likewise, lists the Encratites alongside the Cathari (Novationists) and Apotactites as schismatics, not heretics. In the case of the Encratites, then, even though St. Basil himself called for them to be received by baptism, he permitted the use of economy for schismatics who had maintained the apostolic form of baptism in three immersions in the name of the Holy Trinity.

In Canon 1, St. Basil is clear that those who depart from the unity of the Church lose the Holy Spirit and cannot bestow the Holy Spirit on others through baptism or ordination. To speak of "apostolic succession" among heretics or schismatics, then, is impossible. As Bishop Nikodim (Milas) confirms:

> Thus, the power of a bishop to ordain others, to communicate to them the grace of the priesthood, depends on succession, i.e. on the extent to which he, the subject bishop, has accepted, inherited this power from persons who can lawfully transfer it to him, and insofar as he knows how to keep this inherited power and, in turn, pass it on to others. Once a bishop loses this power, whether as a result of a schism or heresy, then, of course, he is not in a position to transfer it to others, so that in this bishop the succession has ceased, i.e. he lost the inheritance, of which he became

---

147 Epiphanius, *The Panarion, Books II and III,* Anacephalaeosis IV, 4:1,7.
148 Ibid., pp. 1-6.

a partner through consecration, along with other Orthodox bishops. This canonical idea about the sacred hierarchy in the church, touched upon by Basil the Great in this canon, is nothing more than a succinctly formulated teaching of the Holy Scripture, Holy Fathers and teachers of the Church.[149]

In Canon 47, St. Basil confirms the teaching that heretics and schismatics should be baptized despite the fact that they baptize in the name of the Holy Trinity and despite the fact that Rome had forbidden their reception by baptism. St. Basil again states that baptizing all heretics follows the *akriveia* (exactness) of the canons while Rome's position was that of *oikonomia* (economy).

> As for Encratites and Saccophori and Apotactites... we rebaptize such persons. If it be objected that what we are doing is forbidden as regards this practice of rebaptism, precisely as in the case of present-day Romans, for the sake of economy, yet we insist that our rule prevail, since, inasmuch and precisely as it is an offshoot of the Marcionites, the heresy of those who abominate marriage, and who shun wine, and who call God's creation tainted. We therefore do not admit them into the Church unless they get baptized with our baptism. For let them not say that they are baptized in Father and Son and Holy Spirit who assume God to be a bad creator, in a manner vying with the Marcionites and other heresies. So that if this pleases them more Bishops ought to adopt it, and thus establish as a Canon, in order that anyone following shall be in no danger, and anyone replying by citing it shall be deemed worthy of credence.[150]

When St. Basil distinguishes between heresy and schism in Canon 1, commemorates St. Cyprian and St. Firmilian who classified schismatics and heretics together, and then insists that the Encratites be received into the Church by baptism (Canon 47) despite being schismatics (Canon 1), he expresses the patristic

---

149 Milas, *Rules of the Holy Fathers of the Orthodox Church with Interpretations* (in Russian), op. cit.
150 Agapios and Nicodemus, op. cit.

understanding that heretics and schismatics are outside of the Church. As St. John Chrysostom said, schism is just as serious as heresy:

Therefore I assert and protest, that to make a schism in the Church is no less an evil than to fall into heresy.[151]

Canons 1 and 47 of St. Basil completely overturn the claim that the interpretive framework of *akriveia* (exactitude) and *oikonomia* (economy) did not exist prior to St. Nikodemos the Hagiorite in the 18th century. St. Basil clearly held the same ecclesiology as St. Cyprian and believed that to follow the "exactitude" of the canons meant to baptize all heretics and schismatics, in agreement with Apostolic Canons 46 and 47. While St. Basil acknowledged that some bishops in his time did not receive certain heretics by baptism, he understood this as "by economy" and did not endorse this practice, but accepted the use of economy by others at least in cases of schismatics who had maintained the apostolic form of baptism. In St. Basil's 47th Canon he insists that even schismatics who had the same faith in the Holy Trinity and were baptized in three immersions outside of the Church should be received by baptism despite the fact that "present-day Romans" forbade their reception by baptism. St. Basil says the position of Rome was "by economy," and by saying that this was followed by "present-day Romans" he acknowledged that this was not the ancient practice of Rome. Canon 47 of St. Basil was ratified by the Fifth-Sixth Ecumenical Council and not the practice of Rome at the time of St. Basil. For St. Basil, like St. Cyprian, the baptism of the one Church is the only true baptism and the Holy Spirit cannot be bestowed through "baptisms" performed outside of the unity of the Church.

THE SECOND ECUMENICAL COUNCIL, CANON 7 (AD 381)

St. Basil the Great reposed in AD 379, two years prior to the Second Ecumenical Council in AD 381 at which the Symbol of

---

151 John Chrysostom. *Homilies on Ephesians*, Homily XI (NPNF 1/13:107).

Faith (Nicene Creed) was finalized which expressed the Church's belief in "One, Holy, Catholic and Apostolic Church" and "one baptism for the remission of sins." This Council also dealt with the manner by which heretics should be received into the Church. The confession of faith in "One, Holy, Catholic and Apostolic Church" in the context of the reception of various schismatic and heretical groups is significant because the Council declared that such schisms and heresies do not result in many "churches" with many "baptisms," but that there is only one Church, and the baptism which grants remission of sins is to be found only in that Church. Among those who participated in the Council and helped to formulate its canons was St. Cyril of Jerusalem who explicitly taught that heretics should be baptized because their baptisms are not true baptisms.[152]

Canon 7 of the Second Ecumenical Council deals with the subject of receiving various heretics into the Church:

> As for those heretics who betake themselves to Orthodoxy, and to the lot of the saved, we accept them in accordance with the subjoined sequence and custom; viz.: Arians, and Macedonians, and Sabbatians, and Novatians, those calling themselves Cathari (or "Puritans"), and the Aristeri, and the Quartodecimans, otherwise known as Tetradites, and Apollinarians we accept when they offer libelli (i.e., recantations in writing) and anathematize every heresy that does not hold the same beliefs as the catholic and apostolic Church of God, and are sealed first with holy chrism on their forehead and their eyes, and nose, and mouth, and ears; and in sealing them we say: "A seal of a free gift of Holy Spirit." As for Eunomians, however, who are baptized with a single immersion, and Montanists, who are here called Phrygians, and the Sabellians, who teach that Father and Son are the same person, and who do some other bad things, and (those belonging to) any other heresies (for there are many heretics here), especially such as come from the country of the Galatians: all of them that want to adhere to

---

152 Cyril of Jerusalem, *Lectures on the Christian Sacraments*, p. 44. See quote in Chapter 6.

Orthodoxy we are willing to accept as Greeks. Accordingly, on the first day we make them Christians; on the second day, catechumens; then, on the third day, we exorcize them with the act of blowing thrice into their face and into their ears; and thus do we catechize them, and we make them tarry a while in the church and listen to the Scriptures; and then we baptize them.[153]

According to Canon 7, when heretics and schismatics are received into the Church, only then are they joined "to the lot of the saved," indicating that there is no salvation for those separated from the unity of the Church.

In his commentary on this canon, Bishop Gregory (Grabbe) states:

As for the procedure for the reception of heretics, the acceptance of some of them listed at the beginning of the rule as being received without a new baptism does not mean that the baptism performed on them by heretics is recognized as equivalent to baptism in the Orthodox Church, in which it joins people "to the part of those saved," to which they were alien while they were outside the Church.[154]

Canon 7 of the Second Ecumenical Council does not provide a theological explanation for why some heretics were to be received by chrismation rather than baptism. Among those to be received by chrismation were both the Arians, who taught that Christ was human and not divine, and the Quartodecimans who differed from the Orthodox only in that they celebrated Pascha on the 14th day of the month of Nisan and not according to the date prescribed by the First Ecumenical Council. St. Epiphanius of Salamis (+403) said concerning the Quartodecimans that "their doctrine of the Father, the Son, and the Holy Spirit is good and in agreement with ours."[155] Among those to be received by baptism were "Montanists, who are

---

153 Agapios and Nicodemus, op. cit.
154 Grabbe, *The Canons of the Orthodox Church.*
155 Epiphanius, *The Panarion, Book II and III,* Anacephalaeosis IV:50, 24.

here called Phrygians," about whom St. Epiphanius says, "They agree with the holy Catholic Church about the Father, the Son and the Holy Spirit."[156]

St. Theodore the Studite's Epistle 40[157] has been used to claim that St. Theodore offered a theological explanation for why the councils required some heretics to be received by baptism and others by economy. In this epistle, St. Theodore states:

> As for your desire for me to answer in detail about heresies and baptisms, this exceeds the measure of a letter, and, moreover, it would be superfluous to expand on the fact that the God-bearing Epiphanius investigated and described as none of the Fathers. Therefore, read his holy book about this, and from it you will learn what you wish to know... I will briefly answer about those who are being baptized.[158]

St. Theodore the Studite (+826)
from Dionysiou Monastery, Athos
Feast Day: November 11

St. Theodore is referring to *The Panarion* of St. Epiphanius, an encyclopedia of various sects that existed up to the time of St. Epiphanius, but St. Epiphanius does not deal with the topic of how these various groups are to be received into the Church. In this text, St. Epiphanius describes the various heresies referred to in Canon 7 but does not at all imply that any of the sects have grace in their mysteries or "degrees of ecclesiality." In the preface to the text (Proem 1), St. Epiphanius says:

---

156 Ibid. Anacephalaeosis IV:48, pp. 6-7.
157 Theodore the Studite, Epistle 40 (In Russian).
158 Ibid.

Since I am going to tell you the names of the sects and expose their unlawful deeds like poisons and toxic substances, and at the same time match the antidotes with them as cures for those already bitten and preventatives for those who will have this misfortune, I am drafting this Preface for the scholarly to explain the 'Panarion,' or chest of remedies for those whom savage beasts have bitten. It is composed in three Books containing eighty Sects, symbolically represented by wild beasts or snakes. But "one after the eighty" is at once the foundation, teaching and saving treatment of the truth and Christ's holy bride, the Church.[159]

In *The Panarion*, St. Epiphanius refers to the heretical teachings and practices of these sects as "poisons and toxic substances" that are remedied only by exposure to the true faith and reception into the one true Church. Referring to the Song of Songs, St. Epiphanius says that the one Church is, in the words of the Lord, "My dove, my perfect one… the only one"[160] while the eighty sects represent the "eighty concubines"[161] spoken of in the Scriptures. St. Epiphanius states that these sects are called "concubines" because "each one boasts of having 'Christ' inscribed on her" though they "are not his but have taken his name."[162] He refers to them all as false and poisonous, describing the particular heretical teachings and practices of each, but not ascribing significance to "degrees" of heresy or "degrees" of departure from the Church.

St. Theodore says in his Epistle 40 that those whom Canon 7 stated could be received by chrismation "profess both faith and baptism in the Trinity, preserving the special property of each Hypostasis, and not just one that is common to the Three, although they teach heretically about the other."[163] However, in the same epistle, St. Theodore says that the heresies are all connected like a chain:

---

159 Epiphanius, *The Panarion*, Bk. 1, 3.
160 Song of Songs 6:9
161 Song of Songs 6:8
162 Epiphanius, op. cit., Bk. 1, p. 255.
163 Theodore the Studite, Epistle 40, op. cit.

In general, heresies are like some kind of chain woven by a demon: they hold on to one another and all depend on one head - impiety and atheism, although they differ in names, in time, place, quantity, quality, strength and activity.[164]

At the Seventh Ecumenical Council, when a discussion arose about the theological differences between heretics that the ancient canons required to be received by baptism and those that were permitted to be received by economy, St. Tarasius similarly dismissed this discussion saying:

> Evil is evil, especially in matters of the Church, as far as dogmas are concerned, it is all the same to err to a small degree or to a great degree, because in one case and the other the law of God is broken.[165]

In briefly touching upon differences between various heresies addressed by Canon 7, St. Theodore refers in his epistle to the distinction St. Basil the Great made in his first canon between "heresies" and "schisms" (St. Basil says that heretics have a "difference of faith in God itself"[166]) and offers his understanding of the "differences of faith" between those who were required to be baptized and those who were permitted to be received by economy. In the epistle he also refers to the Apostolic Canons and affirms their authority. He treats the matter very briefly, however, and passes on to another subject, having stated at the beginning that the topic could not be fully addressed in a letter. As St. Theodore references St. Basil's first canon and the Apostolic Canons as authoritative, however, it would be incorrect to interpret him in a way that would contradict St. Basil's clear teaching in Canon 1 and Canon 47. While we do not have a more detailed discussion from St. Theodore elsewhere on the subject of the reception of heterodox into the

---

164 Ibid.

165 *Acts of the Ecumenical Councils* (In Russian), vol. 7, 104, Kazan, 1873.

166 Agapios and Nicodemus, op. cit. Canon 1 of St. Basil.

Church, undoubtably from other writings of his, he did not believe that heretics have grace in their mysteries.[167]

As for the reasons why Canon 7 decreed that some heretics were permitted to be received by chrismation instead of baptism, Zonaras (+1145) states:

> These persons therefore, are not rebaptized, because as respects holy Baptism they differ in nothing from us, but are accustomed to be baptized exactly the same as are the Orthodox...[168]

Likewise, Zonaras states regarding those who were required by this canon to be received by baptism:

> As for these and all other heretics, the holy Fathers have decreed that they be baptized. For whether they received holy baptism or not, they have not received it correctly, nor in the form and style prescribed by the Orthodox Church.[169]

While the canons do not give theological explanations for receiving some heretics by baptism and others by economy, Canon 7 explicitly states that the Eunomians must be received into the Church by baptism because they "baptize with a single immersion."[170] Regarding Eunomius, Sozomen records in his *Ecclesiastical History* in the 5th century:

> Eunomius, who had held the church in Cyzicus in place of Eleusius, and who presided over the Arian heresy, devised another heresy besides this, which some have called by his name, but which is sometimes denominated the Anomian heresy. Some assert that Eunomius was the first who ventured to maintain that divine baptism ought to be performed by one immersion, and to corrupt, in this manner, the apostolic

---

167 See quotes in Chapter 6.
168 Agapios and Nicodemus, op. cit., footnote 66 to The 85 Canons of the Holy Apostles.
169 Ibid.
170 Agapios and Nicodemus, op. cit.

tradition which has been carefully handed down to the present day.[171]

The beliefs of the Eunomians were similar to that of Arians, but while the Arians who practiced baptism with three immersions in the name of the Trinity were permitted to be received by chrismation, the Eunomians were required to be baptized since they did not practice the apostolic form of baptism.

St. Nikodemos states in the *Rudder* that differences in the manner of receiving heretics were also influenced by the circumstances of the times rather than theological considerations:

> For the fact is that the Second Ecumenical Synod, as we have said, employed economy and accepted the baptism of Arians and of Macedoniacs with the aim and hope of their returning to the faith and receiving full understanding of it, and also in order to prevent their becoming yet more savage wild beasts against the Church, since they were also a very great multitude and strong in respect of outward things. And, as a matter of fact, they accomplished this purpose and realized this hope.
>
> For, thanks to this economy those men became more gentle towards the Orthodox Christians and returned so far to piety that within the space of a few years they either disappeared completely or very few of them remained.[172]

St. Nikodemos further explains the application of economy at the Council:

> As for the "economy" which certain Fathers employed for a time it cannot be deemed either a law or an example, but if one were to investigate the matter aright, one would finally discover that these heretics whom the Second Ecumenical Council accepted "economically" were mostly persons in holy orders who had been already duly baptized but had

---

171 Sozomen, *Ecclesiastical History*. Book VI, Chapter XXVI (NPNF 2/2:363).
172 Agapios and Nicodemus, op. cit., footnote 66 of the Apostolic Canons.

succumbed to some heresy, and on this account it employed this "economy."[173]

Canon 7 of the Second Ecumenical Council speaks of two methods for receiving heretics into the Church, baptism and chrismation. Those accepted by Chrismation alone were specifically named, and included both Trinitarian heretics and those who celebrated Pascha on a different date than the Orthodox. Thus, we can conclude that such a rule is not about the degree of heresy or being "Trinitarian." Furthermore, the canon shows that reception by chrismation is an economy because it applied to only specifically named groups, whereas baptism applied broadly to "all other heretics."

As Apostolic Canon 50 requires baptism to be done in three immersions in the name of the Holy Trinity, Canon 7 of the Second Ecumenical Council required those heretics to be received by baptism if they practiced a form of baptism that differed from the Orthodox. Thus, the reception of certain heretics by economy in Canon 7 was not based on theories regarding the presence of grace in the baptism of heretics or "degrees of ecclesiality" among various heretics, but on whether or not the heretics preserved the apostolic form of baptism (three immersions in the name of the Holy Trinity). Also, while this canon allows for specific heretics named in the canon to be received by economy if the apostolic form of baptism had been administered outside of the Church, the canon does not require that these heretics be received by economy, nor was it forbidden to baptize them according to *akriveia*.[174] Furthermore, by stating that those from "any other heresies" not named in the canon were to be baptized, Canon 7 affirms that baptism is the standard method of receiving heretics into the Church while reception by chrismation is an exception to that standard and applicable only to specifically named groups.

---

173 Agapios and Nicodemus, op. cit., Interpretation of the Canon of the Council of Carthage under St. Cyprian.
174 Cf. Canon 47 of St. Basil.

THE LOCAL COUNCIL OF CARTHAGE (AD 419)

After the Council of Carthage under St. Cyprian in AD 258, another Council gathered in Carthage in AD 419 which dealt with the Donatists. This Council issued a canon pertaining to the reception of Donatists into the Church, and based on the corrupted Latin text of this canon, some have claimed that this later Council rejected or abrogated the canon of the previous Council of Carthage. This claim is made despite the fact that St. Cyprian and his ecclesiology are not referred to by the AD 419 Council and despite the fact that both councils and their canons were ratified by the Fifth-Sixth Ecumenical Council in Trullo.

Before addressing the canon regarding the reception of the Donatists, another canon (Canon 80) is significant in that it demonstrates that baptism is so essential that if there is any question as to whether a person had been baptized correctly, such a person should be baptized "without any hindrance," lest they inadvertently be deprived of purification and sanctification.

> It has pleased the Council to decree as regarding infants that whenever reliable witnesses cannot be found to declare that they have been baptized beyond a doubt, nor, on account of their age, are the infants themselves able to vouch for any ceremony administered to them, these persons ought to be baptized without any hindrance, lest any such hesitation deprive them of purification and sanctification.[175]

The canon of the Council of Carthage in AD 419 that refers to the reception of Donatists is numbered Canon 57 in the Latin text and Canon 66 in the Greek text. Regarding the Latin and Greek texts, scholar Philip Schaff stated:

> Evidently in the Latin, as we now have it, there are many corrupt passages. In strange contradistinction to this, the Greek is apparently pure and is clear throughout.[176]

---

175 Agapios and Nicodemus, op. cit.
176 "Introductory Note," The Canons of the CCXII Blessed Fathers Who Assembled at

The Latin Canon 57 reads as follows:

> For in coming to faith they [those who were baptized by
> Donatists] thought the true Church to be their own and there
> they believed in Christ, and received the sacraments of the
> Trinity. And that all these sacraments are altogether true and
> holy and divine is most certain, and in them the whole hope
> of the soul is placed, although the presumptuous audacity
> of heretics, taking to itself the name of the truth, dares to
> administer them. They are but one after all, as the blessed
> Apostle tells us, saying: *One God, one faith, one baptism*, and
> it is not lawful to reiterate what once only ought to be
> administered. [Those therefore who have been so baptized]
> having anathematized their error may be received by the
> imposition of the hand into the one Church, the pillar as it is
> called, and the one mother of all Christians, where all these
> Sacraments are received unto salvation and everlasting life;
> even the same sacraments which obtain for those persevering
> in heresy the heavy penalty of damnation.[177]

This translation gives the impression that the mysteries of the
Donatists were viewed as "altogether true and holy and divine."
However, the English translation from the Greek Canon 66 reads
as follows:

> It is decreed that as regards the children being baptized
> by the Donatists, which children have not yet been able to
> realize the ruin resulting from their error, after becoming
> susceptible of the age of discretion, the truth having come
> to be more fully understood, so that they loathe the villainy
> and rascality of those persons, to the catholic Church of
> God which is diffused over the whole world, by virtue of an
> ancient procedure through imposition of the hand let such
> persons be raised out of the error of a name. They ought
> not to be prevented from entering an order of clergy when

Carthage, NPNF 2/14:440.

177 Quoted in Yakovlev, op. cit.

in fact they considered the true Church their own upon joining the faith, and coming to believe in Christ therein, they received the sanctifying gifts of the Trinity, which all it is plainly evident are true and holy and divine; and in these accordingly the soul's every hope exists, notwithstanding that the aforesaid rashness of the heretics impetuously teaches certain things opposed to the name of the truth. For these things are simple, as the holy Apostle teaches by saying: "One God; one faith; one baptism."[178] And what ought to be given but once is something that it is not permissible to repeat; the name of the error being anathematized, through imposition of the hand let them be admitted into the one Church, the one spoken of as a dove,[179] and sole mother of Christians, in whom all the sanctifying gifts, salvifically[180] everlasting and vital, are received, which, however, inflict upon those persisting in the heresy the great punishment of damnation, in order that what to them in the truth was something brighter that they ought to follow for the purpose of gaining everlasting life, might become to those in the error darker and still more damned."[181]

St. Nikodemos the Hagiorite's commentary in the *Rudder* is consistent with the version of the canon above from the Greek:

...for after eschewing the heresy they recognized the catholic and true Church as their own, believed Orthodoxly in Christ, and accepted as true and holy and with unfeigned yearning and love the sanctifying gifts of the Trinity, or, more expressly the undefiled Mysteries, upon which depend all the soul's hope and salvation.[182]

---

178 Ephesians 4:5

179 Song of Songs 6:9

180 English translation modified based on the Greek. "Salvifically" rather than "soterially."

181 Agapios and Nicodemus, op. cit.

182 Ibid.

In other words, while the corrupted Latin text suggests the mysteries of the Donatists are "true and holy and divine," the version in the *Rudder* from the uncorrupted Greek text affirms that the children baptized by Donatists, after coming of age, realizing their error, and joining the Orthodox Church, receive in the Orthodox Church the "sanctifying gifts of the Trinity."

Canon 66 of the AD 419 Council of Carthage did depart from the exactitude of the Council under St. Cyprian by allowing the children of Donatists to be received into the Church by economy (through the laying on of hands or chrismation). The language of the canon, even in Greek, could also be interpreted through an Augustinian lens, but such an interpretation would not have been possible for the Fathers at the Fifth-Sixth Ecumenical Council since St. Augustine's ecclesiology (especially in *Against the Donatists*) was not circulated outside of Africa prior to the 12th century.[183]

Furthermore, the canons of the 419 Council were adopted at Trullo along with the canons of St. Basil, St. Cyprian and the Apostolic Canons. Therefore, the Fathers at Trullo could only have interpreted this canon through the lens of the ecclesiology with which they were familiar, that of St. Basil, St. Cyprian, and the Apostolic Canons. Canon 66 also cannot be assumed to apply more broadly than the circumstances specified in the canon: whether the children of Donatists who were received into the Church could later be ordained in the Church. The Donatists also retained the apostolic form of baptism with three immersions in the name of the Holy Trinity, which made it possible to receive them by economy.

Summary: Among all of the canons of the Church, the version of Canon 66 from the Council of Carthage in AD 419, derived from corrupted Latin manuscripts, is the only canon attributed to the Ecumenical Councils which has been used to make the case that Councils have affirmed "ecclesiality" and the "presence of the Holy Spirit" in the mysteries of schismatics or heretics. The Greek version of the text that the Council adopted, however, does not support this interpretation; and the Fathers of the Fifth-Sixth

---

183 Cowdrey, *The Dissemination of St. Augustine's Doctrine of Holy Orders During the Later Patristic Age*, p. 454.

Ecumenical Council could not have interpreted this canon through the teachings of St. Augustine whose ecclesiology was unknown to them. Canon 80 of the Council also demonstrates the great importance with which Fathers of the Council considered proper reception into the Church by baptism, such that it would be better to baptize someone a second time in the Church rather than risk leaving them without purification and sanctification. The Donatists were permitted to be received into the Church by the laying on of hands (chrismation) and renunciation of heresy (Canon 66) because they baptized in the apostolic form (three immersions in the name of the Holy Trinity), satisfying the canonical presupposition for the application of economy. In cases where it was uncertain as to whether a person had previously received the apostolic form of baptism, the Council, significantly, did not suggest that chrismation or reception of Holy Communion could fill whatever might be lacking in such cases.

FOURTH ECUMENICAL COUNCIL (AD 451)

The Fourth Ecumenical Council gathered in Chalcedon to respond to the Monophysite heresy, which held that Christ had only a single divine nature rather than being one person with two natures, divine and human. Canon 14 of this Council dealt with the topic of mixed marriages (when an Orthodox person marries a heterodox person) and how to receive children from such marriages. The canon reads:

> Inasmuch as Anagnosts [Readers] and Psalts [Chanters] in some provinces have been permitted to marry,[184] the holy Council has made it a rule that none of them shall be allowed to take a wife that is of a different faith. As for those who have already had children as a result of such a marriage, if they have already had their offspring baptized by heretics, let them bring them into the communion of the

---

184 In some provinces it was not permitted for Readers and Chanters to marry after becoming minor clergy.

catholic Church. But if they have not baptized them, let them no longer have any right to baptize them with heretics, nor, indeed, even to contract a marriage with a heretic, or a Jew, or a Greek, unless they first promise and undertake to convert the person joined to the Orthodox Christian to the Orthodox faith. If, on the other hand, anyone transgresses this rule of the holy Council, let him be liable to a Canonical penalty.[185]

The main purpose of this canon was not to discuss the reception of various heretics into the Church but rather to forbid Orthodox from marrying non-Orthodox (heterodox) and to discuss what to do about children from such mixed marriages. While it was forbidden for Orthodox to marry heterodox, if such a marriage had taken place and children were born from such a marriage, this canon states that if the child has not already been baptized by heretics then they must be brought to the Church to be baptized. If the child had not yet been baptized in the Church or by heretics, the canon forbids the parents to allow the child to be baptized by heretics. If the child had already been baptized by heretics, they were to be brought into communion with the Church. However, the canon does not specify how children should be brought into communion with the Church after they had been baptized by heretics. According to the interpretation of St. Nikodemos, the canonist Zonaras states that children baptized by heretics could be received into the Church by chrismation provided that the apostolic form of baptism was administered by the heretics (three full immersions in the name of the Holy Trinity),[186] but St. Nikodemos says that such children should definitely be received by baptism if they had not received the apostolic form of baptism; and that "it would be more correct and safer for them to be baptized" in the Church even if they received the apostolic form of baptism from heretics "seeing that the baptism of all heretics is in the nature of a pollution."[187]

---

185 Agapios and Nicodemus, op. cit., Canon 14 of the Fourth Ecumenical Council.
186 Ibid.
187 Ibid.

THE FIFTH-SIXTH ECUMENICAL COUNCIL IN TRULLO, CANON 95 (AD 692)

The Fifth-Sixth Ecumenical Council (also called the Quinisext Council, the Penthekte Council, or Council of Trullo) was held in AD 692 to establish canons dealing with disciplinary matters that were not addressed in either the Fifth Ecumenical Council (AD 553) nor the Sixth Ecumenical Council (AD 681). The Fifth-Sixth Ecumenical Council was called to supplement the Fifth and Sixth Ecumenical Councils, its canons were ratified by the Seventh Ecumenical Council, and it is considered to be of Ecumenical authority.[188]

Canon 95 of the Fifth-Sixth Ecumenical Council is the last canon from an Ecumenical Council to address the topic of the reception of heretics into the Church. Just as Canon 2 of the Fifth-Sixth Ecumenical Council ratified and accepted the Apostolic Canons and the canons of the previous local and Ecumenical Councils and Holy Fathers, Canon 95 quotes Canon 7 of the Second Ecumenical Council and then addresses additional heretical groups that emerged since the Second Ecumenical Council:

> We accept those from heresies being added to orthodoxy and to the portion of those being saved, according to both the service and custom submitted below. We accept Arians, indeed, and Macedonians and Novations, those calling themselves clean and Aristeri and the Fourteenists, considered Tetradites, and Apollinarists, giving documents and anathematizing all heresies not thinking as thinks the holy, Catholic and Apostolic Church of God, by sealing, that is by anointing first, by holy Myrrh, the forehead and the eyes and the nostrils and the mouth and the ears and sealing them saying: "Seal of gift of Holy Spirit." And concerning the Paulanists, then taking refuge to the Catholic Church, a rule has been set forth to re-baptise them in every case. However, Eunomians, those baptising

---

188 Thornton, *The OEcumenical Synods of the Orthodox Church: A Concise History*, p. 119.

unto one immersion, and Montanists, those hereabouts called Phrygians, and Sabellians, those glorifying [teaching] son-father (modalism) and doing other embarrassing things, and all the other heresies, for there are many hereabout, especially those coming from the Galatian region, all those from them willing to be added to orthodoxy, we receive as Greeks. And the first day we make them Christians, and the second catechizing them then, the third we exorcise them with the act of breathing thrice on their faces and then we baptize them. *And also the Manicheans and the Valentinians and Marcionites, and those out of similar heresies. It is necessary to make documents and to anathematise their heresy, the Nestorians and Nestorius and Eutyches and Dioscorus, and Severus and the remaining exarchs of these heresies and those thinking their things, and all the aforementioned heresies. And thusly to partake of holy communion.*[189]

The portion of the canon prior to the italicized text is nearly identical to Canon 7 of the Second Ecumenical Council. The italicized portion of the canon has various versions and translations which has resulted in some confusion. As Fr. Patrick Ramsey has noted,[190] some versions and translations have been worded in such a way as to imply that the followers of Nestorius, Eutyches, Dioscorus, and Severus were to be received only by confession of faith. However, the penultimate (second to last) sentence can be understood not as a separate means of reception (by confession of faith alone), but as ensuring that the names of these heretics and heresies are added to the documents that all converts sign before being received into the Church, and that these documents

---

189 Ramsey, *Canon 95 - Council of Trullo*. Ramsey also notes that there were some ancient readings of Canon 95 that only required documents of faith, such as St Gregory the Great in a letter to Bishop Quiricus. If this is to be understood as a valid practice, then it can be reconciled with Canon 1 of St. Basil the Great in that Nestorians and Monophysites both baptize and anoint in the same way as the Orthodox Church in the form of each and so neither form needs repeating on reception. Thus, the only issue is correct Faith. This is an exception for only two heresies that anoint with myrrh in the same way as the Orthodox Church. St. Gregory is clear that there is no "power of cleansing" until one is received into the Church.

190 Ibid.

are necessary. In other words, the followers of Nestorius, Eutyches, Dioscorus, and Severus were to be added to the list of heretics mentioned in the previous sentence who were to be received by baptism. The final sentence can be understood as added at the end to affirm the practice of the Church of giving Holy Communion immediately after reception into the Church, thereby completing the canon with reception of Holy Communion which completes the Mystery of reception into the Church. The translation above also agrees with the 12th century canonist Theodore Balsamon who interpreted Canon 95 of the Fifth-Sixth Ecumenical Council as allowing for the reception of heretics by two methods (baptism or chrismation) rather than three (baptism, chrismation, or confession of faith). Balsamon states:

> …according to the text of such a canon, some of the heretics are sanctified by baptism, and others perfected only by holy myron [chrismation].[191]

This translation and interpretation is in agreement with Canon 7 of the Second Ecumenical Council which acknowledges two methods of receiving heretics into the Church (baptism and chrismation) rather than three (baptism, chrismation, or confession of faith) as some versions suggest. This is also in agreement with Canon 1 of St. Basil where he states that while he prefers for all heretics to be received by baptism, if some bishops by economy do not receive heretics by baptism, they "must at all events be anointed" (chrismated) before receiving the Mysteries. The interpretation that the Marcionites are to be baptized along with the Nestorians and Monophysites also agrees with Canon 47 of St. Basil where he states that the Encratites, Saccophori and Apotactites should be received by baptism since they are similar to the Marcionites. This interpretation of Canon 95 was also followed be the Georgian Council of Ruisi-Urbnisi in 1103 and by the 1620 Council of Moscow,[192] both of which will be discussed below.

---

191 Viscuso, *Guide for a Church Under Islam*, p. 34.
192 Dragas, *The Manner of Reception of Roman Catholic Converts into the Orthodox Church*, p. 17.

As in Canon 7 of the Second Ecumenical Council, Canon 95 of the Fifth-Sixth Ecumenical Council requires the Eunomians to be received by baptism since they did not maintain the outward form of baptism commanded by the Apostles in Canon 50 (three immersions in the name of the Holy Trinity), while those who were permitted to be received by economy had retained the apostolic form of baptism. On the necessity of the apostolic form of baptism in three immersions as a precondition for the reception of heretics by economy, and the consequences of applying economy without these preconditions, Fr. George Metallinos summarizes the teachings of Constantine Oikonomos and the Kollyvades Fathers by saying:

> The exercise of *economia* was possible, because there existed the *absolutely necessary* "formal" conditions, i.e. the correct execution of the sacrament by these heretics with three immersions and emersions. The rejection of the single-immersion baptism of the Eunomians, who were classified among the wholly unbaptized, indicates the Council's – and consequently the catholic Church's – condemnation of any alteration in the form of the sacrament of baptism, which alteration is sufficient to render the exercise of *economia* towards these heretics entirely impossible. In this case, according to Oikonomos, "The danger concerning all: they were not born of water and spirit, nor were they through baptism buried with Christ into His death." That is to say, they are unbaptized, and therefore bereft of the regeneration of Christ.
>
> The problem, in the final analysis, is not the disregard or rejection of a mere "form," but something much deeper: namely, disobedience to Christ's command ("...baptizing them..." Mt. 28:19), and unfaithfulness to the Church's tradition. And this tradition, if not held fast in its totality as *pleroma*-fullness of life, runs the risk of becoming estranged, and consequently of losing its total force![193]

---

193 Metallinos, op. cit., p. 63.

That Canon 95 of the Fifth-Sixth Ecumenical Council also required the followers of Eutyches, Dioscorus, and Severus to be received by baptism is also attested to by the Georgian Council of Ruisi-Urbnisi, convened in the year 1103 by St. David the IV, "The Restorer" and King of Georgia. The Council of Ruisi-Urbnisi decreed in Canon 15:

Those of the Armenian heretics, adherents of the *khachetsar* formula,[194] who convert to the Right and Pure Faith, and wish to join the Holy and Catholic Church, and condemn the abominable heresy of one nature, which proclaims in its ignorance that Christ Our True God has one will and one operation, being a union of mingled human and divine natures, and therefore neither divine nor human but something mingled and strange—for them

St. David IV (+1125)
Feast Day: January 26

we decree to be baptized in full, like pagans, for this is the way Great Churches, such as the Antiochian Patriarchate and other Eastern Churches accept them.[195]

---

194 The word *khachetsar* is the Armenian term standing for the formula of Peter the Fuller: "Thou Who wast crucified for us" which was included by the Monophysites in the Trisagion (consequently, the Trisagion read: Holy God, Holy Mighty, Holy Immortal Who wast crucified for us, have mercy on us"). Footnote from the text cited in footnote below.

195 Protopriest John Townsend, *The Holy and Righteous King David the Restorer of Georgia & The Holy and Righteous Queen Tamar of Georgia: Lives, Akathist, Canons, Works*, p. 85.

The Council of Ruisi-Urbnisi attested to the fact that the reception of the Armenian Monophysites by baptism was the practice of the Antiochian Patriarchate and the other "Eastern Churches" at that time. Along with Canon 7 of the Second Ecumenical Council, Canon 95 of the Fifth-Sixth Ecumenical Council reiterated that heretics should be received by baptism or chrismation, that those heretics who were not baptized in the apostolic manner (three immersions in the name of the Holy Trinity) are to be received by baptism, that even some who baptized in three immersions in the name of the Holy Trinity (followers of Nestorius, Eutyches, Dioscorus, and Severus) were to be received by baptism, and that "all the other heresies" not mentioned in the canon should also be received by baptism.

Canon 84 of the Fifth-Sixth Ecumenical Council also reiterates Canon 80 of the AD 419 Council of Carthage, that if there is any question as to whether a person has been correctly baptized, and no witnesses to verify that baptism was correctly administered in the Church, such a person must be baptized lest they possibly be deprived of "purifying sanctification." In the Orthodox Church, we expressly forbid baptism to a person for a second time, if they were already baptized in the Orthodox Church in three full immersions according to the apostolic command; but if a person's Orthodox baptism was not correctly done, then they are to be baptized.

> Closely following the Fathers' institutions, we decree also as concerning infants, whenever there can be found no reliable witnesses who can state beyond a doubt that they have been duly baptized, and neither are they themselves owing to their infancy able to give any information at all in reply to questions respecting the mystagogical rite administered to them, they must be baptized without putting any obstacle in the way, lest any such hesitation may deprive them of such purifying sanctification.[196]

Summary: Canon 95 of the Fifth-Sixth Ecumenical Council reiterated that the Eunomians must be baptized since they did

---

196 Agapios and Nicodemus, op. cit., Canon 84 of the Quinisext Council.

not practice the apostolic form of baptism in three immersions. Canon 84 reiterated that a person who may have been baptized in the Church as a baby should be baptized again if there is any question as to whether the first baptism was done correctly. Canon 2 of the Fifth-Sixth Ecumenical Council, by adopting some canons that insist on baptizing all heretics and other canons which allow exceptions to this rule for certain specifically named heretics, is not contradictory when understood through the interpretive key of exactness (*akriveia*) and economy (*oikonomia*) as explained in Canons 1 and 47 of St. Basil.

THE SEVENTH ECUMENICAL COUNCIL
AND THE RECEPTION OF THE ICONOCLAST CLERGY (AD 787)

The Seventh Ecumenical Council convened in AD 787 to resolve the controversy over the veneration of icons. While the Council did not establish canons pertaining to the reception of heretics into the Church, the fact that the Council accepted some repentant Iconoclast bishops, and allowed for these bishops to continue serving the Church in their orders after their repentance, has been used by some to claim that the Seventh Ecumenical Council acknowledged "ecclesiality" and "the presence of the Holy Spirit" in the mysteries of heretics. The problem with this assertion is that at the time of the Council the Orthodox and Iconoclasts were part of the same Church. The Iconoclasts had not completely broken off from the rest of the Church, nor had the Iconoclast bishops that were permitted to remain bishops in the Church been deposed or anathematized by any council up to that point.

According to Basil Touloumtsis in his book *The Ecclesiological Framework and Presuppositions for the Reception of Heretics According to the Minutes of the Second Ecumenical Council*, there were eleven instances of repentant Iconoclast bishops who were permitted to remain bishops after their repentance without re-ordination, re-chrismation, or re-baptism. All of these bishops had been baptized, chrismated, and ordained within the canonical Church. They were referred to as "heretics" because of their beliefs but not regarding their ecclesiastical status as they had not broken away from the rest of the Church. Prior to the Seventh Ecumenical Council, the Iconoclasts had not been canonically judged, deposed, nor anathematized. These bishops, while teaching heresy, formally belonged to the one Church so there was no question as to the validity of their orders or Mysteries.[197]

This agrees with St. Nikodemos' explanation regarding the economy used in the reception of certain heretics at the Second Ecumenical Council:

> As for the "economy" certain Fathers employed for a time it cannot be deemed either a law or an example, but if one were to investigate the matter aright, one would finally discover that these heretics whom the Second Ecumenical Council accepted "economically" were mostly persons in holy orders who had been already duly baptized but had succumbed to some heresy, and on this account it employed this "economy."[198]

The reception of the Iconoclasts into the Church at the Seventh Ecumenical Council highlights the important distinction between receiving into the Church those who were baptized and ordained before they departed in heresy and schism, and those who were baptized and ordained while in heresy and schism and cut off from the Church. Apostolic Canon 47 forbids a bishop or priest to baptize someone who has already had a "true baptism," meaning a baptism with three immersions (Apostolic Canon 50) in the Orthodox Church. Apostolic Canon 68 states regarding re-ordinations:

> If any Bishop, or Presbyter, or Deacon accepts a second ordination from anyone, let him and the one who ordained him be deposed. Unless it be established that his ordination has been performed by heretics. For those who have been baptized or ordained by such persons cannot possibly be either faithful Christians or clergymen.[199]

---

197 Touloumtsis, *The Ecclesiological Framework and Presuppositions of Reception of Heretics According to the Minutes of the Seventh Ecumenical Council* (In Greek), pp. 342-343.

198 Agapios and Nicodemus, op. cit.

199 Ibid. Apostolic Canon 68.

St. Cyprian of Carthage, while teaching that all heretics and schismatics should be received by baptism, agreed that this would not apply to those who were baptized in the Church and only afterwards departed into schism and heresy:

> Therefore, dearest brother, having explored and seen the truth; it is observed and held by us, that all who are converted from any heresy whatever to the Church must be baptized by the only and lawful baptism of the Church, with the exception of those who had previously been baptized in the Church, and so had passed over to the heretics. For it behooves these, when they return, having repented, to be received by the imposition of hands only, and to be restored by the shepherd to the sheep-fold whence they had strayed.[200]

St. Nikodemos also explains that the Church at the Seventh Ecumenical Council exercised greater economy towards the followers of the heresy than to its leaders:

> ...The Seventh Ecumenical Council also, although it accepted the ordinations of the heretical Iconoclasts (not, however, of the original instigators of the heresy, nor of those who were passionately disposed and not genuinely and truly repenting, as the divine Tarasius said, but rather of those who followed the original instigators and who were truly and genuinely repenting; about this see the interpretation of the epistle of Athanasius the Great to Rufinian) and did not again re-ordain those ordained by them when they had returned to the Orthodox Faith, as is seen in its first act, it nevertheless did this in economy on account of the great multitude of Iconoclasts which was then abundant—just as also the Second Ecumenical Council accepted on account of economy the baptism of certain heretics, as we forementioned. For in fact Patriarch Anatolius, too, was ordained by the heretic Dioscorus and the heretical council around him, and Saint Meletius of

---

200   Cyprian of Carthage, *Epistle LXXIII:12 to Pompey* (ANF 5:389-390).

Antioch by Arians, according to Sozomen (Book 4, Ch. 28), and many others were ordained by heretics, and thereafter they were accepted by the Orthodox. Yet these things are rare and dependent on circumstance, lacking/being inferior in canonical exactitude—and what is rare and what is done dependent on circumstance is not a law of the Church, according to the seventeenth canon of the First and Second Council and Gregory the Theologian and the second act of the council in Holy Wisdom [Hagia Sophia] and that legal maxim which says, "What is contrary to the Canons is not drawn into an example." The second ordinations of the Orthodox are prohibited also by the fifty-seventh canon of Carthage.[201]

When heresies have arisen within the Church historically, complete separation and schism has usually not resulted immediately or universally. As heresies spread, confusion results among the faithful and clergy regarding which bishops are teaching heresy and which bishops are Orthodox. Prior to a formal and synodal condemnation at an authoritative council, confusion may persist regarding the boundaries of the Church. Until a formal condemnation of heretics and heresies at a true council that is guided by the Holy Spirit, until bishops or priests are formally anathematized or deposed, or until the erring party completely breaks off from the rest of the Church in schism, Orthodox and heretics may remain for a time as both belonging to the one Church. A priest or bishop of the Church who begins to believe or teach heresy does not cease to serve grace-filled Mysteries as long as the Church recognizes that priest or bishop as a priest or bishop of the Church. Such a priest or bishop may be liable to condemnation before God for his false beliefs, and spiritually speaking is "outside of the Church" and separated from Christ, but he nevertheless continues to serve true Mysteries as long as he has authority from the Church to do so. If that priest or bishop departs from the Church in schism and ceases to be recognized by

---

201 Agapios and Nicodemus, op. cit. Canon 68 of the Seventh Ecumenical Council.

the Church as a priest of the Church, that heretical priest or bishop then loses the grace and authority to serve true Mysteries.[202]

At the Seventh Ecumenical Council the Iconoclast bishops and priests who did not repent were anathematized and no longer considered true priests and bishops who could bestow the Holy Spirit on others through baptism or ordination. As St. Tarasius said at the Council:

> An anathema is a terrible thing, because it puts a man far away from God, and chases him from the kingdom of heaven, and sends him to the outer darkness.[203]

To suggest there is "ecclesiality" and the "presence of the Holy Spirit" in the mysteries of those who persist in their heresy after formally being anathematized by the Church, after being completely cut off from the Church, and cast into "outer darkness" is impossible. Great importance also lies in distinguishing between the Church's leniency towards those who repent in response to the anathematizing of heresy at a genuine council, and the status of heretics who have been separated from the Church for centuries after such anathemas were declared.

The reception of the Iconoclast bishops in their orders is not applicable to the reception into the Orthodox Church of those heretics who were anathematized by past Councils. The Monophysites were anathematized by the Fourth Ecumenical Council and became completely broken off from the rest of the Church over 1500 years ago. The Third Ecumenical Council (431) and Eighth Ecumenical Council (879-880) under St. Photios anathematized any additions to or subtractions from the Creed, which was aimed at the *Filioque* that had been inserted by the Franks but which had not yet been adopted by the Pope of Rome.[204] The Eighth Ecumenical Council was accepted by the entire Church,

---

202 See Canon 1 of St. Basil and St. Nektarios of Aegina *Concerning the Ethical Perfection of Those Who Conduct the Mysteries,* quoted in Chapter 7 on the teachings of St. Augustine.

203 Mansi, *Proceedings of the Holy Œcumenical Synods* (in Greek), p. 724a.

204 Dragas, *The 8ᵗʰ Ecumenical Council: Constantinople IV (879/880) and the Condemnation of the Filioque Addition and Doctrine.*

including Rome, for nearly 200 years. Rome only rejected the Eighth Ecumenical Council under Pope Gregory VII (Pope from 1073-1085), replacing the Council that occurred under St. Photios with the Ignatian Council (869-870) which had been condemned by the Eighth Ecumenical Council under St. Photios.[205] After the Great Schism, the Latins formally dogmatized the *Filioque* addition to the Creed at the 1274 Council of Lyons, which they adopted as their 9th Ecumenical Council.[206] Since the Great Schism, the Latins have been completely broken off from the rest of the Church and have continued to dogmatize additional heresies. Unlike the Iconoclast bishops who had been baptized and ordained in the one Church, the Latins have been cut off from the Church for nearly 1,000 years, whereas the Protestants who broke off from the Latins have no historical connection to the Orthodox Church.

SUMMARY

The Ecumenical Councils in their decrees and canons present the God-inspired and infallible witness regarding the theological and canonical topics addressed therein. The Canons of the Ecumenical and Local Councils, of the Holy Apostles, and of the Holy Fathers were adopted and ratified by the Fifth-Sixth Ecumenical Council to be "left firm and secure for the care of souls and the cure of diseases." The Seventh Ecumenical Council declared these canons to have been written by men who "having been guided by the light dawning out of the same Spirit, prescribed rules that are to our best interest," and the Council ordered that these canons "remain unwavering and unshakable." The Council also declared that "we too anathematize whomsoever they consign to anathema; and we too depose whomsoever they consign to deposition." From the God-inspired canons that deal directly with the reception of heretics into the Church, we can conclude that:

---

205 Ford, *St. Photios the Great, the Photian Council, and Relations with the Roman Church.*
206 Second Council of Lyons – 1274.

1. Baptism must be performed in the apostolic manner (three immersions in the name of the Holy Trinity).[207]

2. If there is any question as to whether an Orthodox Christian received a correct form of baptism in the Church then he should be baptized without hesitation.[208]

3. Heretics (non-Orthodox or heterodox) who are cut off from the unity of the Church do not receive the Holy Spirit through their mysteries and should be received into the Church by baptism as a rule.[209]

4. The reception of some heretics by chrismation historically was considered reception by economy, an exception to the rule, and its application required that the heretic had already received the apostolic form of baptism (three full immersions in the name of the Holy Trinity).[210]

5. Those baptized outside of the Church could still be received by baptism even if their baptism outside of the Church was done according to the apostolic form.[211]

6. A person who is not correctly baptized in the Orthodox Church risks being deprived of purification and sanctification.[212]

---

207 Apostolic Canon 50.

208 Canon 80 of the AD 419 Council in Carthage, Canon 84 of the Council of Trullo.

209 Apostolic Canon 46 and 47, St. Basil's Canon 1 and 47, Canon 7 of the 2nd Ecumenical Council, Canon 95 of Trullo.

210 Apostolic Canon 50, Canon 80 of the AD 419 Council in Carthage, Canon 84 of the Council of Trullo, Canon 7 of the 2nd Ecumenical Council and Canon 95 of Trullo regarding the Eunomians.

211 Apostolic Canon 46 and 47, St. Basil's Canon 1 and 47, Canon 95 of Trullo regarding the Monophysites and others added to Canon 7 of the 2nd Ecumenical Council.

212 Canon 80 of the AD 419 Council in Carthage, Canon 84 of the Council of Trullo.

When reviewing the teachings of other saints and Fathers on the topic of the reception of the heterodox and the boundaries of the Church, if we find some saints who seemingly contradict the teachings of the Ecumenical Councils on these topics, we should overlook such errors and only hold firmly to those teachings which the Ecumenical Councils have ratified and established as God-inspired and unshakeable.

St. Ignatius of Antioch (+108)
Feast Day: December 20

CHAPTER 6

Other Early Eastern Saints and Fathers
on the Rites of Heretics

Those who oppose the ecclesiology of St. Cyprian and the Ecumenical Councils commonly suggest that the Greek East and Latin West prior to the Schism were substantially different, that the Church in the West was fully Orthodox and patristic in its teachings right up to the Great Schism in 1054, and therefore anything taught by a saint or Father of the West prior to 1054 must be considered Orthodox. This approach is problematic for a number of reasons including the fact that the Great Schism was the culmination of the process of the West falling away from Orthodoxy, and the final falling away cannot be entirely separated from the "small" departures from the apostolic and patristic Tradition which culminated in the Great Schism. Nevertheless, since some claim that the teachings of the Ecumenical Councils represent only the "Eastern view" while the "West" supposedly had a different understanding of ecclesiology and the reception of converts that was equally Orthodox, we will discuss teachings of the saints and Fathers of the East and West separately.

St. Ignatius of Antioch (+108), the great Apostolic Father, taught that only those who belong to the unity of the Church belong to God and those who follow schismatics will not inherit the kingdom of God:

Keep yourselves from those evil plants which Jesus Christ does not tend, because they are not the planting of the Father. Not that I have found any division among you, but exceeding purity. For as many as are of God and of Jesus Christ are also with the bishop. And as many as shall, in the exercise of repentance, return into the unity of the Church, these, too, shall belong to God, that they may live according to Jesus Christ. Do not err, my brethren. If any man follows him that makes a schism in the Church, he shall not inherit the kingdom of God. If any one walks according to a strange opinion, he agrees not with the passion of Christ.[213]

Regarding the teachings of St. Ignatius and other Apostolic Fathers on schism and heresy, Church historian Jaroslav Pelikan observes:

Heresy and schism were closely related because both of them violated the unity of the church. It is interesting that in all seven epistles of Ignatius the church was explicitly called 'holy' only once, while the unity of the church in the bishop was one of the overriding preoccupations of all the epistles, so much so that it seems accurate to conclude that "the most important aspect of the church for the apostolic fathers is its unity."[214]

According to St. Ignatius, everything flows from the unity of the Godhead. As there is one Father, one Lord Jesus Christ, and one Holy Spirit, there is also "one faith, and one preaching, and one Eucharist," and "one baptism; and one Church which the holy apostles established. . . ."[215] Within this unity, which is proved by communion with the bishop, there is the Lord; outside of this unity, God does not dwell.[216] St. Ignatius "knows nothing of any

---

213 Ignatius of Antioch, *Epistle to the Philadelphians*, Ch. III (ANF 1:80).
214 Pelikan, *The Emergence of the Catholic Tradition (100-600)*, p. 159. Pelikan is quoting R. Grant's work *Miracle and Natural Law in Graeco-Roman and Early Christian Thought*, Amsterdam, 1952, p. 137.
215 Ignatius, op. cit., Ch. 4 (long version).
216 Ibid., Ch. 8.

distinction between a visible and an invisible Church. The unity he demands is visible and easily discerned."[217] Therefore, it comes as no surprise that, like the Apostle Paul,[218] he foresaw and warned of wolves in sheep's clothing, meaning schismatics and heretics, rising up to scatter and destroy the flock.[219] These are the enemies of unity and it was obvious that as such they were no longer a part of the Church.[220]

St. Irenaeus of Lyons (+ c. 202) writing some seventy years before the rise of the Novatianists and one hundred and thirty years before the rise of the Donatists, expressed the primitive Church's mind on the subject of heresy and schism with great lucidity. As in St. Ignatius' epistles, it was taken for granted that schismatics and heretics were to be shunned by the faithful, and they were to "cleave to those who keep the Apostles' doctrine."[221] St. Irenaeus would have considered the mysteries performed by a bishop who had

St. Irenaeus of Lyons (+ c. 202)
Feast Day: August 23

been justly defrocked and excommunicated on account of schism or heresy to be inauthentic and void of any spiritual content. It was inconceivable in the early Church to think of a bishop apart from his church and flock.[222] As St. Irenaeus held in common with all of the early Fathers that "the Church was the sole fountain of grace, and that outside it none can be assured of salvation or of sacramental

---

217 Willis, *Saint Augustine and the Donatist Controversy*, p. 94.
218 Acts 20:29.
219 Ignatius, op. cit., *The Epistle to the Antiochians*, Chapter 2 and 6.
220 Ignatius, op. cit., *Epistle to the Philadelphians*, Chapter 3.
221 Ireneaus, *Against Heresies*, 4:26.2-5.
222 Willis, p. 145.

grace, he would have ruled out as entirely worthless the sacraments of schismatics."[223]

As St. Irenaeus taught, the Holy Spirit acts *mysteriologically* in the Church alone:

> "For in the Church," it is said, "God hath set apostles, prophets, teachers," and all the other means through which the Spirit works; of which all those are not partakers who do not join themselves to the Church, but defraud themselves of life through their perverse opinions and infamous behavior. For where the Church is, there is the Spirit of God; and where the Spirit of God is, there is the Church, and every kind of grace; but the Spirit is truth.[224]

St. Irenaeus taught that those who introduce false teachings and who separate from the unity of the Church and the succession of the Apostles will not enter the kingdom of heaven. St. Irenaeus also shows that true apostolic succession requires both the external succession from the Apostles through the laying on of hands, and succession in the "truth."

---

223 Ibid.

224 Irenaeus, *Against Heresies*, 3:24.1. The last phrase is supposed by some today to mean that the Church is coterminous with the Holy Spirit and thus, since the Holy Spirit acts throughout creation, therefore the boundaries of the Church cannot be determined with any certainty. They say that "we know where the Church is, but cannot be sure where the Church is not." But such an interpretation actually is the very opposite of the Saint's meaning. It ignores both the context of the phrase and content of the treatise. Moreover, it stands in contradiction to the mind of the early Church Fathers on the question, of which St. Irenaeus was both a preserver and bearer and exceptional expositor. In the passage in question he begins with the Church and Her identity and location, which is certain, and places the Holy Spirit within Her. In this, he is following the order of the day of Pentecost, when the assembly of those being saved, the Church, was gathered together and the Holy Spirit descended. For, as Fr. Georges Florovsky has written, "the Body of Christ was created and formed already by the Incarnation" (Vol. 14 of Collected Works, pg. 35). There is no identity crisis in St. Irenaeus' thought, no uncertainty as to character or confusion as to boundaries. "The ultimate identity of the Church is grounded in her sacramental structure, in the organic continuity of the body" (Florovsky, Vol. 14 of Collected Works, p. 36). Of all the early fathers, St. Irenaeus stressed this the most. He *knows* where the Church is and it is *within Her* that the Holy Spirit, Who *is truth*, dwells, and, furthermore, as he already stated, *all those are not partakers* of the Holy Spirit *who do not join themselves to the Church* whose boundaries are clearly marked by the company of *apostles, prophets,* and *teachers.*

Wherefore it is incumbent to obey the presbyters who are in the Church, those who, as I have shown, possess the succession from the apostles; those who, together with the succession of the episcopate, have received the certain gift of truth, according to the good pleasure of the Father. But [it is also incumbent] to hold in suspicion others who depart from the primitive succession, and assemble themselves together in any place whatsoever, [looking upon them] either as heretics of perverse minds, or as schismatics puffed up and self-pleasing, or again as hypocrites, acting thus for the sake of lucre and vainglory. For all these have fallen from the truth. And the heretics, indeed, who bring strange fire to the altar of God—namely, strange doctrines—shall be burned up by the fire from heaven, as were Nadab and Abiud. But such as rise up in opposition to the truth, and exhort others against the Church of God, [shall] remain among those in hell, being swallowed up by an earthquake, even as those who were with Chore, Dathan, and Abiron. But those who cleave asunder, and separate the unity of the Church, [shall] receive from God the same punishment as Jeroboam did.[225]

St. Irenaeus writes that only those who are united with the one Church have the Holy Spirit and those who leave the unity of the Church reject the Holy Spirit:

For this gift of God has been entrusted to the Church, as breath was to the first created man, for this purpose, that all the members receiving it may be vivified; and the [means of] communion with Christ has been distributed throughout it, that is, the Holy Spirit, the earnest of incorruption, the means of confirming our faith, and the ladder of ascent to God. For in the Church, it is said, God has set apostles, prophets, teachers, (1 Corinthians 12:28) and all the other means through which the Spirit works; of which all those are not partakers who do not join themselves to the Church, but

---

225   Irenaus of Lyons, *Against Heresies*, Book IV, Ch.26:2 (ANF 1:497).

defraud themselves of life through their perverse opinions and infamous behavior. For where the Church is, there is the Spirit of God; and where the Spirit of God is, there is the Church, and every kind of grace; but the Spirit is truth. Those, therefore, who do not partake of Him, are neither nourished into life from the mother's breasts, nor do they enjoy that most limpid fountain which issues from the body of Christ; but they dig for themselves broken cisterns (Jeremiah 2:13) out of earthly trenches, and drink putrid water out of the mire, fleeing from the faith of the Church lest they be convicted; and rejecting the Spirit, that they may not be instructed. Alienated thus from the truth, they do deservedly wallow in all error, tossed to and fro by it, thinking differently in regard to the same things at different times, and never attaining to a well-grounded knowledge, being more anxious to be sophists of words than disciples of the truth. For they have not been founded upon the one rock, but upon the sand, which has in itself a multitude of stones.[226]

Clement of Alexandria (reposed in the early 200s) is not a saint or Father of the Church but was an influential early Christian writer who expressed the common teaching of the Church that heretics are "destitute of God" and their baptisms are "not proper and true water":

Now he who has fallen into heresy passes through an arid wilderness, abandoning the only true God, destitute of God, seeking waterless water, reaching an uninhabited and thirsty land, collecting sterility with his hands. And those destitute of prudence, that is, those involved in heresies, "I enjoin," remarks Wisdom, saying, "Touch sweetly stolen bread and the sweet water of theft;" (Prov. 9:17)... Then He subjoins: "For so shalt thou pass through the water of another;" reckoning heretical baptism not proper and true water. "And thou shalt pass over another's river," that rushes

226 Ibid., Book III, Ch. XXIV:2 (ANF 1:458).

along and sweeps down to the sea; into which he is cast who, having diverged from the stability which is according to truth, rushes back into the heathenish and tumultuous waves of life.[227]

St. Firmilian, Bishop of Caesarea (+269), who was commemorated by St. Basil in his first canon that was adopted by the Fifth-Sixth Ecumenical Council, taught that heretics who are separated from the Church have no grace in their mysteries:

St. Firmilian of Cæsarea (+269)
Feast Day: October 28

Moreover, all other heretics, if they have separated themselves from the Church of God, can have nothing of power or of grace, since all power and grace are established in the Church where the elders preside, who possess the power both of baptizing, and of imposition of hands, and of ordaining. For as a heretic may not lawfully ordain nor lay on hands, so neither may he baptize, nor do anything holily or spiritually, since he is an alien from spiritual and deifying sanctity... But neither must we pass over what has been necessarily remarked by you, that the Church, according to the Song of Songs, is a garden enclosed, and a fountain sealed, a paradise with the fruit of apples.[228] They who have never entered into this garden, and have not seen the paradise planted by God the Creator, how shall they be able to afford to another the water of the saving lava from the

---

227 Clement of Alexandria. *Stromata*. Book I, Ch. XIX (ANF 2:322).
228 Song of Songs 4:12-13

fountain which is enclosed within, and sealed with a divine seal?[229]

St. Firmilian, in his response to Pope Stephen's teaching that heretical baptism can grant remission of sins despite not having the Holy Spirit, further compares the reception into the Church of heretics by baptism to the apostles' baptism of Jews in the name of the Trinity who had already received the baptism of St. John the Forerunner prior to Pentecost:

> And as Stephen and those who agree with him contend that putting away of sins and second birth may result from the baptism of heretics, among whom they themselves confess that the Holy Spirit is not; let them consider and understand that spiritual birth cannot be without the Spirit; in conformity with which also the blessed Apostle Paul baptized anew with a spiritual baptism those who had already been baptized by John before the Holy Spirit had been sent by the Lord, and so laid hands on them that they might receive the Holy Ghost. But what kind of a thing is it, that when we see that Paul, after John's baptism, baptized his disciples again, we are hesitating to baptize those who come to the Church from heresy after their unhallowed and profane dipping. Unless, perchance, Paul was inferior to the bishops of these times, so that these indeed can by imposition of hands alone give the Holy Spirit to those heretics who come (to the Church), while Paul was not fitted to give the Holy Spirit by imposition of hands to those who had been baptized by John, unless he had first baptized them also with the baptism of the Church.[230]

St. Firmilian also states that the "bare invocation" of the Holy Trinity in baptism is nothing unless the person baptizing has the Holy Spirit and is able to bestow the Holy Spirit on others:

---

229 Firmilian. Epistle LXXIV:7,15 (ANF 5:392-394).
230 Ibid.

That, moreover, is absurd, that they do not think it is to be inquired who was the person that baptized, for the reason that he who has been baptized may have obtained grace by the invocation of the Trinity, of the names of the Father, and of the Son, and of the Holy Ghost... But who in the Church is perfect and wise who can either defend or believe this, that this bare invocation of names is sufficient to the remission of sins and the sanctification of baptism; since these things are only then of advantage, when both he who baptizes has the Holy Spirit, and the baptism itself also is not ordained without the Spirit?[231]

St. Athanasius the Great (+373) became bishop of Alexandria sixty-three years after St. Dionysios of Alexandria. He succeeded St. Alexander, the first to contest against Arius and his heresy. St. Athanasius triumphed against the Arians at the First Ecumenical Council and taught in his works against the Arians that the baptism of heretics is a pollution that does not redeem, even if done in the name of the Holy Trinity:

> For not he who simply says, "O Lord," gives Baptism; but he who with the Name has also the right faith. On this account therefore our Saviour also did not simply command to baptize, but first says, "Teach;" then thus: "Baptize into the Name of Father, and Son, and Holy Ghost;" that the right faith might follow upon learning, and together with faith might come the consecration of Baptism.

> There are many other heresies too, which use the words only, but not in a right sense, as I have said, nor with sound faith, and in consequence the water which they administer is unprofitable, as deficient in piety, so that he who is sprinkled by them is rather polluted by irreligion than redeemed.[232]

---

231 Ibid.
232 Athanasius the Great, *Against the Arians*, Discourse II, Ch. XVIII: 42-43 (NPNF 2/4:371).

St. Athanasius the Great (+ 373)
Feast Day: January 18

St. Athanasius clearly followed the teaching he received from St. Dionysius and Clement of Alexandria before him regarding the baptism of heretics, and he reiterated the teaching in the Apostolic Constitutions that the baptism of heretics is a "pollution."[233] For St. Athanasius, the baptism performed by heretics is not a mere empty form but pollutes the soul, and all that corrupts is the work of the enemy of our salvation. St. Athanasius states that the status of heretical baptism is not simply a question of form and matter, nor correctness of doctrinal confession. It is, and can only be considered as, a spiritual matter of critical importance for ecclesiology and soteriology. Apostasy from Orthodox Faith and Church life reveals not only the loss of a rational grasp of Church dogma and separation from communion with the Church, but a fall into the nets of the evil one and definite spiritual corruption. The consequence of the loss of "sound faith" is that together with the water is also transmitted "pollution from impiety." For, just as the water and Spirit must be together for the one to be redeemed, when water is void of the Spirit, because impiety has intervened to block impartation, that which is imparted is not only a lack of the Spirit but unclean spirits.

St. Cyril of Jerusalem (+386) is renowned for his *Catechetical Lectures* and as an especially authoritative Father with regard to the ancient Church's initiation practices, and he participated in the Second Ecumenical Council which formulated Canon 7 on the reception of various heretics into the Church. In his *Procatechesis* he follows the patristic interpretation of Ephesians 4:5 that there is only

---

233 *Constitutions of the Holy Apostles*, Book VI:III:XV (ANF 7:456-457).

one baptism, that of the one Church, and the baptism of heretics is not a baptism.

St. Cyril of Jerusalem (+ 386)
Feast Day: March 18

> We may not receive Baptism twice or thrice; else it might be said, Though I have failed once, I shall set it right a second time: whereas if you fail once, the thing cannot be set right; for there is one Lord, and one faith, and one baptism [Eph. 4:5]: for only the heretics are re-baptized, because the former was no baptism.[234]

St. Gregory the Theologian (+390) was elected Archbishop of Constantinople by the Second Ecumenical Council and spoke of heretical baptism in the context of his orations against the followers of Eunomius and Macedonius. The main objective of the great preacher and theologian was to maintain the Nicene Faith in the Holy Trinity and bring the followers of heresy back to the True Faith and into the Church.

In the saint's *Discourse on Holy Baptism*, which was given to former Arians (mainly Eunomians) and followers of Macedonius who were now being catechized, he states:

> If you are still limping and are unable to receive the perfectness of the Godhead [of the divinity of the Son and of the Spirit], go and look for someone else to baptize you – or rather to drown you in the baptism: I have no permission to rend the Godhead [to separate the deity of the Son and

234 Cyril of Jerusalem, *Lectures on the Christian Sacraments*, p. 44.

of the Spirit from the Deity of the Father], and to make you dead at the moment of your regeneration [in baptism], that you should have neither the Gift [of baptism] nor the hope born from the grace [of baptism], but in so short a time make shipwreck of your salvation. For whatever you may subtract from the Deity of the Three, you will have overthrown the whole [of the Trinity] and destroyed for yourself the perfection [of baptism].[235]

Along with St. Athanasius, St. Gregory rejects any baptism which does not express the Orthodox Faith. Anyone not baptized in this Faith is baptized into death and deprived of salvation. Any baptism which in any way "subtracts from the Deity of the Three" is no baptism at all, but rather deprives the one being baptized of grace, hope and salvation. This is consistent with the position of the earlier Fathers we have examined that heretical baptism is to the detriment of the one baptized.

St. Gregory does not refrain from stating this positively and clearly in his oration against the Arians and others who deny the Divinity of the Holy Spirit:

Neither will I bear to be deprived of my consecration; *One Lord, One Faith, One Baptism.* If this be cancelled, from whom shall I get a second [baptism]? What say you, you who destroy Baptism or repeat it?[236] Can a man be spiritual without the Spirit? Has he a share in the Spirit who does not

---

235 Gregory the Theologian, Oration XL:XXVI (NPNF 2/7:376), slightly modified translation to more accurately reproduce the meaning of the Greek.

236 St. Gregory here is referring to the Eunomian practice of baptizing everyone, including other Arians, that come to their sect. St. Epiphanius said concerning Eunomius: "He rebaptizes those already baptized, . . . even those from Arians themselves. He rebaptizes them in the name of the uncreated God and in the name of the created Son and in the name of the sanctifying Spirit who is created by the created Son" (*Panarion* 76.54.32-33). By "you who destroy Baptism," St. Gregory may be referring to the fact that the Eunomians introduced baptism in a single immersion, destroying the apostolic form which was to be done in three immersions, and the heretical faith into which the Eunomians baptized others.

honor the Spirit? Can he honor Him who is baptized into a creature and a fellow-servant?[237]

And, further on, St. Gregory continues more resolutely and severely:

I will not allow myself, after having been taught the words of the faithful, to learn also those of the unfaithful; to confess the truth, and then range myself with falsehood; to come down for consecration and to go back even less hallowed; having been baptized that I might live, to be killed by the water, like infants who die in the very birthpangs, and receive death simultaneously with birth. Why make me at once blessed and wretched, newly enlightened and unenlightened, Divine and godless, that I may make shipwreck even of the hope of regeneration?[238]

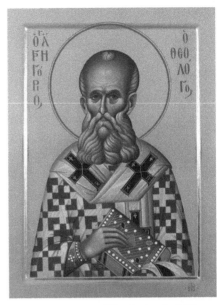

St. Gregory the Theologian (+ 390)
Feast Day: January 25

Clearly, heretical baptism, in this case Arian, Eunomian or Macedonian, is nothing but spiritual death and destruction. One cannot possibly reconcile the Theologian's words here with the idea of the legitimacy, let alone the efficacy, of heretical baptism. Lest one think that St. Gregory imagines that simply holding the Faith in a theoretical sense, apart from initiation into the life of the Church, can make one's baptism salvific, he tells his listeners

237 Gregory the Theologian, Oration 33.17 ("Against the Arians, Concerning Himself").
238 Ibid.

(former followers of Macedonius and Eunomius) that the Mystery of Holy Baptism makes one numbered among the faithful.[239] He also teaches the laver is "is not a mere washing away of sins" but also "a correction of [one's] manner of life."[240] In other words, to be baptized means to become a Christian[241] and outside the Church Christians do not exist:

> Despise not to be and to be called Faithful. As long as you are a Catechumen you are but in the threshold of piety; you must come inside, and cross the court, and observe the Holy Things, and look into the Holy of Holies, and be in company with the Trinity.[242]

To become a Christian means to receive baptism at the hands of one of the Church's approved ministers, not from one who is estranged from the Church:

> [T]o thee let every one be trustworthy for purification, provided that he is one of those who have been approved, not of those who are openly condemned, and not a stranger [αλλότριος] to the Church.[243]

Therefore, for St. Gregory to call his listeners to "be baptized in this faith"[244] is synonymous with calling them to become members of the Church at the hands of the Church. He demands from these former followers of heresy to be "rightly disposed and marked with the good inscription" of the Church's Faith so that he can "make them perfect" with the one baptism of the Church.[245] St. Gregory clearly did not teach that the grace of the Holy Spirit is present in the baptism of heretics.

---

239 Oration 40.11.
240 Oration 40.32.
241 Oration 40.16.
242 Ibid.
243 Oration 40.26.
244 Oration 40.44.
245 Ibid.

St. Maximos the Confessor (+662) triumphed at the Sixth Ecumenical Council. Concerning the Monothelite heretics, who were condemned by a local council in Rome prior to the Sixth Ecumenical Council, St. Maximos said they no longer had true Mysteries:

> They have repeatedly excommunicated themselves from the Church and are completely unstable in the faith. Additionally, they have been cut off and stripped of priesthood by the local council held at Rome. What Mysteries, then, can they perform? And what spirit descends on those whom they ordain?[246]

As with St. Gregory the Theologian, St. Maximos taught that a priest or a bishop only serves true Mysteries when they are united to the Church, but if they are anathematized or deposed by the Church, any mysteries they may serve afterwards are devoid of the Holy Spirit.

St. John of Damascus (+749) defended the veneration of icons and his teaching triumphed at the Seventh Ecumenical Council. He taught that when we receive Holy Communion we commune in the one body of Christ with those who are of the same faith. He says we must take great care neither to give Communion to heretics nor to receive Holy Communion from heretics, lest in doing so we commune with them in their heresy and condemnation. Receiving Holy Communion with other faithful

St. John of Damascus (+ 749)
Feast Day: December 4

---

246 Hieromonk Makarios, *The Life of Our Holy Monastic Father Maximus the Confessor and Martyr*, Vol. 3, p. 380.

is confirmation that we share one faith and are united in the one body of Christ.

> Participation is spoken of; for through it we partake of the divinity of Jesus. Communion, too, is spoken of, and it is an actual communion, because through it we have communion with Christ and share in His flesh and His divinity: yea, we have communion and are united with one another through it. For since we partake of one bread, we all become one body of Christ and one blood, and members one of another, being of one body with Christ.

> With all our strength, therefore, let us beware lest we receive communion from or grant it to heretics; Give not that which is holy unto the dogs, saith the Lord, neither cast ye your pearls before swine (Matt 7:6), lest we become partakers in their dishonour and condemnation. For if union is in truth with Christ and with one another, we are assuredly voluntarily united also with all those who partake with us. For this union is effected voluntarily and not against our inclination. For we are all one body because we partake of the one bread, as the divine Apostle says (1 Cor. 10:17).[247]

St. Theodore the Studite (+826) defended the veneration of icons and also triumphed at the Seventh Ecumenical Council. St. Theodore was very explicit that Communion received from heretics is not the body and blood of Christ but is "poison" that associates the person who receives such Communion with the devil rather than with Christ.

> Communion received from heretics alienates a man from God and associates him with the devil.[248]

---

247 John of Damascus. *An Exact Exposition of the Orthodox Faith.* Book 4, Ch. 13 (NPNF 2/9:84).

248 *The Works of Saint Theodore the Studite*, Vol. II. (In Russian). St. Petersburg, 1908, p. 332, Ep. 220, PG 99:1668

[In the Eucharist] the heretics' bread is not the Body of Christ.[249]

The difference between Orthodox and heretical Communion is the same as the difference between light and darkness. The Orthodox one enlightens, the heretical one darkens; the former unites with Christ, the latter with the devil; the first revitalizes the soul, the second kills it.[250]

Communion from heretical hands is poison, not simple bread.[251]

St. Theodosius of the Kiev Caves (+1074), not long after the Great Schism, wrote that the mysteries of the Latins are lifeless:

St. Theodosius of the Kiev Caves (+1074) Feast Day: May 3

They celebrate the Liturgy, but think that they commit no sin in doing so… They celebrate with a dead substance, thinking that the Lord is dead, while we celebrate the Liturgy with a living body and see the Lord Himself sitting on the right hand of the Father, Who will come again to judge the living and the dead. They [use] dead Latin substances and perform a Liturgy in which there is no life, while we, who bring to the living God a pure and undefiled sacrifice, will attain eternal life. Thus it is written, "He shall reward every man according to his words." … Their faith is perverted and leads to destruction… For there is no eternal life for those living in the faith of the Latins or the Saracens, nor will they share the lot of the saints in the world to come.[252]

---

249 Ibid, p. 596, Ep. 91, PG 99:1597.

250 Ibid, p. 742.

251 Ibid, p. 780.

252 Heppell, *The Holy Paterik of the Kievan Caves Monastery*, vol. 1, pp. 211-213.

SUMMARY

The saints and Fathers quoted above agree with the ecclesiology of the Ecumenical Councils that the Holy Spirit is received only through baptism in the one Church, that those who depart from the unity of the Church do not have the Holy Spirit and cannot bestow the Holy Spirit on others through baptism, ordination, nor the other mysteries. While some of the above quotes refer to Communion offered by heretics, only Mysteries performed within the Church have grace, and the Mysteries are all united in the Church such that what is said about one mystery performed by heretics is applicable to the other mysteries as well. Clearly, there is no basis in any of these quotes for the claim that heretics have "degrees of ecclesiality" or that the Holy Spirit is present in the mysteries of heretics. Saints after the 11th century who upheld this patristic ecclesiology will be discussed later in the text. If some saints have at some times and places deviated from the ecclesiology of the Ecumenical Councils, then we must hold firmly to the consensus of the Fathers who clearly upheld the inspired teachings of the Ecumenical Councils and not follow instead teachings which appear vague and contradictory.

The Three Hierarchs
Feast Day: January 30

St. Augustine of Hippo (+430)
Feast Day: June 15

CHAPTER 7

Western Saints and Fathers
on the Rites of Heretics

Those who do not want to follow the ecclesiology of the Ecumenical Councils often claim that the West had a different ecclesiology than the East and followed Pope St. Stephen of Rome and St. Augustine of Hippo rather than St. Cyprian and St. Basil. The argument is made that since Pope St. Stephen, St. Augustine, and a few others in the West who taught differently from the Eastern Fathers in some respects were glorified as saints, then their teachings are equal in value and authority to the teachings of the saints and Fathers of the East. Some have gone further than this to assert that since the Church has historically permitted the use of economy in certain instances and has not strictly followed St. Cyprian's teaching that all heretics should be received by baptism, the Church thereby chose to follow the teachings of Pope St. Stephen and St. Augustine rather than St. Cyprian. With all this, careful examination is needed regarding the teachings of saints and Fathers of the West on the subject of ecclesiology and the reception of heretics.

TERTULLIAN OF CARTHAGE

Tertullian[253] (+220) was an influential early Christian Latin writer from Roman Carthage who predated St. Cyprian. Tertullian's work

---

253 Tertullian eventually fell into Montanism but there is doubt as to whether he ever

De baptismo is the only treatise still in existence from that period. This text does not express the innovative ideas of one man but rather "the classical doctrine of Christian antiquity,"[254] the common belief of the Church long before Tertullian. His treatise, but also his summary of the four gifts of baptism in his polemic against Marcion,[255] make it clear "that by the end of the second century, if not fifty years earlier, the doctrine of baptism (even without the aid of controversy to give it precision) was so fully developed that subsequent ages down to our own have found nothing significant to add to it."[256]

Tertullian followed the tradition already well established in interpreting Ephesians 4:5. Those who do not have the *one Lord* and *one faith*, cannot, therefore, possess the *one baptism*. Only those in the one Church can possess the one faith and one baptism. While he was not a saint or Father of the Church, he summarized the teachings of the Church in his time as follows:

> There is to us one, and but one, baptism; as well according to the Lord's gospel as according to the apostle's letters, inasmuch as *he says*, "One God, and one baptism, and one church in the heavens." But it must be admitted that the question, "What rules are to be observed with regard to heretics?" is worthy of being treated. For it is to *us* that that assertion refers. Heretics, however, have no fellowship in our discipline, whom the mere fact of their excommunication testifies to be outsiders. I am not bound to recognize in *them* a thing which is enjoined on *me*, because they and we have not the same God, nor one—that is, *the same*—Christ. And therefore their baptism is not one *with ours* either, because it is not *the same*; a *baptism* which, since they have it not duly, doubtless they have *not at all*; nor is that capable of being

---

actually left the Church. See: Geoffrey Dunn, *Tertullian, Early Church Fathers* (New York: Routledge, 2004) p. 6.

254 Willis, p. 166.

255 *Against Marcion*, 1.28.2. The four gifts were: the remission of sins, deliverance from death, regeneration, and the bestowal of the Holy Spirit.

256 Pelikan, *The Emergence of the Catholic Tradition (100-600)*, p. 166. Pelikan is quoting from Earnest Evans' work *Tertullian's Treatise against Praxeas*, London, 1948.

counted which is not *had*. Thus they cannot *receive* it either, because they *have it not*.[257]

Tertullian's words would in his own lifetime receive conciliar approbation. We learn from St. Cyprian that the African Church issued rulings on the matter in a council under the presidency of Bishop Agrippinus of Carthage before St. Cyprian.[258] This council was attended by about seventy bishops drawn from the provinces of Africa and Numidia and would have taken place about AD 213, not long after the repose of St. Irenaeus, toward the end of Tertullian's life and when St. Cyprian was a young boy.[259]

While Tertullian preceded St. Cyprian and upheld the same teaching of the Church regarding the reception of heretics into the Church, St. Stephen the Pope of Rome, St. Augustine, and St. Vincent of Lerins are three saints of the West who most directly disagreed with this teaching.

SAINT CYPRIAN OF CARTHAGE (+258)

St. Cyprian of Carthage was born around AD 200, becoming a Christian in AD 246 and, by popular acclamation, constrained to accept the bishopric of Carthage in AD 248. Even though St. Cyprian had as his "master" Tertullian and shared his views on the status of heretical baptism, "both he and [Tertullian] were inheritors of an even older practice and conviction of the African church."[260] Yet, not only of the African church. St. Cyprian's "characteristics and the key to his whole ministry" are to be found "in the simple and elementary system of organic unity" expressed in the teachings

---

257 Tertullian, *On Baptism*, Ch. 15 (ANF 3, 676).

258 Cyprian, op. cit. Letters 71 (70).4.1; 73 (72).3.1; cf. 70 (69).1.2. St. Augustine also refers to this council, *On the One Baptism*, 13.22; *Against Crescens*, 3.3.3; *On Baptism against the Donatists*, 1.3.12; 4.6. Likewise, St. Vincent of Lerins in his *Commonitorium* makes reference, 1.6.

259 Willis, p. 147. The council was held around 213, Irenaeus reposed around 202 and Tertullian around 220, and St. Cyprian was born between 200 and 210.

260 Evans, Introduction to *De baptismo* of Tertullian.

of St. Ignatius of Antioch.[261] As with St. Ignatius, unity, *the organic unity* of the Body of Christ, lies at the heart of his vision of the Church. Participation in the reality of "the mystery of the kingdom of God"[262] presupposes incorporation through the mysteries into a Living Organism,[263] the Head and members of which form an organic whole,[264] an unbreakable unity, unknown and unavailable "to them that are without."[265]

As Metropolitan John Zizioulas has noted,

> The connection of the "one Church" with the "one eucharist," the "one bishop" and the "one altar," clearly established already in the teaching of Ignatius (Philad., 4; Magn., 7,2; Eph., 5,2; Tral., 7,2, etc.) continues through Cyprian (Ep., 43 [40], 5; De unit., 17,14, etc.) well into the fourth century....[266]

One could and should add to this list the "one baptism,"[267] by which, of course, was understood in this context not the non-repetition of the mystery, but it being *of the Church, unique* to Her.[268] For, just as there are indeed many assemblies called "the church" which are not but synagogues of Satan,[269] and many sacrifices offered[270] which are not the "one sacrifice,"[271] and many called bishops which are not overseers of Christ's flock,[272] and many altars

---

261 Wallis, "Introductory Note to Cyprian," (ANF 5, 542).

262 See Mark 4:11.

263 1 Tit. 3:15

264 1 Cor. 12:12

265 1 Cor. 5:12

266 Zizioulas, *Being as Communion, Studies in Personhood and the Church*, p. 152n.

267 See: Ignatius of Antioch, *Epistle to the Philippians*, 1; Cyprian of Carthage, *Letters*, 69, 70, 72, etc.

268 Cyprian, *Letters*, 73, 11.1. and 70.1.3.

269 See: Rev. 2:9. Ignatius of Antioch, *Letter to the Ephesians*, 5, Cyprian of Carthage, *Letters*, 74.14, 16 (from Firmilian); See also the judgement of Bishop Rogatianus of Nova, preserved in the acts of *The Seventh Council of Carthage under Cyprian*, which assembled in September of 258 A.D. and at which were present eighty-seven bishops from Africa, Numidia, and Mauritania.

270 See: 1 Cor. 10:20; Cyprian of Carthage, *Letters*, 66.2; 69.2.

271 Heb. 10:12

272 See: John 10:12-13; Ignatius of Antioch, *Letter to the Ephesians*, 5, Cyprian of Carthage,

around which is gathered not the eucharistic community;[273] so, too, there are many baptisms which do not baptize by the "one Spirit…into [the] one body,"[274] that is, "into Christ."[275]

St. Cyprian lay great emphasis on the empirical unity of the Church, and in this he "was expressing the conviction of the church catholic from the beginning."[276] Unity for the early Church Fathers meant the organic unity of the Body of Christ as described by the Apostle Paul in his epistles.[277] In focusing on the organic unity of the Church, St. Cyprian was doing little more than following Christ's example, who compared His unity with His disciples to the organic unity of a vine and its branches.[278] St. Cyprian calls forth the organic unity found in creation to illustrate the nature of the Church's unity:

St. Cyprian of Carthage

The sun has many rays, but the light is one; the branches of a tree are many, but the trunk is one, sitting firmly on its root; many streams flow from one source, but although the overflowing resulting from the abundance of waters presents a multiplicity, nevertheless unity is preserved at their origin. Separate a light from its origin, its unity will not allow the existence of a divided light; break a branch from a tree, the

Letters, 54.5.

273 Ignatius of Antioch, Letter to the Ephesians, 5, Letter to the Magnesians, 7, Cyprian of Carthage, Letters, 39.7; 64.3; 66.2; 69.2.

274 1 Cor. 12:13. Ignatius of Antioch, Epistle to the Philippians, 1; Cyprian of Carthage, Letters, 69, 70, 72, etc.

275 Gal. 3:27

276 Pelikan, The Emergence of the Catholic Tradition (100-600), p. 159.

277 Rom. 12:5, 1 Cor. 10:16-17, 1 Cor. 12:12-27, Eph. 4:12-16, Eph. 5:23-25, 30, etc.

278 John 15:1-7

branch thus broken will not be able to grow; cut off a stream from its source, the stream thus cut off will dry up.[279]

These three, then, Christ, Who is the Head, the Church, which is His Body, and the Holy Mysteries, which spring forth from the Body's side,[280] are indissolubly linked together. Moreover, the unity of the mysteries necessarily flows from the unity of the Head with His Body. Just as where the Head is, there is the Body, so too, wherever there is one Mystery, especially the Mystery of initiation, there are all the Mysteries and the Mystery of the Church.[281]

Behind St. Cyprian lie at least two generations of North African teaching, extending to Tertullian and beyond.[282] Although accused by some as being an innovator,[283] he was following both those before him in his See of Carthage (Agrippinus) and renowned teachers and fathers (Ignatius, Irenaeus, Tertullian, etc.). His insistence that Christ, as the Head of the Body, has imparted to the Apostles and their successors *alone* the authority to incorporate new members into His Body is certainly not a conviction unique to him. In this and nearly his entire vision he is simply following the Holy Fathers and Councils before him.

---

279 Cyprian of Carthage, "On the Unity of the Church," p. 5.

280 John 19:34: *But one of the soldiers with a spear pierced his side, and forthwith came there out blood and water.* St. John Chrysostom sums up the Patristic interpretation of this passage: "With this too an ineffable mystery was accomplished: For, 'blood and water came out.' Not simply without a purpose, or by chance, did those founts come forth, but because by means of these two together the Church consists. And the initiated in the Mysteries know it, being by water indeed regenerated, and nourished by the blood and the flesh. Hence the Mysteries take their beginning; that when thou approachest to that awful Cup, thou mayest so approach, as drinking from the very side." (Hom. 85, *P.G.* 59:507 (col. 463)).

281 See Letter 69.2, To Januarius.

282 Frend, *Saints and Sinners in the Early Church*, p. 102.

283 Augustine of Hippo, *On Baptism Against the Donatists*, Book III, chapters 5.7-12.17. Likewise, in our own day there are those who speak of a "strict Cyprianic ecclesiology" as opposed to the "accepted and mainstream" ecclesiology of the Church, as if St. Cyprian was an innovator and, far from being a follower of the Fathers, created his own idea of the Church. As we shall see further on, those who rejected the *consensus patrum* expressed by St. Cyprian were the innovators who became pathfinders to a whole new theology of the Church.

St. Cyprian was "no original theologian . . . [or] theological pioneer."[284] He taught what he was taught by Tertullian and his predecessors, and this was not seen as a weakness but as strength and a duty. In the second and third centuries all were in agreement that wherever the true Church existed, it and only it could dispense the living water of God's grace to his people. This view was taken for granted by most, not debated, and not peculiar to St. Cyprian, as is sometimes presented today.[285]

Therefore, unsurprisingly the famous saying attributed to St. Cyprian, "He cannot have God for his Father, who has not the Church for his mother," actually belongs to his teacher, Tertullian (and is later repeated by St. Augustine).[286] This is indicative of St. Cyprian's fidelity to the witness of the Fathers. His aim was to pass on what he had been given, namely, the "faith which was once delivered unto the saints."[287]

He held that the unity of the Body of Christ was clearly the will of God and expressed both in Christ's high-priestly prayer (Matt. 17:18) and His words to the Apostle Peter (John 21: 15-17). The uniqueness of the Church was also clear in the baptismal service itself.[288] Within this unity man could be sure He was doing the will of God; outside of this unity, salvation was at best doubtful. Hence the famous line: "extra ecclesiam nulla salus."[289]

Following St. Ignatius, St. Cyprian held the bishop to be the focal point of the visible unity of the Church. As Jaroslav Pelikan has written:

> For both Ignatius and Cyprian, moreover, the bishop was the key to authentic unity, and schism was identified as party spirit in opposition to him. Therefore the efforts

---

284 Willis, p. 96.

285 See, for instance: Meyendorff, Paul, "Toward Mutual Recognition of Baptism," in *Baptism Today: Understanding, Practice, Ecumenical Implications*, p. 204.

286 See: Tertullian, *De orat.* II, St. Cyprian, *De unit.* VI, and St. Augustine, *C. Litt. Pet.* III, 10.

287 Jude 1:3

288 See Letter 75, To Magnus. St. Cyprian cites the baptismal interrogation of the candidate as an example of the confession of faith in one church: "Dost thou believe the remission of sins and life eternal through the holy Church?"

289 Letter 73.21, To Jubaianus.

to superimpose on the second and third centuries the distinction made by Augustinism and especially by the Reformation between visible and invisible churches have proved quite ineffectual . . . on earth there was only one church, and it was finally inseparable from the sacramental, hierarchical institution.[290]

Breaking with the bishop, violating the unity of the Church, is the sin of schism—a renunciation of Christ and rebellion against the will of God. Schism, however, cannot divide the Church, which is indivisible, but it does separate the instigators of schism from the Church, making them apostates, cutting themselves off from the holy people of God.

In St. Cyprian's view, which was shared universally, there is no distinction between irregular and invalid ministrations (which St. Augustine will later introduce) because every Mystery emanates from, and is inseparably linked to, the Mystery of the Church.[291] He who is cut off from the Church has nothing he can impart.

St. Cyprian has been wrongly understood by some, most likely due to the Donatists' commandeering of his words and authority, as saying that the administrator himself imparts forgiveness and the Holy Spirit (*ex opere operantis*). However, this is a grave misreading of the Saint's writings. Cyprian's fundamental thought, however, was that these gifts are found in the Church and the minister is to be understood as the agent of the Church.

The problem with accepting heretical baptism, however, is not merely its being outside the boundaries of the Church. St. Cyprian recognizes, as do many other Fathers after him, that the waters of heretical baptism are not only unprofitable, benign and neutral; they are rather blasphemous and detrimental. He calls heretical baptism "adulterous and unhallowed water."[292]

Like his predecessor Agrippinus, and the fathers in Asia Minor, St. Cyprian called together bishops of the North African church to judge the matter of the reception of heterodox into the Church.

---

290 Pelikan, *The Emergence of the Catholic Tradition (100-600)*, p. 161.
291 Ibid, p. 103.
292 Letter 72.1, To Jubaianus.

The first such council took place in AD 255 and consisted of twenty-one bishops, the second in AD 256 with seventy-one bishops and the third in September of that same year with eighty-seven bishops. In this last council especially, the bishops were unanimous in expressing the *consensus patrum* of the time, declaring the Church as the *sole* dispenser of the Holy Mysteries.[293]

ST. STEPHEN POPE OF ROME (+257)

Pope St. Stephen did not share St. Cyprian's vision and view of the Church. After the second council called by St. Cyprian, bishops were sent to Rome to convey the synodical letter and decisions. Stephen did not even grant them an audience. Rather, he answered by sending a letter in which he berated St. Cyprian harshly, "calling him a false Christian, a false apostle, and a deceitful worker."[294] At the same time he wrote to the bishops in Asia Minor who supported the African Church's decision, threatening them with excommunication if they persisted in their support of the practice of baptizing heretics. It was in response to the fanatical stance of Pope Stephen that the last and largest of the three councils in Carthage was called.

Pope Stephen's letters have not been preserved, providentially. We know portions of his teaching through the writings of others. St. Cyprian quotes St. Stephen as saying:

> If any one, therefore, come to you from any heresy whatever, let nothing be innovated (or done) which has not been handed down, to wit, that hands be imposed on him for repentance; since the heretics themselves, in their own proper character, do not baptize such as come to them from one another, but only admit them to communion.[295]

---

293 See Chapter 5 above on the Local Council of Carthage under St. Cyprian.

294 Firmilian, Epistle LXXIV:26 (ANF 5:397).

295 Cyprian of Carthage, Epistle LXXII to Pompey, op. cit.

St. Cyprian claimed that St. Stephen "forbade one coming from any heresy to be baptized in the Church; that is, he judged the baptism of all heretics to be just and lawful."[296] Regarding St. Stephen's claim that reception of heretics by baptism is an "innovation," St. Cyprian responds:

> Let nothing be innovated, says [Pope Stephen], nothing maintained, except what has been handed down. Whence is that tradition? Whether does it descend from the authority of the Lord and of the Gospel, or does it come from the commands and the epistles of the apostles? For that those things which are written must be done, God witnesses and admonishes, saying to Joshua the son of Nun: "The book of this law shall not depart out of thy mouth; but thou shalt meditate in it day and night, that thou mayest observe to do according to all that is written therein (Joshua 1:8)." Also the Lord, sending His apostles, commands that the nations should be baptized, and taught to observe all things which He commanded. If, therefore, it is either prescribed in the Gospel, or contained in the epistles or Acts of the Apostles, that those who come from any heresy should not be baptized, but only hands laid upon them to repentance, let this divine and holy tradition be observed. But if everywhere heretics are called nothing else than adversaries and antichrists, if they are pronounced to be people to be avoided, and to be perverted and condemned of their own selves, wherefore is it that they should not be thought worthy of being condemned by us, since it is evident from the apostolic testimony (Titus 3:11) that they are of their own selves condemned? So that no one ought to defame the apostles as if they had approved of the baptisms of heretics, or had communicated with them without the Church's baptism, when they, the apostles, wrote such things of the heretics. And this, too, while as yet the more terrible plagues of heresy had not broken forth; while Marcion of Pontus

---

296 Ibid.

had not yet emerged from Pontus, whose master Cerdon came to Rome,—while Hyginus was still bishop, who was the ninth bishop in that city,—whom Marcion followed, and with greater impudence adding other enhancements to his crime, and more daringly set himself to blaspheme against God the Father, the Creator, and armed with sacrilegious arms the heretical madness that rebelled against the Church with greater wickedness and determination.

But if it is evident that subsequently heresies became more numerous and worse; and if, in time past, it was never at all prescribed nor written that only hands should be laid upon a heretic for repentance, and that so he might be communicated with; and if there is only one baptism, which is with us, and is within, and is granted of the divine condescension to the Church alone, what obstinacy is that, or what presumption, to prefer human tradition to divine ordinance, and not to observe that God is indignant and angry as often as human tradition relaxes and passes by the divine precepts, as He cries out, and says by Isaiah the prophet, "This people honoureth me with their lips, but their heart is far from me. But in vain do they worship me, teaching the doctrines and commandments of men (Isaiah 29:13)." Also the Lord in the Gospel, similarly rebuking and reproving, utters and says, "Ye reject the commandment of God, that ye may keep your own tradition (Mark 7:13)." Mindful of which precept, the blessed Apostle Paul himself also warns and instructs, saying, "If any man teach otherwise, and consent not to the wholesome words of our Lord Jesus Christ, and to His doctrine, he is proud, knowing nothing: from such withdraw thyself (1 Tim. 6:3-5)."[297]

While claiming that the more ancient tradition is to receive heretics without baptizing them, St. Stephen does not appear to offer any proofs for this claim, and St. Cyprian rejects St. Stephen's claim completely, stating that St. Stephen is following a mere

---

297 Ibid.

human tradition that contradicts the command of the Lord and the teaching of the Apostles (Canon 95 of the Fifth-Sixth Council also acknowledged that the Council under St. Cyprian in Carthage was following "the custom handed down to them" as demonstrated in Chapter 5).

Regarding St. Stephen's assertion that the Church should not receive heretics by baptism since heretics do not baptize those who leave the Church and join them, St. Cyprian replies:

> To this point of evil has the Church of God and spouse of Christ been developed, that she follows the examples of heretics; that for the purpose of celebrating the celestial sacraments, light should borrow her discipline from darkness, and Christians should do that which antichrists do. But what is that blindness of soul, what is that degradation of faith, to refuse to recognise the unity which comes from God the Father, and from the tradition of Jesus Christ the Lord and our God! For if the Church is not with heretics, therefore, because it is one, and cannot be divided; and if thus the Holy Spirit is not there, because He is one, and cannot be among profane persons, and those who are without; certainly also baptism, which consists in the same unity, cannot be among heretics, because it can neither be separated from the Church nor from the Holy Spirit.[298]

St. Cyprian contends that the Church must receive heretics based on the commandments of the Lord, the teachings of the Apostles, and the ecclesiology of the Church and not on how heretics happen to receive those coming to them from the Church. St. Cyprian further questions Pope Stephen's teaching, asking:

> But as no heresy at all, and equally no schism, being without, can have the sanctification of saving baptism, why has the bitter obstinacy of our brother Stephen broken forth to such an extent, as to contend that sons are born to God from the baptism of Marcion; moreover, of Valentinus and Apelles,

---

298 Ibid.

and of others who blaspheme against God the Father; and to say that remission of sins is granted in the name of Jesus Christ where blasphemy is uttered against the Father and against Christ the Lord God?[299]

According to St. Cyprian, Pope Stephen even received Marcionites and Valentinians without baptizing them. St. Dionysius of Alexandria relates that Pope Stephen threatened to break communion with those who insisted on receiving heretics into the Church through baptism:

> [Pope Stephen] therefore had written previously concerning Helenus and Firmilianus, and all those in Cilicia and Cappadocia and Galatia and the neighboring nations, saying that he would not commune with them for this same cause; namely, that they re-baptized heretics. But consider the importance of the matter.
>
> For truly in the largest synods of the bishops, as I learn, decrees have been passed on this subject, that those coming over from heresies should be instructed, and then should be washed and cleansed from the filth of the old and impure leaven. And I wrote entreating him concerning all these things.[300]

St. Firmilian wrote to St. Cyprian expressing his full agreement with St. Cyprian and his rejection of the position of Pope Stephen, even calling Pope Stephen a "Judas" and a "schismatic" for threatening to break communion with all those who insisted that heretics must be received by baptism:

> But although we have received the favour of this benefit on account of Stephen, certainly Stephen has not done anything deserving of kindness and thanks. For neither can Judas be thought worthy by his perfidy and treachery wherewith he wickedly dealt concerning the Saviour, as

299 Ibid.
300 Eusebius, *The Church History of Eusebius,* Book VII, Ch. V (NPNF 2/1:294-295).

though he had been the cause of such great advantages, that through him the world and the people of the Gentiles were delivered by the Lord's passion.

But let these things which were done by Stephen be passed by for the present, lest, while we remember his audacity and pride, we bring a more lasting sadness on ourselves from the things that he has wickedly done. And knowing, concerning you, that you have settled this matter, concerning which there is now a question, according to the rule of truth and the wisdom of Christ; we have exulted with great joy, and have given God thanks that we have found in brethren placed at such a distance such a unanimity of faith and truth with us. For the grace of God is mighty to associate and join together in the bond of charity and unity even those things which seem to be divided by a considerable space of earth... For even as the Lord who dwells in us is one and the same, He everywhere joins and couples His own people in the bond of unity, whence their sound has gone out into the whole earth, who are sent by the Lord swiftly running in the spirit of unity; as on the other hand, it is of no advantage that some are very near and joined together bodily, if in spirit and mind they differ, since souls cannot at all be united which divide themselves from God's unity.[301]

St. Firmilian continues, saying that it is a "foolish" assertion of Pope Stephen that the apostles forbade the reception of heretics by baptism. He criticizes Pope Stephen for allowing even the followers of Marcion, Valentinus, Appelles, and Basilides to be received into the Church without baptizing them, and again says that Rome does not follow the tradition of the apostles but the teachings of men:

And indeed, as respects what Stephen has said, as though the apostles forbade those who come from heresy to be baptized, and delivered this also to be observed by their successors, you have replied most abundantly, that no one

---

is so foolish as to believe that the apostles delivered this, when it is even well known that these heresies themselves, execrable and detestable as they are, arose subsequently; when even Marcion the disciple of Cerdo is found to have introduced his sacrilegious tradition against God long after the apostles, and after long lapse of time from them. Apelles, also consenting to his blasphemy, added many other new and more important matters hostile to faith and truth. But also the time of Valentinus and Basilides is manifest, that they too, after the apostles, and after a long period, rebelled against the Church of God with their wicked lies. It is plain that the other heretics, also, afterwards introduced their evil sects and perverse inventions, even as every one was led by error; all of whom, it is evident, were self-condemned, and have declared against themselves an inevitable sentence before the day of judgment; and he who confirms the baptism of these, what else does he do but adjudge himself with them, and condemn himself, making himself a partaker with such?

But that they who are at Rome do not observe those things in all cases which are handed down from the beginning, and vainly pretend the authority of the apostles; any one may know also from the fact, that concerning the celebration of Easter, and concerning many other sacraments of divine matters, he may see that there are some diversities among them, and that all things are not observed among them alike, which are observed at Jerusalem, just as in very many other provinces also many things are varied because of the difference of the places and names. And yet on this account there is no departure at all from the peace and unity of the Catholic Church, such as Stephen has now dared to make; breaking the peace against you, which his predecessors have always kept with you in mutual love and honour, even herein defaming Peter and Paul the blessed apostles, as if the very men delivered this who in their epistles execrated heretics, and warned us to avoid them. Whence it appears that this tradition is of men which maintains heretics, and asserts that they have baptism, which belongs to the Church alone.[302]

According to St. Firmilian, Pope Stephen taught that the baptism of heretics grants remission of sins even without receiving the Holy Spirit. St. Firmilian then speaks of the Council of Iconium where all those from Galatia, Cilicia, and neighboring countries gathered and affirmed that all heretics should be baptized. He demonstrates that the authority to ordain and the authority to baptize are one, that we cannot say that remission of sins occurs through the baptism of heretics if the Holy Spirit does not work through their baptisms, and how can we say that heretics have the authority and power to grant remission of sins through baptism but cannot confer ordination?

> But, moreover, you have well answered that part where Stephen said in his letter that heretics themselves also are of one mind in respect of baptism; and that they do not baptize such as come to them from one another, but only communicate with them; as if we also ought to do this... Moreover, all other heretics, if they have separated themselves from the Church of God, can have nothing of power or of grace, since all power and grace are established in the Church where the elders preside, who possess the power both of baptizing, and of imposition of hands, and of ordaining. For as a heretic may not lawfully ordain nor lay on hands, so neither may he baptize, nor do any thing holily or spiritually, since he is an alien from spiritual and deifying sanctity. All which we some time back confirmed in Iconium, which is a place in Phrygia, when we were assembled together with those who had gathered from Galatia and Cilicia, and other neighbouring countries, as to be held and firmly vindicated against heretics, when there was some doubt in certain minds concerning that matter.

---

302 Ibid. Epistle LXXIV:5-6 (ANF 5:391).

And as Stephen and those who agree with him contend that putting away of sins and second birth may result from the baptism of heretics, among whom they themselves confess that the Holy Spirit is not; let them consider and understand that spiritual birth cannot be without the Spirit.[303]

Moreover, what is the meaning of that which Stephen would assert, that the presence and holiness of Christ is with those who are baptized among heretics? For if the apostle does not speak falsely when he says, "As many of you as are baptized into Christ, have put on Christ (Gal 3:27)," certainly he who has been baptized among them into Christ, has put on Christ. But if he has put on Christ, he might also receive the Holy Spirit, who was sent by Christ, and hands are vainly laid upon him who comes to us for the reception of the Spirit; unless, perhaps, he has not put on the Spirit from Christ, so that Christ indeed may be with heretics, but the Holy Spirit not be with them…

For it follows that they must be asked by us, when they defend heretics, whether their baptism is carnal or spiritual. For if it is carnal, they differ in no respect from the baptism of the Jews, which they use in such a manner that in it, as if in a common and vulgar laver, only external filth is washed away. But if it is spiritual, how can baptism be spiritual among those among whom there is no Holy Spirit? And thus the water wherewith they are washed is to them only a carnal washing, not a sacrament of baptism.[304]

St. Firmilian continues, claiming that by threatening to break communion with those who insist on baptizing all heretics, Pope Stephen is excommunicating himself and is behaving as a schismatic.

Do not deceive yourself, since [Pope Stephen] is really the schismatic who has made himself an apostate from the communion of ecclesiastical unity. For while you think that

---

303 Ibid. Epistle LXXIV:7-8 (ANF 5:391-392).
304 Ibid. Epistle LXXIV:12-13 (ANF 5:393).

all may be excommunicated by you [Pope Stephen], you have excommunicated yourself alone from all...[305]

St. Firmilian accuses Pope Stephen of breaking with a great multitude of bishops throughout the whole world, testifying to the fact that many bishops in the East required heretics to be received into the Church by baptism.

> [Pope Stephen] disagreed with so many bishops throughout the whole world, breaking peace with each one of them in various kinds of discord: at one time with the eastern churches, as we are sure you know; at another time with you who are in the south...[306]

Pope Stephen seemed to agree with St. Cyprian and St. Firmilian that the Holy Spirit is not received by heretics outside of the Church, so he was not in agreement with those in the Orthodox Church today who criticize the teaching of St. Cyprian and claim to follow Pope Stephen while asserting that heterodox mysteries have "the presence of the Holy Spirit." Rather, St. Stephen seemed to believe that remission of sins is granted by heretical baptism without the Holy Spirit, and heretics receive the Holy Spirit through the laying on of hands when they are received into the Church.

In response to Pope Stephen, St. Cyprian clearly taught that the Holy Spirit is received through baptism and not through the laying on of hands:

> No one is born by receiving the Holy Spirit through the imposition of hands, but through baptism. As in the case of the first man, Adam, only by being already born does he receive the spirit: it was after God had moulded him that He breathed into him through his face the breath that gave him life. Some one must already be in living existence to be able to receive the Spirit; otherwise he cannot receive it. Birth, in the case of Christians, is at their baptism so that the giving

---

305 Ibid. Epistle LXXIV:24 (ANF 5:396).
306 Ibid. Epistle LXXIV:25 (ANF 5:396).

birth in baptism and sanctification exists with the bride of Christ alone.[307]

The opposition of Pope Stephen and the Church in Rome to baptizing heretics may have been a reaction to the fierce criticism against Pope Callistus I of Rome (+222) who baptized a second time those who were already baptized in the Church but who had fallen into grievous sins.[308] The Marcionites in Rome had similarly been criticized by St. Epiphanius (+403) for introducing rebaptism in Rome in a similar manner, baptizing in the Church those who had already been baptized in the Church and afterwards fell into grievous sins.[309] Rightly did St. Hippolytus of Rome (+236) and St. Epiphanius oppose this practice of baptizing a person twice in the Church, which St. Cyprian also spoke against; but in opposing this practice, Rome by the time of Pope Stephen appears to have overcorrected by refusing to baptize anyone joining the Church who was baptized by heretics.

Prior to Pope Stephen, Pope Cornelius (+253), who also died as a martyr, relayed how he and all of the clergy spoke against the ordination of the priest Novatus on account of the fact that he had been baptized by affusion (pouring) during a time of severe illness. This demonstrates that Rome at this time did uphold the necessity of being baptized in three immersions in the name of the Holy Trinity. Pope Cornelius relates that when a bishop ordained Novatus to the priesthood:

> This had been resisted by all the clergy and many of the laity; because it was unlawful that one who had been affused on his bed on account of sickness as he had been should enter into any clerical office.[310]

---

307 Cyprian of Carthage, *Letters*, Epistle LXXIII:7 to Pompey (ANF 5:388).

308 Hippolytus, *Philosophumena*. Ed. by M. Marcovich. (Patristische Texte und Studien, 25.). 9.2.12 and 9.3.13. Quoted in Beek, *Heretical baptism in debate*, p. 552.

309 Epiphanius, *Panarion* 3.42; Williams, F. 1987. The *Panarion* of Epiphanius of Salamis. Book 1. (Sect. 1- 46). Leiden: Brill.: pp. 272-274. Quoted in Beek, *Heretical baptism in debate*, p. 553.

310 Eusebius, *The Church History of Eusebius*, Book VI, Ch. XLIII:17.

Pope Stephen was succeeded by Pope Xystus in Rome. St. Dionysius of Alexandria (+265) wrote to Pope Xystus defending the decision to baptize heretics and saying this decision was decreed by the "largest synods of the bishops." St. Dionysius refers to the fact that he had written to Pope Stephen "entreating him concerning all these things," and that the practice of receiving heretics by baptism should therefore not be dismissed. He further refers to priests Dionysius and Philemon who were priests of Rome that "formerly had held the same opinion as Stephen." This priest Dionysius who no longer shared the view of St. Stephen on the reception of heretics into the Church succeeded Pope Xystus as the next Pope of Rome, indicating that after Pope Stephen the official policy in Rome regarding the reception of heretics likely changed and was closer to the view of St. Dionysius of Alexandria and St. Cyprian. As Eusebius records in his *Ecclesiastical History:*

> But Stephen, having filled his office two years, was succeeded by Xystus. Dionysius wrote him a second epistle on baptism, in which he shows him at the same time the opinion and judgment of Stephen and the other bishops, and speaks in this manner of Stephen:
>
> "[Pope Stephen] therefore had written previously concerning Helenus and Firmilianus, and all those in Cilicia and Cappadocia and Galatia and the neighboring nations, saying that he would not commune with them for this same cause; namely, that they re-baptized heretics. But consider the importance of the matter.
>
> "For truly in the largest synods of the bishops, as I learn, decrees have been passed on this subject, that those coming over from heresies should be instructed, and then should be washed and cleansed from the filth of the old and impure leaven. And I wrote entreating him concerning all these things...
>
> "I wrote also, at first in few words, recently in many, to our beloved fellow-presbyters, Dionysius and Philemon, who

formerly had held the same opinion as Stephen, and had written to me on the same matters."[311]

Pope Stephen of Rome is venerated as a saint by the Orthodox Church on account of his martyrdom, but the Church did not adopt his teaching concerning baptism and the reception of the heterodox. His sufferings for the faith are rightly honored in his Life as found in *The Great Synaxaristes* (Lives of the Saints), yet his Life appropriately concludes with the following regarding his teaching on baptism:

> A saint can make a mistake, or can even fall away from the Faith at one point in his life, as he is human and no individual is guaranteed not to fall away or go astray. It is possible for an individual father to say something erroneous by accident, perhaps in heated controversy, or from some other cause, which is why we refer to the Church's declarations, decrees, endorsements, and the consensus of the holy fathers in lieu of that for assurance.[312]

St. Cyprian was also glorified by the Church as a martyr but his teachings were embraced and ratified by the Ecumenical Councils and he is honored in the hymnography of the Church not only for his martyrdom but also for his ecclesiology. In the Kontakion for the feast of St. Cyprian of Carthage, the Church proclaims:

> We honour you, O Cyprian,
> as a true shepherd who with your sacred words and divinely-wise doctrines
> has shown us the boundary-stones marking out the one Church of Christ.
> Even unto death you bore witness with courage;
> wherefore, we extol you as a hierarch and martyr.
> Entreat Christ that we all be saved.

---

311 Eusebius, *The Church History of Eusebius,* Book VII, Ch. V (NPNF 2/1:294-295).

312 "Hieromartyr Stephen I, Pope of Rome," *The Great Synaxaristes of the Orthodox Church, August,* p. 98.

St. Jerome (+420)

St. Jerome has been referenced as a critic of St. Cyprian's teaching on the reception of heretics by baptism, particularly based on his text *The Dialogue Against the Luciferians*. In this text, St. Jerome speaks of Noah's ark as a type of the Church and says that the Ark contains both clean and unclean animals, just as the wheat grows up with the tares in the parable of the Lord.[313] St. Jerome then says, concerning the Church:

> While the householder slept the enemy sowed tares among the wheat, and when the servants proposed to go and root them up the master forbade them, reserving for himself the separation of the chaff and the grain (Rom. 9:22,23, 2 Tim. 2:20,21). There are vessels of wrath and of mercy which the Apostle speaks of in the house of God. The day then will come when the storehouses of the Church shall be opened and the Lord will bring forth the vessels of wrath; and, as they depart, the saints will say (1 John 2:19), "They went out from us, but they were not of us; for if they had been of us, they would no doubt have continued with us." No one can take to himself the prerogative of Christ, no one before the day of judgment can pass judgment upon men. If the Church is already cleansed, what shall we reserve for the Lord (Prov. 14:12)? "There is a way which seemeth right unto a man, but the end thereof are the ways of death." When our judgment is so prone to error, upon whose opinion can we rely?[314]

Truly, within the unity of the Church, there are not only holy people who are faithful to the Church's dogmatic teaching but also sinners and those with heretical views. However, St. Jerome fails to distinguish between those who remain within the body of the Church despite their personal sins or heretical beliefs and those

---

313 Matt. 13:24-30
314 St. Jerome, *The Dialogue Against the Luciferians,* 22 (NPNF 2/6:331-332).

who are removed from the body of the Church through schism or the anathematization of heresy and heretics by a council of the Church. If those who remain in the unity of the Church partake of the true and grace-filled Mysteries while in a state of sin or while maintaining heretical beliefs, they receive true Mysteries but unto their condemnation, and so remain spiritually outside of communion with the Church while nevertheless partaking of true Mysteries. Those who have not yet departed from the

St. Jerome (+420)
Feast Day: June 15

Church (in schism) or been removed from the Church (through discipline) receive the true Mysteries of the Church unworthily; they are reconciled through repentance and need not be baptized again. However, those who have broken off from the unity of the Church do not serve true Mysteries (Canon 1 of St. Basil). Those who received a baptism outside of the Church have not received a true mystery and so may be received into the Church by baptism.

St. Jerome asks on whom we, on earth, can rely to separate the wheat from the tares prior to the Final Judgment. Of course such authority "to bind and to loose"[315] was given by the Lord to the Apostles, and discerning wheat from tares prior to the Final Judgment has especially been taken up by God-bearing Fathers whose teachings were adopted by the Ecumenical Councils. The Ecumenical Councils, guided by the Holy Spirit, proclaimed "anathema" against those who persist in soul-destroying heresies, and in this way, tares were cast out of the field of the Church to prevent their proliferation.

St. Jerome continues:

---

315 Matt 17:18

Cyprian of blessed memory tried to avoid broken cisterns and not to drink of strange waters: and therefore, rejecting heretical baptism, he summoned his African synod in opposition to Stephen, who was the blessed Peter's twenty-second successor in the see of Rome. They met to discuss this matter; but the attempt failed. At last those very bishops who had together with him determined that heretics must be re-baptized, reverted to the old custom and published a fresh decree.[316]

St. Jerome honored St. Cyprian as "of blessed memory" and refers to the Council of Carthage held under St. Cyprian in AD 258 which "reverted to the old custom and published a fresh decree" opposing the decree of Pope Stephen. In the Prologue to the Council of Carthage held in AD 258 under St. Cyprian, St. Nikodemos states that this was the third council held in Carthage since AD 255 which was concerned with the reception of heretics into the Church. The decree of the second council of Carthage was sent to Pope Stephen who then held a council in Rome to oppose that decree. A third council was then held in Carthage to reject the decree of Pope Stephen and affirm the "old custom" of receiving heretics by baptism.[317] The Fifth-Sixth Ecumenical Council purposefully ratified this third council in Carthage in AD 258 as a statement of Orthodox and apostolic ecclesiology, in opposition to Pope Stephen's council at Rome which was not ratified by the Ecumenical Councils.

After commemorating St. Cyprian, St. Jerome then asks how should heretics therefore be received into the Church? He cites many examples of those who went astray in the New Testament who were then called to repentance, including the churches in the Apocalypse that were rebuked,[318] and then argues that since in the New Testament many who were in error were called to repentance but no mention is made of reconciling them to the Church through

---

316 Jerome, op. cit., 23 (NPNF 2/6:332).
317 Agapios and Nicodemus, op. cit. Concerning the Holy Synod Held in Carthage in the Time of Cyprian: Prologue.
318 Revelations 2-3

baptism, "repentance unaccompanied by baptism ought to be allowed valid in the case of heretics."[319]

St. Jerome then says,

> If, however, those men who were ordained by Hilary, and who have lately become sheep without a shepherd, are disposed to allege Scripture in support of what the blessed Cyprian left in his letters advocating the re-baptization of heretics, I beg them to remember that he did not anathematize those who refused to follow him. At all events, he remained in communion with such as opposed his views.[320]

St. Jerome does not say that St. Cyprian was wrong but says that since St. Cyprian did not break communion with Pope Stephen and others who opposed the reception of heretics by baptism, then reception of heretics by repentance should at least not be seen as justification for breaking communion. He then speaks of the practice in Rome of even receiving the Manicheans without requiring that they be baptized (Canon 95 of the Fifth-Sixth Council later decreed that they must be received by baptism).

St. Jerome continues,

> But if anyone thinks it open to question whether heretics were always welcomed by our ancestors, let him read the letters of the blessed Cyprian in which he applies the lash to Stephen, bishop of Rome, and his errors which had grown inveterate by usage. Let him also read the pamphlets of Hilary on the re-baptization of heretics which he published against us...[321]

St. Jerome sides with St. Cyprian in his letters against Pope Stephen and says that Pope Stephen's "errors... had grown inveterate by usage." Yet, he then refers to the First Ecumenical Council as allowing for the reception of heretics by repentance and without requiring that they be received by baptism. While St. Jerome

---

319 Jerome, op. cit., 24 (NPNF 2/6:332).

320 Ibid. 25 (NPNF 2/6:333).

321 Ibid. 27 (NPNF 2/6:333-334).

reposed in AD 420, he wrote this text in AD 379, two years prior to the Second Ecumenical Council, which is why he mentions only the First Ecumenical Council and does not take into consideration Canon 7 of the Second Ecumenical Council discussed in Chapter 5; this allowed for some named heretics to be received by economy while saying those belonging to "any other heresies" should be received by baptism, thereby acknowledging that baptism was the standard for the reception of heretics into the Church.

St. Jerome concludes this text saying that while there have been different practices for receiving heretics into the Church, the most important thing is to "remain in that Church which was founded by the Apostles and continues to this day," for those "called Christians" who are outside of the unity of the one Church are "not the Church of Christ, but the synagogue of Antichrist."[322]

In this text, St. Jerome does not say that St. Cyprian was in error but rather affirms that it is also acceptable to receive heretics by repentance and the laying on of hands. However, St. Jerome did not suggest that heretics receive the Holy Spirit through their baptisms outside of the Church. Since St. Jerome wrote *The Dialogue Against the Luciferians* before the Second Ecumenical Council, he does not address the portion of Canon 7 which required the Eunomians to be received by baptism because they no longer baptized in three immersions in the name of the Holy Trinity. As mentioned above, St. Jerome also does not address the distinctions between those who receive true Mysteries in the Church despite their sins and heretical beliefs, and those who receive rites from heretics who are separated from the Church in schism. St. Jerome concludes by upholding the necessity of remaining in the unity of the Church and of not departing into schism and heresy by joining a "synagogue of Antichrist". The Canons adopted by the Ecumenical Councils after St. Jerome further clarify that baptism is the standard for receiving heretics into the Church while providing specific criteria for the application of economy.

---

322 Ibid. 28 (NPNF 2/6:334).

St. Augustine of Hippo (+430)

St. Augustine wrote more than any other Latin saint or Father
on the subject of baptism and ecclesiology. St. Augustine's work *On
Baptism: Against the Donatists* has been said by Latins after the Great
Schism to represent the views of the West prior to the Schism. In
this work, St. Augustine says:

> Nor is the water "profane and adulterous" over which
> the name of God is invoked, even though it be invoked
> by profane and adulterous persons; because neither the
> creature itself of water, nor the name invoked, is adulterous.
> But the baptism of Christ, consecrated by the words of the
> gospel, is necessarily holy, however polluted and unclean its
> ministers may be; because its inherent sanctity cannot be
> polluted, and the divine excellence abides in its sacrament,
> whether to the salvation of those who use it aright, or to the
> destruction of those who use it wrong.[323]

St. Augustine here clearly contradicts the Apostolic Canons and
those Fathers who spoke of the baptism of heretics as a "pollution."
However, he is correct that sinful priests and bishops serve true
Mysteries if they remain united with the Church and have not
departed from the unity of the Church into schism and heresy.
However, St. Augustine draws an incorrect analogy by reasoning
that if sinful priests within the Church serve genuine Mysteries,
and those Mysteries are not defiled by the sins of the priest; then
heretics outside of the Church must also have genuine Mysteries
that are not defiled by their heresy.

> We do not, therefore, "acknowledge the baptism of heretics,"
> when we refuse to baptize after them; but because we
> acknowledge the ordinance to be of Christ even among evil
> men, whether openly separated from us, or secretly severed
> whilst within our body, we receive it with due respect, having

---

323 Augustine of Hippo, *On Baptism: Against the Donatists*. Book III, Ch. 10 (NPNF
     1/4:439).

corrected those who were wrong in the points wherein they went astray. However as I seem to be hard pressed when it is said to me, "Does then a heretic confer remission of sins?" so I in turn press hard when I say, "Does then he who violates the commands of Heaven, the avaricious man, the robber, the usurer, the envious man, does he who renounces the world in words and not in deeds, confer such remission? If you mean by the force of God's sacrament, then both the one and the other; if by his own merit, neither of them. For that sacrament, even in the hands of wicked men, is known to be of Christ; but neither the one nor the other of these men is found in the body of the one uncorrupt, holy, chaste dove, which has neither spot nor wrinkle. And just as baptism is of no profit to the man who renounces the world in words and not in deeds, so it is of no profit to him who is baptized in heresy or schism; but each of them, when he amends his ways, begins to receive profit from that which before was not profitable, but was yet already in him."[324]

St. Augustine also says:

> Whereas the reason why the Catholic Church should not administer again the baptism which was given among heretics, is that it may not seem to decide that a power which is Christ's alone belongs to its members, or to pronounce that to be wanting in the heretics which they have received within her pale, and certainly could not lose by straying outside.[325]

By stating that the Mysteries belong to Christ and not to the Church, St. Augustine seems to separate the head (Christ) from His body (the Church). Christ sent down the Holy Spirit upon the Apostles at Pentecost and they were given power and authority to administer the Mysteries within the Church and to appoint bishops and priests to do the same. Christ did not give such authority to all

---

324 Ibid. Book 4, Ch. 4.
325 Ibid. Book 3, Ch. 11.

people indiscriminately, but to the Apostles and to the bishops and priests who succeeded them, who remained in the unity of Christ's body and in the apostolic faith. The Church cannot be separated from Christ because "the Church is Christ Himself."[326]

St. Nektarios of Aegina (+1920) agrees with St. Augustine that the sins of a priest or bishop do not affect the grace of the Mysteries, yet he states quite clearly that the grace of the Mysteries belongs only to the Church and to those priests and bishops who have received the authority from the Church to serve the Mysteries:

> The ethical perfection of the liturgizing priest and the degree of his faith do not contribute at all to the completion of the Mysteries, because even if he is lacking these, he is an instrument of the Church who acts on behalf of the Church, and it is God Who gives the grace in the interest of the Church. If a priest is unworthy, he will give an account for his own audacity; however, the Mysteries still take place and are perfected.

> If the ethical perfection and faith of a priest were completely necessary in order for the Mysteries to be performed, then it would be uncertain as to whether or not salvation existed within the Church, and whether or not She is the one Holy Catholic and Apostolic Church, the spotless bride of Christ which received the order to conduct the Mysteries He entrusted to Her in order to eternally perpetuate the redeeming work of the Savior. Because who, from them who deem necessary the ethical and religious qualifications of priests in order for the Mysteries to be performed, would be convinced that the Church preserved the priesthood and the grace to perform the Mysteries within Herself for twenty centuries since the establishment of the Church? Who would be able to guarantee that all the ordinations of the priests and archpriests that have been conducted through the centuries were actually performed by ethical and faithful archpriests? Certainly no one.

---

326 Paisios the Athonite, *With Pain and Love for Contemporary Man*, p. 361.

If the Mysteries remained incomplete and imperfect due to the absence of a priest's or archpriest's ethical and religious qualifications, and if grace did not descend during baptism and ordination, then they who have been baptized would still remain unbaptized, while the priests and archpriests would also be non-clerics. And then the Church would remain deprived of sacred persons and of all the grace given to Her by the Apostles. But things are not so. The ethical and religious quality of the priests in no way contributes to the completion of the Mysteries; everything depends on the Church, because only She received the grace of redemption and sanctification, and only She conducts the Mysteries through her sacred instruments.[327]

St. Nektarios then quotes St. Gregory the Theologian (+390) that the Mysteries performed by priests and bishops of the Church are not impacted by their individual sins or false opinions unless the Church condemns or deposes them. Again, the Mysteries belong to the Church and not to those who depart from the Church in schism or who are deposed or condemned by the Church:

All [priests and bishops] are trustworthy for your purification, as long as he is among them who have received the authority to forgive sins, and as long as he has not been openly condemned. You who seek healing, do not judge your judges; do not examine the value of them who purify you, and do not make distinctions regarding them who give you birth... the grace of baptism is one.[328]

St. Paisios the Athonite (+1994) similarly states that true priests of the Church cease to serve true Mysteries if they are suspended from the priesthood:

If a priest is suspended from his duties, he retains the priesthood, but the Mysteries are no longer activated

---

327 Nektarios of Aegina, *Concerning the Ethical Perfection of Those Who Conduct the Mysteries,* translated from Greek.
328 Gregory the Theologian. Oration 40.26. Quoted in Ibid.

through him. The priest has no power. The most important thing is Grace. If Grace is reinstated, then the Mysteries will be valid.[329]

If a priest of the Church who has been given the authority to serve true and saving Mysteries loses this authority by being suspended, and the Holy Spirit ceases to work through the mysteries of the suspended priest, how can a priest serve true and grace-filled Mysteries who has left the unity of the Church (Latins, Monophysites, etc.) or who had never received such authority from the Church in the first place? If a priest or bishop who is recognized as such by the Church and who remains in the unity of the Church begins to teach heresy, the Mysteries they serve on behalf of the Church are not affected though they commune unto condemnation on account of their heresy. Yet, as St. Basil explains in his Canon 1, when a priest or bishop departs from the unity of the Church, he loses the Holy Spirit and can no longer bestow the Holy Spirit on others through baptism or ordination. In *Against the Donatists*, St. Augustine fails to distinguish between baptisms performed in the Church by unworthy priests for unworthy people, and baptisms performed outside of the Church. He also fails to distinguish between priests and bishops who privately teach heresy within the Church but who have not been condemned or deposed by the Church, and those who are ordained by heretics and who preach heresy outside of the Church on account of departing in schism or being deposed.

On the teaching of St. Augustine that grace is received through the baptisms of heretics though they do not receive remission of sins as long as they remain outside of the unity of the Church, St. Hilarion Troitsky comments:

> Augustine makes the strange assumption that presumably at the moment of baptism, and only at that moment, the Holy Spirit operates outside the Church as well. The sins of the person being baptized – so goes Augustine's reasoning – are forgiven but return upon him at once. He who is baptized outside the Church passes as it were through a narrow

---

329 Paisios the Athonite, *With Pain and Love for Contemporary Man*, p. 360.

zone of light and again enters darkness. While he passes through the zone of light, he is cleansed of his sins, but since immediately after baptism he returns to the darkness of dissent, his sins return immediately upon him.[330]

St. Hilarion rightly asks, "Why is the Church's Baptism to be found among the schismatics, although only at the moment of its accomplishment? For the schismatic is converted not to the Church but to the schism."[331]

St. Augustine, even in *Against the Donatists*, makes the distinction that while heretics have baptism the Church is not found among the heretics, but he makes the problematic assertion that since the Holy Spirit can withdraw from those baptized in the Church on account of sin, heretics outside of the Church can have baptism even if the Holy Spirit has withdrawn from them due to their heresy:

> And so, as baptism can continue in one from whom the Holy Spirit withdraws Himself, so can baptism continue where the Church is not.[332]

In his writings *Against the Donatists*, St. Augustine closely followed Bishop Optatus of Milevis who also wrote against the Donatists a generation prior. St. Augustine refers to Bishop Optatus in his book *On Christian Doctrine* along with St. Cyprian:

> And what else have many good and faithful men among our brethren done? Do we not see with what a quantity of gold and silver and garments Cyprian, that most persuasive teacher and most blessed martyr, was loaded when he came out of Egypt? How much Lactantius brought with him? And Victorious, and Optatus, and Hilary, not to speak of living men![333]

---

330 Troitsky, *The Unity of the Church*, pp. 29-30.
331 Ibid. See also Heers, *The Ecclesiological Renovation of Vatican II*, pp. 82-83.
332 Augustine of Hippo, *Against the Donatists*, Bk. 5, Ch. 23-33 (NPNF 1/4:475).
333 Augustine of Hippo, *On Christian Doctrine*, Bk. 2, Ch. 40.

In writing against the Donatists, Bishop Optatus claims, as did St. Augustine after him, that baptism belongs to God and not to the Church. Through the Holy Trinity a person is baptized and it matters little who performs the baptism:

It is clear that in the celebration of this Sacrament of Baptism there are three elements, which you will not be able either to decrease or diminish, or put on one side. The first is in the Trinity, the second in the believer, the third in him who operates. But they must not all be weighed by the same measure. For I perceive that two are necessary, and that one is quasi-necessary. The Trinity holds the chief place, without whom the work itself cannot be done. The faith of the believer follows next. Then comes the office of the "Minister," which cannot be of equal authority. The first two remain always unchangeable and unmoved. For the Trinity is always Itself; and the Faith is the same in everyone. Both [the Trinity and Faith] always preserve their own efficacy. It will be seen, therefore, that the office of the minister cannot be equal to the other two elements [in the Sacrament of Baptism], because it alone is liable to change...

The Name of Baptism is but one... The "Ministers" can be changed; the Sacraments cannot be changed. Since therefore you see that all who baptise are labourers, not lords, and that the Sacraments are holy through themselves, not through men, why do you claim so much for yourselves? Why is it that you try to shut God out from His own gifts? Allow Him to bestow those things, which are His own. For that gift, which belongs to God, cannot be given by man. If you think otherwise, you are endeavouring to make of no effect the words of the Prophets and the promises of God, by which it is proved that it is God, not man, who cleanses.[334]

Optatus, like St. Augustine, taught that since the gift of baptism is given by the Holy Trinity irrespective of the person performing

---

334 Optatus of Milevis, *Against the Donatists* (1917) Book 5, Ch. 4., pp. 203-245.

the baptism, a person baptized in heresy cannot be received by baptism.[335] However, Optatus in the same book distinguishes between schismatics and heretics, considers the Donatists schismatics, and states that there are no Mysteries among the heretics. Optatus criticizes the Donatists for classifying schismatics and heretics together, agreeing that heretics do not have Mysteries while schismatics do:

> To return to your book, you have said that the Endowments of the Church cannot be with heretics, and in this you have said rightly, for we know that the churches of each of the heretics have no lawful Sacraments, since they are adulteresses, without the rights of honest wedlock, and are rejected by Christ, who is the Bridegroom of One Church, as strangers. This He Himself makes clear in the Canticle of Canticles. When He praises One (Song of Songs 6:9), He condemns the others because, besides the One which is the true Catholic Church, the others amongst the heretics are thought to be churches, but are not such. Thus He declares in the Canticle of Canticles (as we have already pointed out) that His Dove is One, and that she is also the chosen Spouse, and again a garden enclosed, and a fountain sealed up (Song of Songs 4:12)...

> But to my surprise you have thought good to attach yourselves to those who certainly are schismatics, for in denying the Endowments of the Church both to those who are heretics, and also to schismatics, you have denied them to yourselves.

> Amongst other things you have said that schismatics have been cut off, like branches, from the Vine, and that they have been reserved, marked off for punishment, like dried wood, for the fires of Hell...

> All these things might well be true of heretics alone, since they have falsified the creed, for amongst them one has

---

335 Ibid. Book 5, Ch. 3.

said that there are two Gods, though God is One; another wishes the Father to be recognised in the Person of the Son; another robs the Son of God of His Flesh, through which the world has been reconciled to God, and there are yet others of the same kind, who admittedly are separated from Catholic Sacraments. Wherefore you should regret that you have coupled schismatics with such men as these, for, when you thought that you were attacking others, you failed to observe how wide is the gulf between schismatics and heretics, and turned the sword of judgement upon yourself.

This is the reason that you do not see which is the Holy Church, and have in this way made confusion of everything...

You see, then, my brother Parmenian, that none but heretics only—who are cut off from the home of truth—possess "various kinds of false Baptisms with which he, who is stained, cannot wash, nor the unclean cleanse, nor the destroyer raise, nor he, who is lost, free, nor the guilty man give pardon, nor the condemned man absolve."...

Wherefore, since all these things are justly denied to heretics, why did you think well to deny them to yourselves as well, who clearly are schismatics, for you have gone outside? For our part we were willing that in this matter heretics alone should be condemned, but so far as lies with you, you have chosen to strike yourselves, together with them, in one condemnation.[336]

While Optatus says that baptism belongs to God and not man, and the Holy Trinity works through the baptism despite the minister, he appears to apply this to baptisms performed by priests in the Church or those who are in schism, but not baptisms performed by heretics, since heretics have "false baptisms" and are "separated from Catholic sacraments."

---

336 Ibid. Book 1, Ch. 10 and 12.

Important to note within the writings of Optatus and St. Augustine against the Donatists is that the Donatists were seen by many as schismatics rather than heretics. The Donatists believed that the operation of the Holy Spirit through the Mysteries was dependent upon the personal holiness of the priest or bishop administering the Mysteries. The Donatists otherwise held to the same faith as the Orthodox and practiced baptism in the apostolic manner (three immersions in the name of the Holy Trinity). Perhaps it was the insistence of the Donatists to baptize those who were already baptized in the Church that led the opponents of Donatism to forbid receiving Donatists into the Church by baptism so as not to encourage the Donatists in this practice.

In other writings of St. Augustine, he states more clearly that the Holy Spirit does not work through the mysteries of those outside of the unity of the one Church:

> [They] cannot seek the Holy Spirit, except in the body of Christ, of which they possess the outward sign outside the Church, but they do not possess the actual reality itself within the Church of which that is the outward sign, and therefore they eat and drink damnation to themselves (1 Cor. 11:29). For there is but one bread which is the sacrament of unity, seeing that, as the apostle says, "We, being many, are one bread, and one body (1 Cor. 10:17)." Furthermore, the Catholic Church alone is the body of Christ, of which He is the Head and Saviour of His body (Eph. 5:32). Outside this body the Holy Spirit gives life to no one seeing that, as the apostle says himself, "The love of God is shed abroad in our hearts by the Holy Ghost which is given unto us (Rom. 5:5);" but he is not a partaker of the divine love who is the enemy of unity. Therefore, they have not the Holy Spirit who are outside the Church; for it is written of them, "They separate themselves being sensual, having not the Spirit (Jude 1:19)."[337]

---

337 Augustine of Hippo, Letter 185, Ch. 11:50.

The term "valid" that many use in reference to mysteries outside of the Church is derived principally from St. Augustine.[338] However, St. Augustine did not teach that "valid" mysteries outside of the Church were "fruitful," nor that they granted remission of sins as Pope Stephen taught. Rather, he taught that "although sacraments administered outside the Church were valid, they were wholly devoid of the Holy Spirit."[339]

In Homily 21 of St. Augustine on the New Testament, he clearly states that there is no Holy Spirit and no remission of sins outside of the unity of the Church and that baptisms performed by heretics and schismatics are mere forms lacking life, like dead branches broken from a tree:

> Wherefore whosoever are baptized in the congregations or separations rather of schismatics or heretics, although they have not been born again of the Spirit, like as it were to Ishmael, who was Abraham's son after the flesh; not like Isaac, who was his son after the Spirit (Gal. 4:9), because by promise; yet when they come to the Catholic Church, and are joined to the fellowship of the Spirit which without the Church they beyond doubt had not, the washing of the flesh is not repeated in their case. For "this form of godliness" was not wanting to them even when they were without; but there is added to them "the Unity of the Spirit in the bond of peace," which cannot be given but within. Before they were Catholics indeed, they were as they of whom the Apostle says, "Having a form of godliness, but denying the power thereof (2 Tim. 3:5)." For the visible form of the branch may exist even when separated from the vine; but the invisible life of the root cannot be had, but in the vine. Wherefore the bodily sacraments, which even they who are separated from the Unity of Christ's Body bear and celebrate, may give "the form of godliness;" but the invisible and spiritual power of godliness cannot in any wise be in

---

338 See Heers, *The Ecclesiological Renovation of Vatican II*, Ch. 4.

339 Cowdrey, *The Dissemination of St. Augustine's Doctrine of Holy Orders During the Later Patristic Age*, p. 480.

them, just as sensation does not accompany a man's limb, when it is amputated from the body.

And since this is so, remission of sins, seeing it is not given but by the Holy Spirit, can only be given in that Church which hath the Holy Spirit.[340]

Those who claim that there is "the presence of the Holy Spirit" and "ecclesiality" in the mysteries of heretics do not actually follow St. Augustine or Pope Stephen but the ecclesiology of the Post-Schism Latin West that was based primarily on selections from St. Augustine *Against the Donatists* as interpreted by the Latin Scholastics.

In *Against the Donatists*, St. Augustine disagrees with St. Cyprian's teaching while commending him for not breaking communion with those who disagreed with him.[341] St. Augustine, however, claimed that St. Cyprian's teaching was rejected by an authoritative "plenary council."[342] Here he is referring to the Council of Arles in 314 which states in Canon 9:

> Concerning the Africans who use their own special law in that they practice rebaptism, it is resolved that if any come to the church from heresy, they question him on the creed (used at his baptism), and if they consider him to have been baptized into the Father and the Son and the Holy Spirit, let him only receive the laying on of hands so that he receive the Holy Spirit; but if when questioned he does not solemnly confess this Trinity, let him be baptized.[343]

The Council in Arles did not provide a dogmatic explanation for the reception of heretics by the laying on of hands, nor did it imply that heretics have "ecclesiality" and the "presence of the Holy Spirit" in their mysteries. Rather, while disagreeing with St. Cyprian and the Council of Carthage under him that all heretics

---

340 Augustine of Hippo, *Sermon XXI*:32-33 (NPNF 1/6:329).

341 Augustine of Hippo, *Against the Donatists*, Bk. 3, Ch. 1-1 (NPNF 1/4:436).

342 Ibid., Bk. 2, Ch. 9.-14., note 1246 (NPNF 1/4:431, note 7).

343 Munier, *Concilia Galliae a.314-a.506*, 9-13. The Canons from the Council of Arles (AD 314).

should be received by baptism, the Council of Arles nevertheless stated that heretics receive the Holy Spirit not through their heretical baptism but only when they are received into the unity of the Church. So, the ecclesiology of St. Cyprian was not opposed by the Council of Arles despite the Council's opposition to the implications of this ecclesiology for the reception of heretics into the Church. Furthermore, the Council of Arles was never accepted and ratified as an authoritative council by the Ecumenical Councils. The influence of the writings of Bishop Optatus *Against the Donatists* and the mistaken belief regarding the authority of the Council of Arles may have played a substantial role in St. Augustine's opposition to receiving all heretics by baptism.

In the East, interest in St. Augustine developed only many centuries after his falling asleep. Some major works of his (at least *De Trinitate*) were translated by Maximus Planudes near the turn of the 14th century,[344] but a few decades later Augustine's writings began to receive a more serious treatment through the work of two brothers: Demetrios Kydones and Prochoros Kydones. Regarding these brothers, however, it is significant that they both resisted St. Gregory Palamas and rejected the teaching of hesychasm.[345] The Council of 1368 which canonized Palamas also condemned both brothers who eventually apostatized to the Latin faith.[346] While it is uncertain when *Against the Donatists* was translated into Greek, it also received very little attention in English until relatively recently. In Philip Schaff's edition of the text, the translator (J. R. King, M.A.) believed there were no English translations prior to his which was done in 1870.[347] This suggests that St. Augustine's text concerning the Donatists was not widely known and valued in the East, nor more recently in the English-speaking West, which calls into question the claim that this text has historically been viewed as authoritative on the subject of ecclesiology. In general, Augustine's influence in the pre-Schism West is found in minor ways (usually

---

344 Britannica, "Maximus Planudes."

345 Britannica, "Demetrius Cydones."

346 Ibid.

347 King, "Writings in Connection with the Donatist Controversy," Preface (NPNF 1/4:406).

terminology), but there is little indication of any comprehensive acceptance of his teachings on ecclesiology or other errors until the Carolingian Franks.[348] For the East, he was generally unknown and was not venerated until St. Nikodemos included him in the Synaxarion in the 18th century,[349] due to the absence of writings by or about him in Greek for most of Church history.

Despite disagreements regarding how heretics should be received, the important point to reiterate is that Pope Stephen, St. Augustine, St. Cyprian, and St. Firmilian agreed that the Holy Spirit only works through the Mysteries of the one Church and not through the mysteries of heretics. Metropolitan John (Zizioulas) recognized this when he stated:

> [Pope Stephen] and Cyprian seem to be in essential agreement; for both accept that the Holy Spirit is not given to those who are baptized outside of the Catholic Church. We can in consequence accept that the consciousness of the "Catholic Church" which Cyprian formulated as a result of the schisms did not differ in essence from that of those who disagreed with him on the issue of baptism. And, therefore, that insofar as the sources allow us to know, this consciousness was that of all the Churches of the middle of the third century.[350]

St. Vincent of Lerins (+450)

St. Vincent of Lerins in his *Commonitory* claims that Bishop Agrippinus of Carthage who preceded St. Cyprian was the first who taught that those baptized in schism and heresy should be received into the Church by baptism, that this practice was "contrary to the rule of the universal Church," that Pope Stephen of Rome objected to this practice as an "innovation," and that the Council of Carthage

---

348 See Romanides, *Franks, Romans, Feudalism, and Doctrine*, Part 2.

349 Rose, *The Place of Blessed Augustine in the Orthodox Church*, p. 78.

350 Metropolitan John (Zizioulas), *Eucharist, Bishop, Church: The Unity of the Church in the Divine Eucharist and the Bishop During the First Three Centuries*, Part 2.

under St. Cyprian that required heretics and schismatics to be received by baptism was afterwards annulled. He was particularly critical of this teaching because heretics had used the writings of St. Cyprian to justify baptizing into heresy those who had been baptized in the Church. Thus, he says that St. Cyprian and those in the Church who agreed with him "will reign with Christ" while the heretics who agreed with him and baptize into heresy those who were baptized in the Church "will have their portion in Hell."[351]

St. Vincent (+450)
Feast Day: May 24

Regarding the Council of Carthage under Bishop Agrippinus in the early part of the third century, St. Cyprian states:

[R]emission of sins cannot be given save in the Church, nor can the adversaries of Christ claim to themselves anything belonging to His grace. Which thing, indeed, Agrippinus also, a man of worthy memory, with his other fellow-bishops, who at that time governed the Lord's Church in the province of Africa and Numidia, decreed, and by the well-weighed examination of the common council established: whose opinion, as being both religious and lawful and salutary, and in harmony with the Catholic faith and Church, we also have followed. And that you may know what kind of letters we have written on this subject, I have transmitted for our mutual love a copy of them, as well for your own information as for that of our fellow-bishops who are in those parts. I bid you, dearest brother, ever heartily farewell.[352]

The Fifth-Sixth Ecumenical Council states that the decision of the Council of Carthage under St. Cyprian to baptize all heretics and schismatics was "in accordance with the custom handed down to them."[353] While the council under Bishop Agrippinus may have

---

351 Vincent of Lerins, *The Commonitory*, Ch. 6 (NPNF 2/11:135).

352 Cyprian of Carthage, *Epistle LXX*:3-4 (ANF 5:378).

353 Agapios and Nicodemus, op. cit. Canon 2 of the Quinisext (Fifth-Sixth) Ecumenical Council.

been the first council in Carthage to formally establish that heretics should be baptized, it is unlikely that Bishop Agrippinus introduced this as a new teaching but was rather following what had been the tradition in Carthage since apostolic times, as attested to in Apostolic Canons 46 and 47. As we have demonstrated previously, St. Firmilian and St. Dionysius of Alexandria affirmed that the practice of baptizing all heretics was accepted not only in Carthage but in Cilicia, Cappadocia, Galatia, and the neighboring nations among the "largest synods of the bishops."[354] Like St. Augustine, St. Vincent may have also assumed that the Council of Arles which allowed heretics to be received by the laying on of hands, provided they had been baptized in the name of the Holy Trinity, was an authoritative council. Like St. Augustine and St. Jerome, St. Vincent also seemed to be unaware of the Second Ecumenical Council and the Apostolic Canons.

OTHER LATIN SAINTS AND FATHERS & THE INFLUENCE OF ST. AUGUSTINE IN THE WEST

While St. Augustine wrote more on the topic of the reception of heretics into the Church than any other Latin Father aside from St. Cyprian, the topic is touched on by St. Ambrose of Milan, St. Gregory the Great and St. Leo the Great.

St. Ambrose of Milan (+397), the teacher of St. Augustine, referred to the baptism of heretics as a "pollution," just as does Apostolic Canon 47, St. Athanasios the Great, and other Fathers quoted previously:

> ...now all are made whole; or more exactly, the Christian people alone, for in some even the water is deceitful (Jer. 15:18). The baptism of unbelievers [heretics] heals not but pollutes.[355]

---

354 Eusebius, *The Church History of Eusebius*, Bk. VII, Ch. V (NPNF 2/1:294-295).
355 Ambrose of Milan, *On the Mysteries*, Ch. IV.23 (NPNF 2/10:320).

St. Gregory the Great (+604) did not require that all converts be received by baptism, yet he taught that the baptisms performed by heretics are empty forms that are only filled with the Holy Spirit when the heretics are united to the One Church:

> The Monophysites and others are accepted only through the confession of the true faith, since the holy baptism, which they received from the heretics, then receives the power of purification in them, when they (Arians) receive the Holy Spirit through the laying on of hands, and these (Monophysites) unite with the bosom of The Holy Ecumenical Church through the confession of the true faith.[356]

St. Leo the Great (+461), who triumphed against the Monophysites at the Fourth Ecumenical Council, also affirms that heretics do not have any grace in their mysteries, which are only "bare forms":

> For they who have received baptism from heretics, not having been previously baptized [in the one Church], are to be confirmed by imposition of hands with only the invocation of the Holy Ghost, because they have received the bare form of baptism without the power of sanctification. And this regulation, as you know, we require to be kept in all the churches, that the font once entered may not be defiled by repetition, as the Lord says, "One Lord, one faith, one baptism." And that washing may not be polluted by repetition, but, as we have said, only the sanctification of the Holy Ghost invoked, that what no one can receive from heretics may be obtained from catholic priests.[357]

After Pope Stephen, the Latin saints and Fathers generally taught that heretics baptized in the name of the Holy Trinity may be received into the Church through the laying on of hands, but that the Holy Spirit is not present in the baptism of heretics and

356 Gregory the Great, *Letter from Pope St. Gregory I to Catholicos Kirion I.*
357 Leo the Great, *Letter CLIX:VIII. To Nicaetas, Bishop of Aquileia* (NPNF 2/12:103-104).

that heretics only receive the Holy Spirit and remission of sins when they are received into the unity of the Church. This position, however, still raises the important question from St. Firmilian that if the Holy Spirit and remission of sins is not granted through the baptism of heretics, then why is the baptism of heretics considered something sacred or spiritual that cannot be repeated?

> For it follows that they must be asked by us... whether their baptism is carnal or spiritual. For if it is carnal, they differ in no respect from the baptism of the Jews, which they use in such a manner that in it, as if in a common and vulgar laver, only external filth is washed away. But if it is spiritual, how can baptism be spiritual among those among whom there is no Holy Spirit? And thus the water wherewith they are washed is to them only a carnal washing, not a sacrament of baptism.[358]

After St. Augustine, the Latins were confronted with the challenge of reconciling St. Augustine's teachings on Holy Orders with the reality of Church discipline. In his writings against Parmenian, St. Augustine stated that heretics who are baptized outside of the Church should not be baptized when received into the Church, so heretics who were ordained as priests or bishops outside of the Church should not be "re-ordained" when received into the Church.[359] After St. Augustine, little reference was made to his teachings on this topic in the West, and there is little evidence that his writings against the Donatists were circulated outside of Africa prior to the 12th century.[360]

> During the twelfth and thirteenth centuries, the doctrine of holy orders which Augustine expressed in such passages as this, became firmly accepted as the foundation of western thought and practice. But the seven centuries which intervened saw a long history of reordinations, and an

---

358 Firmilian, *Epistle LXXIV*.13 (ANF 5:393).
359 Cowdrey, p. 448.
360 Cowdrey, p. 454.

underlying uncertainty about the validity of sacraments, and especially of ordinations, that were administered outside the Church.[361]

Generally, in the West starting with Pope Stephen, baptism was seen as distinct from the other Mysteries, and while many in the West continued to believe that heretics have "valid" baptisms and should not be received into the Church by baptism, it was not generally believed that heretics could ordain anyone; so those who were ordained outside of the Church were often required to remain as layman after being received into the Church or they were re-ordained.[362] This separation of baptism from the other Mysteries, and treating as something sacred and unrepeatable that which is not the work of the Holy Spirit, poses many problems from the standpoint of ecclesiology.

THE ECCLESIOLOGY OF THE PRE-SCHISM WEST
IN THE LIGHT OF THE ECUMENICAL COUNCILS

A tradition seemed to develop fairly early in Rome to not receive by baptism those who had received the form of baptism in the name of the Holy Trinity from schismatics and heretics. Despite the difference in practice from that of St. Cyprian, the ecclesiology of St. Cyprian was essentially the same as that of St. Augustine and others saints and Fathers in the West, namely, that the Holy Spirit does not work through the mysteries of heretics who are outside of the Church.

Examined in the light of the Ecumenical Councils, it was St. Cyprian who was commemorated for his ecclesiology by both St. Basil in his Canon 1 (along with St. Firmilian) and in Canon 2 of the Fifth-Sixth Ecumenical Council. The Fifth-Sixth Ecumenical Council also ratified Apostolic Canons 46 and 47 that requires heretics to be baptized, as well as Canon 7 of the Second Ecumenical Council that requires several specific heretics to be baptized along

361 Ibid., p. 448.
362 Ibid., pp. 463-481.

with "all the other heresies" not named by the canon. Canon 95 of the Fifth-Sixth Ecumenical Council which was ratified by the Seventh Ecumenical Council reiterated Canon 7 of the Second Ecumenical Council, upholding baptism as the standard means of receiving heretics into the Church. St. Basil acknowledged in his Canon 47 that Rome had forbidden the reception by baptism of those who received baptism in the name of the Holy Trinity from heretics, yet he calls the teaching of Rome an "economy" and insists that heretics baptized in the name of the Trinity should still be received by baptism.

While Pope Stephen and St. Augustine contended that the Marcionites and Valentinians should not be received into the Church by baptism (nor the Eunomians according to St. Augustine),[363, 364] Canon 95 of the Fifth-Sixth Ecumenical Council decreed that all of these heretics should be baptized. While the Fifth-Sixth Ecumenical Council ratified the Council of Carthage under St. Cyprian and St. Basil commemorated St. Cyprian and St. Firmilian for following the "exactitude" of the canons by requiring the baptism of heretics, the Ecumenical Councils did not praise any of the saints or Fathers in the West for their ecclesiology nor for their teachings on the reception of heretics. While St. Augustine believed the Council of Arles to be an authoritative council and St. Vincent of Lerins said the Council of Carthage contradicted the universal tradition regarding the reception of heretics, the Ecumenical Councils passed over the Council of Arles in silence and did not ratify it as an authoritative council.

When the Fathers of the Ecumenical Councils formulated canons on the reception of heretics, it was primarily St. Basil whose writings were employed, developing more canons from his writings than from any other saint or Father. While certain Latin saints and Fathers were spoken of approvingly by the Ecumenical Councils when their writings were correct and useful for opposing various heresies, the Councils did not adopt as canons any of the writings of Pope Stephen, St. Jerome, St. Augustine, St. Vincent, nor any of the

---

363 Firmilian. op. cit. Epistle LXXIV:5-6.
364 Augustine of Hippo, *Against the Donatists*, Bk. 3, Ch. 15-20.

Latin saints. Yet, the Seven Ecumenical Councils which occurred before the Great Schism were fully adopted by Rome and continue to be commemorated by the Latins as Ecumenical Councils up to the present time.

St. Photios the Great (+893) said in response to the claim that the Church should follow Sts. Augustine, Jerome, and Ambrose who, it was claimed, taught that the Holy Spirit proceeds from the Father and the Son (though he did not believe they actually taught this[365]):

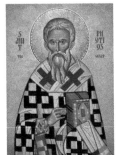

St. Photios the Great
(+893)
Feast Day: February 6

> If ten or even twenty Fathers have said this, 600 and a numerous multitude have not said it. Who is it that offends the Fathers? Is it not those who, enclosing the whole piety of those few Fathers in a few words and placing them in contradiction to councils, prefer them to the numberless rank (of other Fathers)? Or is it those who choose as their defenders the many Fathers? Who offends holy Augustine, Jerome, Ambrose? Is it not he who forces them to contradict the common Master and Teacher, or is it he who, doing nothing of the sort, desires that all should follow the decree of the common Master?[366]

St. Photios continues:

> Have there not been complicated conditions which have forced many Fathers in part to express themselves imprecisely, in part to speak with adaptation to circumstances under the attacks of enemies, and at times out of human ignorance to which they also were subject?... If some have spoken imprecisely, or for some reason not known to us, even deviated from the right path, but no question was put to them nor did anyone challenge them to learn the truth – we

---

365 Photios the Great, *The Mystagogy of the Holy Spirit*, p. 93.
366 Photios the Great, *Letter to the Patriarch Aquileia*, Quoted in Fr. Seraphim Rose, op. cit., p. 66.

admit them to the list of Fathers, just as if they had not said it, because of their righteousness of life and distinguished virtue and their faith, faultless in other respects. We do not, however, follow their teaching in which they stray from the path of truth... We, though, who know that some of our Holy Fathers and teachers strayed from the faith of true dogmas, do not take as doctrine those areas in which they strayed, but we embrace the men.[367]

In the *Rudder*, St. Nikodemos quotes St. Augustine, St. Jerome, St. Ambrose and other Latin Fathers approvingly in many instances, expressing the highest regard for them. As already mentioned, St. Nikodemos in the 18th century included the Life of St. Augustine in his Synaxarion (Collection of the Lives of the Saints) for the first time, and he is credited for St. Augustine being added to the Greek and Russian calendars.[368] Yet, as to why the Fifth-Sixth Ecumenical Council did not ratify any of the local councils in the West aside from the two synods in Carthage, St. Nikodemos states:

> Note also that, inasmuch as the Latins declaim against this Synod because it did not mention the local Synods held in the West, nor the Canons of the Latins that had been collected by Bartholomew Carantzas and many others before him; we reply as follows to this objection. We point out that the Synod enumerated those Canons of Synods and Fathers which were in use in the Church, but at the same time also recognized and accepted all the Canons of local Synods and regional Synods held in the West that agreed with the Canons of the Ecumenical Synods. And, in general, just as the Fifth Ecumenical Synod recognized and accepted the declarations of St. Augustine and of St. Ambrose, not, to be sure, in general, but only as many as pertained to the right faith and had been issued in refutation of heretics. So do we too recognize and accept whatever is right and correct in what the Synods held in the West have declared, but not

---

367 Ibid., pp. 66-67.
368 Ibid., p. 78.

everything, seeing that the Pope of Rome has decreed many things therein that are strangely incongruous.

Hence it must be remembered that most of the local Synods and regional Synods held in the West erred and spoke amiss; and, indeed, to them was due the addition to the Creed that was the first and worst of evils and the primary and incipient cause of the schism.[369]

On St. Augustine and the few Fathers of the West who may have held views contrary to the consensus of the Holy Fathers, Fr. Seraphim (Rose) further states:

With regard to Blessed Augustine in particular, it cannot be doubted that his teaching missed the mark in many respects: with regard to the Holy Trinity, grace and nature, and other doctrines...

To some extent, the faults of Augustine's teaching are the faults of the Western mentality, which on the whole did not grasp Christian doctrine as profoundly as the East. St. Mark of Ephesus makes a particular remark to the Latin theologians at Ferrara-Florence which might be taken as a summary of the differences between East and West: "Do you see how superficially your teachers touch on the meaning, and how they do not penetrate into the meaning, as for example do John Chrysostom and Gregory the Theologian and other universal luminaries of the Church?"[370]

When speaking of the consensus of the saints and Fathers about a topic which has been thoroughly addressed by the Ecumenical Councils, one absolutely cannot claim that a teaching is Orthodox which some saints may have held if that teaching contradicts the canons and teachings of the Ecumenical Councils.

---

369 Agapios and Nicodemus, op. cit. Quinisext (Fifth-Sixth) Ecumenical Council, footnote 13.

370 Rose, op. cit., pp. 86-87.

The ecclesiology of St. Cyprian and St. Firmilian is completely consistent with the Apostolic Canons and the consensus of the Fathers in the East and West. The Ecumenical Councils, while acknowledging the Council of Carthage under St. Cyprian to be a local council, did not reject this Council nor did it pass over it in silence as it passed over so many other local councils in the East and West that could have been ratified. Rather, the Council under St. Cyprian was upheld as divinely inspired. St. Cyprian's ecclesiology was fully embraced by the Church even if exceptions were made, by economy, in the practical application of this ecclesiology in the reception of specific converts. Despite these important differences between these saints on the subject of the reception of heretics into the Church, the point to reiterate is that the saints of the East and West agreed that there is only one Church and the Holy Spirit does not work through the mysteries of heretics unto purification, illumination, and theosis (salvation).

St. Cyprian of Carthage

СТЫЙ ѲЕѠѴЛКТЪ АРХІЕПКОПЪ ѠХРДСКІЙ

Blessed Theophylactus of Ochrid (+1107)
Feast Day: December 31

CHAPTER 8

The Principle of Economy
Prior to St. Nikodemos the Hagiorite

St. Nikodemos's use of "exactitude" (*akriveia*) and "economy" (*oikonomia*) to explain why the Church has historically required some heretics to be received by baptism while allowing others to be received by chrismation has been criticized by some as supposedly an 18th century innovation. For this reason, to further demonstrate that St. Nikodemos did not develop this terminology and criteria is important and, rather, he was faithfully following the Fathers, the Councils, and the canonists which preceded him. Those who reject this interpretive key inevitably see the canons on the reception of converts as contradictory, conflicting, or in need of an innovative theory to explain how the Fifth-Sixth Ecumenical Council somehow rejected canons which it explicitly ratified.

The Lord established the rule for the reception of converts when he said to the Apostles:

> Go therefore and make disciples of all the nations, baptizing them in the name of the Father and of the Son and of the Holy Spirit, teaching them to observe all things that I have commanded you; and lo, I am with you always, even to the end of the age.[371]

---

371 Matthew 28:19-20

The Apostles and their successors are to whom the Lord gave His commandment to baptize, to "make disciples of all nations" and to teach their disciples "all things that I have commanded you." The Lord did not give the command to the multitudes that they should go forth and baptize, but to the Apostles. Those who are not successors to the Apostles by the laying on of hands and by continuing in the apostolic faith, are not and cannot be disciples of Christ. Heretics who are cut off from the Church cannot unite their followers to the Church.

As demonstrated previously, Apostolic Canons 46 and 47 set the standard for the reception of heretics into the Church by stating that heretics must be baptized. When St. Basil in his first canon acknowledges that some bishops do not receive heretics by baptism, he says that this is "out of economy" while he is obliged "to serve the Canons with exactitude [akriveia]." Canon 47 of St. Basil states that the "Encratites and Saccophori and Apotactites" must be baptized despite the fact that they practice baptism according to the apostolic form (three immersions in the name of the Holy Trinity) and despite the fact that Rome forbade them to be received by baptism. St. Basil specifically states that Rome's position is one of economy. By allowing certain named heretics to be received by economy while declaring that those from "all the other heresies" should be received into the Church by baptism, Canons 7 of the Second Ecumenical Council and Canon 95 of the Fifth-Sixth Ecumenical Council affirm that the reception of heretics by baptism is the standard, the rule, and exceptions to this rule are by economy.

According to the Oxford Dictionary of Byzantium, economy (oikonomia) has three primary meanings. The first meaning is "the wise or responsible management, 'stewardship,' or administration of something." The second meaning is theological and "based on the idea of relationship between righteous God and sinful man that required God's dispensations of GRACE and mercy culminating in the 'economic' sacrifice of the Son." Finally, "oikonomia referred to moral concession as opposed to the rule of order or TAXIS." It further says that this "prudent disposition of church stewardship... aims at the general well-being of the Christian community and each individual—as long as doctrine or truth is not compromised." The Dictionary says that while debates have arisen in the history of the Church about when and how to apply *oikonomia* in particular contexts, "the principle of *oikonomia* was never denied by anyone."[372]

While St. Basil says in his first canon that it is best to follow the "exactitude of the canons" and receive heretics and schismatics by baptism, he acknowledged that pastoral reasons, rather than dogmatic or ecclesiological explanations, could allow for the Encratites to be received by a method other than baptism if requiring them to be received by baptism would hinder their conversion. The canonist Hieromonk Matthew Blastares in the 14th century explained that St. Basil, by not insisting as strongly as St. Cyprian that all schismatics and heretics must be received by baptism, did so out of economy, since the circumstances of St. Basil's time were different from those of St. Cyprian's.[373] In other words, Blastares recognizes St. Cyprian's teaching on the manner of reception as the canon/rule and deviations from St. Cyprian to be by economy.[374]

The 12th century canonist, Monk John Zonaras, comparing the decision of the Seventh Canon of the Second Ecumenical Council to St. Cyprian states that the Ecumenical Council "makes an exception for certain heretics."[375] However, an exception implies that there is a standard, a rule that the exception deviates from, hence the distinction between *akriveia* (exactitude) and *oikonomia* (economy).

Blessed Theophylact (+1107) discusses the temporary and circumstantial nature of economy in his commentary on Galatians 5:11, where he explains that St. Paul circumcised Timothy "by economy" but did not preach circumcision as a rule to be followed by the rest of the Church.

---

372 Kazhdan, *The Oxford Dictionary of Byzantium*, Vol. 3, pp. 1516-1517.

373 Σύνταγμα τῶν θείων καὶ ἱερῶν κανόνων 6 [Athens, repr. 1966 of 1859], p. 18. Cited from Patrick Viscuso, "A Late Byzantine Theology of Canon Law," Greek Orthodox Theological Review 3 [1989], p. 207.

374 Important to remember, however, is when St. Basil in his first canon accepts the decisions of other bishops to receive certain groups into the Church through economy, he was referring to schismatics (i.e. Encratites) who baptized in three immersions in the name of the Holy Trinity and who did not teach heresy regarding the Trinity.

375 Pogodin, *On the Question of the Order of the Reception of Persons into the Orthodox Church*.

"Well," the false apostles argue, "did you not circumcise Timothy?" "Yes, I did," Paul replies, "but only by economy. It is one thing to circumcise once, on a particular occasion and for a certain reason, and quite another to preach circumcision for everyone"... [St. Theophylact explains:] But one who circumcises a man by economy, does so not because circumcision is a good thing in and of itself, but because it is useful to do so in this particular circumstance.[376]

St. Theodore the Studite speaks about the danger of condescending too much, of exceeding the appropriate application of economy, such that economy becomes the rule, the holy canons are undermined, and lawlessness prevails:

And what is more than this [acceptable application of economy], it will be, forgive me, no longer economy, but the guilt of lawlessness and the transgression of divine canons. For the limit of economy, as you know, is not to completely violate any regulation, and not to go to extremes, and not to cause harm to the most important thing in the case when a small indulgence can be made according to time and circumstances.[377]

Canon 29 of the Fifth-Sixth Ecumenical Council gives an example of the principal of economy, applied to another ecclesiastical issue, as a temporary and not an eternally binding measure:

The Canon of the Fathers that met in Carthage prescribes that the holy rites of the sacrificial altar, unless performed by men under a fast, are not to be celebrated at all, except on one day of the year on which the Lord's Supper is celebrated, perhaps having decided to employ such an economy of the divine Fathers on account of certain pretexts advantageous to the Church in such seasons. Since there is nothing to

---

376 Theophylact of Ohrid, *The Explanation of the Epistle of Saint Paul to the Galatians*, pp. 69-70.
377 Theodore the Studite. Epistle 24.

compel us to abandon exactitude,[378] we decree, pursuantly to the traditions of the Apostles and of the Fathers, that the fasting during the Thursday which falls in the last week in Great Lent must not be omitted, and the whole fast of Great Lent dishonored by being prematurely broken.[379]

Just as with St. Basil's 1st and 47th Canons, Canon 29 of the Fifth-Sixth Ecumenical Council describes the deviation from the rule as by economy and that such economy must have been employed because it was in the best interest of the Church at that time. Canon 29 also recognizes that the reasons for this economy no longer applied so the exactitude of the rule should be reinstated.

Dealing with another matter of ecclesiastical order, that of the preparation of candidates for consecration to the episcopacy, Canon 17 of the First-Second Council states that decisions made out of economy, or exceptions made in rare circumstances, cannot be made a law of the Church.

> Since we have been occupied with matters of ecclesiastical good order, it behooves us to decree also this, that henceforth none of the laymen or monks shall be allowed to ascend to the height of the episcopacy precipitately and multitudinously as in a stampede, but, on the contrary, by being duly examined with reference to the various ecclesiastical degrees or grades, let them thus attain to ordination to the episcopacy. For even if hitherto and up till now some laymen and some monks, owing to need or want demanding it, have been enabled to attain to the honor of the episcopate immediately and without further ado, and they have distinguished themselves for virtuousness and have exalted their churches, yet the fact is that what is of rare occurrence cannot be made a law of the Church; we therefore decree that this shall no longer be done hereafter and henceforth, but that the ordinee must pass through the priestly degrees in a logical manner by

---

378 English modified based on the Greek.
379 Agapios and Nicodemus, op. cit. Quinisext Council, Canon 29.

fulfilling the required length of service of each order before proceeding to the next higher rank.[380]

The canons of the Councils and writings of the Fathers which have allowed for the reception of specific heretics by economy has not been accompanied by language forbidding the baptism of those same heretics. Apostolic Canon 47 which forbids a bishop or priest from baptizing anew anyone who had a "true baptism" has not been understood by the Fathers as applicable to the reception of heretics who had been baptized in heresy, since the only "true baptism" is that which is performed by a priest or bishop of the one Church, while the baptisms of heretics are "a pollution" and mere empty form. Even if a heretic receives a baptism with three full immersions in the name of the Holy Trinity outside of the Church, the Church is not obligated to receive such heretics by economy (St. Basil's Canon 47). Again, the Georgian Council of Ruisi-Urbnisi in 1103 required Monophysites to be received by baptism despite the fact that they had been baptized in the apostolic manner, with three immersions in the name of the Trinity, and this Council stated that this was how Antioch and all the Eastern Church received Monophysites at that time.[381]

The application of economy has presuppositions that are required by the canons. As economy means a deviation from the rule based on the needs of the times, economy can never replace the rule, *oikonomia* cannot become *akriveia*. When the presuppositions for the application of economy are lacking, economy cannot be applied. When the presuppositions are in place for the canonical application of economy, economy can be applied if necessary but is not mandatory, as "All things are lawful for me, but not all things are helpful; all things are lawful for me, but not all things edify."[382] Canon 7 of the Second Ecumenical Council, Canon 95 of the Fifth-Sixth Ecumenical Council in Trullo, and Apostolic Canon 50 show that the apostolic form of baptism must be applied (three

---

380 Agapios and Nicodemus, op. cit. Canon 17 of the First-Second Council..
381 Townsend, *The Holy and Righteous King David the Restorer of Georgia & The Holy and Righteous Queen Tamar of Georgia: Lives, Akathist, Canons, Works*, p. 85.
382 1 Cor. 10:23

immersions in the name of the Trinity) and heretics who have not received the apostolic form of baptism (i.e. the Eunomians) must be received by baptism. The Church, however, is not required to receive by economy those baptized in the correct form outside of the Church if doing so is neither necessary nor beneficial (cf. St. Basil, Canon 47 and Council of Ruisi-Urbnisi). This principle of economy and *akriveia* is not the "invention" of St. Nikodemos but is the principle embedded in the canons ratified by the Ecumenical Councils and in the teachings of the Fathers.

St. Hilarion (Troitsky) the Hieromartyr and Confessor,
Archbishop of Vereya (+1929)
Feast Day: December 15

CHAPTER 9
Reception of Heretics and the Great Schism

Since the time of the Apostles, to baptize meant to immerse (βαπτίζω) three times in water in the name of the Holy Trinity as stated in Apostolic Canon 50. In the book, *A History of the Modes of Christian Baptism*, James Crystal, a Protestant minister, studied the texts of the Ecumenical Councils and all of the local councils of the East and West, including those not ratified by the Fifth-Sixth Ecumenical Council in Trullo, as well as the rubrics of East and West before and after the Great Schism to understand how baptism has been performed since apostolic times. He concluded that aside from a single exception (the Arian controversy at the time of St. Gregory the Great), baptism by three full immersions was rule in both the East and the West prior to the Great Schism.[383]

---

383 In Spain in the 6th century, St. Gregory the Great acknowledged that it was the tradition of the Church to baptize in three immersions, but since the Arians in Spain had used baptism in three immersions to symbolize dissimilar substances in the Trinity, St. Gregory expressed the opinion that baptizing in a single immersion may be preferable at that time and place in order to distinguish the Orthodox from the Arians and to symbolize the consubstantiality of the Holy Trinity in the face of Arian heresy. St. Gregory's opinion that single immersion baptism was acceptable contradicted the view of Pope Pelagius before him who said that baptism in three immersions was expressly taught by Christ. After St. Gregory, baptism in three immersions was again reinstated in Spain. The rest of the Church did not accept St. Gregory's opinion, and the Fifth-Sixth Ecumenical Council after him reaffirmed the teaching of Canon 7 of the Second Ecumenical Council which condemned the single immersion baptism practiced by the Eunomians. See Crystal, *A History of the Modes of Christian Baptism*, pp. 146-148.

Just before the Great Schism, some Latins began to change the form of baptism so the Greeks began to baptize Latins who had not been baptized according to the apostolic form. Crystal states:

> The mode of baptism was a prolific source of discord between the East and the Roman See. The Greeks uniformly resisted any attempt to alter it. Michael Cerularius in the eleventh century brings it as a charge against the Latins, that they baptize by one immersion. The contest seems to have waxed warm between them, for we find Humbert, the Papal legate, complaining that the Greeks "like the Arians, rebaptize those who had been baptized in the name of the Holy Trinity, and especially the Latins, and that, like the Donatists they asserted that, with the exception of the Greek Church, the Church of Christ and true sacrifice and baptism had perished from the earth."[384]

The accusation of Cardinal Humbert that the Greeks were baptizing the Latins was included among the reasons why Patriarch Michael of Constantinople was formally excommunicated by the Latins in 1054,[385] demonstrating that the Greeks were "correctively"[386] baptizing those whom the Latins had "baptized" with a single immersion prior to any formal schism or excommunication between the Greeks and Latins. The Greeks, according to Humbert, were "especially" baptizing Latins but also other heretics who had been baptized in the name of the Holy Trinity, demonstrating that the Greeks did not consider it incorrect

---

384 Ibid, p. 149

385 Will and North, "A Brief or Succinct Account of What the Ambassadors of the Holy Roman and Apostolic See Did in the Royal City attributed to Cardinal Bishop Humbert of Silva Candida."

386 The term "corrective baptism" has been used to describe those who are baptized in the Orthodox Church after having been received into the Church in a way that is not canonically correct, either because the "baptism" performed in the Orthodox Church did not consist of three full immersions, or because reception into the Church was by another method that was not justified by the canonical presuppositions for the application of economy. Since such people have never received baptism in three immersions in the Orthodox Church, "corrective baptism" is simply baptism for those who have never received a true baptism in the Church.

to baptize those who were baptized in the name of the Holy Trinity by heretics. Fr. George Dragas notes:

> Already at the time of the great Schism (1054) the baptism of the Latins came under severe criticism. The Ecumenical Patriarch Michael Kerularios[387] wrote on that occasion to Patriarch Peter of Antioch, about the deviations of the Western Church from the ancient tradition and included in them "the unlawful administration of Baptism."[388] The problem was the Roman Catholic practice of single immersion, which had been condemned by the ancient canons...
>
> The renowned canonist Theodore Balsamon, who in 1193 argued on the basis of Canon 7 of the Second Ecumenical Council that Latin baptisms, based on one immersion, ought to be considered as invalid because their case was similar with that of the Eunomians, shared the view of Kerularios.[389]

That the Orthodox re-baptized Roman Catholics after the Schism of 1054 is also confirmed by the 4th canon of the Western Council of Lateran IV, which was summoned in 1215 by Pope Innocent III.[390] In the 13th century, especially after the sacking of Constantinople by the crusaders in 1204, the practice of re-baptizing Western converts to Orthodoxy was intensified. Metropolitan Germanos of Ainos pointed out that the reason for this strict practice was the violent aggression, which the Western Church showed towards the Eastern Church at that time. Part of that aggression was

---

387 Also translated as "Cerularius."

388 PG 104:744. Quoted in Dragas, *The Manner of Reception of Roman Catholic Converts into the Orthodox Church*, p. 236 (3 online).

389 Ralli-Potle, Syntagma... Kanonôn, vol. 2, p. 10. Quoted in Ibid.

390 See Mansi, Sacrorum Conciliorum... Collectio, tom. 22, p. 1082 In cl. 990 we read: "Baptizatos etiam a Latinis et ipsi Graeci rebaptizare ausu temerario praesumebant: et adhuc, sicut acceptimus, quidam opere hoc non verentur." Quoted in Ibid. See also Medieval Sourcebook.

the attempt to proselytize the Orthodox by using various devious means, including the declaration of the union of the two Churches through a pseudo-synod. In 1222 the (lawful) Patriarch of Constantinople, Germanos II, who was based at Nicaea because of the sacking of the Royal City by the crusaders, wrote a treatise[391] which identifies three types of Western Baptism: the authentic and Apostolic one, which is acceptable to the Orthodox, the Baptism of single immersion, and the Baptism by affusion (pouring) or aspersion (sprinkling), which are highly questionable. At the time of Michael Palaiologos (1261), Meletios the Confessor exposed the invalidity of the Latin Baptism that was based on single immersion and suggested by implication the re-baptism of the Latin converts.[392]

St. Hilarion (Troitsky)

During the 13th century re-baptizing Latin converts was a universal practice in Russia... Thus, Pope Honorius

---

391 This is mentioned by Leo Allatius in his De Concessione..., p. 712: "De azymis, purgatorio, et de tribus modis administrandi baptisma." Constantine Oikonomos cites this reference and adds that the Latin baptism by affusion (kat' epichusin) should be repeated (p. 465). See also Miklosich-Mueller, Acta et Diplomatica Patriarchatus Constantinopolitani, tom. ii (1862) p. 81. Quoted in Ibid.

392 PG 144: 22. Germanos of Ainos, Peri tou kyrous... bibliography below (1952) p. 304. Quoted in Ibid.

III (1216-1227) and Pope Gregory IX (1241) accuse the Russians for re-baptism practices.[393]

In the first half of the 14th century (around 1335) Matthaios Vlastaris underlines the same problem.[394] In 1355 Patriarch Kallistos of Constantinople (1350-4, 1355-63) writes to the clergy of Trnovo that those Latins who have been baptized by single immersion should be re-baptized.[395, 396]

St. Hilarion (Troitsky) also cites many historical examples of Orthodox requiring the Latins to be received by baptism following the Great Schism.

At the very beginning of the twelfth century, a Serbian prince, the father of Stefan Nemanya, was forced to baptize his son with the baptism of the Latins, but later rebaptized him in the Orthodox fashion when he returned to Rascia.[397]

The bishop of Cracow, Matthew, in a letter of 1130 to Bernard, the Abbot of Clairvaux, invites him to concern himself with the conversion of the Russians to Latinism and affirms that the Russians rebaptize Latins.[398]

It is well known how kindly Ludwig VII was received by Manuel I in Constantinople in 1147; however, the description

---

393 Cf. M. Jugie, Theologia Dogmatica... bibliography below (1930), p. 92. Quoted in Ibid.

394 Patriarch Dositheos, Tomos Katallagês..., p. 144. Cited by Germanos of Ainos, op. cit. Quoted in Ibid.

395 "He calls the baptism by one immersion most improper and full of impiety (pragma atopôtaton kai dussebeian anameson). His view is based on the Apostolic canons which clearly state that those baptized by one immersion (eis mian katadusin) are not baptized (hôs mh baptisthentas) and should be rebaptized (anabaptêzesthai parakeleuontai)." See Miklosich-Mueller, Acta et Diplomatica patriarcharum..., I (1860) p. 439. Cf. Kattenbusch, Lehrbuch der vergleichenden Confessionskunde, Freiburg 1892, p. 404. Quoted in Ibid.

396 Dragas, Ibid.

397 E. E. Golubinsky, A Brief Sketch of the History of the Orthodox Churches of Bulgaria, Serbia, and Rumania. Moscow, 1871, p. 551. Quoted in Troitsky, The Unity of the Church and the World Conference of Christian Communities.

398 E. E. Golubinsky. History of the Russian Church, vol. 1, 2, Moscow, 1904, p. 807. Quoted in Troitsky, op. cit.

of his journey to the East, Odo de Dioglio mentions that the Greeks rebaptized Latins.[399]

In 1232, Pope Gregory IX wrote to the Polish clergy not to permit the marriage of Roman Catholic women to Russians, who have them rebaptized according to their own rite...[400]

In Russian sources there is testimony of the baptism of Latins from the fourteenth century. Our chronicles for 6841 (1333) report that Grand Duke Ivan Danilovich married his son Semyon: "From Lithuania they brought a princess for him by the name of Augusta, and in holy baptism she was called Anastasia."[401]

On the views of the Russian Orthodox Church towards Latins and Protestants in the period between 1240-1589, Metropolitan Macarius of Moscow wrote in his *History of the Russian Church*:

> Our relations with the Roman Church retained their former character. We looked at the Latins as apostates from the true faith, schismatics and heretics...

> The Russians - we repeat after the foreigners themselves who visited our fatherland at that time - only recognized themselves as true Christians, and all other Christians, including Protestants and Latins, were considered heretics..., and all not only Catholics, but equally, Protestants and others were re-baptized if they accepted Orthodoxy.[402]

It was not only the Orthodox after the Great Schism who taught that all heretics should be received into the Church by baptism. Despite the teachings of St. Augustine and the Scholastics

---

399 De Ludov. VII profectione in Orientem. Ed. Chiffeletius, Paris 1660, p. 34. A. Pichler, Geschichte der Kirchlichen Trennung Zwischen dem Orient und Occident. 1. Band Muenchen 1864, s. 288 Amn. 7. Quoted in Troitsky, op. cit.

400 Historica Russiae monimenta, V. 1, XXXIV, p. 31. Quoted in Troitsky, op. cit.

401 Voskresensky Chronicle, A Complete Collection of Russian Chronicles, vol. 7, St Petersburg, 1857, pp. 204. The Patriarchal, or Nikon's Chronicle, Complete Collection of Chronicles, vol. 10. St. Petersburg, 1885, p. 206. Quoted in Troitsky, op. cit.

402 Bulgakov, *History of the Russian Church*, Part 3, Ch. 9 (In Russian).

regarding "valid mysteries" outside of the Church, the baptism of Orthodox by the Latins also "occurred rather frequently in the Middle Ages,"[403] even though the Orthodox practiced baptism with three immersions in the name of the Trinity.

> In the middle of the fourteenth century, for example, when the Byzantine Emperor John V Cantacuzene went to Hungary to negotiate an alliance, King Louis of Hungary demanded as a preliminary condition that the Emperor and his suite should undergo Baptism at the hands of Roman clergy. And when Louis conquered large tracts of Bulgaria, Latin missionaries proceeded systematically to rebaptize the Orthodox there: it is said that eight Franciscan friars administered Baptism to no less than 200,000 persons in the course of fifty days.[404]

St. Hilarion further demonstrates that in the 15th century the practice of receiving Latins by baptism was "the rule in the Russian Church." Among other historical references, he states how Tsar Ivan IV in the 16th century, while courting the niece of Queen Elizabeth I of England, wrote to the Queen's ambassador that the princess must first accept Orthodoxy and be baptized before they could marry. In 1590, Queen Elizabeth complained that English merchants in Russia "were forced to be baptized anew, when they had already been received into Christianity through baptism."[405]

> Nicholas Varkoch, ambassador of the Emperor of the Holy Roman Empire, who was in Russia in the year 1593, testifies in the description of his journey, "If baptized Christians happen to convert to their faith, they must allow them (the

---

403 North American Orthodox-Catholic Theological Consultation, *Baptism and 'Sacramental Economy': An Agreed Statement of the North American Orthodox-Catholic Theological Consultation.*

404 Ware, *Eustratius Argenti*, pp. 67-68.

405 Journal of the Imperial Russian Historical Society, Bk. 38, p. 105. St. Petersburg. Quoted in Troitsky, op. cit.

Russians) to baptize them again, since the Muscovites doubt that our baptism is genuine...".[406]

And here is what we read in the encyclical letter of June 14, 1613 of Sylvester, Archbishop of Vologda, to the Archangelsk priest Bartholomew: "When this letter reaches you, you, together with your fellows, the priests and deacons of Archangelsk, shall order those foreigners to prepare themselves for baptism. And you shall baptize them into our true Orthodox Christian faith according to the canons of the holy Apostles and the holy Fathers; you shall command them everywhere to curse and renounce their faith, to deny heathenism and to turn to the true God; after baptism and Communion, you shall also order them to fast as much as possible."[407]

St. Hilarion also quotes from the letter sent to the Polish King Sigismund III in 1610 by St. Hermogenes the Patriarch of Moscow on behalf of "the metropolitans, archbishops, bishops, archimandrites, abbots, and all the council of the Church" offering the Polish Latin Prince Vladislav the Russian tsardom. Acknowledging that Prince Vladislav had been baptized by the Latins, St. Hermogenes, in the name of the entire Russian Orthodox Church, made it clear that Prince Vladislav must first be baptized into the Orthodox Church before he could become Tsar.[408]

By the time of the Great Schism, it was common for Orthodox to baptize those who had been baptized by the Latins prior to the Schism using a single immersion. After the Great Schism, it was the common practice among the Greeks

---

406 Russian trans, in *Reading in the Imperial Society of History and Antiquities for 1874*, book 4, pp. 33-34, 135. Quoted in Troitsky, op. cit.

407 Chronicle of the Studies of the Archeographic Commission, (Issue) No. 2, St. Petersburg, 1862, p. 64. Troitsky, op. cit.

408 Collection of Government letters and Agreement preserved in the Governmental College of Foreign Affairs. Part II, Moscow 1814, no. 201, pp. 408, 411, 413, 414, 416, 418, 421. Quoted in Troitsky, op. cit.

and the Russians to receive the Latins and other heretics into the Orthodox Church only by baptism.

St. Hermogenes of Moscow

Ὁ ἍΓΙΟΣ   ΜΑΡΚΕ   Ὁ ΕΥΓΕΝΙΚΟΣ

St. Mark of Ephesus (+1444)
Feast Day: January 19

CHAPTER 10

St. Mark of Ephesus and the
1484 Council of Constantinople

While the baptism of Latins and other heretics was the common practice throughout the Orthodox Church prior to St. Mark of Ephesus, the position of St. Mark and the 1484 Council in Constantinople appear as exceptions to this rule. St. Hilarion states regarding the position of St. Mark:

> In the fifteenth century...[t]he reception of Latins into the Church was accomplished by chrismation. Such a practice was determined upon also at the council of Constantinople in 1484... It is remarkable that the Greek writers of the fifteenth century prove by the chrismation of Latins upon their being received that these latter are heretics. "The ordinances of piety say," writes St. Mark of Ephesus, "that even those who in the least fall away from the Orthodox faith are called heretics and are also subject to the statutes against heretics. And why do we anoint with chrism those of them who unite themselves to us? Obviously, it is because they are heretics." Here St. Mark of Ephesus bears witness that Latins were only chrismated. But this does not at all mean that he considers them as belonging to the Church. He speaks clearly and definitely on this question. "We," he says, "have cut them off and cast them out from the

common body of the Church… We have abandoned them as heretics, and thus separated ourselves from them." St. Mark of Ephesus refers to the 7th Canon of the Second Ecumenical Council in proof of the fact that Latins are received into the Church as were the ancient heretics and that therefore they are likewise heretics.[409]

While St. Mark stated that the Latins were at that time received by chrismation, one must also note that he still viewed Latins as "cut off" and "cast out… from the common body of the Church." The economy which was followed in these times, which was based on the means of reception allowed for Arians and other heretics at the Second Ecumenical Council and the Fifth-Sixth Ecumenical Council in Trullo, did not coincide with any declaration of "ecclesiality" or the "presence of the Holy Spirit" in the mysteries of Latins. By this time, the Latins had not yet universally abandoned the practice of baptizing in three immersions, so the canonical presuppositions for the application of economy remained mostly intact among the Latins. As noted in *A History of the Modes of Christian Baptism*:

> At that council [at Florence], AD 1439, a passage at arms occurred between Mark of Ephesus on the side of the Greeks, and Gregory the monk and Protosyncellus[410] on that of the Latins. Mark laid to the charge of the latter that they had "two baptisms, one administered by trine immersion, and the other by pouring water upon the top of the head." To which Gregory replies, "That there are two baptisms, no one ever asserted, for holy baptism is one,"… "and that the trine immersion is necessary is evident, for thus has it been handed down by the saints, to signify the three days' burial of the Lord. So, indeed, it has been handed down, and so the rituals of the Latins teach that it shall be observed."[411]

---

409 Troitsky, op. cit.

410 Gregory Mammas was the confessor of the Emperor John VIII Paleologos. He opposed St. Mark of Ephesus at the Council of Florence, defended Latin teachings, and signed the false union with the Latins. See Ostroumoff, *The History of the Council of Florence*.

411 Crystal, *A History of the Modes of Christian Baptism*, p. 106.

Furthermore:

> We have already alluded… to the fact that Gregory the
> Monk, at Florence, in 1439, states that the Latin rituals still
> enjoined trine immersion. Yet, notwithstanding this latter
> statement, the views of Aquinas and his coadjutors were
> gradually leavening that body. The rituals seem, until quite
> a later period, perhaps until the Reformation, to enjoin trine
> immersion as the rule. The single [immersion], however,
> and the compends [sprinkling or pouring] were brought in
> little by little until, at the Reformation, they had become the
> ordinary modes in certain countries.[412]

Regarding whether three (trine) immersions continued in the
West alongside other modes, Crystal notes:

> All the Westerns, however, were not justly liable to the
> charge of wholly altering the mode, for we know that, long
> after the disruption, the trine was the rule in some countries,
> and in England even until the Reformation.[413]

With regard to the reception of Latins, St. Mark cited Canon 7
of the Second Ecumenical Council but did not discuss this or any
of the other relevant canons in detail, nor did he explain why the
Latins should be classified among those whom the canon allows to
be received by chrismation rather than among those required to be
baptized. Archimandrite Ambrose (Pogodin) mentions the unique
context of St. Mark of Ephesus' words which help understand why
he applied such economy at that time:

> St. Mark of Ephesus wrote these things at a time when the
> Orthodox Church was subject to massive aggression from
> the Roman Catholics — at a time when her very existence,
> in human terms, was questionable. This was one of the most

---

412 Ibid, p. 152.
413 Ibid, p. 149.

critical epochs if not the critical epoch in the history of the Orthodox Church.[414]

The 1484 Council in Constantinople was convened after the repose of St. Mark of Ephesus to officially declare the Council of Ferrara-Florence a false council and the Latins to be heretics, and to call back to the Orthodox Church those former Orthodox who began to commemorate the Latin Pope of Rome following the false council.[415] In its decrees, including that the Latins should be received by chrismation, the "Latins" in question were primarily Uniates who had submitted to the Pope of Rome[416] but otherwise retained the Orthodox form of baptism and who confessed the Orthodox faith.

Such an application of economy was made by St. Mark of Ephesus and the 1484 Council at that time, as St. Nikodemos explains, because the Orthodox feared Latin aggression if Latins were required to be received by baptism in large numbers; considering the military power of the Latins during this period, their violence towards the Orthodox in the Fourth Crusade, and the continued aggression of the Latins after the Fourth Crusade. St. Nikodemos explains:

> So when it is taken into account that up to that time, according to the testimonies of the same enemies, the Easterners had been baptizing them, it is plain that it was for the sake of a great economy that they later employed the expedient of chrism simply because our race could not afford, in the plight in which it then was in, to excite the mania of the papacy; and in addition there is such evidence in the fact that they then abrogated and invalidated all the evils done in Florence, and there was much rage among the Latins on this account. Now the need of economy having

---

414 Pogodin, *On the Question of the Order of Reception of Persons into the Orthodox Church, Coming to Her from Other Christian Churches*, Ch. 1.

415 Runciman, *The Great Church in Captivity*, p. 228.

416 See Nelson, *The Decrees of the Fifth Lateran Council (1512–17): Their Legitimacy, Origins, Contents, and Implementation*.

passed away, exactitude and the Apostolic Canons must have their place.

So those preceding us also employed economy and accepted the baptism of the Latins... because Papism, or Popery, was then in its prime and had all the forces and powers of the kings of Europe in its hands, while on the other hand, our own kingdom was breathing its last gasps. Hence it would have become necessary, if that economy had not been employed, for the Pope to rouse the Latin races against the Eastern, take them prisoners, kill them, and inflict innumerable barbarities upon them.

But now that they are no longer able to inflict evils upon us, as a result of the fact that divine Providence has lent us such a guardian that he has at last beaten down their brow, now I say, that the fury of Papism (Roman Catholicism) is of no avail against us, what need is there any longer of economy? For there is a limit to economy, and it is not perpetual and indefinite.[417]

The same explanation is also given by St. Athanasios Parios that:

Those who propound the so-called synodal decree of 1484, which received Latin converts by chrismation, do not understand that the churchmen of that time were using *economia*, and that they thus formulated their decree because of the Papacy's agitation and tyranny... Now the season of *economia* has passed... and the papal fury no longer has any power over us.[418]

Despite the words of St. Mark of Ephesus and the decision of the Council of 1484, Greeks continued to receive Latins by baptism after this time and prior to the 1755 Decree of the Patriarchs of Constantinople, Jerusalem, and Alexandria. Quoting Constantine Oikonomos, Fr. George Metallinos states:

---

417 Agapios and Nicodemus, op. cit., footnote 66 to the Canons of the Holy Apostles.
418 Metallinos, op. cit., p. 91.

For even after this [1484] Council, "neither did the Latin baptism seem acceptable... nor did [the Orthodox] think of the Latins as having priesthood, referring to the innovation regarding the rite which again had spread in many places." Hence, despite the synodally given solution and the composition of a special service [for receiving Latins], "the East, aiming with conviction at the *acrivia* of the holy Ecumenical Councils," in practice received Western converts by baptism, for they saw no benefit arising from the concession made by *economia*, but rather "harm... to the simpler and afflicted Orthodox."[419]

Latins who visited Greece in the 17th century confirmed that Latins were still being baptized by the Orthodox at that time:

Caucus, Latin Archbishop of Corfu, begins his long list of the "Errors of the Modern Greeks"... by stating, "They re-baptise all the Latins that embrace their Communion."[420]

Also in the 17th century, the Latin priest Richard Simon observed:

As to the re-baptising of the Latins, it is certain that they have done it in other Places, besides Corfou; and that because of the Enmity they bear towards them, looking upon all their Ceremonies as abominable.[421]

Another French Latin priest named Francois Richard wrote in 1657:

A number of Greeks do not regard our baptism as good and valid; and although this heresy does not prevail so much on the islands of the Archipelago as in the towns of the mainland, none the less some are to be found who rebaptize those of us Franks who wish to pass over to their rite.[422]

---

419 Ibid. p. 89.
420 Simon, *The Critical History of the Religions and Customs of the Eastern Nations*, p. 5. Quoted in Ware, *Eustratios Argenti*, p. 67.
421 Ibid.
422 Richard, *Relation*, p. 139. Quoted in Ibid.

St. Mark of Ephesus and the 1484 Council permitted the Latins, particularly those who were previously Orthodox and who had united with the Pope of Rome, to be received by chrismation but the Latins at that time had not yet abandoned the canonical presuppositions for their reception by economy (the apostolic form of baptism by three immersions in the name of the Holy Trinity). These decisions in the 15th century were not accompanied by any declarations of "ecclesiality" or "grace" in the mysteries of Latins. Rather, the Latins were referred to explicitly as "heretics" who were "cut off" from the Church. Furthermore, the Greeks at that time did not consider the words of St. Mark of Ephesus nor the decision of the 1484 Council to be binding with regard to the reception of Latins, as Latins continued to be received by baptism after these declarations. The official decision in 1755 by the Patriarchs of Constantinople, Jerusalem, and Alexandria to baptize Latins and all other converts demonstrates that the words of St. Mark of Ephesus and the decision of the 1484 Council were not universally accepted. St. Nikodemos, St. Athanasios Parios, and others in the 18th century acknowledged that the economy practiced by St. Mark and the 1484 Council was due to the fierce aggression of the Pope at that time, and that the need for economy no longer applied since the Pope no longer posed such a military threat.

St. Hermogenes, Patriarch of Moscow (+1612)
Feast Days: February 17 & May 12

CHAPTER 11

The 1620 Moscow Council

While the Russian Church historically required all heterodox converts to be baptized, this decision was formally codified by the Moscow Council of 1620 under Patriarch Philaret[423] of Moscow who sought to follow the policies of Hieromartyr Hermogenes the Wonderworker and Patriarch of Moscow and All Russia. Regarding this period, the Russian Elder John (Krestiankin) (+2006) relates:

> In the 17th century, the sword put by Rome into the hand of the false Tsarevich Demetrius passed through Rus, deposed the tsar, and demanded that Russia be betrayed to the will of the Polish king who received secret instructions from Rome to carefully but steadily lead the Russian Church to submission to the Pope, that is, to Unia...
>
> At that terrible moment, Russia was saved by her Patriarch. Not only did he not sign the letters of surrender, but he sent the letters all over Rus, revealing to the Russians the essence of the events taking place and encouraging the Russians to raise up weapons and fight. Patriarch Hermogenes was martyred and canonized as a saint. And as if drawing a conclusion from the history of Russia of that period, the

---

423 Patriarch Philaret of Moscow was the father of Tsar Michael I, the first Russian Tsar from the House of Romanov.

next Russian Patriarch Filaret said: "Latin papists are the worst of all heretics, for they accepted into their law all of the condemned heresies of all the ancient Greek, Hagarene, heretical faiths; and fall under that part of the 95th Canon [of the Fifth-Sixth Ecumenical Council in Trullo] which deals with heretics." These, pay attention, are not the words of an ordinary person, but of Patriarch Filaret...

Elder John
(Krestiankin) (+2006)

The 17th century and the 20th are different times, but the deeds are the same. And the deeds reveal and bring to witness the Catholic falsehood committed by them with fanatical hatred, in which Uniate Catholics destroy Orthodox churches, Orthodox people, subjecting them to reproach and terrible persecution - up to violent death. These are indisputable facts of our time."[424]

Elder John said that St. Hermogenes saved Russia at this time from the Latins who sought to subject Russia to the Pope even through the use of violence. He also stated that the Latins and Uniates in the 20th century had not changed since the 17th century but still use the same violent means to force the Orthodox into subjection to the Pope.

After the repose of St. Hermogenes, Patriarch Philaret of Moscow called the 1620 Council after learning that Latins from Poland had been received by chrismation with the blessing of Metropolitan Jonah of Sarsk and Podonsk, contrary to the canons of the Church and the historic practice of the Russian Church. Patriarch Philaret reminded the Metropolitan that Patriarch Ignatius of Moscow before him had been deposed specifically for receiving a Latin convert by chrismation in violation of Apostolic Canons 46 and 47. The 1620 Council was called to ensure such a violation of the canons would not occur again. St. Hilarion relates:

---

424 Krestiankin, *One Faith, One Baptism, One God and Father of All* (In Russian).

In view of all these testimonies, I think that it would be an inaccuracy to call the decision of the Council of Moscow of 1620 an innovation. Indeed, the Council of 1620 itself looked on its decision not as a novelty, but as a confirmation of an old custom. Patriarch Philaret himself speaks of the incentives to the decision of 1620...

Patriarch Philaret... recalls how St. Ermogen [Hermogenes] sent him to Vladislav "to make him Tsar, and to baptize him into our true Orthodox Christian faith of the Greek canon. And our father, the great, most holy Patriarch Ermogen, gave me a script from the Canons of the holy Apostles and the holy Fathers, for the strengthening of us all, and as an answer against the heretics of many different heretical faiths, why they should be baptized."

The Patriarch speaks of how he studied the canons and understood "that all heretics of every different heretical faith are deprived of the true, holy baptism, which is of water and the Holy Spirit. For this reason it is proper for all those who come to the Orthodox Christian faith from heretical faiths to be baptized perfectly with holy baptism..." "But how do you, in this imperial city of Moscow, undertake to introduce and establish that which is in opposition to the canons of the holy Fathers, the seven Ecumenical Councils, the Local Councils and the holy Patriarchs; why do you not order those coming to you from the Latin faith to be baptized in three immersions and why do you not investigate the deviation of their heresy, but instead command only that they be anointed with Holy Chrism. . . ?"

"I, the humble, do not even wish to hear of your newly introduced heretical delusion, since it is not in accordance with the divine canons that you introduce and teach new heresies, saying that it is not proper that those papists be baptized, and affirming that you do this in accordance with the canons of the holy Fathers..." "For from the years of the Grand Duke St. Vladimir of eternal memory, who enlightened all Great Russia with holy baptism received from the Greeks, and even until today, in the year 7128, no one among us has dared commit such a scandalous act of heresy, except Ignatius, the dethroned Patriarch and yourself.

"Since the beginning of the state of Moscow until now, there has never been a case where Latin heretics and heretics of other faiths were not baptized, except for the case of Ignatius the Patriarch, who was deposed from his episcopal throne."[425]

Patriarch Philaret's instructions regarding the baptism of all converts were printed in the *Trebnik* (service book) for laymen as expressing the official position of the Russian Church. Metropolitan Macarius of Moscow in his *History of the Russian Church* relates that at the 1620 Council a collection of all of the relevant canons were read to Metropolitan Jonah of Sarsk and Podonsk regarding the reception of heretics into the Church, and that these canons had been compiled by St. Hermogenes the Patriarch and Wonderworker of Moscow and All Russia with some additions from Patriarch Philaret.[426]

He also said that he himself, Philaret, on the orders of Hermogenes, then tried to study the rules of the holy apostles and fathers and came to the conclusion that all heretics of various heretical faiths do not have true baptism and therefore those who come to Orthodoxy from all heretical faiths must be baptized again with perfect baptism...[427]

At the 1620 Council, after Metropolitan Jonah listened to the reading of the relevant canons and the explanation of Patriarch Philaret, he repented and signed the declaration that Latins and all heretics are to be received by baptism.

---

425 *Trebnik for Laymen*, 1639 edition, pp. 399 and ff. Quoted in Troitsky, op. cit.
426 Bulgakov, *History of the Russian Church*, Part 5, Chapter 3 (In Russian).
427 Ibid.

Finally, Jonah obeyed before the great Council… and asked for forgiveness, confessing that he understood the 95th canon of the Sixth Ecumenical Council [Fifth-Sixth Ecumenical Council in Trullo] in this way "by simplicity, and not by intention," promised to be of one mind with Patriarch Philaret and with all the consecrated Council and said: "And to your conciliar election from the rules of the holy apostle and holy Fathers to the Latin heresy about baptism, I want to attribute with my hand and according to this your conciliar writing I want to do." The patriarch, seeing the contrition and petition of Jonah, his repentance and tears, and after consulting with other bishops, removed the spiritual prohibition from him and blessed him to continue to celebrate the liturgy. The synodical exposition was signed by all the hierarchs present, including Jonah, in the house of the Most Pure Theotokos on the 4th day of December 1620. In this exposition, Patriarch Filaret did not establish any new rule or rules for the Russian Church, but only tried to confirm the long-standing custom of re-baptizing Latins in the event of their conversion to Orthodoxy.[428]

St. Hilarion further relates that Patriarch Philaret required even Uniates who were baptized with the Orthodox form of baptism in three immersions to be received by baptism since they had been baptized by heretics:

> In 1621 Patriarch Philaret issued a decree on how the White Russians should be examined: which of them to baptize, which to chrismate, and which neither to baptize nor chrismate.[429] It was indicated that those baptized by the Uniates should be baptized with three immersions "because they were baptized by an apostate who prays to God for the Pope."[430] But upon writing this directive, the Patriarch also confesses that "we have not introduced a new tradition,

---

428 Ibid.
429 *Trebnik for Laymen*, 1639, pp. 427 and ff. Referenced in Troitsky, op. cit.
430 Ibid., p. 431.

but only renewed and strengthened the ancient one."[431]

All these affirmations of Patriarch Philaret have a genuine historical foundation. This is the reason why even the foreigners who were in Moscow after 1620, when recalling the rebaptism of Latins, do not speak as though this practice had just recently appeared... Baron Augustine Maierberg, who was in Moscow in 1661, reports without any stipulations that "the Muscovites believe that baptism has no power unless the baptized person is completely immersed three times, according to the custom of the ancient Church. For this reason, when someone baptized according to the Latin faith goes over to the Muscovite faith, they rebaptize him by triple immersion, as one not baptized according to the ritual of the Church; they even dissolve a marriage contracted by him beforehand, considering that he was unlawfully led to the other sacraments, having not entered the Church by the sacred door of baptism. They at once anoint the baptized with chrism, not placing any value on Latin chrismation, considering it ineffectual."[432]

St. Hilarion (Troitsky)

Fr. George Dragas confirms the testament of St. Hilarion that the earliest practice of the Russian Orthodox Church and

---

431 Ibid., p. 429.

432 *Readings in the Society of History and Antiquities, 1873*, article 3, pp. 77-78. Quoted in Troitsky, op. cit.

the Patriarchate of Constantinople was to baptize all Latins and Protestants.

> The earliest norm in Russia for the reception of Western Christians, first Roman Catholics and later Protestants, into the Orthodox Church was by (re-)baptism. In doing this, the Russian Church was in line with the Church of Constantinople. The Popes Honorius III (1216-1227) and Gregory IX (1227-1241) reproached the Russians for re-baptizing the Latins. This position was officially and synodically instituted by a Synod summoned in Moscow by Patriarch Philaret Nikititch in 1620. This Synod stipulated the rebaptism of Latins, Uniates and the Orthodox of Little Russia (Ukraine) who had been baptized by Uniate priests. Another Synod summoned in Moscow by the same Patriarch in 1621 reiterated the same position. The main arguments for this position were as follows:
>
> 1) The Trullan Canon 95 specifies that heretics are to be re-baptized in order to enter into the Church.
>
> 2) Latins are heretics and as such they must be re-baptized.
>
> 3) Re-baptism of heretics is specifically ordered by the apostolic canons 46 and 47.
>
> 4) All Russian Orthodox Bishops have followed the practice of re-baptizing Latin converts.
>
> 5) All Ecumenical Patriarchs have concurred with this practice.[433]

The 1620 Council dealt not only with how the Latins should be received into the Orthodox Church but also decreed that Orthodox who were "baptized" by Orthodox priests by pouring should afterwards be baptized with three immersions.

---

433 Dragas, op. cit.

Another issue at the council was the question of the reception of "Belarusians," those who came to the Muscovite state from Lithuania. The Council decreed that those baptized by a non-Orthodox priest should be completely baptized, those who were baptized in three immersions and anointed with chrism from an Orthodox priest should be allowed into Eucharistic communion and considered Orthodox, those who were baptized by pouring and anointed with chrism from an Orthodox priest should be baptized in three immersions [i.e. they received "corrective baptisms"]... The decree on "Belarusians" was signed on December 16, 1620. The decisions of the council were published several times in the Great Potrebnik: in 1623, 1624, 1625, 1633, 1636, 1642, 1647, 1651....

"Belarusians" coming from Lithuania, baptized by pouring, were baptized again by immersion. In 1623-24, only a few dozen "Belarusians" were accepted. Among them were Orthodox abbots, hieromonks and monks. Pouring baptism was not recognized at the reception - everyone was re-baptized, and then, if necessary, re-ordained. In 1630, the Uniate Archbishop Afinogen Kryzhanovsky was baptized. In the beginning, he had a purely Orthodox ordination up to and including the rank of archimandrite...[434]

Concerning these decisions, including the instruction that those "baptized" into the Orthodox Church by pouring must be baptized with three immersions:

[The] Patriarch and the Council make the remark that they do not introduce a new tradition, but update and strengthen the old one, following the commandments of the holy apostles and holy fathers, but they do not give these commandments themselves.[435]

---

434 *Local Council of 1620 Moscow* (In Russian).
435 Bulgakov, op. cit. Part 5, Ch. 3.

Patriarch Philaret was succeeded by Patriarch Joseph in 1634. Shortly after becoming Patriarch he was forced to deal with the many scandals involving Archbishop Joseph Kurtsevich of Suzdal. This Archbishop Joseph was accused of many terrible things, including violence, sending people out to rob the faithful, eating meat, and keeping prostitutes. He was eventually called to a council to be tried for the accusations against him. As Metropolitan Macarius relates:

> After listening to all these testimonies and taking into account that Joseph himself had not been baptized until now (i.e., through a threefold immersion), like other heretics of the Papist or Lutheran faith, the fathers of the Council decided to remove from him the hierarchical dignity and panagia and recognized that Joseph was unworthy not only to bear the hierarchical dignity, but also to be in communion with the faithful, but should be "in the rank of weeping and sobbing"... Having stated all this in his letter to the Siya Monastery, Patriarch Joseph ordered that the monastery authorities gather all their priests and monks, put the former Archbishop Joseph before them and read the letter sent to everyone, and then removed from Joseph the hierarchal dignity and panagia and clothed him in black dress and... Hilarion Lopukhin, who was with Joseph, took him to the Solovetsky Monastery according to the sovereign's letter.[436]

In 1643, his successor (also by the name of Joseph) took part in a lengthy exchange regarding Lutheranism when the Tsar initiated negotiations with King Christian IV of Denmark with the hope of Danish prince Voldemar marrying Tsarina Irina Mikhailovna. In order to marry the Tsarina, Prince Voldemar was required to first be baptized in three immersions:

> On April 21, a messenger from the patriarch [Joseph] appeared to the king's son and said: "The sovereign father, the most holy Joseph, the patriarch of Moscow and all Russia... sent a letter to your Majesty, under his seal, in

---

436 Ibid.

order to invite you to lovingly make an answer." In the letter, the patriarch urged the prince not to be stubborn, to obey the king of the sovereign and unite with him in faith, then briefly explained the difference between the Orthodox confession and the Lutheran, and finally again urged the prince to accept Orthodoxy and be baptized in three immersions, adding that he would take the sin upon himself, if the prince considers it a sin...[437]

When this exchange did not seem productive, an open oral debate was organized on May 28th of the same year, and the prince's Lutheran Pastor Filgober participated and defended "baptism" by pouring.

The Russians, for their part, spoke and wrote in response to the pastor: it is by no means all the same in baptism whether to immerse, pour or sprinkle; in baptism, according to the apostle, we are buried with Christ unto death (Rom. 6:3,4), and this burial is possible only through immersion in water, and not through pouring it over or sprinkling it... That is why the rules of the holy apostles, holy councils and holy fathers unanimously command to baptize in three immersions... The Greek βάπτισμα, "baptism," means precisely "immersion" and only "immersion"... while dousing or sprinkling is called differently in Greek... St. John the Baptist baptized the people and Christ Himself not by water, but in water - ἐν ὕδατι, as all the evangelists testify (Matt. 3:11; Mk. 1:8; Lk. 3:16; Jn. 1:26), therefore, through immersion, and not through pouring or sprinkling... Baptism is indeed not repeated, but only true baptism, that is, through threefold immersion. And the pouring baptism performed by the Lutherans is not true, but heretical, and therefore even "there is no baptism at all, but rather desecration," and those baptized with such baptism are not only not forbidden to be baptized again but are commanded to be baptized (Apostolic Canons 47 and 50)... You don't even have the

---

437 Ibid.

> sacred rank of ordaining, according to tradition... We know
> that you... are neither holy nor ordained with the laying on
> of the hand of the priesthood, and you yourself are neither
> baptized nor consecrated: how can you baptize and sanctify
> others? And how can you sanctify and baptize others when
> you yourself have not been sanctified by anyone?[438]

Prince Voldemar's father, King Christian IV of Denmark,
also inquired of Patriarch Parthenios I of Constantinople about
Lutheran baptism at the same time.

> The Patriarch [Parthenios of Constantinople] conferred
> with many learned people, including the famous teacher
> Meletios Sirigus at that time, and convened a Council,
> at which, after many investigations and consultations, it
> was decided that Lutheran baptism was not baptism and
> Lutherans should be baptized again, because they are not
> baptized through three immersions, but only sprinkled, and
> not with water, but with defiled water, and their very priests
> are not consecrated.[439]

In the end, however, Prince Voldemar did not consent to be
baptized Orthodox and was not allowed to marry Tsarina Irina
Mikhailovna.

St. Hermogenes of Moscow and the Russian Orthodox Church
prior to 1667 followed the Apostolic Canons and the teachings of
St. Cyprian in requiring all heretics to be received into the Church
by baptism with three immersions. At the 1620 Council, the Russian
Church was so insistent on the necessity of triple immersion baptism
that even Orthodox priests, hieromonks, and abbots who had been
received into the Orthodox Church by pouring were required
to be baptized by three immersions ("correctively"). St. Hilarion
(Troitsky), and Metropolitan Macarius of Moscow in his *History
of the Russian Church*, thoroughly demonstrate that the Russian
Church before 1667 understood that all heretics must be received

---

438 Ibid.
439 Ibid.

into the Orthodox Church by baptism in three immersions; and that baptisms done by heretics and baptisms performed in the Orthodox Church by pouring or sprinkling are not true baptisms. The Russian Church also understood that only a priest or bishop of the Church can perform true baptisms and that there are no true baptisms outside of the Orthodox Church. Apostolic Canon 47 that forbids priests and bishops to "baptize anew anyone that has had a true baptism" was understood as applicable only to those who had already been baptized in the Orthodox Church with three immersions in the name of the Holy Trinity.

St. Hermogenes of Moscow

Council of Trent (1545–1563)

CHAPTER 12

The Patriarchates Under the Ottomans and Latin Influences on Orthodox Theology

Constantinople fell to the Muslim Ottomans in 1453, after the repose of St. Mark of Ephesus in 1444 and prior to the 1484 Council in Constantinople. The Ottoman Empire continued to expand and by 1520 the Patriarchates of Constantinople, Antioch, Jerusalem, and Alexandria were under Ottoman rule. The Orthodox suffered tremendously under the Ottomans, were taxed heavily, and theological study was very difficult. While there were Orthodox during this time that continued to study the Fathers and maintained patristic teaching, many Orthodox seeking theological education attended Latin and Protestant theological schools abroad and became influenced by heterodox beliefs.

In *The Orthodox Church*, Metropolitan Kallistos Ware says:

> Yet alongside this traditionalism [of that period] there is another and contrary current in Orthodox theology of the seventeenth and eighteenth centuries: the current of western infiltration. It was difficult for the Orthodox under Ottoman rule to maintain a good standard of scholarship. Greeks who wished for a higher education were obliged to travel to the non-Orthodox world, to Italy and Germany, to Paris, and even as far as Oxford. Among the distinguished Greek theologians of the Turkish period, a few were self-taught,

but the overwhelming majority had been trained in the west under Roman Catholic or Protestant masters.

Inevitably this had an effect upon the way in which they interpreted Orthodox theology. Certainly Greek students in the west read the Fathers, but they only became acquainted with such of the Fathers as were held in esteem by their non-Orthodox professors. Thus Gregory Palamas was still read, for his spiritual teaching, by the monks of Athos; but to most learned Greek theologians of the Turkish period he was utterly unknown. In the works of Eustratios Argenti (died c.1758), the ablest Greek theologian of his time, there is not a single citation from Palamas; and his case is typical. It is symbolic of the state of Greek Orthodox learning in the last four centuries that one of the chief works of Palamas, *The Triads in Defense of the Holy Hesychasts*, should have remained in great part unpublished until 1959.

There was a real danger that Greeks who studied in the west, even though they remained fully loyal in intention to their own Church, would lose their Orthodox mentality and become cut off from Orthodoxy as a living tradition. It was difficult for them not to look at theology through western spectacles; whether consciously or not, they used terminology and forms of argument foreign to their own Church. Orthodox theology underwent what the Russian theologian Fr. Georges Florovsky (1893-1979) has appropriately termed a *pseudomorphosis*. Religious thinkers of the Turkish period can be divided for the most part into two broad groups, the "Latinizers" and the "Protestantizers." Yet the extent of this westernization must not be exaggerated. Greeks used the outward forms which they had learned in the west, but in the substance of their thought the great majority remained fundamentally Orthodox. The tradition was at times distorted by being forced into alien moulds – distorted, but not wholly destroyed.[440]

---

440 Ware, *The Orthodox Church*, pp. 92-93.

Metropolitan Kallistos acknowledges that while those who attended non-Orthodox theological schools at this time did not necessarily lose their Orthodoxy completely (though many did convert to Protestantism or Papism), Orthodox who studied at heterodox schools were only exposed to Fathers who were popular among the heterodox professors, and such studies with the heterodox often led to a "distorted" Orthodoxy. There was a real risk of these Orthodox Christians "losing their Orthodox mentality" and being cut off from "Orthodoxy as a living tradition." The living tradition of patristic learning and the patristic way of life was nevertheless maintained on Mt. Athos during this time and among those who remained in contact with Athos.

Following the Pan-Orthodox rejection of the false Council of Florence, the Latins increased their efforts to convert Orthodox. The Latins established The Society of Jesus (the Jesuits) in 1540 to convert the Orthodox to subservience to the Pope of Rome both through outward missionary activity and by obtaining secret declarations of allegiance to the Pope. Between 1545 and 1563, the Latins held the Council of Trent at which a number of teachings were formally adopted that are contrary to the teachings of the Fathers and the Ecumenical Councils on mysteries outside of the Church and the Apostolic form of baptism. The canons of the Council of Trent state:

On the Sacraments in General

CANON IX.-If any one saith, that, in the three sacraments, Baptism, to wit, Confirmation, and Order, there is not imprinted in the soul a character, that is, a certain spiritual and indelible Sign, on account of which they cannot be repeated; let him be anathema.

CANON XI.-If any one saith, that, in ministers, when they effect, and confer the sacraments, there is not required the intention at least of doing what the Church does; let him be anathema.

On Baptism

CANON IV.-If any one saith, that the baptism which is even given by heretics in the name of the Father, and of the Son, and of the Holy Ghost, with the intention of doing what the Church doth, is not true baptism; let him be anathema.[441]

These canons state that baptism by heretics in the name of the Trinity constitute a "true baptism" that leaves an "indelible sign" which can never be repeated, and states that the "intention" of the heretic conducting the baptism influences whether or not the baptism is true.

In the Catechism of the Council of Trent, for the first time the Latins formally adopted the teaching that three immersions are unnecessary in baptism and that pouring or sprinkling were equivalent to immersion. Following this 16th century Latin council, due to the convenience of pouring and sprinkling compared to performing baptism by full immersion, pouring and sprinkling became the norm among the Latins. The Catechism of the Council of Trent states:

Administration of Baptism

What has been said on the matter and form, which are required for the essence of the Sacrament, will be found sufficient for the instruction of the faithful; but as in the administration of the Sacrament the legitimate manner of ablution should also be observed, pastors should teach the doctrine of this point also.

They should briefly explain that, according to the common custom and practice of the Church, Baptism may be administered in three ways, by immersion, infusion or aspersion.

Whichever of these rites be observed, we must believe that Baptism is rightly administered. For in Baptism water is used

---

441 Council of Trent, Ch. 7, On the Sacraments, First Decree & Canons.

to signify the spiritual ablution which it accomplishes, and on this account Baptism is called by the Apostle a laver. Now this ablution is not more really accomplished by immersion, which was for a considerable time the practice in the early ages of the Church, than by infusion, which we now see in general use, or by aspersion, which there is reason to believe was the manner in which Peter baptized, when on one day he converted and gave Baptism to about three thousand souls.

It is a matter of indifference whether the ablution be performed once or thrice. For it is evident from the Epistle of St. Gregory the Great to Leander that Baptism was formerly and may still be validly administered in the Church in either way. The faithful, however, should follow the practice of the particular Church to which they belong.[442]

The Latins here turned entirely against the teachings of the Holy Apostles, the Canons of the Ecumenical Councils, and the consensus of the Fathers based on the single rare case of St. Gregory the Great[443] and baseless assumptions regarding whether or not the Apostle Peter was able to baptize by immersion.

At the Council of Trent, the Latins primarily followed Thomas Aquinas who, aside from St. Augustine, has had the most significant impact on Latin theology after the Great Schism. In his *Summa Theologica*, Aquinas states in Article 7, in response to the question "Whether immersion in water is necessary for Baptism?":

I answer that, in the sacrament of Baptism water is put to the use of a washing of the body, whereby to signify the inward washing away of sins. Now washing may be done with water not only by immersion, but also by sprinkling or pouring. And, therefore, although it is safer to baptize by immersion, because this is the more ordinary fashion, yet Baptism can

---

442 *The Catechism of the Council of Trent*, The Sacrament of Baptism, Administration of Baptism.
443 See footnote 383.

be conferred by sprinkling or also by pouring, according to Ezekiel 36:25: "I will pour upon you clean water," as also the Blessed Lawrence is related to have baptized. And this especially in cases of urgency: either because there is a great number to be baptized, as was clearly the case in Acts 2 and 4, where we read that on one day three thousand believed, and on another five thousand: or through there being but a small supply of water, or through feebleness of the minister, who cannot hold up the candidate for Baptism; or through feebleness of the candidate, whose life might be endangered by immersion. We must therefore conclude that immersion is not necessary for Baptism.

… Christ's burial is more clearly represented by immersion: wherefore this manner of baptizing is more frequently in use and more commendable. Yet in the other ways of baptizing it is represented after a fashion, albeit not so clearly; for no matter how the washing is done, the body of a man, or some part thereof, is put under water, just as Christ's body was put under the earth.[444]

In Article 8 of *Summa*, Aquinas deals with the question of, "Whether trine immersion is essential to Baptism?" The objections raised include that even St. Augustine spoke about threefold immersion in baptism, but that St. Gregory the Great allowed a single immersion.

On the contrary, Gregory wrote to the Bishop Leander: "It cannot be in any way reprehensible to baptize an infant with either a trine or a single immersion: since the Trinity can be represented in the three immersions, and the unity of the Godhead in one immersion."

I answer that as stated above… washing with water is of itself required for Baptism, being essential to the sacrament: whereas the mode of washing is accidental to the

---

444 Aquinas, *Summa Theologica*, Part 3, Question 66, Article 7.

sacrament. Consequently, as Gregory in the words above quoted explains, both single and trine immersion are lawful considered in themselves; since one immersion signifies the oneness of Christ's death and of the Godhead; while trine immersion signifies the three days of Christ's burial, and also the Trinity of Persons.[445]

Yet Aquinas then states that deviations from triple immersion were a rare exception, that it is a sin to baptize in any way other than by three immersions, but pouring and sprinkling are nevertheless "valid," and that the intention of the person baptizing matters as to the "validity" of the baptism.

> But now that this motive has ceased, trine immersion is universally observed in Baptism: and consequently anyone baptizing otherwise would sin gravely, through not following the ritual of the Church. It would, however, be valid Baptism.

> ...As stated above... the intention is essential to Baptism. Consequently, one Baptism results from the intention of the Church's minister, who intends to confer one Baptism by a trine immersion.[446]

In Article 9, Aquinas reiterates the Latin teaching that, "Those heretics who have been baptized in the confession of the name of the Trinity are to be received as already baptized when they come to the Catholic Faith."[447]

Aquinas wrote his *Summa Theologica* in the 13th century, but his views were not immediately adopted by all Latins. Aquinas said on one hand that sprinkling and pouring were permissible, and on the other hand that baptism in three immersions was "more frequently in use and more commendable" and "universally observed"; and that deviations from baptism in three immersions are only a sin to the administering priest while retaining their "validity." By the time of the Council of Trent in the 16th century, the Latins went

---

445 Ibid, Article 8.
446 Ibid.
447 Ibid., Article 9.

beyond even Aquinas by formally equating sprinkling and pouring to immersion. This is also the period during which the Protestant Reformation occurred and the Protestants followed the Latins in their abandonment of the Apostolic form. St. Ignatius Brianchaninov (+1867) commented with regard to the Latin and Lutheran departure from the Apostolic form of baptism:

> Indeed, many delusions have crept into the Roman Church. Luther would have done well if, having rejected the errors of the Latins, he had replaced these errors with the true teaching of the Holy Church of Christ; but he replaced them with his own delusions; some of the errors of Rome he fully followed and some he strengthened... Luther followed the error of the

St. Ignatius Brianchaninov (+1867)
Feast Day: April 30

Latins in relation to the performance of the sacrament of Holy Baptism, which, according to the testimony of the Latins themselves, was performed in the West until the 12th century with a triple immersion, and not pouring.[448] In the Gospel of Matthew (28:19), where the Lord commands His disciples to teach all nations by baptizing them, the word βαπτίζοντες is used in the Greek text, which in Russian means immersing. This word is used in other places of the New Testament in the Greek text, which speaks of baptism.[449]

---

448 While there were cases of the Latins performing baptism with a single immersion in the 11th century, these cases were rare.

449 Brianchaninov, *Collected Works* (In Russian), Vol 4, p. 444.

By the 16ᵗʰ century, many Orthodox Christians studying in Latin and Protestant universities were influenced by these teachings concerning ecclesiology and baptism, and spread these heterodox teachings among the local Orthodox churches to which they returned. Even Orthodox who did not study abroad in heterodox institutions picked up such heterodox teachings from those who did attend these institutions. The Orthodox Christians today who speak of "valid baptism" among heretics, who equate pouring and sprinkling to immersion, and who teach that "water and the invocation of the Holy Trinity" are all that is necessary for a baptism to be "valid" and unrepeatable, base these teachings not on the Fathers and Councils of the Orthodox Church but on Latin Scholasticism and the false Latin Council of Trent.

The teaching of Aquinas and the Council of Trent are not only important for understanding the roots of the ecclesiology adopted by many Orthodox Christians who do not accept the patristic teachings on ecclesiology and the reception of converts, but are also important for explaining why there was an even greater need to insist on receiving Latins (and Protestants) into the Orthodox Church by baptism after the 16ᵗʰ century, since by that time they had officially abandoned the Apostolic form of baptism. Just as the Ecumenical Councils required the Eunomians to be received by baptism since they practiced baptism with only a single immersion, after the Council of Trent the Latins were increasingly referred to as Eunomians and received by baptism accordingly.

Regarding the danger of Orthodox Christians studying at heterodox institutions, and the possibility of adopting and spreading heterodox teachings as a result, St. Paisios the Athonite relates the following story about a man who came to ask for the saint's blessing to study theology in Italy:

> A man came to see me to receive a blessing to go to Italy for Liturgical studies and write a dissertation. "Are you in your right mind?" I asked him. "You want to do your dissertation with the Jesuits, and you are coming to me to get a blessing?" Those people are clueless! The teachers there are Jesuits, Uniates, I don't know what all! We must be very careful.

This is what our young people do. They go to England, France and other countries to study; they catch all kinds of "European viruses," and write dissertations. They study the Greek Fathers in translation, from translations prepared by foreigners. Sometimes, the translators, either because they could not correctly render the meanings and nuances or because they had made a calculated decision not to, added their own erroneous notions. Our own Orthodox scholars, who have learned foreign languages and studied abroad, catch these foreign "viruses," these erroneous notions, and then bring them back here when they return, and even go on to teach them. Of course, if one is careful, it is easy to separate the gold from the amber.[450]

St. Paisios described much of what took place in Orthodox theology under the Ottomans. Many Orthodox who studied in heterodox institutions remained in the Orthodox Church while adopting and spreading heterodox beliefs and practices that are not in agreement with the Ecumenical Councils and the consensus of the Holy Fathers. Of course, as St. Paisios says, not all who have studied with the heterodox have become "infected" by their false teachings, but such study can be dangerous, and as Metropolitan Kallistos points out, such study can lead to the loss of an "Orthodox mentality" as a result of being cut off from "Orthodoxy as a living tradition."

---

450 Paisios the Athonite, *With Pain and Love for Contemporary Man*, p. 337.

St. Paisios the Athonite (+1994)
Feast Day: July 12

Council of Moscow (1666-1667)

CHAPTER 13

The 1666-1667 Moscow Council

OVERVIEW OF THE COUNCIL

The 1666-1667 Council in Moscow was called by Tsar Alexis I of Russia primarily to bring Patriarch Nikon of Moscow to trial after he abandoned the patriarchal throne, with the goal of formally removing him as patriarch and electing a new patriarch. For this to occur, patriarchs and bishops from other local churches were required. The liturgical reforms of Patriarch Nikon, supported by Tsar Alexis I, resulted in the Old Believer schism that was also a major focus of this council's deliberations. Significantly, this council also completely changed the teaching of the Russian Church regarding the reception of converts.

The Moscow Patriarchate received its autocephaly from the Patriarchate of Constantinople in 1593. Following this decree, Patriarch Nikon of Moscow sought to bring Russian liturgical practice into conformity with Greek practice. Since the printing press had only been invented in the 15th century, and liturgical manuscripts had been hand copied for centuries, variations in manuscripts were common, and slight differences in liturgical texts and rubrics emerged in various Orthodox lands. For example, in Russian practice the sign of the cross was made by two fingers rather than three as did the Greeks, the Russians said two alleluias after the reading of the Psalms rather than three alleluias as the Greeks, and the Russian services contained more priestly petitions than the services of the Greeks. Patriarch Nikon, eager to establish liturgical unity with the Greeks, requested that Tsar Alexis call a council in 1654 to authorize the undertaking of a formal correction of service books. This council convened and decreed that the Moscow liturgical books were to be corrected using "ancient Greek and Slavonic books."[451]

The liturgical reforms carried out by Patriarch Nikon with the full support of Tsar Alexis caused a great deal of confusion which led to a tragic schism. Since the Greek bishops had largely submitted to the Latin Pope of Rome at the 15th Century Council of Ferrara-Florence, many Russians were suspicious of the Orthodoxy of the Greeks at that time and resisted the proposal to correct Russian liturgical books based on Greek texts. Furthermore, instead of carrying out the reforms according to the ancient Greek and Russian manuscripts as the 1654 Council instructed, the Russian

Patriarch Nikon of Moscow
(+1681)

liturgical texts were corrected based on contemporary Greek texts published in Venice, the territory of Latin heretics. As Silvester Medvedev, who was involved in the correction of the liturgical texts at that time, stated about the advocates of liturgical reform:

> They did not want to agree with the ancient Greek and Russian books, by which our saints have achieved salvation, but they liked the Greek books, newly-printed in foreign lands, and followed them.[452]

---

451 Stroev, *Opisanie Knig Tolstova I Tsarskago*, p. 155-158. Quoted in Meyendorff, *Russia, Ritual, and Reform*, p. 46.

452 Medvedev, 9, quoted in Ibid., p. 55.

As Bishop Alexander of Viatka protested at the 1666 Moscow Council:

> The new *Trebnik* does not agree with either the Kievan, or the previous Moscow editions. From where does truth come if we must use Greek books published in Venice? We must not accept customs and rules from Greeks living unwillingly among the Latins.[453]

When Patriarch Nikon wrote to Constantinople hoping to receive approval for his liturgical reforms prior to the council, Patriarch Paisios of Constantinople replied stating that it is commendable to strive for unity of faith and to avoid schisms over differences in practices which "have nothing to do with the chief articles of faith":

> But if it happens that a certain church differs from another in certain practices which are not important and essential to faith, or which have nothing to do with the chief articles of faith, but only in insignificant practices, such as for example the time for celebrating the liturgy, or which fingers a priest uses to give the blessing, and the like, then this should not cause any division, as long as one and the same faith is preserved. This is because our church did not receive the entire present *typicon* from the beginning, but little by little.[454]

Despite such cautionary language from Constantinople and objections from bishops in Russia, Patriarch Nikon and Tsar Alexis forcefully imposed ill-advised reforms onto the Russian Church, resulting in a serious conflict and tragic schism. By 1658, however, Patriarch Nikon ceased pushing the reforms, left his position as patriarch, and went to live as a simple monk. In the absence of a patriarch, Tsar Alexis took control and pushed ahead with the liturgical reforms with great zeal.[455] Tsar Alexis sought to depose

---

453 Gorskii-Nevostruev, v. 2:4, No. 294, f. 14, quoted in Ibid., p. 54.

454 Paisios of Constantinople, p. 315, quoted in Ibid., p. 56.

455 The most complete description of the events is found in Makarii, Istoriia, v. 12, pp. 311-325. An eyewitness account by the Boyar Aleksei Nikitich Trubetskoi, who was sent by the tsar to find out why Nikon was abandoning his throne, is published in

and replace Patriarch Nikon but knew that this decision would have to come from a Pan-Orthodox Council, so he invited bishops from other local churches to attend the Council in 1667 to adopt the liturgical reforms and depose Patriarch Nikon.

At this Council in 1667, the "Old Believers" who refused to accept the liturgical reforms but wished to use the liturgical texts and practices handed down to them by countless Russian saints before them, were tragically branded as "heretics" and the council formally endorsed their persecution.

> The two-fingered sign of the Cross, for example, was branded as Arian, Nestorian, Apollinarian... It was seen as a Trinitarian heresy, because the three folded fingers (representing, for the Old Believers, the Trinity) are uneven in size.[456]

Even the Old Rite version of the Jesus Prayer* ("Lord Jesus Christ, Son of God, have mercy on us") was branded as an Arian heresy by this council![457]

At this same Council of 1666-1667, according to Metropolitan Macarius of Moscow in his *History of the Russian Church*, "[t]he rite for the reception of Latins into the Orthodox Church was now completely changed."[458]

As St. Hilarion states:

> The old Russian practice, confirmed by the Council of 1620, was changed at the Council of Moscow of 1667. This is understandable. The Council of 1667 is distinguished for the fact that, led by Greeks often of dubious worth, it condemned everything, even in the minor rites of the Russian Church, that deviated from Greek practice. And till now the curse hastily placed by the Council on the Old-Russian rite, as on a heresy, still causes turmoil in the Russian

---

DELO, pp. 15-16, quoted in Ibid., p. 64.

456 Deianiia 1666-1667, pt. 2, ff. 3v-7v., quoted in Ibid., p. 71.

457 Ibid., f. 33-33v. The reason for this is unclear, Ibid., p. 71.

458 Quoted in Pogodin, *On the Question of the Order of Reception of Persons into the Orthodox Church, Coming to her from Other Christian Churches*, Ch. 2.

Church. Obsequious in relation to the secular government, the Greeks were at that time ready even to proclaim the principle that the State is superior to the Church and only the protest of the Russian hierarchy prevented such a solution of the problem of the mutual relations of Church and State.[459]

St. Hilarion continues:

> Concerning the rebaptism of Latins the Council of 1667 decided: it is not proper to rebaptize Latins, but, after they foreswear their heresies and confess their sins and submit a written statement, let them be anointed with the holy and great chrism and let them be administered the holy and most pure Mysteries and thus be united to the Holy, Catholic and Apostolic Church. But the Council could bring only the decision of the Council of Constantinople of 1484 and the words of St. Mark of Ephesus in support of its decree. It is worthy of note that the decision of the Council of 1667 did not immediately change the Russian rule of practice for receiving Western Christians; at the end of the seventeenth and at the beginning of the eighteenth century they were still rebaptized.[460]

St. Hilarion proceeds to cite references and accounts showing that Latins continued to be received by baptism after the 1667 Council at least into the 18th century, since this was the ancient practice of the Russian Church and the reception of Latins by chrismation was widely considered an innovation. He then states regarding the 1667 decision:

> The decisions of the Church and authoritative Church writers demanded the chrismation of Latins. Receiving Latins without chrismation is only a local custom of the Russian Church which was introduced under the influence of the Trebnik of Peter Mogila and was even prompted

459 Troitsky, op. cit.
460 Ibid.

by the theological spirit of [Roman] Catholicism itself. Everything which is the sad result of the influence of Latin scholasticism in our theology cannot be, of course, more authoritative than the teaching of the ancient Church and the direct heir of Her grace-filled gifts — the Eastern Church.[461]

Refusing to acknowledge the authority of the 1667 Council, those who remained on the Old Rite continued to adhere to the decrees of the 1620 Moscow Council and required that all heretics be received by baptism.[462] Those who opposed the decisions of the 1667 Council were justified in many of their objections, but the resulting schism and the extremist positions held on both sides of the schism (with those on each side labelling as heretical the small differences in service texts and rituals of the other side), has had lasting tragic consequences. Eventually, the Russian Church would revoke all of the anathemas against the Old Rite from this Council, but would stop short of declaring the entire council false, including its innovative teaching on the reception of converts.

THE AUTHORITY OF THE 1666-1667 MOSCOW COUNCIL

As the 1666-1667 Moscow Council completely changed the method of receiving Latins into the Church and formally anathematized those who refused to accept the liturgical reforms of Patriarch Nikon and Tsar Alexis, and because those in the Russian Church today who insist on receiving Latins and Protestants by chrismation or confession of faith rely primarily on this council, the authority of this council remains an important question. Regarding the Old Rite and the Nikonian reforms, how could a council anathematize Orthodox who wanted to continue using the liturgical books that had been handed down to them over centuries? How could the Russian liturgical customs followed by so many Russian saints for centuries now be considered heretical?

---

461 Ibid.
462 Local Council of 1620 Moscow, op. cit.

In 1928, Hieromartyr Andrew, Archbishop of Ufa[463] (+1937) warned those in Russia under the Soviet regime to beware of false bishops, recounting the many false councils of the past and the many saints who were persecuted by false bishops who "for the sake of their own welfare are ready to sell the truth and strangle their brothers." Among these false councils, St. Andrew includes the council of 1667, saying:

St. Andrew of Ufa
(+1937)
Feast Day:
September 4

As is known, the history of the Russian Church falls into two parts, which are very different from each other as pertains to the character of the Church authorities. The first part was before the schism of the Old Believers and the second was after the notorious Council of 1667, which blessed and approved all of the violence of the Tsars against the religious conscience of the subjects. During the reign of Tsar Peter the Great, these violations and the torture of Christians was cynically savage.

Peter hated the appearance of any type of freedom or independence among his subjects, and being a firm atheist himself, he drove out faith in others with a fanatical cruelty. That's why, before Tsar Peter, unworthy bishops were found only as a rare exception, and after his upbringing – on the contrary – genuine church bishops began to be found only on very rare occasions...

---

463 Hieromartyr Andrew tonsured into monasticism St. Luke the Surgeon, Archbishop of Simferopol and Crimea. When St. Luke was a priest in Tashkent in Uzbekistan the clergy and faithful there were left without a bishop. The clergy assembled and elected St. Luke (who was then Fr. Valentine) to the episcopacy due to his spiritual manner of life and defense of the Faith. Archbishop Andrew of Ufa was in Tashkent in exile at the time and tonsured Fr. Valentine into monasticism, giving him the name Luke. Since Archbishop Andrew could not consecrate him to the episcopacy by himself, as the canons require that at least two bishops perform such a consecration, Archbishop Andrew sent St. Luke to the town of Penjikent to be consecrated by Bishop Daniel (Troiitsky) of Volkhov and Bishop Basil (Zummer) of Suzdal who had been sent there in exile. Marushchak, op. cit., 28-30.

Therefore, we will bypass even the frightening Council of 1667, when 2 Eastern Patriarchs accepted enormous bribes in order to carry out the will of the unhinged mind of Tsar Alexis Mikhailovich, and cursed the entire history of the Russian Church with all of the Saints of the Russian land...[464]

Hieromartyr Andrew said these words as an archbishop of the Russian Orthodox Church and was not an Old Believer.

Regarding the liturgical reforms mandated by the 1667 Council, which included anathemas against any who would oppose these reforms, Paul Meyendorff explains:

The prefaces to the Nikonian liturgical books present Nikon's reform as both a "correction," and a "return to the sources." This has been taken at face value in the vast majority of the literature on the subject. Our study has shown the reality of the matter to be quite different, for, in fact, the reform consisted simply in replacing existing Russian practice with 17th century Greek usage. No ancient manuscripts, Greek or Slavonic, were, or could have been, used, for the very simple reason that none of them contained the changes which the Nikonian reformers introduced into the Muscovite books.[465]

The 1667 Council did not end the Old Believer schism, but through its baseless anathemas and endorsement of violent persecution of all who opposed the liturgical reforms, the schism became more deeply entrenched. Some who opposed the council were put to death, including Archpriest Avvakum Petrovitch who was burned at the stake.[466] A church council in November of 1681 decreed that all unrepentant dissidents be turned over to civil courts for condemnation and execution.[467] This persecution made reconciliation nearly impossible.

---

464 Andrew of Ufa: "On Bishops and Catascops (1928)."
465 Meyendorff, *Russia, Ritual, and Reform*, p. 219.
466 Ware, *Orthodox Church*, pp. 109-110.
467 AAK, iv, no. 75 (pp. 705-706), cited in Cracraft, *The Church Reform of Peter the Great*, p. 74.

As time passed, the Russian Orthodox Church began to acknowledge that many of the decisions of the 1666-1667 council were erroneous, and finally in 1971 the anathemas against the Old Rite were formally revoked. An official report to the Synod at this time concluded:

> Patriarch Nikon in changing the liturgical rubrics and rites according to his modern Greek models, proceeded from the erroneous view that "the differences that exist between us and the Greeks corrupt our faith," and the elimination of these differences he considered a matter as necessary as "cleansing Orthodoxy from heresies and sins."

> Groundless judgments at the Councils of 1656 and 1667 about the old rites of pre-Nikonian times, as allegedly containing heretical meaning, gave reason to see in the anathemas and definitions of these Councils a condemnation of the old rites in themselves.[468]

The official report goes on to explain that the decisions of 1666-1667 which were understood as anathematizing the Old Rite, which had been used for centuries in Russia, were later understood by the Russian Church as only anathematizing those who went into schism because of the Nikonian reforms and who anathematized these reforms as heretical. Official documents, decrees and councils in Russia starting from AD 1765 are cited which affirmed that the liturgical books printed before the 1667 Council were indeed Orthodox and salvific. Finally, this council in 1971 formally decreed that the anathemas of 1667 against the Old Russian Rites and those who adhered to them should be considered null and void.[469]

Similarly, in 1974 the Russian Orthodox Church Outside of Russia, which was not at that time in communion with the Moscow Patriarchate due to the influence of the atheist Soviet regime over the ecclesiastical life of the Russian Church, issued a similar decree which included the decision:

---

468 "On the Abolition of Oaths to Old Rites" (In Russian).
469 Ibid.

To consider the interdicts and anathemas imposed in the past of the Councils of 1656 and 1667, and also by certain individuals who took part in the Councils, because of misunderstandings, as null and void and rescinded AS IF THEY HAD NEVER BEEN.[470]

While revoking the 1667 anathemas against the Old Rite and declaring the foundation of this council to be erroneous, the Russian Church has not gone so far as to reject the entire council as false, nor has the Russian Church formally revoked the decision made at the council to receive Latins by chrismation which departed from the ancient practice of the Russian Church. While the 1667 Council aligned contemporary Russian practice with the practice of contemporary Greeks, unfortunately the more ancient practice of baptizing Latins was not restored in Russia in 1756 when the patriarchs of Constantinople, Alexandria, and Jerusalem decreed that all converts "from the West" should be received by baptism. Instead, the Russian Church moved further from the canonical and patristic criteria for the reception of converts by eventually allowing Latins to be received by confession of faith, without baptizing or chrismating them.[471] Latin priests would also be received "in their orders" in the Russian Church, without them being baptized, chrismated, and ordained in the Orthodox Church.[472]

Despite removing the anathemas against the Old Rite, many Old Believers still refuse to reunite with the Russian Orthodox Church in part due to the lingering influence of heterodox Latin teachings in the Russian Church, including the areas of ecclesiology and the reception of converts. St. Ignatius (Brianchaninov) (+1867), referring especially to the Latinized influences on iconography and chanting in Russia, explains that such departures from Orthodox standards continue to be a cause of temptation and scandal for the Old Believers, hindering the healing of the schism:

---

470 ROCOR Synod of Bishops, *The Decision of the Council of Bishops of the ROCOR Concerning the Old Ritual.*
471 Pogodin, op. cit., Ch. 2.
472 Ibid.

However, one should not blame the [Old Believer] schismatics for everything. Western enlightenment has flooded into Russia so strongly that it also invaded the Church and violated its Eastern Orthodox character... These violations of the Eastern Orthodox character tempt schismatics and grieve the sons of the Church, who have thoroughly studied Christianity.[473]

St. Ignatius clarified that such "violations of the Eastern Orthodox character" did not completely corrupt the "essence of Christianity" and expressed the hope that such violations "can be eliminated very soon" since "Russia no longer obeys and blindly imitates Europe."[474] However, to understand how the Old Believer schism, the extensive Latinization, and the complete change in the policy of the reception of converts occurred in Russia in the 17th century, one needs to understand the conflict between the Possessors and Non-Possessors which led to the suppression of the hesychastic* tradition in Russia, resulting in this vulnerability to heterodox teachings.

POSSESSORS, NON-POSSESSORS, AND THE SUPPRESSION OF THE HESYCHASTIC TRADITION IN RUSSIA

The conflict between the Possessors, represented by St. Joseph of Volokolamsk (+1515), and the Non-Possessors, represented by St. Nilus Sorsky (Nil Sora) (+1508) and the Transvolgan Elders, revolved initially around whether ownership of land by monasteries was counter to the monastic ideals of poverty and detachment from material things. Yet, their disagreement over landownership was just one of the areas which distinguished the two groups. St. Nilus represented traditional Athonite hesychastic monasticism while St. Joseph represented a form of monasticism that was more externally focused on liturgical precision and social obligations such as caring for the sick and the poor. St. Joseph and the Possessors taught that

---

473 Brianchaninov, *Collected Works*, Vol 4, pp. 466-467.
474 Ibid.

if heretics refuse to repent, the Church should call upon the State to imprison, torture, or even kill unrepentant heretics while St. Nilus and the Non-Possessors considered heresy a spiritual matter that should be resolved by the Church without the force or coercion of the State.[475]

St. Nilus Sorsky
(+1508)
Feast Day: May 7

In general Nilus drew a clearer line than Joseph between the things of Caesar and the things of God. The Possessors were great supporters of the ideal of Moscow the Third Rome; believing in a close alliance between Church and State, they took an active part in politics, as Sergius [of Radonezh] had done, but perhaps they were less careful than Sergius to guard the Church from becoming the servant of the State. The Non-Possessors for their part had a sharper awareness of the prophetic and other-worldly witness of monasticism. The Josephites were in danger of identifying the Kingdom of God with a kingdom of this world; Nilus saw that the Church on earth must always be a Church in pilgrimage. While Joseph and his party were great patriots and nationalists, the Non-Possessors thought more of the universality and Catholicity of the Church.

Nor did the divergences between the two sides end here: they also had different ideas of Christian piety and prayer. Joseph emphasized the place of rules and discipline, Nilus the inner and personal relation between God and the soul. Joseph stressed the place of beauty in worship, Nilus feared that beauty might become an idol: the monk (so Nilus maintained) is dedicated not only to an outward poverty, but to an absolute self-stripping, and he must be careful lest a devotion to beautiful icons or Church music comes between him and God...

---

475 Ware, *The Orthodox Church*, pp. 104-106.

Nilus... was chiefly interested not in liturgical but in mystical prayer: before he settled at Sora he had lived as a monk on Mount Athos, and he knew the Byzantine Hesychast tradition at first hand.[476]

Regarding the Transvolgan Elders and St. Nilus, Fr. George Florovsky writes:

St. Joseph of Volokalamsk (+1515)

Feast Days: September 9 & February 13

The Transvolgan Elders built an incomparable school for spiritual vigil, which provided a spiritual and moral preparation for theology... St. Nil of the Sora was a "silent one" (bezmolvnik). He had no need to speak or teach. Although not a thinker, writer, or theologian, Nil appears in history precisely as an 'elder' [starets*] or teacher. He was a teacher of silence, an instructor and guide for "mental construction" in the spiritual life.

Upon comparison with the wider contemplative tradition of Greece and Byzantium or after comparison with the Philokalia [Dobrotoliubie], one discovers nothing new in St. Nil... He lives in the patristic tradition. That tradition lives and is alive in him...

Nil of the Sora came from and remained confined to the ascetical and contemplative tradition of the ancient and Byzantine Church... St. Nil laid particular stress on the ascetical guidance, experience, and advice of "wise and spiritual men."[477]

The conflict between the Possessors and Non-Possessors came to a head when the Non-Possessors spoke out against Tsar Basil III for unjustly divorcing his wife. The Tsar responded by imprisoning the leading Non-Possessors and closing the Transvolgan hermitages,

476 Ibid.
477 Florovsky, *Ways of Russian Theology*, Ch. 1.

driving the hesychastic tradition underground.[478]
St. Maxim the Greek (+1556), an educated
Athonite monk who labored at that time in
Moscow translating ecclesiastical texts, was
among the Non-Possessors who were imprisoned
and oppressed.[479]

St. Maximos the
Greek (+1556)
Feast Day: January 21

The Russian Church rightly saw good
things in the teaching of both Joseph
and Nilus, and has canonized them both.
Each inherited a part of the tradition
of Saint Sergius [of Radonezh], but no
more than a part: Russia needed both the
Josephite and the Transvolgan forms of
monasticism, for each supplemented the other. It was sad
indeed that the two sides entered into conflict, and that the
tradition of Nilus was largely suppressed: without the Non-
Possessors, the spiritual life of the Russian Church became
one-sided and unbalanced. The close integration which
the Josephites upheld between Church and State, their
Russian nationalism, their devotion to the outward forms
of worship—these things were to lead to trouble in the next
century.[480]

The triumph of the Possessors and suppression of the hesychastic
tradition of the Non-Possessors led to a one-sided focus on liturgical
precision, an equating of small liturgical differences with heresy,
and the use of the State to imprison and violently persecute those
who were branded as heretics. Without proper emphasis on noetic
prayer*[481], those who studied academic theology were vulnerable to
the influences of Latin scholasticism which resulted in theological
and ecclesiological confusion, and the adoption by many of a
heterodox *phronema*.

---

478 Ware, *The Orthodox Church*, pp. 104-106.
479 Zernov, *The Russians and Their Church*. Ch. 6.
480 Ware, *The Orthodox Church*, pp. 104-106.
481 Ware, *The Orthodox Church*, p. 113.

Latin Influence in Russian Theology and Ecclesiology in the 17ᵀᴴ Century

The change in the practice of receiving Latins into the Russian Orthodox Church at the 1667 Council was marked not only by a departure from Russian Orthodox practice up to that time, but also coincided with the widespread influence of Post-Schism Latin teachings, and the influence on the council of what St. Hilarion referred to as Greeks "of dubious worth."[482]

For the first time in the history of the Orthodox Church, this council decreed that Latins who were baptized by pouring did not need to be received by baptism and that pouring was a valid form of baptism, agreeing thereby with the 16ᵗʰ century Latin Catechism of the Council of Trent that formally accepted baptism by aspersion and affusion as equal to baptism by triple immersion.[483] Furthermore, while previous saints and councils in Russia employed Apostolic Canon 47 to depose priests and bishops for receiving Latins by chrismation (since Latins are heretics), the 1667 Council boldly turned the canon on its head and threatened to depose those who baptized Latins, as if baptizing Latins violated the Apostolic prohibition against administering baptism twice within the Church![484] This was the first time that a council of Orthodox bishops declared that baptizing heretics violates Apostolic Canon 47 and the Nicean Creed which forbid a second baptism.

The 1666 Council was attended by Patriarch Paisios of Alexandria and Patriarch Macarius III of Antioch and bishops from Russia and other local churches. The patriarchal throne of Moscow was vacant. Of the two patriarchs and the other bishops in attendance, Patriarch Macarius III of Antioch had the greatest influence over the council, both in pushing for the liturgical reforms prior to the council and in overturning the decision of the 1620

---

482 Troitsky, op. cit.

483 Catechism of the Council of Trent, The Sacrament of Baptism.

484 Russian Faith, *Acts of the Consecrated Council of the Russian Old Orthodox Church, held on April 10-13 (23-26) n.st. 2015* (In Russian).

Council that required the baptism of Latins and other heretics. As Metropolitan Macarius of Moscow states:

> All Russian bishops were invited to this new Council along with the metropolitan of Kazan. The Antiochian Patriarch Macarius again insisted that the Latins should not be re-baptized when converting to Orthodoxy and had a heated argument with the Russian hierarchs. He tried to convince them by making references to their own books of Canons. To support his argument, he presented an extract from some ancient Greek book brought from Mt. Athos, which made a detailed analysis of the subject, and in this way compelled the Russian bishops to submit, however reluctantly, to the truth. This extract, signed by Macarius, was presented to the sovereign (Tsar Aleksei Mikhailovich), translated into Russian, printed and handed out. The Tsar issued an Ukaz that prohibited the baptism of Poles and others belonging to the same faith. Not satisfied with all this Macarius, who soon left Moscow, sent a letter to Nikon about the same matter. Along with this Patriarch Macarius wrote to Patriarch Nikon that "the Latins must not be re-baptized: they have the seven sacraments and all seven Councils, and they are all baptized correctly in the name of the Father, Son and the Holy Spirit with an invocation of the Holy Trinity. We must recognize their baptism. They are only schismatics, and schism does not make a man unfaithful and unbaptized. It only separates him from the Church. Mark of Ephesus himself, who opposed the Latins, never demanded their re-baptism and accepted their baptism as a correct one."[485]

Uncertainty surrounds the identity of this "ancient Greek book from Mt. Athos" that was supposedly used by Metropolitan Macarius in his efforts to change the practice of the Russian Church. The persuasiveness of Patriarch Macarius of Antioch and the reference

---

485 Makarii of Moscow, *History of the Russian Church* (In Russian), v. XI, p. 232., 196-197. Quoted in Pogodin, op. cit.

to St. Mark of Ephesus, however, apparently swayed the council to "reluctantly" agree to this change despite the "heated argument" Russian hierarchs had in opposition to Patriarch Macarius' position. As St. Hilarion has demonstrated, the baptism of Latins and all heretics continued after this council since Russia had been receiving heretics by baptism for centuries. Along with this decision of the council, no detailed examination of the relevant canons has come down to us. While Patriarch Macarius relied on St. Mark of Ephesus as the authority for this decision, he misrepresented St. Mark by saying that Latins are "only schismatics" when St. Mark clearly taught that the Latins were heretics. He also claimed that St. Mark referred to the baptism of Latins as "correct," when in fact St. Mark stated that they are heretics and should be chrismated. St. Mark said nothing about the baptism of Latins being "correct" or "true" or having grace.

Metropolitan Macarius of Moscow continues in his summary of the Acts and Decrees of the 1666-1667 Council:

> The Council fathers carefully reviewed Patriarch Philaret Nikitich's statute and came to the conclusion that the laws were incorrectly interpreted and applied to the Latins. They then referred to earlier Council statutes whereby it was forbidden to re-baptize even Arians and Macedonians in the event of their coming into Orthodoxy, and even more so, the fathers said, Latins must not be re-baptized. They referred to the Council of the four Eastern Patriarchs held in Constantinople in 1484, which decreed not to re-baptize Latins upon their coming into Orthodoxy, but only to anoint them with Chrism, and which even composed the actual rite for their reception into the Church. They referred to the wise Mark of Ephesus who, in his epistle addressed to all Orthodox, offers the same teaching and decreed:

> "Latins must not be re-baptized but only after their renunciation of their heresies and confession of sins, be anointed with Chrism and admit them to the Holy Mysteries and in this way

bring them into communion with the holy, catholic Eastern Church, in accordance with the sacred canons."[486, 487]

The reference to St. Mark of Ephesus is to his Encyclical "To All Orthodox Christians on the Mainland and in the Islands."[488] However, St. Mark nowhere says in this encyclical, or anywhere else, that it was "forbidden" to baptize Latins or that Latins "must not be (re)baptized." He simply said, "it is necessary to anoint with chrism" the Latins because "they are heretics." In fact, St. Mark refers to the Latins repeatedly as "heretics" in this encyclical despite the false claim of Patriarch Macarius of Antioch at the 1666-1667 Council that the Latins were only schismatics.

When Metropolitan Macarius of Moscow relates that the 1666-1667 council "referred to earlier Council statutes whereby it was forbidden to re-baptize even Arians and Macedonians in the event of their coming into Orthodoxy," this also misrepresents the canons of the Ecumenical Councils. As discussed in Chapter 5, the Second and Fifth-Sixth Ecumenical Councils permitted Arians and Macedonians to be received by chrismation, but no council forbade their reception by baptism. Not a single canon of any Ecumenical Council forbade the reception of heretics by baptism.

Patriarch Macarius of Antioch who pressured the Russian Church to stop baptizing had secretly submitted allegiance to the Pope of Rome prior to attending the Moscow Council. Regarding the influence of the Latins in Antioch at the time of Patriarch Macarius, and his submission to the Pope of Rome prior to the council, historian Steven Runciman states:

> It was in the Patriarchate of Antioch that Rome enjoyed its greatest success. While the Patriarchs of Alexandria and Jerusalem seemed to have worked well during the sixteenth and seventeenth centuries with their brothers of Constantinople, the Patriarchs of Antioch seem to have felt

---

486 *Acts of the Moscow Councils 1666-1667* (In Russian), Moscow, 1893, pp. 174-175. Quoted in Ibid.

487 Makarii of Moscow, p. 786. Quoted in Ibid.

488 Mark of Ephesus, "The Encyclical of St. Mark of Ephesus," p. 53-59.

some jealousy and preferred to go their own way. It was an area in which Catholic missionaries had worked since the time of the Crusades and in which they were well established. In 1631 the Patriarch Ignatius II of Antioch made an informal act of submission to Rome. His successors, Euthymius II and Euthymius III, were both on the friendliest terms with Roman missionaries; and Euthymius III's successor, Macarius III, who reigned from 1647 to 1672, not only sent his secret submission to Rome in 1662 but also publicly toasted the Pope as his Holy Father at a dinner at the French Consulate at Damascus later that year.[489, 490]

Prior to the 1666-1667 Council, Patriarch Macarius III of Antioch arrived in Aleppo and:

In view of the tireless charity of the [Latin] missionaries during the months of the 1661 famine, [Patriarch Macarius] publicly praised the Roman Church and "invited the consul (Picquet) and the missionaries to his church to listen to the Liturgy and allow his people to see that the Franks were in the true path of salvation, as he noted in the sermon which he preached in Arabic."[491] He also sent a letter (dated September 30, 1661) to Consul Picquet and asked him to personally give it to Pope Alexander VII. The letter was sent with Arabic manuscripts of the Euchologion and Horologion so that they could be printed at the Congregation for the Propagation of the Faith printing press. The consul was in Rome before May 22, 1662. On that date the contents of this letter were communicated to the general assembly of the cardinals of the Congregation for the Propagation of the

489 Runciman, *The Great Church in Captivity*, p. 234.

490 See also: Rabbath, A. *Documents inedits pour server a l'histoire due Christianisme en orient*, 2 vols., Paris and Beirut, 1905-21. p. 466. Quoted in Ware, *Eustratios Argenti*, p. 29.

491 Cf. Rabbath, I, pp. 456-459: "Brève relation de la Mission d'Alep in 1662 adressée aux âmes dévotes par les Supérieurs des Missions des RR.PP. Capucins, Carmes et Jésuites" Cf. Rustum (p. 99) which corrects the erroneous Arabic translation of this text made by Bacha (Voyage, pp. 119 ff). Quoted in Raheb, *Conception of the Union in the Orthodox Patriarchate of Antioch*. phoenicia.org/orthodox-antioch-union.html.

Faith: "The patriarch of the Greeks of Antioch expressed a great desire of (coming) to see His Holiness the pope, but since distance did not permit him, he prays that God bring to a good conclusion his belief on the subject of the union of the Holy Church, wishing that it would be easy with the help of God and the Holy Virgin, although it seems to be difficult (to realize). He also asks His Holiness to pray for the poor Christians who are reduced at the present time to extreme misery. He compares the flourishing situation of the ancient Church of the East to its actual very disastrous state and attributes this great change to the fact of being separated from the Roman Church. Now he has the resolve to finding all the ways for reunion because this separation had not been caused by any heresy, but by haughtiness. It is true that it is necessary to proceed secretly in order to avoid many disturbances. For these reasons he says that Mr. Picquet will expose his designs to His Holiness. He praises the rare virtues (of this consul), particularly his piety toward the poor, his zeal and his efforts for the conversion of heretics, and he declares that if this virtuous man was left there (in Near East), he would arrange the union of the nations to perfection."[492]

On December 14, 1663, Patriarch Macarius wrote a letter to the Roman Congregation of the Congregation for the Propagation of the Faith saying:

> You have observed that the Roman Church is mother of all the faithful, that it loves the children of the Greeks for whom it has built a college and that it loves the Christians of the East for whom it always cared for by sending priests to enlighten them and instruct them. We understand that, my brothers. For this reason we implore our Creator and our Lord Jesus Christ, head of the Holy Church, that He strengthen the Roman Church, elevate its grandeur, consolidate it for the end of ages and guard our master and

---

492 Raheb, Ibid.

our father, the honored pope, its head
and our head over all, wishing that you be
always preserved from all evil. Amen.[493]

Patriarch Macarius III
of Antioch
(+ c. 1672)

So, the Patriarch who led the decision at the
1666-1667 Moscow Council that the Russian
Church should no longer receive Latins by
baptism, claiming the authority of St. Mark of
Ephesus for this decision, had secretly submitted
to the Pope and confessed his belief that the Pope
was his "master," "father," and "head over all." Patriarch Macarius,
then, was of one mind with the Unionist Patriarch about whom St.
Mark of Ephesus said:

> I am absolutely convinced that the farther I stand from
> him and those like him, the nearer I am to God and all
> the saints; and to the degree that I separate myself from
> them am I in union with the Truth and with the Holy
> Fathers, the Theologians of the Church; and I am likewise
> convinced that those who count themselves with them stand
> far away from the Truth and from the blessed Teachers of
> the Church.[494]

Other influential figures in the 1666-1667 Moscow Council
include Metropolitan Paisios (Ligarides) and Bishop Simeon of
Polotsk. Regarding Metropolitan Paisios (Ligarides), Fr. George
Florovsky states:

> Paisios Ligarides (1609-1678) was a brilliant but deceptive
> scholar and an absolutely shameless opportunist. Educated
> at Rome and ordained a Uniate prelate, he travelled
> throughout the Orthodox East diving into any situation where
> an opportunity for riches presented itself, and held various
> positions in the Orthodox Church (such as metropolitan
> of Gaza) while receiving regular missionary stipends from
> Rome. He played a major role in the history of the Russian

493 Ibid.
494 Mark of Ephesus, *Address of St. Mark of Ephesus on the Day of His Death*, p. 104.

Church of this time, first ingratiating himself with Nikon and then becoming the chief spokesman for his opponents and the orchestrator of the Council of 1666-1667...

Before the Great Council of 1666-1667 Ligarides had produced forged documents which named him the patriarch of Constantinople's legate for the council. Tsar Aleksei sent a special envoy to Dionysios to find out the truth of the matter, but because Ligarides' fall would be too harmful to Nikon's opponents and personally embarrassing to the tsar Dionysios' reply was kept secret and Ligarides continued to function.[495]

Ligarides, the "orchestrator of the Council of 1666-1667" was:

[O]rdained in Rome by the West Russian Uniate Metropolitan, Rafail Korsak. In his estimation and report, Leo Allatius, a dignitary of St. Athanasius, declared that Paisios was "a man prepared to lay down his life and give up his soul for the [Roman] Catholic faith." Paisios returned to the Levant as a missionary. The Propaganda Fide also later sent him to Wallachia. There, however, he made a close acquaintance with Patriarch Paisios of Jerusalem and accompanied him to Palestine. Soon afterward he became Orthodox metropolitan of Gaza. All this time Ligarides played a dual role. Greed served as his guiding passion. He tried to convince the Propaganda Fide of his fidelity and asked that his suspended missionary stipend be restored. No one believed him. The Orthodox also distrusted Ligarides, seeing in him a dangerous papist. He soon fell under a ban and was still under it when he arrived in Moscow. When asked about Ligarides during Nikon's trial in Moscow, Patriarch Dionysios of Constantinople replied that "Ligarides' scepter is not from the throne of Constantinople, and I do not consider him Orthodox, for I hear from many that he is a papist and a deceiver." Nevertheless, he played a decisive

---

495 Florovsky, *Ways of Russian Theology*, Notes 40 and 87.

role at the Great Council of 1667... Nikon was not entirely wrong when in reply he dubbed the tsar a "Latinizer" and the boyars and hierarchs "worshippers of Latin dogmas."[496]

Patriarch Macarius III and Metropolitan Paisios (Ligarides) had also adopted the Latin practice of selling indulgences for the remission of sins.[497]

Regarding Bishop Simeon of Polotsk, his close association with Paisios (Ligarides) and his role in the council:

> He was entrusted with the "arrangement" of the agenda for the councils of 1666 and 1667 and instructed to translate Paisios Ligarides' polemical tracts...[498]

Bishop Simeon also wrote a book called "The Rod of Government" which summarized the work of the council. The council reviewed and approved the book of Bishop Simeon, it was published with the blessing of Patriarchs Paisios and Macarius, and was presented to the Tsar.[499] This book contains a number of problematic teachings, including that a child receives their soul 40 days after conception.[500]

Florovsky says concerning Bishop Simeon's approach to theology:

> In preparing his own textbooks, Simeon relied on Latin works... He developed only knowledge of Latin and obviously knew no Greek... "Unable to read Greek books, he read only Latin ones and believed only Latin innovations in thought to be correct." His work was always guided by Latin and Polish books, that is, "by the thoughts of men like Scotus, Aquinas, and Anselm."[501]

---

496 Ibid.

497 Axarloglou, et al., *A Cartel that Lasts for Centuries*, p. 36.

498 Florovsky, *Ways of Russian Theology*, Ch. 3, Kievan Learning in Muscovy.

499 Bulgakov, op. cit., Part 5, Chapter II.

500 Russian Faith, "Was the Great Moscow Council of 1666-1667 heretical?" Part 1 (In Russian).

501 Florovsky, op. cit. Florovsy is here quoting Vladimir Osten. The footnote Florovsky provides says "Vladimir Ivanovich Osten (1854-1911) was a professor of literature

Florovsky says that among the Latin heresies that Bishop Simeon publicly taught included transubstantiation, the "western view concerning the transformation of the sacraments during the liturgy, that is, the Words of Institution" (rather than during the invocation of the Holy Spirit or epiclesis), a view which was rejected by other Orthodox as the "bread worshipping" heresy.[502] According to Florovsky, Bishop Simeon and his student Dimitri Medvedev

Fr. Georges Florovsky (+1979)

"not only embraced individual 'Latin' opinions, but there was also something Latin in their spiritual demeanor and make up."[503] Bishop Simeon and Medvedev were both anathematized by the 1690 Council in Moscow for their heretical teachings.[504]

Regarding this period, St. Hilarion writes:

> From the seventeenth century, Russian theology begins to fall under Latin influence. Kievan practice in the seventeenth century was different from the Muscovite. In the Trebnik (Book of Needs) of Peter Mogila an idea, unknown to the ancient Church, intrudes: That there is some sort of validity to mysteries performed outside the Church. In this Trebnik it is said of Lutherans and Calvinists that "it is not at all proper to rebaptize them since they are baptized," and of Latins: "But as for these, not only do we not baptize them, but

---

at the University of St. Petersburg. His article on Simeon Polotskii appears in *Khristianskoe chtenie*, 1907, no. III."

502 Ibid.

503 Ibid.

504 *Russian Faith*, "Was the Great Moscow Council of 1666-1667 heretical?" Part 1 (In Russian).

if they have been chrismated by their own, we do not anoint them with holy chrism." In the Trebnik of Peter Mogila, a dogmatic foundation is placed under a practice, which in the ancient Church was admitted only according to the considerations of Church economy. Baptism, chrismation, and priesthood are not repeated because supposedly "they leave a stamp, that is an indelible seal or a sign upon the soul of the recipient."[505] "For baptism signs or seals the soul of the person baptized such that he is known to be a sheep of the flock of Christ, and is written in the book of life; chrismation signs or seals the chrismated person such that he is distinguished from the unchrismated, being inscribed in the ranks of the warriors of Christ." But how can one be a sheep outside the one flock of Christ? How can one be a soldier of Christ while waging war against the Church of Christ? It is in Latin theology with its *opus operatum* that the source of this theory of the validity of mysteries performed outside the one Church of Christ lies, a theory which has been adopted by certain of the new Russian theologians.[506]

In his *Symbolic Texts in the Orthodox Church*, Russian Orthodox Archbishop Vasily (Krivoshein) of Brussels states regarding the Confession of Peter Mogila:

Compiled originally in Latin by the Metropolitan of Kyiv Peter Mogila and his closest collaborators - Isaiah Kozlovsky and Sylvester Kossov, approved in 1640 at the Council in Kiev, convened by Peter Mohyla [Mogila], it was sent for approval to the Patriarch of Constantinople Parthenius and submitted by the latter for consideration to the Local Council in Iasi in 1641-1642. There, the Latin text was translated into Greek colloquial language by the learned theologian Meletios Sirigus. He fairly remade it,

---

505 This language of "indelible seal" is from the Latin Council of Trent, Chapter 7, On the Sacraments, First Decree & Canons. For more, see: Heers, *The Ecclesiological Renovation of Vatican II*, pp. 71-84.

506 Troitsky, op. cit.

throwing out or changing the most obvious Latin deviations from the Orthodox faith of the original text, such as, for example, about the time of the change of the Holy Gifts, about purgatory, etc. This alteration was done, however, very hastily, and even Meletius Sirig himself, although he was a staunch opponent of the Roman Catholic Church, was, as a graduate of the University of Padua, under Latin influence in theology. Naturally, the "cleansing" he carried out in the Latin text of Met. Peter Mohyla [Mogila] could not be sufficient, and the Greek Orthodox Confession, even in such a corrected form, still remains the most Latinized text from the symbolic monuments of the 17th century. In this revised form, it was approved in Constantinople by a patriarchal letter dated March 11, 1643, signed by four Eastern patriarchs and 22 bishops and sent by Met. Peter Mogila in Kyiv. The latter, however, did not agree with the changes made to the text and refused to accept and publish the corrected Orthodox Confession sent to him. Instead, he published in 1645 his "Small Catechism," where he again returns to his Latin errors. Be that as it may, the Orthodox Confession remained unknown in the Russian Church until 1696, when it was translated in Moscow from Greek into Church Slavonic under Patriarch Adrian.[507]

Archbishop Vasily provides a thorough evaluation of the many problems with this Confession of Peter Mogila but some of the general observations he makes in summary include:

> Turning now to the very content of the Orthodox Confession, it can be said that, basically and essentially, it is, of course, an Orthodox symbolic monument of its era and in all controversial issues that separate the Orthodox from Roman Catholics, such as, for example, Filioque, papal primacy, or with Protestants, as the veneration of holy icons and relics, the invocation of saints, the sacraments, etc., it always adheres to Orthodox teaching. This is quite

---

507 Krivoshein, *Symbolic Texts in the Orthodox Church* (In Russian).

understandable, otherwise it would have been rejected by the
Orthodox Church, and not signed by so many patriarchs and
bishops. This does not prevent it from being a vividly Latin
document in form, and sometimes in content and spirit...
The Orthodox Confession fully assimilates Latin scholastic
terminology, such as, for example, the matter and form of the
sacrament, the intention (intentio) of the performer of the
sacrament as a condition for its validity, transubstantiation
(transsubstantiatio), the Aristotelian doctrine of substance
and accidents to explain transubstantiation, the doctrine
of the celebration of the sacraments *ex orere orerato* etc...
Latin is the teaching of the Orthodox Confession about the
"indelible seal" of the priesthood... With a few exceptions...
in the Orthodox Confession there are almost no references
to the Holy Fathers - a characteristic sign of separation from
the patristic tradition, which is felt throughout the theology
of this symbolic monument.[508]

The influence of Post-Schism Latin Scholasticism on Russian
Orthodox theology occurred principally through the Theological
School in Kiev and the person of Peter (Mogila). Florovsky states:

The main point is that taken as a whole the Orthodox
Confession [of Peter Mogila] is little more than a
compilation or adaptation of Latin material, presented in
a Latin style. Indeed, Mogila's Confession can justly be
categorized as one of the many anti-Protestant expositions,
which appeared throughout Europe during the Counter
Reformation or Baroque era. Certainly, the Confession was
more closely linked to the Roman Catholic literature of its
day than to either traditional or contemporary spiritual life
in the Eastern Church.

...It was not so much the doctrine, but the manner of
presentation that was, so to speak, erroneous, particularly
the choice of language and the tendency to employ any and

---

508 Ibid.

all Roman weapons against the Protestants even when not consonant in full or in part with Orthodox presuppositions. And it is here that the chief danger of Mogila's Latin "pseudomorphosis" or "crypto-Romanism" surfaces. The impression is created that Orthodoxy is no more than a purified or refined version of Roman Catholicism. This view can be stated quite succinctly: "Let us omit or remove certain controversial issues, and the rest of the Roman theological system will be Orthodox." Admittedly, in some ways this is true. But the theological corpus that is thereby obtained lacks or sorely reduces the native genius and the ethos of the eastern theological tradition.

For those opposed to the pressures by Mogila's followers for a Latin education there were good reasons for the suspicion that this was Uniatism. Were not the Orthodox partisans of a Latin orientation time and again in conference or negotiation with active Uniates, anticipating a compromise to which both sides could wholeheartedly adhere? Did they not more than once discuss a proposal to join all Orthodox believers in the region, Uniates and non-Uniates alike, under the authority of a special West Russian patriarch, simultaneously in communion with Rome and Constantinople? And was not Mogila himself always promoted for this august office by the Uniate side of the talks? This was, of course, hardly without his knowledge. Rutskii, the Uniate metropolitan, did not doubt for a moment that Mogila was "inclined to the Unia." It is certainly significant that Mogila never voiced doctrinal objections to Rome. In dogma, he was privately, so to speak, already at one with the Holy See. He was quite ready to accept what he found in Roman books as traditional and "Orthodox." That is why in theology and in worship Mogila could freely adopt Latin material. The problem for him, the only problem, was jurisdiction. And in the solution of this problem his outlook and temperament dictated that practical concerns would be decisive: ecclesiastical and political "tranquility," "prosperity," and "good order." For in the practical realm everything is relative. Things can be arranged and agreed upon. The task is one for ecclesiastical tacticians.

Probably the most representative figure of this final chapter in the Mogila era in Kievan intellectual history was Ioasaf Krokovskii (d. 1718), reformer, or even second founder, of the Kievan school... At Kiev, he taught theology

Metropolitan Peter Mogila of Kiev and Gallich (+1646)

according to Aquinas and centered his devotional life — as was characteristic of the Baroque era — on the praise of the Blessed Virgin of the Immaculate Conception. It was under his rectorship that the student "congregations" of the Kiev Academy known as Marian Sodalities arose, in which members had to dedicate their lives "to the Virgin Mary, conceived without original sin" ("Virgini Mariae sine labe originali conceptae") and take an oath to preach and defend against heretics that "Mary was not only without actual sin, venal or mortal, but also free from original sin,".... The veneration of Panagia and Theotokos by the Orthodox is by no means the same. It is grounded in a spiritual soil of an altogether different kind."

On the legacy of Peter Mogila, Florovsky says,

But however Mogila's motives are interpreted, his legacy is an ambiguous one... Under his guidance and rule the Orthodox Church in West Russia emerged from that state of disorientation and disorganization wherein it had languished ever since the catastrophe at Brest. On the other hand, the Church he led out of this ordeal was not the same. Change ran deep. There was a new and alien spirit, the Latin spirit in everything. Thus, Mogila's legacy also includes a drastic "Romanization" of the Orthodox Church. He brought Orthodoxy to what might be called a Latin "pseudomorphosis." True, he found the Church in ruins and had to rebuild, but he built a foreign edifice on the ruins. He founded a Roman Catholic school in the Church, and for generations the Orthodox clergy was raised in a Roman Catholic spirit and taught theology in Latin. He "Romanized" the liturgies and thereby "Latinized" the mentality and psychology, the very soul of the Orthodox people. Mogila's "internal toxin," so to speak, was far more dangerous than the Unia. The Unia could be resisted, and had been resisted, especially when there were efforts to enforce it. But Mogila's "crypto-Romanism" entered silently and imperceptibly, with almost no resistance. It has of course often been said that Mogila's "accretions" were only external, involving form not substance. This ignores the truth that form shapes substance, and if an unsuitable form does not distort substance, it prevents its natural growth. This is the meaning of "pseudomorphosis." Assuming a Roman garb was an alien act for orthodoxy. And the paradoxical character of the whole situation was only increased when, along with the steady "Latinization" of the inner life of the Church, its canonical autonomy was steadfastly maintained.[509]

While Peter Mogila is credited with helping Orthodox resist the Unia and submission to Rome, he nevertheless led many Orthodox into a *phronema*, outlook, and spiritual disposition that was not patristic but was that of the Latin Scholastics after the Great Schism. This alien Latin spirit inevitably impacted ecclesiology and the understanding about the reception of converts. Fr. John Erickson, in his work, "The Challenge of our Past: Studies in Orthodox Canon Law and Church History," notes the following:

> Since the time of Peter Mogila in the seventeenth century, many Orthodox theologians would say that non-Chalcedonians, Roman Catholics and mainstream Protestants have a "valid baptism," i.e., baptism in the name

---

509 Florovsky, op. cit., Ch. 2.

of the Trinity, and thus are to be received without rebaptism; but that the Protestants at least do not have "valid orders," whether because of a break in "apostolic succession" or because of a defect of intention, and thus cannot be received as clerics without ordination. This explanation, of course, depends heavily on Augustine's arguments against the Donatists as developed by the scholastics and codified after Trent. The sacraments are regarded as valid *ex opera operato* if certain objective conditions are met, though this does not necessarily make them licit or fruitful. Thus, while the non-Chalcedonians have "valid orders," they do not have the lawful exercise thereof.

These days this approach to sacramental theology is frequently criticized by Orthodox theologians as hopelessly Latinized.[510]

Such references to "valid mysteries" and the significance of "apostolic succession" and "intention" in the context of the reception of heretics into the Church, which Fr. John identifies as "hopelessly Latinized," are terms frequently employed in the canonical commentaries of Bishop Nikodim (Milas) that were discussed previously, as well as in the writings of some saints and ecclesiastic writers after the 17th century. As was seen in the canonical commentaries of Bishop Nikodim (Milas) discussed in the context of the Apostolic Canons, the attempt to reconcile the irreconcilable— the patristic ecclesiology adopted by the Ecumenical Councils with the teachings of the Post-Schism Latin Scholastics—leads to contradiction, confusion, and incoherence.

SUMMARY

The absence of patristic and hesychastic *phronema* in the Russian Church in the mid-17th century led to the dogmatization of liturgical

---

510 Erickson, *The Reception of Non-Orthodox into the Orthodox Church: Contemporary Practice*, pp. 5-6.

rubrics which culminated in the Old Believer Schism and the baseless anathemas of the 1667 Council, as well as to the deep infiltration of Latin Scholasticism into Russian theology which contributed to the decision to forbid the reception of Latins by baptism. This decision regarding the reception of the Latins was based on a misrepresentation of the canons of the Ecumenical Councils concerning the reception of heretics into the Church, and a misrepresentation of the teachings of St. Mark of Ephesus primarily by Patriarch Macarius III of Antioch who had confessed his allegiance to the Pope of Rome prior to this Council. Understanding the conditions which led to the spread of heterodox Latin Scholastic teachings in Russia during this period is critical in order to understand how it was possible for such teachings to be held by some Russian saints after the 17th century.

St. Mark of Ephesus

ΠΑΤΡΙΑΡΧΗΣ

ΕΛΕΩ ΘΕΟΥ   ΔΟΣΙΘΕΟΣ   ΤΗΣ ΑΓΙΑΣ ΠΟΛΕΩΣ   ΙΕΡΟΥΣΑΛΗΜ

Patriarch Dositheos II of Jerusalem (+1707)

CHAPTER 14

Patriarch Dositheos and the 1672 Council of Jerusalem

The influence of Latin Scholasticism on Orthodox theology was not only limited to Russia but also influenced the ancient Patriarchates that were under the Ottomans. In a weakened state in terms of theological learning, and the pursuit of theological education at heterodox schools in the West, led many such Orthodox to direct confrontation with both Latin and Protestant teachings. Often, Latin polemical sources were used by Orthodox in an effort to defend against Protestant teachings, and sometimes Protestant polemical sources were used by Orthodox in an attempt to defend against Latin teachings. While Peter Mogila's Confession represented an attempt to defend Orthodox teaching against the Unia, but employed almost exclusively Latin texts and Scholastic terminology, the Confession of Patriarch Dositheos and the 1672 Council in Jerusalem similarly employed Latin scholastic terminology to confront Calvinist teachings that were ascribed to Patriarch Cyril (Lucaris) of Constantinople. Regarding the Latinizing influences of that time, Metropolitan Kallistos states:

> The Latinizing tendency is found most notably in two other seventeenth century Confessions... the one by Peter of Mogila, Metropolitan of Kiev from 1633 to 1647, the other by Dositheos, Patriarch of Jerusalem from 1669 to 1707...

[U]nder Latin influence Peter and Dositheos deviate at some points from the main stream of Orthodox tradition...[511]

The history and authority of the Confession of Patriarch Dositheos and the 1672 Council in Jerusalem are complicated by the number of corrections and revisions that have been made since 1672. The first edition of the Confession was sent in 1723 by the Orthodox Patriarchs to the Anglican Non-Jurors through Russia as representing an Orthodox response to Calvinism.[512] Prior to his repose, Patriarch Dositheos acknowledged errors in that edition and had made several corrections which were not incorporated into the version that was sent on behalf of the Patriarchates. St. Philaret of Moscow also made several corrections to the original version but his version was not published in Russian until 1846.[513]

Archbishop Vasily (Krivoshein) discusses the 1672 Council of Jerusalem and the Confessions of Dositheos thoroughly in his *Symbolic Texts in the Orthodox Church* and identifies many similar problems as are found in the writings of Peter Mogila:

> Another symbolic monument of the 17th century has almost the same Latinizing character – The Confession of Faith of the Jerusalem Patriarch Dositheus, better known to us (in conjunction with other documents) under the name "Epistle of the Patriarchs of the Eastern Catholic Church on the Orthodox Faith." The reason for the compilation of this Confession was the confessional disputes between Roman Catholics and Calvinists in France. Both sides sought to prove that their dogma was shared by the Eastern Orthodox. And since in the Near and Middle East the interests of the Roman Catholics were defended by France, and the Calvinists by Holland, the ambassadors of these powers in Constantinople put pressure on the Patriarchate of Constantinople in order to obtain from it a text of confession of faith favorable for the confession they represent, in order to use it to fight the

---

511 Ware, *Eustratius Argenti*, p. 11.
512 Bernatsky, *Dositheus II Notar* (In Russian).
513 Ibid.

enemy. So, the Church would have revealed its negative attitude towards the Calvinist Confession of Cyril Lukar, gathered there in January 1672...

As is well known, [the Confession of Dositheos] is a response to the Confession of Cyril Lukar and follows exactly, one might say, "slavishly," his text, contrasting the

Patriarch Cyril I (Lucaris) of Constantinople

Orthodox teaching with his statements in the same order and on the same points... [It is] directed exclusively against Calvinists and does not at all speak of Roman Catholic errors. The reader gets the impression that the heretics - the Calvinists (Patriarch Dositheos writes about them in non-ecumenical terms) did not revolt and secede from the Roman Catholic Church, but from the Orthodox and that in general there are only Orthodox and Protestants, and there are no Roman Catholics or their teaching completely coincides with the Orthodox. In general, the Confession of Dositheus, like the Confession of the Eastern Church (Peter Mohyla [Mogila]), expounds, of course, the Orthodox teaching, otherwise it could not have been approved by the four Eastern patriarchs, but expresses it in forms borrowed from the Latins and with many deviations from Orthodox tradition in detail. So, it, following the Latin scholasticism, teaches about different types of grace - anticipatory grace (*gratia praevenies*), special grace (*specialis*), contributing grace (*cooperativa*). Such a distinction is alien to patristic tradition. Latin terminology is particularly common in the doctrine of the Eucharist. We can say that here Dositheus even surpasses Peter Mogila in his passion for Latin. Here is a typical example: "After the consecration of bread and wine, the essence (substance) of bread and wine no longer remains, but the very Body and Blood of the Lord under the form and image of bread and wine, or, which is the same, in the accidents of bread and wine." According to the Roman Catholic model, the sacrament of chrismation is called the word confirmation. The teaching of the Confession also has a Roman Catholic character about the indelibility of the priesthood, about the division of the Church into heavenly and militant... Theological doctrine of redemption as in the Orthodox Confession, it is completely undeveloped, almost absent, everything is limited to a few texts, so it is difficult to understand what convictions Dositheus holds here. He probably considered the question of redemption to be outside the framework of the anti-Calvinist controversy and did not consider it necessary to dwell on it. But what especially "jars" the Orthodox feeling in the Confession of Dositheus is the prohibition for the laity to read Holy Scripture, especially Old Testament. In defense of this prohibition, Dositheus refers to the experience of the Church, which allegedly became convinced of the harm resulting from the reading of Holy Scripture by the laity, and tries to justify it by asserting that, as Scripture itself says, salvation comes from "hearing the word of God," and not from reading it... Needless to say, the "experience" referred to here is the "experience" of the Roman Catholic, not the Orthodox Church. There it is understandable, because the church system, and indeed the teaching of the Roman Catholic Church, is really not in agreement with Scripture, and the laity should not know this, but in Orthodoxy this is not so, he has nothing to fear from Holy Scripture... It is interesting to note that in the Russian translation of the Confession of Dositheus, made in 1838 by Metropolitan Filaret, the passage about the prohibition of the laity to read the Bible is omitted.

Yes, Patriarch Dositheus realized and openly acknowledged over time the shortcomings of his Confession and in its third edition (Iasi, 1690) made a number of changes and additions to it directed against the Roman Catholics, about which he, in his original text, as we have already said, does not speak. So, he changed Article 18, where a doctrine close to the Roman doctrine of purgatory developed, spoke out, though indirectly, against the doctrine of the pope as the head of the Church ("a mortal man cannot be the eternal head of the Church" - Article 10), added to the original the text prohibition "to add or subtract anything to the text of the Creed," etc. All this undoubtedly improves the original version of the Confession. But at the same time, it turns it into only a personal document, since at the "Council" in Bethlehem [the original uncorrected version] was approved... All this limits the significance of the Confession of Dositheus as a conciliar document. And its numerous theological shortcomings, as well as the random nature of its occurrence, encourage us to look at it more as a historical monument of the 17th century symbolic content, rather than as an authoritative and binding symbolic text of enduring significance.[514]

On the Confession of Patriarch Dositheos and the Confession of Peter Mogila from this period, Archbishop Vasily states "they do not withstand the criterion of comparison with the 'ancient ecumenical teachings' either in terms of accuracy or in terms of the level of theological thought."[515] Neither of these Confessions were given much attention in Russia until the 1830s when the Jesuit educated Count Protasov, the chief procurator of the Holy Synod, promoted their study. Outside of Russia, these Confessions have been given very little attention by other local Orthodox churches.[516]

Despite lack of patristic teaching in the Confession of Patriarch Dositheos, and its limited authority and historical importance, those

---

514 Krivoshein, op. cit.
515 Ibid.
516 Ibid.

who oppose the patristic ecclesiology of the Ecumenical Councils refer to Decree 15 of the Confession to promote acceptance of Latin Scholastic ecclesiology. The unusual wording of this decree has led to considerable confusion and debate. According to one English translation, the decree states:

> Moreover, we reject as something abominable and pernicious the notion that when faith is weak the integrity of the Mystery is impaired. For heretics who renounce their heresy and join the Catholic Church are received by the Church; although they received their valid Baptism with weakness of faith. Wherefore, when they afterwards become possessed of the perfect faith, they are not again baptized.[517]

This translation, which is similar in English and Russian, has led some to understand this as stating that heretics have "valid baptism" and it is "abominable and pernicious" to receive such heretics into the Orthodox Church by baptism. However, such a conclusion is erroneous when read in context and when translated from the Greek. The Greek text reads as follows:

> ἔτι ἀπορρίπτομεν ὡς κάθαρμά τι καὶ μίασμα τὸ ·λιπῶς γὰρ ἐχούσης τῆς τῆς ζημιοῦται ἡλοκληρία τοῦραρα. Οἱ γὰρ αἱρετικοί, οὓς τὴν αἵρεσιν ἀποσεισαμένους καὶ προστεθέντας τῇ καθολικῇ ἐκκλησίᾳ, δέχεται ἡ ἐκκλησία· καίτοι ἐλλιπῆ ἐσχηκότες τὴν πίστιν τέλειον ἔλαβον τὸ βάπτισμα· ὅθεν τελείαν ὕστερον τὴν πίστιν κεκτημένοι οὐκ ἀναβαπτίζονται.[518]

According to Fr. Theodore Zisis, Honorary Professor of the Faculty of Theology at the University of Thessaloniki and Monk Seraphim (Zisis), former secretary of the Patriarch of Jerusalem Theophilos III, a more accurate translation from the Greek is:

---

517 Robertson, *The Acts and Decrees of The Synod of Jerusalem*, p. 139.

518 Ogorodnik, *Perfect Baptism of 'Imperfect in the Faith': What Is the 'Epistle of the Eastern Patriarchs' Really Talking About?* (In Russian).

> We also reject, as something unclean and polluted, the teaching that some imperfection of faith prevents the celebration of the sacrament. For heretics - whom the Church accepts after they renounce heresy and join the Catholic Church - despite their imperfect faith, they receive perfect baptism, and therefore, when they further acquire perfect faith, they are not rebaptized.[519]

As Fr. Theodore and Monk Seraphim point out, in the 15th Decree, Patriarch Dositheos is not addressing the topic of the "validity" of the baptism of those outside of the Orthodox Church but is addressing the question of whether the operation of the Holy Spirit in the Mystery of baptism relies on the degree of faith of the person being baptized. When Patriarch Dositheos rejects the belief that "some imperfection of faith prevents the performance of the sacrament," he is not referring to the dogmatic faith or canonical status of the one performing the baptism but only the degree of faith of the person being baptized. Here, "imperfect faith" refers to the degree to which the person being baptized trusts in God, not the person's dogmatic understanding at the time of baptism in the Orthodox Church. A heretic can renounce his heresy, fully embrace all of the dogmas of the Orthodox Church, and be baptized in the Orthodox Church by an Orthodox priest while still lacking in faith and trust in God; and this lack of faith does not prevent the Holy Spirit from working through the Mystery of Baptism in the Orthodox Church. If a person's "weakness of faith" or "imperfect faith" prevented the Mystery of baptism from taking place, then one could be tempted to think that after a person is baptized in the Orthodox Church and later grows in faith and trust in God, their Orthodox baptism may need to be repeated. This repetition of an Orthodox baptism is considered "unclean and polluted," or even "abominable," to use the former translation.[520]

This interpretation is clear from the context of Decree 15, from the other decrees of Patriarch Dositheos, and from the Confession

---

519 Ibid.
520 Ibid.

attributed to Cyril Lucaris that Patriarch Dositheos was responding to. Decree 15 is in direct response to Chapter 15 of the Calvinist Confession attributed to Patriarch Cyril which states:

Hieromartyr Cyril I (Lucaris)
of Constantinople (+1638)

> We believe that there are in the Church Evangelical Mysteries [Sacraments of the Gospel Dispensation], which the Lord delivered in the Gospel, and that these are two. For so many were delivered unto us; and the Institutor delivered no more. And that these consist of a word and of an element; and that they are seals of God's promises, and procure grace, we hold firmly. But that the Mystery be perfect and entire, it is necessary that the earthly matter and the external act concur with the use of that earthly thing, which was instituted by our Lord Jesus Christ, united with sincere faith; for when faith is wanting in the receivers the entire Mystery is not preserved.[521]

The claim of the Calvinists was that the sincerity and strength of the faith of the person participating in the Mystery was needed for grace to work through the Mystery, a belief that later led some Protestants to reject infant baptism altogether. Immediately before the words quoted above from Patriarch Dositheos in Decree 15, he objects to the same thinking with regard to the Mystery of Holy Communion:

---

521 Robertson, op. cit., pp. 200-201.

> And the [sanctifying of the Holy Communion] necessarily precedeth its use. For if it were not perfect before its use, he that useth it not aright could not eat and drink judgment unto himself (1 Cor. 11: 26, 28, 29); since he would be partaking of mere bread and wine. But now, he that partaketh unworthily eateth and drinketh judgment unto himself; so that not in its use, but even before its use, the Mystery of the Eucharist hath its perfection.[522]

When Patriarch Dositheos in the same decree speaks of heretics receiving a "perfect baptism" he is speaking of a baptism performed according to the apostolic form (three immersions in the name of the Trinity) in the Orthodox Church. Dositheos further states in Decree 16:

> Now the manner of Baptism is pure water, and no other liquid. And it is performed by the Priest only, or in a case of unavoidable necessity, by another man, provided he be Orthodox, and have the intention proper to Divine Baptism.[523]

While Patriarch Dositheos introduces the Latin Scholastic concept of "intention" as impacting the "validity" of baptism, he nevertheless states that baptism must be done by an Orthodox priest, and if in cases of emergency where no priest is available, baptism may be done by a layman if he is Orthodox. This is the same instruction given centuries later in 1912 by St. Raphael of Brooklyn to his Orthodox flock living amidst Anglicans.[524] If the Holy Spirit is present in heterodox baptisms, but this grace is not fruitful due to heresy and schism and only becomes fruitful when the heterodox are united with the one Church (as St. Augustine taught in *Against the Donatists)*, then there is no reason why an Orthodox Christian in an emergency could not have their child baptized by heretics while otherwise remaining in communion with the Orthodox Church.

---

522 Ibid., p. 138.

523 Ibid., p. 141.

524 Kohanik, op. cit.

Further on in Decree 16, Patriarch Dositheos states:

> Moreover, Baptism imparteth an indelible character, as doth also the Priesthood. For as it is impossible for any one to receive twice the same order of the Priesthood, so it is impossible for any one rightly baptized to again be baptized, although he should fall even into myriads of sins, or even into actual apostasy from the Faith. For when he is willing to return unto the Lord, he receiveth again through the Mystery of Penance the adoption of a son, which he had lost.[525]

Here, Patriarch Dositheos is clearly stating again that those "baptized rightly" in the Orthodox Church should not be baptized again in the Orthodox Church even if they fall into sins or apostasy. He is not dealing here with those who were baptized by heretics and were then received into the Church.

Furthermore, Patriarch Dositheos was in favor of baptizing Latins who had received baptism in only a single immersion, and referred to Latins who had been baptized this way as "unbaptized" with reference to the necessity of baptizing in the apostolic form (three immersions):

> For they who (without necessary cause) are not baptized with three emersions and immersions are in danger of being unbaptized. Wherefore the Latins, who perform baptism by aspersion, commit mortal sin.[526]

The claim that Patriarch Dositheos believed in the "validity" of baptism among heretics, or "ecclesiality" or "presence of the Holy Spirit" among the Calvinists to whom he was responding, cannot be reconciled with these words addressed by the 1672 Synod in Jerusalem "To all Orthodox Bishops everywhere...[and] all pious and Orthodox Christians":

---

525 Robertson, op. cit., p. 143.
526 Dositheos of Jerusalem, *Dodekavivlos*, 525. Quoted in Metallinos, op. cit., p. 93.

It is to be noted, therefore, that the leaders of these heretics, well knowing the doctrine of the Eastern Church, declare that she maintaineth the same as they themselves do in what concerneth God and divine things; but of set purpose do they malign us, chiefly to deceive the more simple. For being severed, or rather rent away from the Westerners, and consequently being absolutely rejected by the whole Catholic Church, and convicted, they are manifestly heretics and the chiefest of heretics. For not only have they become, from motives of self-love, propounders of new and silly dogmas (if it is allowable to call what are really only fables dogmas); but are entirely external to the Church, as having no kind of communion whatever with the Catholic Church, as hath been said. And as fearing lest those who have unhappily listened to them might perhaps be converted, they have thought how they might give utterance to this most transparent lie, that what they hold concerning the faith that the Eastern Church holdeth – God in his marvellous providence permitting this, and shewing that he who is not adorned with the Church's name, cannot even be called a Christian, much less be a Christian; and teaching them that they should, therefore, join the Catholic Church, though they have not understood this.[527]

In Decree 10, Patriarch Dositheos states that heretics are "forsaken by the Holy Spirit."

The High Priest... preaches the Sacred Gospel, and contends for the Orthodox faith, and those that refuse to hear he casts out of the Church as heathens and publicans (Matt. 18:17), and he puts heretics under excommunication and anathema, and lays down his own life for the sheep...

But it is well said by one of the Fathers, that it is not easy to find a heretic that has understanding. For when these forsake the Church, they are forsaken by the Holy Spirit,

---

527 Robertson, op. cit., p. 8-9.

and there remains in them neither understanding nor light, but only darkness and blindness.[528]

The Confession of Patriarch Dositheos approved by the 1672 Council and by the Eastern Patriarchs is a heavily Latinized text that is full of Scholastic terminology that is not in full agreement with the consensus of the Holy Fathers and the Ecumenical Councils. The Confession of Dositheos is interesting as an Orthodox response to Calvinist teaching in the heavily Latinized theological context that many Orthodox found themselves in during the 17th century, but its lack of patristic teaching limits its value as a thoroughly Orthodox Confession. Regarding the subject of the reception of heterodox, however, the Confession has largely been misinterpreted by those in the Orthodox Church who would like to adopt and promote the heterodox ecclesiology of the Latin Scholastics. Clearly, from the Confession and from the *Dodecavivlos* of Patriarch Dositheos, he did not believe that heretics have grace in their mysteries and did believe that Latins who had not been baptized in the apostolic form (three immersions in the name of the Holy Trinity) should be baptized. A few decades after the repose of Patriarch Dositheos, he would be succeeded by Patriarch Parthenios of Jerusalem who would sign the 1755 Encyclical declaring that all heretics must be received by Holy Baptism.

---

528 Ibid., pp. 128-129.

Church of the Holy Sepulchre, Jerusalem (woodcut)

St. Auxentios of Mount Katirli (+1757)
Feast Day: February 14

CHAPTER 15

The 1755 Council of the Three Patriarchs

St. Mark of Ephesus stated that Latins in the 15th Century were to be received by chrismation, referring to the Seventh Canon of the Second Ecumenical Council. The 1484 Council of Constantinople decreed that Latins who were formerly Orthodox but who had submitted to the authority of the Latin Pope of Rome following the Council of Florence should be received back by chrismation. Canon 7 of the Second Ecumenical Council that St. Mark referenced when instructing that Latins (or Uniates) be chrismated also required the Eunomians to be received by baptism, since the Eunomians did not practice baptism with three immersions. However, following the 16th century Latin Council of Trent at which the Latins formally declared sprinkling and pouring as equal to baptism with three immersions, the practice of sprinkling and pouring became the standard method of Latin "baptism." This official departure from the apostolic form of baptism led the Orthodox patriarchs of Constantinople, Alexandria, and Jerusalem to formally declare in 1755 that heterodox converts from the West (including the Protestants which by that time also departed from the apostolic form of baptism) were to be received into the Orthodox Church only by baptism. This followed a 1722 Council between Constantinople, Antioch, and Jerusalem.[529] This decision was also

---

529 This serves as evidence the Patriarch of Antioch was in agreement with the Encyclical of 1755. See Dragas, "The Manner of Reception of Roman Catholic Converts into

prompted by the increasing Latinization discussed in the previous section on Patriarch Dositheos of Jerusalem and a coinciding departure from the patristic *phronema*[530] among many Orthodox under Ottoman rule.

After the Fall of Constantinople and during the expansion of the Ottoman Empire in the East, relations between the Latins and Orthodox were mixed. Unable to provide theological education, some Orthodox sought support from the Latins and even invited Latin preachers to instruct the faithful. This, however, inevitably led to confusion, loss of Orthodox identity, and a blurring of the boundaries of the Church. When the Latins took advantage of this close cooperation to deceptively convince Orthodox laity and clergy to secretly pledge allegiance to the Pope of Rome, something had to be done to clarify the boundaries of the Church and remove the heretical Latin influences.

> The attitude of the Greek bishops is intelligible enough: they needed preachers and confessors; their own clergy were for the most part simple and ill-educated; the Latin missionaries were incomparably better qualified to give instruction and spiritual direction. But what was the attitude of the missionaries towards the Orthodox who came to them for confession? Sometimes they encouraged them to make an act of submission to the Roman Catholic Church, but more often – particularly when their penitents were ignorant and uneducated – they gave them absolution without embarking on any matters of religious controversy... The Orthodox not only welcomed the western missionaries when they arrived, but frequently took the initiative and invited them to come.[531]

Along with the theological confusion that resulted, the Latins' use of this close relationship to secretly convert the Orthodox led to a deterioration in relations between Latins and Orthodox.

---

the Orthodox Church" p. 9.

530 *Phronema* is a Greek term which loosely means "outlook" or "worldview."

531 Ware, *Eustratius Argenti*, pp. 21-22.

The Venetian occupation of the Peloponnese (1685-1718) was in part to blame. In the areas which they took from the Turks, the Venetians, without actively persecuting the Orthodox, yet did all they could to promote the Roman cause. Orthodox churches, converted by the Turks into mosques, were now recovered for Christian worship, but instead of being restored to their previous Orthodox owners they were assigned to the Latins. Large numbers of Latin clergy were introduced and new Latin bishoprics were created; at the same time the Venetians interfered in the appointment of Orthodox bishops, prevented many of the sees from being filled, and tried to abolish the dependence of the Orthodox dioceses upon the Patriarchate of Constantinople. The Greeks saw the Latin cause advanced, while their own was systematically undermined; they found themselves in a worse position under Christian Venetians than under infidel Turks, and like the Grand Duke Lukas Notaras before the fall of Constantinople, they not unnaturally concluded "better the Moslem turban than the Latin mitre"... The same kind of thing also happened elsewhere...

But there was another and far more important reason for the hardening of the Orthodox attitude around this time. The Orthodox authorities, while prepared to make use of the Latin missionaries, had at the outset little desire to become Roman Catholics. But the missionaries were gifted and persuasive advocates for the Papal cause: friendship with them inevitably produced converts to the Roman Catholic faith, and the Orthodox gradually came to realize with alarm how numerous and influential these converts were. Here, then, was another factor which caused an increase in hostility – the success of Latin penetration and propaganda.

Matters were made worse by the policy of concealment which the western clergy adopted. The missionaries, when they collaborated with the Orthodox, had naturally but one ultimate aim – the reconciliation of the Eastern Church to the see of Rome. But they realized that the best way to achieve their purpose was not to embark at once upon official negotiations, still less to undertake an open and aggressive proselytism among Orthodox congregations, but rather to win the confidence of the Greeks, to infiltrate among them, and so work upon them from within.[532]

Cyril V of Constantinople (+1775)

Latins would convince the Orthodox laity and clergy to continue attending Orthodox services and remaining outwardly Orthodox while pledging their allegiance to the Pope of Rome secretly. The Latins were even able to convince some patriarchs to submit letters of allegiance to the Pope.[533]

During this time of Latin intrigue and widespread confusion regarding the boundaries of the Church, the 1755 Encyclical was issued by Patriarch Cyril V of Constantinople, "the hesychast patriarch,"[534] along with the patriarchs of Alexandria and Jerusalem. When Patriarch Cyril decreed in 1750 that all Latins should be received by baptism, controversy resulted. His successor, Paisios II, sought to change this decision but the faithful rose up and forcefully removed him from the Patriarchate and demanded that Cyril be reinstated. Patriarch Cyril was installed again as patriarch "to the unbounded joy of the common people."[535]

St. Auxentios of Mount Katirli (+1757) was a great ascetic and miracle worker and the spiritual father of Patriarch Cyril.

532 Ibid., pp. 23-24.
533 Ibid., pp. 26-29.
534 Metallinos, op. cit., p. 34.
535 Ware, *Eustratios Argenti*, pp. 72-73.

St. Auxentios preached many sermons about the need for all converts to be received by baptism and many of the faithful rallied in support of Patriarch Cyril's decree.[536] As the controversy continued, Patriarch Cyril convened together with Patriarch Matthew of Alexandria and Patriarch Parthenios of Jerusalem and all Palestine to issue the 1755 Encyclical. The purpose of the council was to resolve the question, "When heretics

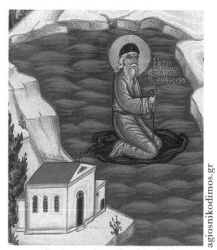

St. Auxentios using his cloak
as a boat to cross the sea

come over to us, are their baptisms acceptable, given that these are administered contrary to the tradition of the holy Apostles and divine Fathers, and contrary to the custom and ordinance of the catholic and apostolic Church?"[537] This was the first official decree signed by multiple Patriarchs dealing directly with the issue of the loss of the apostolic form of baptism among the Latins and Protestants following the 16th Century Latin Council of Trent. The decree stated:

> We, who by divine mercy were raised in the Orthodox Church, and who adhere to the canons of the sacred Apostles and divine Fathers, recognize only one Church, our holy, catholic, and Apostolic Church. It is her Mysteries, and consequently her baptism, that we accept. On the other hand, we abhor, by common resolve, all rites not administered as the Holy Spirit commanded the sacred Apostles, and as the Church of Christ performs to this day. For they are the inventions of depraved men, and we regard them as strange and foreign to the whole Apostolic

---

536 "Saint Auxentios the ascetic in Kartilio" (In Greek).
537 Metallinos, op. cit., pp. 134-136.

tradition. Therefore, we receive those who come over to us from them as unholy and unbaptized. In this we follow our Lord Jesus Christ who commanded His disciples to baptize "in the name of the Father, and the Son, and the Holy Spirit"; we follow the sacred and divine Apostles who order us to baptize aspirants with three immersions and emersions, and in each immersion to say one name of the Holy Trinity; we follow the sacred Dionysios, peer of the Apostles, who tells us: "to dip the aspirant, stripped of every garment, three times in a font containing sanctified water and oil, having loudly proclaimed the threefold hypostasis of the divine Blessedness, and straightway to seal the newly baptized with the most divinely potent myron [i.e. chrism], and thereafter to make him a participant in the super-sacramental Eucharist"; and we follow the Second and Penthekte [Fifth-Sixth] holy Ecumenical Councils, which order us to receive as unbaptized those aspirants to Orthodoxy who were not baptized with three immersions and emersions, and in each immersion did not loudly invoke one of the divine hypostases, but were baptized in some other fashion.

We too, therefore, adhere to these divine and sacred decrees, and we reject and abhor baptisms belonging to heretics. For they disagree with and are alien to the divine Apostolic dictate. They are useless waters, as Sts. Ambrose and Athanasios the Great said. They give no sanctification to such as receive them, nor avail at all to the washing away of sins. We receive those who come over to the Orthodox faith, who were baptized without being baptized, as being unbaptized, and without danger we baptize them in accordance with the Apostolic and synodal Canons, upon which Christ's holy and Apostolic and catholic Church, the common Mother of us all, firmly relies.[538]

---

538 Ibid.

The 1755 Encyclical was in full agreement with St. Hermogenes of Moscow in the early 17th century and the 1620 Moscow Council, and it formally upheld the practice of receiving all heretics by baptism that was in force in Russia prior to the 1667 Council and in Constantinople prior to the 15th century. According to historian Steven Runciman,

> The Patriarch of Antioch would have [signed the 1755 Encyclical], had he not been on an alms-seeking visit to Russia and had his throne not been snatched in his absence by a usurper.[539]

This decree was thereby signed by the future successor of Patriarch Paisios of Alexandria who was one of the two patriarchs who participated in the 1667 Moscow Council, and the future successor of Patriarch Dositheos of Jerusalem who led the 1672 Council of Jerusalem. In 1933, the Holy Synod of the Patriarchate of Antioch issued a formal decree that all converts received in its jurisdiction should be received by baptism, thereby also adopting policy expressed in the 1755 Encyclical.[540] Tsar Peter I had abolished the Moscow Patriarchate in 1721, replacing it with a German Lutheran model of synodal government,[541] and the Russian Church continued to receive converts according to the Latin Scholastic teachings of Peter Mogila.

While the 1755 Encyclical declared that those not baptized with three immersions must be received by triple immersion baptism as was decreed regarding the Eunomians in the Second Ecumenical Council and the Fifth-Sixth Ecumenical Council in Trullo, St. Athanasios Parios emphasized that the Latins were even "worse than the Eunomians" because the Eunomians at least used a single immersion, whereas the Latins did not immerse at all.[542] Fr. Daniel

---

539 Runciman, *The Great Church in Captivity*, p. 358. But according to Ware, Antioch wished Cyril V had the support of the metropolitans of his synod. See Ware, *Eustratios Argenti: A Study of the Greek Church under Turkish Rule*, p. 76. With this political difficulty in Antioch, such a position is understandable given the political issues in Constantinople at the same time.

540 See *Echos d'Orient*, vol. xxxiii, Paris, 1934, pp. 368-370. Quoted in Ware, *Eustratios Argenti*, p. 106.

541 Ware, *The Orthodox Church*, p. 114.

542 Metallinos, op. cit., p. 79.

Sysoev in Russia also spoke about the agreement between the 1755 Council and the 1620 Moscow Council:

> Likewise, the 91st canon of St. Basil the Great specifically calls the custom of triple immersion a mystical apostolic tradition. The heretics' violation of this standard, according to the 7th canon of the 2nd and the 95th canon of the 6th Ecumenical Councils, was sufficient grounds for their rebaptism. It is true that both church tradition and the canons (7th canon of the Council of Neocaesarea) provide for baptizing a person through effusion in exceptional (and only exceptional) circumstances. But the Church rejects as false reasoning any attempt to make this practice standard. The most striking example of this is the resolutions of the Council of Constantinople in 1755 (to this day in force on Athos) and the Moscow Council of 1620, which reject the validity of Latin baptism specifically because Rome normalized baptism by pouring or even sprinkling.
>
> It is no accident that the 1848 Encyclical of the Eastern Patriarchs calls the introduction of sprinkling instead of immersion the "vile spawn" of the filioque heresy and an "innovation contradictory to the Gospel." In the same way, all the Russian works opposing Catholicism denounce this innovation of the Western Church as un-Orthodox. The venerable Kollyvades fathers (Nicodimos of the Holy Mountain, Macarius of Corinth, and others) considered it impossible to recognize Catholics and Lutherans as baptized specifically because the sacrament was performed by sprinkling.[543]

As St. Nikodemos explained in the *Rudder*, by this time the Latins had to be received by baptism because their "baptisms" could not be accepted by exactitude nor by economy. By exactitude, the Latins should be baptized since they are heretics and heretics

---

543 Sysoev, *Catechetical Talks*, pp. 330-331.

cannot serve true Mysteries (St. Basil's first canon), and since by economy "they do not observe the three immersions which have to be administered to the one being baptized, as the Orthodox Church has received instructions from the Holy Apostles from the beginning."[544] Economy cannot be applied where the apostolic form of baptism is not found, according to Canon 7 of the Second Ecumenical Council and Canon 95 of the Fifth-Sixth Ecumenical Council in Trullo.

The 1755 Encyclical of the Three Patriarchs has not been revoked and it remains the last official statement on

St. Nikodemos the Hagiorite

the reception of converts signed by multiple patriarchs. It is also the only official declaration on the reception of converts since the Ecumenical Councils which takes proper account of the relevant canons of the Ecumenical Councils and addresses the necessity of baptism being performed in three immersions in the name of the Trinity. The decision of the 1755 Council was defended by St. Nikodemos the Hagiorite, the Kollyvades Fathers and especially by the Greek and Athonite saints and elders up to the present time. Unlike the 1667 Council of Moscow, which the 1755 Encyclical passed over in silence, the 1755 Encyclical conformed to, rather than contradicted, the Apostolic Canons and the decisions of the Ecumenical Councils. The decree was also welcomed by the faithful as confirming apostolic tradition rather than being forced on the faithful using violence as had been done in 1667.

544 Agapios and Nicodemus, op. cit., footnote 66 to The 85 Canons of the Holy Apostles.

While the Russian Church in 1667 was eager to conform to modern Greek practice rather than to the ancient tradition of the Orthodox Church, it ended up following bishops who were influenced by heterodox Latin teachings instead. By 1755 the Russian Church had already set its own course based on the 1667 Council and the heterodox ecclesiology enshrined in the *Trebnik* of Peter Mogila and did not look back. Fr. Ambrose (Pagodin) writes on the history of the reception of converts in the Russian Church:

> Since 1718 the Spiritual Council [Synod] decreed not to re-baptize Protestants who were baptized in the name of the Holy Trinity. From that time the Russian Church never returned to the re-baptism of Latins, Lutherans, Anglicans and Calvinists. Later the Russian Church decreed that confirmed Roman Catholics and chrismated Armenians be received by the third rite, i.e., through confession and repudiation of heresy. Lutherans, Calvinists and other Protestants who were baptized by triple immersion (or by pouring), to be received by the second rite, i.e., by chrismation and repudiation of heresy. They were chrismated because in the first place they do not have such a sacrament and secondly, they do not have a priesthood based on apostolic succession. Anglicans and Episcopalians are likewise received through the second rite because it is questionable (as Metropolitan Philaret of Moscow wrote) whether their church has preserved apostolic succession.[545]

Unfortunately, while revoking the anathemas of the 1667 Council against the Old Believers, admitting to the baselessness of these anathemas and to the harm which resulted from the Council, the Russian Church has not formally renounced the 1667 Council in its entirety, nor the Latin Scholastic teaching on the reception of heterodox into the Church that was adopted by this council. Whereas the 1667 Moscow Council decreed that Latins should be chrismated based on the (misunderstood) words of St. Mark of Ephesus, by 1718 the Church in Russia moved even further away

---

545 Pogodin, *On the Question of the Order of the Reception of Persons into the Orthodox Church.*

from the patristic and canonical basis for the reception of heretics by allowing Latins to be received by confession of faith alone, even if they were not previously baptized in three immersions, disregarding the necessity of the apostolic form of baptism.

SUMMARY

The 1755 Council, with its encyclical, signed by the Patriarchs of Constantinople, Jerusalem, and Alexandria is the last official decision on the reception of converts signed by multiple Patriarchates. It is also the only decision on the reception of converts that has been made since the Ecumenical Councils which took full account of all of the relevant canons of the Ecumenical Councils. 1755 was also the first council after the Ecumenical Councils to fully address the widespread departure of the Latins and Protestants from the apostolic form of baptism after the 16th century Latin Council of Trent. The 1755 Encyclical has not been revoked but rather its decision to receive all converts by baptism was defended and upheld by St. Nikodemos, the Kollyvades Fathers, and charismatic saints and elders up to our own time.

St. Paisius Velichkovsky (+1794)
Feast Day: November 15

CHAPTER 16

Patristic and Scholastic Ecclesiology
After the 17ᵗʰ Century

Latin Scholastic theology had a tremendous influence on Orthodox theology in Russia through Peter Mogila and the Kiev Academy, and on Orthodox theology outside of Russia through the Latin schools that were attended by Orthodox from the territories under Ottoman rule. The extent of this Latin influence in and beyond Russia was such that it should be no surprise that writings of some saints after this period continued to exhibit such heterodox influences. When the Synod of the Russian Orthodox Church adopted a position on the reception of Latins and Protestants in the 17ᵗʰ century that was based on Latin Scholastic ecclesiology, and this ecclesiology was taught in the Orthodox theological academies, it should come as no surprise that there would be holy people that assumed such teachings were Orthodox.

In the 19ᵗʰ and 20ᵗʰ centuries, efforts were made within and outside of Russia to return to patristic sources and remove the corruptions of Latin Scholasticism.[546] The return to patristic teaching of this period went hand in hand with the hesychastic revival brought about by the Kollyvades Fathers including the Russian St. Paisius (Velichkovsky).

---

546 Krivoshein, op. cit.

St. Paisius (Velichkovsky) (+1794)

In Russia, the ecclesiastical, spiritual, and theological climate of mid-17th to 18th centuries was marked by heterodox influences in all aspects of Church life—theology, iconography,[547] chanting, prayer, and spiritual life. Under Tsar Peter I, and throughout the 18th century, monasticism was persecuted.

> From the beginning of the 18th century, a century-long period of persecution began for monasticism... Peter I called [monasticism] "gangrene of the state," and considered the monks to be parasites and rogues. Spiritual life in the state froze more and more. State power quickly and clearly acquired a secular, non-ecclesiastical character. At a superficial glance, it might have seemed that monasticism was finally dying. The spiritual principle was persecuted everywhere... And, indeed, state reforms, directed primarily against monasticism, lead to the most unfortunate consequences.[548]

It was through St. Paisius (Velichkovsky) and his spiritual successors that a patristic and spiritual renewal took place in Russia and throughout the Orthodox world in the 19th century.

> The second part of the Synodical period, the nineteenth century, so far from being a period of decline, was a time of great revival in the Russian Church. Men turned away from religious and pseudo-religious movements in the contemporary west, and fell back once more upon the true spiritual forces of Orthodoxy. Hand in hand with this revival in the spiritual life went a new enthusiasm for missionary work, while in theology, as in spirituality, Orthodoxy freed itself from a slavish imitation of the west.

---

547 St. John the Wonderworker sharply criticized the changes to iconography that took place during this period. See John of Shanghai and San Francisco, *A Discourse on Iconography*.

548 Optina Pustyn, *History of the Monastery*, Page 2, Section 3 (In Russian).

It was from Mount Athos that this religious renewal took its origin. A young Russian at the theological academy of Kiev, Paissy Velichkovsky (1722-1794), repelled by the secular tone of the teaching, fled to Mount Athos and there became a monk.[549]

When the Prefect of the theological academy of Kiev asked St. Paisius why he was leaving, he replied:

> The first reason is that, having the firm intention to become a monk and realizing the uncertainty of the hour of death, I wish as soon as possible to receive the tonsure. The second reason is that from outward learning I do not see any benefit for my soul, hearing only the names of pagan gods and wise men – Cicero, Aristotle, Plato… Learning wisdom from them, people today have become completely blinded and have stepped away from the right path; they pronounce lofty words, but within they are full of darkness and obscurity, and all their wisdom is only on their tongues. Seeing no benefit from such teaching, and fearing lest I myself be corrupted by it, I have abandoned it. Finally, the third reason is this: I have noticed that, like worldly functionaries, they live in great honor and glory, adorn themselves with expensive garments, travel on splendid horses and in fine carriages – I do not say this in judgment of them, may this not be! I only fear and tremble lest I myself, after learning outward wisdom and becoming a monk, should fall into yet a worse infirmity. Behold, it is for all these reasons that I have abandoned outward learning.[550]

St. Paisius' experience at the Academy was just over 100 years after its establishment by Peter Mogila. After spending time on Mt. Athos, St. Paisius went to Romania, and eventually his disciples would bring the patristic and hesychastic tradition to Russia which would lead to a spiritual and monastic revival:

---

549 Ware, *Orthodox Church*, p. 117.
550 Metrophanes, *Blessed Paisius Velichkovsky: The Man Behind the Philokalia*, p. 30.

In 1763 [St. Paisius] went to Romania
and became Abbot of the monastery of
Niamets, which he made a great spiritual
center, gathering round him more than
500 brethren. Under his guidance, the
community devoted itself specially to the
work of translating Greek Fathers into
Slavonic. At Athos Paissy had learnt at
first hand about the Hesychast tradition,
and he was in close sympathy with his
contemporary Nicodemus.[551] He made a Slavonic translation
of the Philokalia, which was published at Moscow in 1793.
Paissy laid great emphasis upon the practice of continual
prayer — above all the Jesus Prayer — and on the need for
obedience to an elder or starets...

St. Paisius
Velichkovsky

Paissy himself never returned to Russia, but many of his
disciples traveled thither from Romania and under their
inspiration a monastic revival spread across the land. Existing
houses were reinvigorated, and many new foundations
were made: in 1810 there were 452 monasteries in Russia,
whereas in 1914 there were 1,025... [This tradition] was
marked in particular by a high development of the practice
of spiritual direction. Although the "elder" has been a
characteristic figure in many periods of Orthodox history,
nineteenth-century Russia is par excellence the age of the
starets.

The first and greatest of the startsi of the nineteenth century
was Saint Seraphim of Sarov (1759-1833)... Seraphim is
rightly regarded as a characteristically Russian saint, but he
is also a striking example of how much Russian Orthodoxy

---

551 St. Paisius actually preceded St. Nikodemos on the Holy Mountain and left the Holy
Mountain before St. Nikodemos arrived in 1775. However, they were close in time,
both helped to spread the *Philokalia* and revive hesychasm, and both were of the same
mind regarding ecclesiology and the reception of converts.

has in common with Byzantium and the universal Orthodox tradition throughout the ages...

After his death the work was taken up by another community, the hermitage of Optina. From 1829 until 1923, when the monastery was closed by the Bolsheviks, a succession of *startsy* ministered here, their influence extending like that of Seraphim over the whole of Russia... While these elders all belonged to the school of Paissy [Velichkovsky] and were all devoted to the Jesus Prayer, each of them had a strongly marked character of his own...[552]

Nicolas Zernov writes in *The Russians and their Church*:

[St. Paisius] inaugurated a spiritual revival which raised the religious life of Russia to new heights comparable to those attained at the time of St. Sergius of Radonezh in the fourteenth century. Paisi was steeped in the teaching of the ancient Fathers and ascetics, and he had an outstanding gift for sharing his experience and knowledge with others. He was elected Abbot of the monastery of Niamets in Moldavia, where he gathered round him more than five hundred monks. Many of his disciples became great experts in the art of spiritual direction. These elders ("Startsy" in Russian) were men distinguished by their understanding of the most intricate problems of human life, and by their power to help others along the road of perfection. Many of them returned to Russia after the death of their teacher, and spread far and wide the best tradition of Orthodox monasticism, which had been obscured since the time of the [Old Believer] Schism...

Two of Paisi's disciples, Theodor (d. 1817) and Kleopa (d. 1822), formed a link between him and the most famous centre of "Starchestvo" or spiritual direction in the nineteenth and twentieth centuries — the "Optina Pustyn." This monastery

---

552 Ware, *Orthodox Church*, pp. 117-120.

became famous throughout Russia for its succession of inspired "elders:" Leonid (1768-1841), Makari (1788-1860), Amvrosi (1812-91), Iosif (d. 1911), Nektari (d. 1928), Anatoli (d. 1922), were the best known among them. These wise teachers of Christianity attracted a ceaseless stream of visitors from all corners of the land."[553]

Synaxis of the Saints of Optina
Feast Day: October 10

The influence of St. Paisius and the revival of hesychasm and spiritual life in Russia was primarily due to the publication and dissemination of his writings by the Optina Hermitage which was only made possible through the intervention of St. Philaret of Moscow.

Elder Macarius, others at Optina, and the Optina library collected many handwritten translations of St. Paisius (Velichkovsky)... From today's perspective, it is hard to imagine that then, in officially Orthodox Russia, the idea of publishing these manuscripts seemed like a daring innovation, and Elder Macarius doubted its feasibility for censorship reasons. Indeed, in 1793 in St. Petersburg, through the efforts of the St. Petersburg and Novgorod Metropolitan Gabriel (Petrov-Shaposhnikov); and later, for about 50 years, not a single Orthodox book was published, with the exception of liturgical books. The book market was overflowing with Catholic and Protestant books, the "Zion Herald" was published, preaching outright hatred of Christianity. And

---

553 Zernov, *The Russians and Their Church.* Ch. 15.

all this was printed with the permission of censorship in an Orthodox state.

Thanks to the appeal of the Kireevskys to St. Philaret, Metropolitan of Moscow, this obstacle was overcome, and in 1847 the first book of the Optina edition was published— "The Life and Writings of the Moldavian Elder Paisius Velichkovsky"... The Optina publishing house was a kind of repetition of the work of the Elder Paisius himself, who gathered around him a translation circle. And in a short time, a number of exemplary books for spiritual reading and reflection were introduced into Russian readership.[554]

The life of Elder Leonid of Optina (+1841), the first of the clairvoyant Optina elders, illustrates the bewilderment with which their hesychastic way of life was met by the surrounding monasteries and by the metropolitan at that time, long after the hesychastic Non-Possessors were suppressed in Russia. As the wisdom, prayerfulness, and clairvoyance of the elders became known, monastics and laity flocked to the monastery for spiritual advice. The large numbers of visitors and the jealousy and bewilderment of nearby monasteries led to a formal investigation of the monastery by Metropolitan Ambrose of Novgorod and St. Petersburg, but when Fr. Hilarion of Tikhvin Monastery arrived to question the elders, he left amazed by their wisdom.[555]

Other great saints and hierarchs of Russia who were influenced by the life and legacy of St. Paisius (Velichkovsky) include St. Ignatius (Brianchaninov) and St. Theophan the Recluse.[556]

It was not only the *Philokalia* and the living tradition of hesychasm and spiritual eldership that St. Paisius helped to revive in the Slavic world as the Kollyvades Fathers had done in the Greek world, but also a return to a patristic understanding of the canons, the boundaries of the Church, and the reception of converts. As recorded in his life, St. Paisius "was so apprehensive about heresies

554 Optina Pustyn, *Blessed Optina* (In Russian).
555 Sederholm, *Elder Leonid of Optina*, pp. 28-34.
556 McGuckin, *Illumined in the Spirit: Studies in Orthodox Spirituality*, pp. 263-280.

and schisms that all who were converted, whether from sects or from the western Latin heresies, he baptized."[557]

In a letter to a Uniate priest, St. Paisius implored him:

> Depart from the Unia as speedily as possible, lest death overtake you in it and you be numbered among the heretics and not among the Christians... And not only go away yourself, but advise others to go away also, if in your conscience you know that they will hear you. And if they will not hear you, then at least depart yourself from the nets of the enemy and be united in soul and heart with the Holy Orthodox Church, and thus, together with all [the faithful] holding the inviolate faith and fulfilling the commandments of Christ, you will be able to be saved.[558]

St. Paisius (Velichkovsky) corresponded with Fr. Dorotheos Voulismas and the Kollyvades Fathers regarding the reception of converts into the Church and agreed with them that all converts should be baptized with three full immersions.[559, 560] St. Paisius was the spiritual father of Voulismas, the reviewer of the *Rudder* of St. Nikodemos appointed by the Patriarch of Constantinople. At the request of St. Paisius, Voulismas prepared a defense for the reception of Latins and Uniates by baptism, which was then translated into Romanian and published. The teachings of St. Paisius and the Kollyvades Fathers on patristic ecclesiology and the reception of converts would have limited influence in Russia, however, due to the official position of the Holy Synod which was based on Latin Scholastic teachings, and the tremendous censorship that the Holy

---

557 Metrophanes, op. cit., p. 158.

558 Ibid., p. 202.

559 See in Greek *Οι Κολλυβάδες και ο Δωρόθεος Βουλησμάς. Το ζήτημα της "ανακρίσεως" του Πηδαλίου και του Κανονικού* (Ιερά Μονή Παναγίας Χρυσοποδαριτίσσης Νεζερών). *The Kollyvades and Dorotheos Voulismas. The Case of the Examination of the Pedalion and the Canonikon (Holy Monastery of Panagia Chrysopodaritissa of Nezeron).* An English translation of this text will be published in the future by Uncut Mountain Press.

560 See also Heers, "St. Nikodemos, the Rudder and the Reception of Converts into the Orthodox Church: A Look at the Correspondence Between the Kollyvades Fathers & Dorotheos Voulismas."

Synod in Russia undertook during this time to ensure that nothing contrary to the Holy Synod's official teachings would be published.

ST. IGNATIUS (BRIANCHANINOV) (+1867)

St. Ignatius (Brianchaninov) was an inheritor of the hesychastic and patristic tradition of St. Paisius (Velichkovsky) and made a major contribution to the restoration of patristic teaching in Russia. In his early years, before entering the monastic life, St. Ignatius met and became acquainted with Elder Leonid of Optina. St. Ignatius had great love for Elder Leonid, and while St. Ignatius was a hieromonk prior to his consecration to the episcopacy, he had hoped to join the Optina monastery, but this never transpired.[561] He corresponded with Elder Leonid and Elder Macarius of Optina and helped with the material support of the monastery and with the publication of patristic texts.[562] St. Ignatius was consecrated bishop in 1857, but after serving for four years he resigned to live the rest of his life in seclusion.[563] St. Ignatius was a prolific writer and his writings constantly refer to and summarize the writings of the Holy Fathers. While he is perhaps best known for his writings on monasticism (*The Arena*) and the Jesus Prayer, he wrote about many other topics as well, including the topics of schism and heresy.

St. Ignatius (Brianchaninov) (+1867)
Feast Day: April 30

---

561 Stavitskaya, "St. Ignatius (Brianchaninov) and Optina Hermitage" (In Russian).

562 Optina Pustyn, "Correspondence of St. Ignatius (Brianchaninov) with the Optina Elders and Other Fathers and Brothers of the Optina Hermitage."

563 Ware, "Introduction." See Brianchaninov, *The Arena*, vii.

Regarding schism and heresy, like the saints and Fathers before him, St. Ignatius does not speak of "degrees of heresy." Rather, "schism" is said to be a break in the unity of the Church where there is no change to dogmas or Mysteries, while "heresy" constitutes a change to the dogmas and Mysteries:

> A schism is a violation of complete unity with the Holy Church, with the exact preservation, however, of the true teaching about dogmas and sacraments. Violation of unity in dogmas and sacraments constitutes heresy.[564]

After explaining how the Latins and Protestants have altered the dogmas and Mysteries of the Church, St. Ignatius states that for one to be saved one must receive the true Mysteries in the true Church where the true dogmas have been maintained.

> So, for those who want to be saved, first it is necessary that he correctly believes in God, that he belongs to the Orthodox Church, that in its bosom he is baptized, chrismated, cleansed of sins by repentance, and communes of the Holy Mysteries of Christ. Secondly, as the Lord said to the young man, it is necessary for him to keep the commandments of God.[565]

St. Ignatius further states that heretics and schismatics change the dogmas and Mysteries of the Church out of pride, that such distortions constitute blasphemy, and that those who distort the dogmas and Mysteries of the Church belong to the devil. Since heretics and schismatics already belong to the devil, the devil leaves them alone and does not create additional trials and temptations for them, and for this reason schismatics and heretics may appear virtuous.

> But the essential manifestation of pride in heretics and schismatics is that, having rejected the knowledge of God and divine worship, revealed and taught by God Himself,

---

564 Brianchaninov, *Collected Works*, Vol 4, p. 466 (In Russian).
565 Ibid., p. 320.

they strive to replace them with self-willed and blasphemous divine services. Infected with heresy and schism, the devil does not care to tempt with other passions and obvious sins. And why should the devil tempt him and fight with him who, through the medium of mortal sin—heresy—has been killed by eternal death and already while alive is the property of the devil?[566]

Furthermore, St. Ignatius emphasizes that to find salvation one must belong to the Orthodox Church and obey the teachings of the Church. He also says that outside of the unity of the Church, no amount of prayer and ascetical labor will bear spiritual fruit.

> Whoever wants to be saved must belong to the one holy Orthodox Church, be her faithful son, and obey her institutions in everything. If someone does not obey the Church, if someone has separated from the Church, if someone is a schismatic; then no matter how many prostrations he makes, no matter how much he fasts, no matter how much he prays, he will not be saved. The Lord compared the one who disobeys the Church with an idolater: if anyone disobeys the Church, He said, let him be to you like a pagan and a publican (Matt. 18:17).[567]

While these quotes do not deal specifically with the reception of converts, they demonstrate that St. Ignatius (Brianchaninov) shared the same ecclesiology of the Fathers of the Church that saw nothing salvific in the mysteries performed outside of the unity of the Church. He clearly considers Latins and Protestants to be heretics, and as noted in Chapter 12, lists the departure of Latins and Protestants from the apostolic form of baptism as an example of their corruption of the Mysteries.

---

566 Ibid., p. 457.
567 Ibid., p. 357.

St. Philaret of Moscow (+1867)

St. Philaret
of Moscow (+1867)

St. Philaret of Moscow helped facilitate the patristic and hesychastic revival in Russia by blessing the Optina Hermitage to publish and distribute the life and teachings of St. Paisius (Velichkovsky) and other important spiritual books. While St. Philaret was educated in Latin, he labored to end the use of Latin in theological education in Russia. With St. Philaret, as with some other saints of that period, we find a mixture of both patristic and Latin Scholastic teachings, just as we saw also in the canonical interpretations of Serbian Bishop Nikodim (Milas). Attempts to reconcile patristic and Latin Scholastic teachings, however, has often resulted in contradictions and irreconcilable statements. For instance, in his "Longer Catechism," St. Philaret of Moscow states in response to the question:

> What is most essential in the administration of Baptism?

> Trine immersion in water, in the name of the Father, and of the Son, and of the Holy Spirit.[568]

Yet, with regard to the reception of Anglicans into the Orthodox Church, St. Philaret says:

> A member of the Anglican Church, who has definitely received a baptism in the name of the Father, and of the Son, and of the Holy Spirit, even though it be by effusion (pouring), can, in accordance with the rule accepted in the Church of Russia (which the Church of Constantinople considers to be a form of condescension), be received into the Orthodox Church without a new baptism, but the sacrament of chrismation must be administered to him,

---

568 Philaret of Moscow, *The Longer Catechism of the Eastern Orthodox Church*, p. 125.

because confirmation, in the teaching of the Anglican Church, is not a sacrament.[569]

St. Philaret says that three immersions are "essential" in the administration of baptism, but then states that Anglicans could be received by chrismation even if their Anglican "baptism" was done by pouring. He does not explain or elaborate on this apparent contradiction. He then states that Anglicans should be chrismated, not because of what the canons and Fathers teach about the reception of heretics and schismatics into the Church, but because the Anglicans do not believe that chrismation is a sacrament, as if the views of heretics about their own mysteries should influence how the Church should view the mysteries of heretics. However, we have not seen from St. Philaret a detailed examination of the relevant canons and patristic teachings covered in this text so uncertainty exists in how he reconciled these views with the teachings of the Ecumenical Councils. Very likely, he simply followed the decisions of the Holy Synod of the Russian Church following the 1667 Council.

St. Theophan the Recluse (+1894)

St. Theophan the Recluse was another Russian saint of the 19ᵗʰ century who contributed to the patristic and hesychastic renewal in Russia. Like St. Ignatius (Brianchaninov), he was also consecrated as a bishop but a few years later resigned to live in seclusion where he wrote books and answered correspondence. Also, like St. Ignatius, St. Theophan's writings are full of patristic teaching and he is likewise best known for his writings on the spiritual life and the Jesus Prayer. However, one private letter from St. Theophan (dated February 28, 1888) has unfortunately been used by some to claim that St. Theophan believed there is grace in heterodox mysteries and that he held a Latin Scholastic ecclesiology. In this letter, St. Theophan states:

---

569 Birchall, *Embassy, Emigrants, and Englishmen*, p. 607.

In a letter dated February 10, you asked for my opinion on the views of a certain person that the Catholic Church is not heretical...

You and I are private individuals; and in their opinions they must conform to the decision of the Orthodox Church. It seems Our Holy Church is indulgent towards Catholics - and recognizes the power not only of the baptism of the Catholic and other sacraments, but also of the priesthood, which is very significant. Therefore, it is better for us to refrain both from asking these questions and from solving them. One thing [that] should be kept in mind is that one should not go over to the Catholics, because aspects of their confession of faith and church order have been corrupted or changed, departing from what is most ancient. I can't say more than that.[570]

St. Theophan ends his letter with the exhortation "Save yourself!"

A shortened version of this quote, provided without any context, has been shared by proponents of Latin Scholastic ecclesiology which is surprising for a number of reasons. From the context, the letter to St. Theophan appears to have been from an Orthodox layperson asking about an article written by a priest or bishop stating that Latins are not heretics. The reader wants to know if St. Theophan agrees with the author. St. Theophan does not respond directly to the question about whether Latins are heretics but only acknowledges what the Holy Synod has officially taught. He then states that the priest or bishop writing the article has to conform to the position of the Holy Synod, that the position of the Synod on Latins is "significant," and as "private individuals" there is little value in either St. Theophan or the layman occupying themselves much with this issue. Here, St. Theophan may have been referring to the censorship rules in Russia that will be discussed later in the text which prevented the publication of views contrary to the

---

570 Theophan the Recluse, *Collection of Letters of St. Theophan* (In Russian). Issue 7, Letter 1181, pp. 201-202.

official teaching of the Synod. St. Theophan concludes the letter by saying that one should not join the Latins due to the corruptions they have introduced to the faith and practice of the Church.

St. Theophan the Recluse (+1894)
Feast Day: January 6

Overall, St. Theophan's reply is very short and does not make a case for why Latins are heretics or not, nor does he discuss his views on how Latins and other heretics should be received into the Church, as this question was not posed to him. He also states that the teaching of the Russian Synod on the topic is "significant," but he does not say the position is correct. In responding as he did, St. Theophan is choosing not to get involved in opposing the author of the article in question nor the teachings of the Synod, and is encouraging the person writing to also not get involved in the matter. Surprisingly, while this letter treats the topic only vaguely, some have upheld the letter as supposed proof that St. Theophan adopted a Latin Scholastic ecclesiology when St. Theophan has expressed himself more clearly on the topic of ecclesiology elsewhere.

Writing to an Orthodox layperson who was tempted to follow a Protestant minister, St. Theophan states:

> Learn then, and believe deeply that Divine Grace is offered and received in no other way than through the Divine Mysteries that are performed by the Apostles and their successors, as the Lord Himself ordained in the Church.[571]

St. Theophan also taught:

---

571 Theophan the Recluse, *Preaching Another Christ: An Orthodox View of Evangelicalism*, p. 36.

"If any man shall say to you, Lo, here is Christ; or, lo, He is there; believe him not (Mark 13:21)." Christ the Lord, our Savior, having established upon earth the Holy Church, is well pleased to abide in it as its Head, Enlivener, and Ruler. Christ is here, in our Orthodox Church, and He is not in any other church. Do not search for Him elsewhere, for you will not find Him. Therefore, if someone from a non-Orthodox assemblage comes to you and begins to suggest that they have Christ—do not believe it. If someone says to you, "We have an apostolic community, and we have Christ," do not believe them. The Church founded by the Apostles abides on the earth—it is the Orthodox Church, and Christ is in it. A community established only yesterday cannot be apostolic, and Christ is not in it. If you hear someone saying, "Christ is speaking in me," while he shuns the [Orthodox] Church, does not want to know its pastors, and is not sanctified by the Sacraments, do not believe him. Christ is not in him; rather another spirit is in him, one that appropriates the name of Christ in order to divert people from Christ the Lord and from His Holy Church. Neither believe anyone who suggests to you even some small thing alien to the [Orthodox] Church. Recognize all such people to be instruments of seducing spirits and lying preachers of falsehoods.[572]

It would be wrong to uphold St. Theophan's vague reply in one personal letter as supposedly being more representative of his beliefs on the topic of ecclesiology than his clearly stated words elsewhere that "Christ is here, in our Orthodox Church, and He is not in any other church."

---

572 Theophan the Recluse, "St. Theophan the Recluse Adopted an Ecumenistic Ecclesiology?"

St. Hilarion (Troitsky) (+1929)

The writings of St. Hilarion (Troitsky) on ecclesiology and the history of the reception of the heterodox by the Russian Orthodox Church have been referenced throughout this text, yet the post-17th century movement in Russia to return to a patristic ecclesiology cannot be spoken of without reference to St. Hilarion's significant role and influence. St. Hilarion obtained a Master's Degree from the Moscow Theological Academy in 1913 after having already obtained a Ph.D. in theology.[573] His extensive master's thesis is published in English under the title *On the Dogma of the Church: An Historical*

St. Hilarion (Troitsky)

Overview of the Sources of Ecclesiology. This text, which in English is approximately 600 pages with over 2,000 footnotes, includes a detailed examination of the teaching concerning the Church according to the New Testament and the saints and Fathers of the first four centuries after Christ, with particular attention given to the writings of St. Cyprian and St. Augustine.

St. Hilarion's text under the title "The Unity of the Church and the World Conference of Christian Communities" was written in 1917 in response to the fourth letter written by Robert H. Gardiner to Archbishop Anthony (Khrapovitsky) (Archbishop Anthony later became the first hierarch of the Russian Orthodox Church Outside of Russia).[574] Robert Gardiner was a lay Protestant

---

573 Troitsky, *On the Dogma of the Church*, pp. 11-12.
574 Troitsky, *The Unity of the Church and the World Conference of Christian Communities.*

Episcopalian who, along with Episcopalian Bishop Charles Henry Brent, founded the ecumenical Faith and Order Movement[575] which led to the establishment of the World Council of Churches in 1948. St. Hilarion was in full agreement with Archbishop Anthony (Khrapovitsky) regarding the boundaries of the Church and the absence of grace in sacraments performed outside of the Orthodox Church. In his extensive letter to Mr. Gardiner, St. Hilarion discusses the history of the reception of the heterodox into the Russian Church and clearly explained how the dogma concerning of the unity of the Church did not allow for a belief in the activity of the Holy Spirit in sacraments performed outside of the Orthodox Church. As St. Hilarion wrote to Mr. Gardiner:

> Membership in the Church is determined by the unity with the Church. It cannot be otherwise, if only because the Church is not a school of philosophy. She is a new mankind, a new grace-filled organism of love. She is the body of Christ. Christ Himself compared the unity of His disciples with the organic unity of a tree and its branches. Two "bodies" or two trees standing side by side cannot be organically related to each other. What the soul is to the body, the Holy Spirit is to the Church; the Church is not only one body but also One Spirit. The soul does not bring back to life a member which has been cut off, and likewise the vital sap of a tree does not flow into the detached branch. A separated member dies and rots away. A branch that has been cut off dries up. These similes must guide us in a discussion of the unity of the Church. If we apply these similes, these figures of a tree and a body, to the Church, any separation from the Church, any termination of the unity with the Church will turn out to be incompatible with membership in the Church. It is not the degree of the dogmatic dissent on the part of the separated member that is important; what is significant in the extreme is the fact of separation as such, the cessation itself of the unity with the Church. Be it a separation on the

---

575 Armentrout and Slocum, "Gardiner, Robert Hallowell." *An Episcopal Dictionary of the Church.*

basis of but a rebellion against the Church, a disciplinary insubordination without any dogmatic difference in opinion, separation from the Church will for the one that has fallen away have every sad consequence.[576]

Regarding St. Basil the Great's teaching contained in his first canon that was adopted by the Fifth-Sixth Ecumenical Council of Trullo, on those separated from the unity of the Church, St. Hilarion says:

> If the mysteries are valid outside the one Church of Christ, if the fullness of the ecclesiastical life in grace is not limited to the boundaries of the Church, then there exist several churches and not semi-churches, then the ninth article of our Creed should be dropped. There can be no semi-churches of any kind. I think Bishop Success expressed the perfect truth when he said at the Council of Carthage in 256: "*Haereticis aut nihil aut totum licet*" — heretics should be allowed either nothing or everything. If the Latin priests are as we are, if their laying on of hands is identical with that which we receive through the grace of God, if they bestow on their flock the same grace-filled gifts as we do, then why is Catholicism a different church from our Orthodox one? What reason can I have, I, a priest in the Church of Christ, for avoiding ecclesiastical communion with Latin bishops? Why do I not join them in celebrating the Divine Liturgy, why do I not partake with them of one Body of Christ? If the recognition of the beneficence of the Latin hierarchy and its religious rites does not contradict the truth of Church unity, then I must, bound by my conscience, enter into unity with the Latins at once, appealing to my brethren to do the same and censuring them in case of resistance on their part. I must moreover preach to the laity that they may receive the Eucharist also in a Polish or a French church. No, the truth of ecclesiastical unity does not recognize the grace of the mysteries administered within extra-ecclesiastical

---

576 Troitsky, *The Unity of the Church and the World Conference of Christian Communities*, op. cit.

communities. It is impossible to reconcile Church unity with the validity of extra-ecclesiastical sacraments.[577]

After examining in detail the teachings of Pope Stephen and St. Cyprian on the reception of heretics and schismatics into the Church, St. Hilarion acknowledges that Pope Stephen "is not very far from the thoughts of Cyprian," for while Pope Stephen taught that heretics and schismatics receive remission of sins through baptisms performed outside of the Church, he nevertheless taught that heretics and schismatics do not receive the Holy Spirit until they are received into the Church. Regarding the disagreement between Pope Stephen and St. Cyprian on the reception of heretics and schismatics into the Church, however, St. Hilarion says:

> Of the two points of view—Cyprian's and Stephen's—I dare say that one can be fully satisfied only with the viewpoint of St. Cyprian. Here the unity of the Church is preserved and a possible condescension and independence of words and formulae is given. Stephen preserves the unity of the Church only in the thought that heretics and schismatics do not have the Holy Spirit and therefore, upon their reception into the Church, it is indispensable to perform the laying-on of hands for the transmission of the gifts of the Holy Spirit. But this thought, which is expressed still more decisively in the *Liber de rebaptismate*, belittles and even makes poorly understood the meaning of baptism. In the *Liber de rebaptismate*, the grace-filled gifts of the Holy Spirit are considered the exclusive property of the Church, but baptism performed in the name of Jesus is common to the Church and to others. Such a baptism washed only the body and, outside the Church, remains without benefit on the Day of Judgment. But what sort of mystery is this? How can a mystery be performed without the grace of the Holy Spirit? If the grace giving baptism of the Holy Spirit is permitted

---

577 Ibid.

outside the Church, then it is completely impossible to preserve the unity of the Church.[578]

Regarding the consequences of the Great Schism of 1054 and its implications for the discussion of the legitimacy of the Anglican hierarchy, St. Hilarion states:

> Those among the Russian theologians who discuss the legitimacy of the Anglican hierarchy start out from that supposedly indisputable position that the former Latin bishops of England were true grace-filled bishops of the Church, and therefore, for a positive solution of the problem, it is sufficient simply to prove the continuity of succession in ordination. But, according to the canon of St. Basil the Great, from bishops of a community outside the Church, as were the Latin bishops before the English Reformation, it was impossible to receive grace, which had already run dry in Catholicism from the date of 1054.[579]

St. Hilarion said regarding the historical reception of the Latins into the Orthodox Church that from the Great Schism up to the 18ᵗʰ century, the common practice among the Greeks and Russians was to receive Latins by baptism. He said that if Latins have true and grace-filled baptism, one would have to conclude that all of the Greek and Russian saints and clergy for so many centuries who required the Latins to be received by baptism would be guilty of blasphemy and violation of Apostolic Canon 47. St. Hilarion also states that historical cases of receiving Latins by chrismation alone in no way suggests that the Latins have grace-filled baptisms:

> Does the reception of Latins without baptism mean that they are members of the same Church to which I belong? But then, how will I regard my Church, which now recognizes Latins as Her members, possessing Her gifts of grace, and then begins to baptize them [after the Great Schism], like pagans and Jews? If all Latins are to be baptized, why

---

578 Ibid.
579 Ibid.

can Arab Roman Catholics not be baptized?[580] What did St. Ermogen [Hermogenes], Patriarch of Moscow, who received a martyr's death from the Latins, do when he demanded the baptism of Prince Vladislav? Did he not, in spite of the tenth article of the Symbol of Faith, require a second baptism? If the rebaptism of Latins was a second baptism, then do not hundreds of Orthodox hierarchs deserve to be deposed, according to the 47th Apostolic Canon: "If a bishop or presbyter shall baptize again one rightly having baptism or shall not baptize one polluted by the ungodly, let him be deposed, as one mocking the Cross and death of the Lord and not distinguishing priests from pseudo-priests." No, I cannot dare to think that the local Churches, Greek and Russian, have throughout the course of centuries mocked and are mocking the Cross and death of the Lord. If sacraments outside the Church are valid and grace-bestowing, one can only accept them; then to change the practice of receiving converts, as did the Greeks and the Russians from the eleventh century to the eighteenth, means to blaspheme and to be subject to anathema. I cannot recognize my own Church as having blasphemed or blaspheming. For this reason one must seek explanation for Church practice in relation to the Latins only in the considerations of Church economy, and not in the dogmatical understanding of the unity of the Church of Christ. The Eastern Church, just as the ancient Church, has not gone astray or erred. For although at times for the sake of the profit of human souls, She has made a condescension by not requiring that a new rite of baptism be performed upon converting Latins, even though their rite differs from the Orthodox in its external aspect (sprinkling).[581]

---

580 St. Hilarion is here referencing the inconsistency of the Russian Orthodox Church in the reception of converts after the 1666-1667 Council.

581 From the full text by St. Hilarion, it is clear that he is not saying that the Latins who were previously "baptized" by sprinkling should be received by a manner other than baptism. Rather, St. Hilarion acknowledges in this text that the historic practice of the Russian Church was to receive all converts by baptism and to require the

She has nevertheless retained immutably Her dogmatical understanding of the unity of the Church. The decisions of the Church and authoritative Church writers demanded [at least] the chrismation of Latins. Receiving Latins without chrismation is only a local custom of the Russian Church which was introduced under the influence of the Trebnik of Peter Mogila and was even prompted by the theological spirit of Catholicism itself. Everything which is the sad result of the influence of Latin scholasticism in our theology cannot be, of course, more authoritative than the teaching of the ancient Church and the direct heir of Her grace-filled gifts — the Eastern Church.[582]

After explaining that the historic practice of the Russian Church prior to 1667 was to receive all heretics by baptism, and after demonstrating that sacramental grace can only be found in the Orthodox Church, St. Hilarion refers to the 79th Canon of the Council of Carthage in AD 419 (Canon 77 in the *Rudder*) as an exception to the requirement to receive all heterodox by baptism. Apostolic Canon 68 states that a person ordained in the Church must not be re-ordained, but those ordained by heretics should not serve as clergy in the Church without being ordained in the Church. St. Hilarion refers to Canon 79 (77) of Carthage which allowed the Donatists in Africa to be received in their orders despite Apostolic Canon 68, since the Donatists were schismatics and not heretics (they maintained the same external forms of baptism and ordination as the Orthodox and the same dogmas), the Donatists were present in large numbers in Africa, and there was a great need for Orthodox priests in Africa. With regard to the Anglicans and Canon 79 (77) of Carthage, St. Hilarion states:

---

baptism by three immersions of even those who had been "baptized" by sprinkling or pouring by Orthodox priests. He is saying here that when the Russian Church in the 17th century departed from the ancient practice of baptizing all converts, and even allowed Latins who were "baptized" by sprinkling to be received by a method other than baptism, that the Russian Church nevertheless understood that there were no true and grace-filled sacraments outside of the Orthodox Church.

582 Troitsky, *The Unity of the Church and the World Conference of Christian Communities*, op. cit.

Obviously, both councils[583] are of one mind in this: that there are no hierarchs outside the Church, even in schism, and that no ordination outside the Church has charismatic sacramental meaning. However, according to the considerations of Church economy, for the sake of the peace of the Church, schismatic clergy may be received in their rank with the expectation that, for union with the Church, the Lord grants them the grace of priesthood even without the repetition of the rite, which was already correctly performed although without grace. To understand the 79th canon of the Council of Carthage otherwise is, to all appearance, quite impossible.[584]

At the end of his letter to Mr. Gardiner, St. Hilarion references Canon 79 (77) of Carthage as a canonical precedent for reception of clergy in their orders, though clearly this canon does not apply to Anglicans because the Anglicans are heretics rather than schismatics,[585] and unlike the Donatists the Anglicans have not preserved the same external rites of baptism, chrismation, and ordination as the Orthodox.[586]

St. Hilarion was consecrated Bishop of Verey, a vicariate of the Moscow diocese, in 1920. While he was first imprisoned for three months by the Bolsheviks in 1919, in 1923 he was sentenced to three years in prison for his opposition to the schismatic renovationists

---

583 Council of Carthage in AD 419 and the "council beyond the sea" to which St. Hilarion refers.

584 Troitsky, *The Unity of the Church and the World Conference of Christian Communities*, op. cit.

585 This is much more obvious in the 21st century than it was in 1917 when St. Hilarion wrote these words, however historically the Anglicans have adopted the *Filioque* heresy (that the Holy Spirit proceeds from the Father *and the Son*) and have not accepted the theology of the Nine Ecumenical Councils.

586 Like St. Tikhon of Moscow, St. Hilarion was perhaps optimistic that the Anglicans might become increasingly Orthodox in their theology and *phronema* despite being outside of the Church and without the grace of priesthood and the holy sacraments, and that the reception of the Anglicans into the Church en masse could become a real possibility. Unfortunately, as time passed, the Anglicans increasingly distanced themselves from the teachings and practices of the Apostolic Church such that their mass reception into the Orthodox Church as St. Hilarion envisioned has become an impossibility.

and their "Living Church." From 1923 until his repose in 1929 he was transferred to various prisons and, due to the harsh conditions and diseases to which he was exposed in prison, he reposed at the mere age of 43.[587]

St. Hilarion was formally glorified by the Russian Orthodox Church as a Hieromartyr, yet the Church glorifies him not only for his martyrdom but for his God-inspired teachings, as a "new Chrysostom" and "most subtle theologian," particularly for his defense of the dogma concerning the unity of the Church and the boundaries of the Church. The Church in its hymnography on the feast of St. Hilarion expresses with one mind and one voice concerning him:

What shall we call thee, O holy master? Initiate of the profundity of the Church, most subtle theologian, lover of the majesty of the Church, zealot of the wisdom of the Fathers, preacher like unto Chrysostom, converser with the angels. The mind is at a loss what to call thee, for thou art the confirmation of the Church of Russia, the glory of the Russian land, the boast of the martyrs.[588]

O divinely-wise Hilarion, who didst enlighten thy mind with the grace of the Holy Spirit, thou didst refute the wicked ones who disputed with thee, and didst confirm the truth of Orthodoxy. Where is the wise man, where the scribe, where the disputer of this world? By thy discourse on the Cross thou hast put to shame the wisdom of the world![589]

Thou didst enlighten the eyes of thy heart, O blessed Hilarion; wherefore, thy theology had its source in thy piety, and thou wast shown to be a new Chrysostom, confirming the truth of Orthodoxy and guiding all the faithful to salvation.[590]

---

587 Snychev, "The Life of Hieromartyr Hilarion (Troitsky), Archbishop of Verey".
588 Aposticha Doxastikon in the Vespers service to St. Hilarion.
589 Third Stichera at "Lord I have cried..." in the Vespers service to St. Hilarion.
590 Seventh Stichera at "Lord I have cried..." in the Vespers service to St. Hilarion.

Thou wast shown to be a new apostle in the godless world, O divinely-wise Hilarion, didst preach Christ's self-abasement on the Cross, didst come to know the mystery of the Church, and didst make clear the mysteries of the final judgment.[591]

With thy divine wisdom, O holy Hilarion, fill my benighted and passion-fraught mind, that I may hymn thy manner of life, thy virtues and struggles, crying out with the faithful: Rejoice, our all-good advocate; rejoice, inspired theologian! Rejoice, thou who didst attain the depths of the mystery of the Church; rejoice, thou who didst declare that in the Church alone is the path of salvation! Rejoice, thou who didst put to shame the subtle machinations of thy wicked disputers; rejoice, thou who like lightning didst vanquish the rapacious heretics! Rejoice, mighty defender of the patriarchate; rejoice, faithful preserver of the legacy of the Fathers! Rejoice, true confessor of Christ; rejoice, victim slaughtered for the Church! Rejoice, O Hilarion, our glory and confirmation![592]

The Church's commemoration of St. Hilarion as a divinely inspired teacher of the Church's ecclesiology is certain from his Apolytikion:

O Hilarion, warrior of Christ, glory and boast of the Church of Russia, thou didst confess Christ before the perishing world, hast made the Church steadfast by thy blood, and having acquired divine understanding, hast proclaimed unto the faithful: Without the Church there is no salvation![593]

St. Seraphim (Sobolev) of Sofia (+1950)

St. Seraphim of Sofia in Bulgaria was a staunch defender of the Faith and an outspoken critic of Ecumenism. He was originally from

---

591	First Troparia of Ode 4 in the Orthros Canon to St. Hilarion.
592	Oikos in the Orthros service to St. Hilarion.
593	Apolytikion to St. Hilarion.

Ryazan in Russia and was consecrated a bishop in Russia before being transferred to Bulgaria.[594] Regarding whether it is possible for heretics to be part of the Church, St. Seraphim taught:

St. Seraphim of Sofia (+1950) Feast Day: February 13

> Our Church has never considered heretics to be part of it, of the Body of Christ itself. And how is it possible to consider this ecumenical point of view as Orthodox, when the Ecumenical Councils have always anathematized heretics, as excommunicated from the Church?...

> But most of all, Orthodox ecumenists sin against the ninth article of the Creed... when they include heretics in this Holy Church. The Church is called Holy because it is the dispenser of the grace of the Holy Spirit, which is communicated to believers in the sacrament of chrismation when they are baptized...

> And also at the Ecumenical Councils, the words of our Lord, spoken to the apostles and their successors, who are at the head of the Orthodox Church, the bishops, were realized: "Amen, I say to you: if you bind on earth, they will be bound in heaven, and if you loose on earth, they will be allowed in heaven" (Matt. 17:18). It is clear that these divisions reach to heaven itself...

> Then, the dogmatic resolutions of the Ecumenical Councils with an anathema against heretics were issued on the basis of the apostolic words: "it seemed good to the Holy Spirit, and to us" (Acts 15:28). Consequently, the rulings against heretics came not only from the Holy Fathers of the Ecumenical Councils, but also from the Holy Spirit Himself. Significant in this case are the words of Christ, spoken during His appearance to the disciples after the

---

594 Women's Monastery of the Protection of the Most-Holy Theotokos, "Archbishop Seraphim of Bulgaria."

resurrection: "Receive the Holy Spirit. If you forgive the sins of any, they are forgiven them; if you retain the sins of any, they are retained" (John 20: 22-23).

It is clear that the anathema of the Ecumenical Councils, which was based on the words of Christ, was imposed on heretics jointly: both from the Holy Spirit and from the Church. The question is, can these dogmatic divisions not even reach the Holy Spirit, as they came from Him?

But this is not all. From the words of Christ: "whatever you bind on earth will be bound in heaven," it is clear that the anathema against heretics, i.e. their excommunication from the Church, passes into the future life and that all heretics after death go to hellish torments...

It is difficult to say where the more Orthodox ecumenists depart from the Orthodox Church - whether in their writings, or by attending ecumenical conferences? This presence is in its essence a betrayal of our Orthodox dogmatic teaching about the Church, expressed in the ninth article of the Creed.[595]

St. Seraphim proceeds to quote the Apostolic Canons and the interpretation of canonist Bishop John of Smolensk, and quotes St. Cyprian of Carthage affirming that heretics will not come to the Church if we mislead them into thinking that they have genuine Mysteries:

But such joint prayer is forbidden by the holy canons of our Church. The 10th Apostolic Canon says.

"If anyone prays with someone who has been excommunicated from church fellowship, even if it is in the house, let him be excommunicated."

And in the 45th Apostolic Canon it says:

---

595 Seraphim of Sofia, *Orthodox Teaching About Grace* (In Russian).

"A bishop, or presbyter, or deacon, having prayed only with heretics, may he be excommunicated. If he allows them to act in any way, as if they were servants of the Church, let him be deposed."

In his interpretation of this last canon, Bishop John of Smolensk says: "The canons strive not only to protect the Orthodox from the infection of the heretical spirit, but also to protect them from indifference to the faith and the Orthodox Church, which can easily arise from communion with heretics in matters of faith. Such a situation, however, does not in the least contradict the spirit of Christian love and tolerance, which distinguishes the Orthodox Church, since there is a big difference - to endure those who have gone astray in the faith ... and live with them in external civil communion, or enter into religious contact with them indiscriminately, such that we no longer try to convert them to Orthodoxy."

Regarding the interpretation of the above canons by Bishop John of Smolensk, one must bear in mind the words of St. Cyprian, Bishop of Carthage, who says that heretics will never come to the Church if they are strengthened by us in the conviction that they also have a church and sacraments.[596]

While St. Seraphim expresses himself here according to sound patristic teaching regarding the problems of Ecumenism, elsewhere he adopts the ecclesiology of St. Augustine which contradicts the ecclesiology of the Ecumenical Councils:

We have seen that the baptismal regenerating grace in its various manifestations is inherent only in the Orthodox Church. Therefore, this grace, or something else, the Kingdom of God, is the most important essential feature that distinguishes Orthodox Christians from pagans and Jews, since they do not have this grace. Although the latter is

---

596 Ibid.

communicated in Catholicism, nevertheless, here too there is no Kingdom of God in the manifestations of the grace of the Holy Spirit, since this grace is not saving here, i.e. cannot be revealed in its manifestations, due to the heresies inherent in Catholicism. And this is understandable, because Apostle Paul said: "If we or an angel from heaven preaches any other gospel to you than what we have preached to you, let him be anathema (Gal 1:8)." In view of this, although according to apostolic succession, inner regenerating grace is communicated in Catholicism through the sacraments of baptism and chrismation, but, by virtue of the indicated words of St. Paul, it does not act there, and those who have received this grace are separated from it, or rather, from its saving action. This grace, although it remains in Catholicism, due to the fact that the Divine gifts are immutable, but it is no longer effective and not saving.

As for Protestantism, there is neither apostolic succession nor the sacrament of Chrismation. Consequently, there are no gifts of the Holy Spirit there, and along with this, there can be no manifestations of them at all. It is clear that in Protestantism there is no Kingdom of God or the active grace of the Holy Spirit, either in its essence or in its manifestations. Therefore, inner regenerating grace is the most important feature by which we, Orthodox Christians, differ from both Catholics and Protestants.[597]

St. Seraphim makes clear in his writings that there is only one Church, that man can only be inwardly regenerated through the Mysteries of the Orthodox Church, and that man can only become a saint and inherit eternal life in the Orthodox Church. St. Seraphim also understands the Apostolic Canons against prayer with heretics as applying equally to Latins, Protestants, and other contemporary heretics and agrees with St. Cyprian that there are no true mysteries outside of the Church. Yet, despite all of this, he

---

597 Seraphim of Sofia, *Distortion of Orthodox Truth in Russian Theological Thought*, pp. 254–256. Quoted in Ibid.

nevertheless expresses the Post-Schism Latin Scholastic teaching, based loosely on St. Augustine, that claims "apostolic succession" exists outside of the unity of the Church and such "succession" can transmit sacramental grace, even if that grace does not work in and through those who are separated from the unity of the Church. This teaching unfortunately contradicts Canon 1 of St. Basil which was ratified by the Ecumenical Councils and states that those who separate from the unity of the Church lose the Holy Spirit and become laymen, unable to bestow the Holy Spirit on others through baptism or ordination.[598] As can be seen here, even such a seemingly small influence of Latin Scholastic teaching can undermine the patristic teaching of the Ecumenical Councils concerning the charismatic boundaries of the Church and the reception of converts.

St. Luke the Surgeon, Archbishop of Simferopol and Crimea (+1961)

St. Luke, Archbishop of Simferopol and Crimea was tonsured into monasticism by Hieromartyr Andrew, Archbishop of Ufa, who blessed him to be consecrated to the episcopacy. St. Luke was consecrated as a bishop on May 31, 1923 by Bishop Daniel (Troiitsky) of Volkhov and Bishop Basil (Zummer) of Suzdal who were in exile in the town of Penjikent. Hieromartyr Tikhon, Patriarch of Moscow, was informed and approved of the legitimacy of St. Luke's consecration.[599]

In addition to insisting on the absolute necessity of baptizing in three full immersions,[600] St. Luke understood that deviations from this practice were the result of Latin influence from the days of the Unia. Furthermore, he considered that those who have been baptized by pouring or sprinkling (or in any form other than

---

598 See also Jude 1:19 and quotes from St. Irenaeus of Lyons and other saints and Fathers in Chapter 6.

599 Marushchak, op. cit., pp. 28-30.

600 See relevant section in Chapter 3 under Apostolic Canon 50.

three immersions) are not baptized and must be baptized in three immersions:

St. Luke (the Surgeon) Archbishop of Simferopol and Crimea (+1961) Feast Day: June 11 New Style & May 29 Church Calendar

In the western and southwestern regions of Russia, the forcibly introduced union with the Catholic Church led to the fact that baptism by pouring took root there; and in all other regions of Russia, all priests correctly baptize by immersion. Western baptism by pouring, unfortunately, has also penetrated into the Crimean region, and I must declare for the last time that I consider it a duty, bequeathed to me by God, to eradicate baptism by pouring in my diocese. According to the true proverb "the beginning of trouble is hard," some priests who do not have the fear of God, having become accustomed to baptizing by pouring, come to the point that even pouring is replaced by pouring water or even sprinkling only the head of the baptized person standing in their clothes. Those wickedly "baptized" in this way, of course, must be re-baptized, for the Sacrament has not been performed over them.[601]

St. Luke was outspoken about the many abuses that were taking place in his diocese in the performance of the Mystery of Baptism and insisted that it is better not to baptize a person than to receive a person into the Church without baptizing them in three full

---

601 Luke, Archbishop of Simferopol and Crimea, St. op. cit. Decree dated January 12, 1955.

immersions, saying, "one must resolutely insist on immersion and those who stubbornly refuse are to be left unbaptized."[602]

On Dec 10, 1959, St. Luke issued a decree to all priests in the Crimean diocese that they should cease from using the term "rebaptized" when referring to the baptism of those who were previously baptized incorrectly. He insisted that when those who are incorrectly baptized are afterwards baptized correctly (by three full immersions in the name of the Holy Trinity), the person is being baptized and not "rebaptized," since what was previously done was not a baptism.[603]

If St. Luke was so insistent that those baptized in the Orthodox Church by a method other than three full immersions in the name of the Holy Trinity are not baptized and are in need of being baptized in three full immersions, how much more so should the heterodox be received into the Church through triple immersion baptism who never received the apostolic form of baptism outside of the Church?

FR. GEORGE FLOROVSKY (+1979)

Fr. George Florovsky was one of the most influential Orthodox scholars and academic theologians of the 20th century. One of his best-known writings, made popular by those involved in the Ecumenical Movement, is his article on "The Limits of the Church." While Florovsky in this article encourages Orthodox to make use of St. Augustine's ecclesiology, he nevertheless acknowledges that St. Cyprian's ecclesiology was adopted by the Orthodox Church even if the logical implications of his ecclesiology for the reception of converts was not always followed with exactitude:

The historical influence of Cyprian was continuous and powerful. Strictly speaking, in its theological premises the

---

602 Ibid. Decree dated June 6, 1952. Of course, St. Luke was not opposed to deviating from the requirement to baptize by three immersions in cases of emergency where immersion is impossible, as cited in Chapter 3.

603 Ibid. Decree of December 10, 1959.

teaching of St Cyprian has never been disproved.... But the practical conclusions drawn by Cyprian have not been accepted and supported by the consciousness of the Church. One may ask how this was possible, if his premises have been neither disputed nor set aside.[604]

Florovsky does not offer a solution to the question of why the Church has allowed the use of economy in some cases while also accepting the ecclesiology of St. Cyprian, a dilemma which only arises when one does not understand and accept the principles of *oikonomia* and *akriveia* that are found in the canons of the Ecumenical Councils (i.e. Canon 46 and 47 of the Holy Apostles, Canon 1 and 47 of St. Basil). Instead of examining St. Cyprian's ecclesiology in the context of the consensus of the Fathers and the Ecumenical Councils, Florovsky identifies the dilemma posed by the use of economy and then shifts from St. Cyprian's ecclesiology to the ecclesiology of St. Augustine in search of a solution.

In his thorough review of Florovsky's article, Bishop Athanasius (Yevtich) of Zahumlje and Herzegovina states:

Florovsky presents the position of Saint Cyprian, then quickly passes over to the opinion of Saint Augustine and accepts his ecclesiological views without adequate critical thought. In particular, it seems he adopts the views on *ex opera operato* and *opera operantis*, and recommends that the Orthodox accept Augustine's opinion concerning the limits of the Church, where the charismatic and canonical boundaries do not coincide. On the other hand, the analysis of Saint Cyprian which Fr. Florovsky provides is one-sided. Fr. George Florovsky did not carefully examine, in parallel to the texts of Cyprian, his very important letter to Saint Firmilianus of Caesarea (230-268), the predecessor of Saint Basil, and also the letter to Saint Dionysius of Alexandria. These two Fathers, both contemporaries of Saint Cyprian, do not accept the opinion of Augustine and Pope Stephen of Rome. For without a doubt they speak about coinciding

---

604 Florovsky, *The Limits of the Church.*

charismatic and canonical limits of the Church even if they do not refer to them in this manner...

When Florovsky examines the works of Cyprian, and especially those of Metropolitan Anthony Khrapovitsky, (who as we said, considers the canonical and charismatic limits of the Church to be the same), sometimes we have the impression that he exaggerates. Likewise, it appears, when he talks about the practice of the Church in relation to the reception of heretics. For example, the then young theologian and priest George Florovsky observes, "One may ask who gave the Church this right..." to accept heretics in this manner, meaning here the application of ecclesiastical economy instead of the exactitude supported by Cyprian. In other words, the practice of the Church does not impose on all heretics to be re-baptized, as Saint Cyprian demanded. To such a question, we dare juxtapose the following counter-question: Who gave the right to Fr. Florovsky to put such questions to the Church? Or in other words, to direct this question to Basil the Great, the great hierarch, theologian and canonist of the Church, whose opinion on the application of economy in the acceptance of heretics is what the Church ultimately applies. This position of his concerning the use of economy does not indicate an acceptance of a "Church outside the limits of the Church" (a phrase belonging to Fr. Florovsky), because economy of the Church, the act of acceptance of heretics to the Church... was conveyed perfectly in the canonical letter of Basil the Great to Amphilochios of Iconium (Epistle no. 188). It is apparent that ecclesiastical economy has been taken into consideration in a much greater degree than Fr. Florovsky assumes. Florovsky concludes that the economy of the Church is simply a pedagogical – pastoral measure, related simply to the philanthropy of the Church.

As if philanthropy is something arbitrary, an unimportant detail![605]

Bishop Athanasius proceeds to discuss the patristic understanding of ecclesiology in the light of St. Basil, St. Firmilian, St. Dionysius of Alexandria, St. Athanasius the Great and other Fathers.

In other writings, Florovsky expresses himself more clearly regarding the boundaries of the Church. In his article, "The House of the Father," for instance, Florovsky writes:

> Indeed, not only mystically, but also historically, division in faith always appeared through schism and falling away, through separation from the Church... There is no and can be no "partial" Christianity — "can it be Christ was divided?" There is only One, Holy, Catholic, Apostolic Church — a single Father's House; and the believers, as St. Cyprian of Carthage said, "do not have any other home than the one Church."[606]

Here, Florovsky does not express the belief that there is "ecclesiality" or "partial Christianity" outside of the unity of the Church, and again emphasizes that the ecclesiology of the Church is that of St. Cyprian. While Florovsky's "Limits of the Church" article has been popular and influential, it sadly fails to express the ecclesiology of the Fathers and of the Ecumenical Councils, instead exchanging patristic ecclesiology for the teachings of St. Augustine that were promoted by the Latin Scholastics after the Great Schism.

Fr. Daniel Sysoev (+2009)

Fr. Daniel Sysoev upheld the ecclesiology of the Fathers and the Ecumenical Councils in many of his writings, and spoke of the necessity of baptism in three immersions, yet also affirmed the position of the Russian Synod on the reception of heretics which is at odds with these teachings. Regarding the ecclesiology of the

605 Yevtich, *Fr. George Florovsky on the Boundaries of the Church.*
606 Florovsky, *The House of the Father.*

Church and whether there is grace in the mysteries of heretics, Fr. Daniel states:

Fr. Daniel Sysoev
(+2009)

> Yes, I am certain that the Orthodox Church is the one path to God, and that he who has no part with her cannot be saved. Why? The New Testament gives the answer. Christ left behind not a Book, and not a set of doctrines, but the Church, the visible Church, with clear boundaries, defined by one faith, one baptism, joint communion of His Body and Blood (and not by symbols, as those of your [Protestant] confession believe), governed on earth by the successors of the apostles the bishops and presbyters.[607]

> Do the Protestants, who have distorted the teaching on salvation, who teach wrongly about baptism, the Eucharist, and the Church, and some of whom preach unconditional predetermination – do they rightly glorify God (that is, are they Orthodox)?

> No. Hence, according to Galatians they are heretics, and consequently are at risk of perishing eternally.[608]

> Dear N, If you remain with the Baptists, you will destroy your soul. Heretics do not inherit the kingdom of God (Gal 5:20-21). If you enter the Church, however, the Holy Spirit will teach you all things.[609]

> The question of schism has long ago been resolved by the Church. The very first canon of St. Basil the Great states that the streams of grace cease to flow for schismatics and their sacraments are devoid of the power of the Holy Spirit.

---

607 Sysoev, *Letters*, Letter 82, p. 90.

608 Ibid., Letter 89, p. 101.

609 Ibid., Letter 90, p. 103.

Hence, all who have received false sacraments in schismatic communities have received nothing.[610]

Fr. Daniel affirmed St. Basil's first canon that those who depart from the Church do not have the Holy Spirit and cannot bestow the Holy Spirit on others through baptism or ordination. Commenting on Canon 95 of the Fifth-Sixth Ecumenical Council that "all other heretics" not named in the canon should be baptized, Fr. Daniel states:

> According to the 7th canon of the 2nd Ecumenical Council and the 95th canon of the Council of Trullo, "... all other heretics, all of them who desire to be united to Orthodoxy, we receive as pagans. On the first day we make them Christians, on the second – catechumens, then on the third we exorcise them, with the threefold breathing into their faces and ears; and thus we catechize them, and oblige them to abide in the Church, and listen to the Scriptures, and only then do we baptize them. The same holds for the Manicheans, the Valentinians, the Marcionites, and like heretics."[611]

However, Fr. Daniel then presents how the Russian Church received various heterodox groups:

> Incidentally, here we might list those Christian heretics who must be received into the Church through holy baptism. These include all Protestants except the Lutherans, Reformed Protestants, Anglicans, and Old Catholics. This, firstly, is because Protestants reject the regenerative power of holy baptism. They are convinced that baptism is merely a rite of loyalty, and not a birth of water and the Spirit. This is why we cannot acknowledge their rite as a sacrament. Secondly, the Baptists, Pentecostals, and other sectarians (such as the Church of Christ – the so-called 'Boston movement') that baptize through single immersion, which is expressly forbidden by the 7th canon of the 2nd Ecumenical Council,

---

610 Ibid., Letter 92, p. 104.
611 Sysoev, *Catechetical Talks*, pp. 302-303.

while others (such as the Methodists) baptize through aspersion (sprinkling), so that frequently not a single drop of water falls on the person being "baptized."…

The baptisms of Old Believer doctrinarians also cannot be acknowledged, if there are no sure witnesses that the rite was properly performed. The fact is, there is a whole range of priestless Old Believer practices that radically distort the form of the sacrament.[612]

Fr. Daniel here is correct that the 95th canon of the Fifth-Sixth Ecumenical Council taught that "all the other heresies" not named by this canon are to be baptized, which shows reception of heretics by baptism is the rule, and deviations from this rule are by economy. He is also correct about St. Basil's first canon that those who depart from the unity of the Church cannot bestow the Holy Spirit on others. In the discussion of Apostolic Canon 50 previously in the book, Fr. Daniel is also quoted as stating that, "Baptism by triple immersion is expressly required by the Word of God," and he refers to the 1620 Moscow Council and 1755 Council of the Three Patriarchs to illustrate this position. However, when describing the reception of different heretical groups into the Church he says Lutherans, Reformed Protestants, Anglicans, and Old Catholics do not need to be received into the Church by baptism because they believe their baptism has regenerative power. St. Basil's first canon, which was adopted by the Fifth-Sixth Ecumenical Council and which Fr. Daniel previously affirmed, states that those who depart from the unity of the Church do not bestow the Holy Spirit on others through baptism and that there is no regenerative power in the mysteries of heretics. Why should the Church receive heretics based on what the heretics believe about their own baptisms rather than on what the Church believes regarding baptisms performed outside of the unity of the Church? This seems similar to the reasoning of Pope Stephen that the Orthodox should not baptize heretics because the heretics baptize the Orthodox. St. Cyprian

---

612 Ibid.

rightly criticized this reasoning of Pope Stephen, as the Church should not base what it does on what heretics do.[613]

Fr. Daniel illustrates another contradiction when stating that Baptists and other Protestants should be received by baptism since they do not practice baptism in the apostolic form (three immersions in the name of the Trinity) while not addressing the fact that the Lutherans, Reformed Protestants, Anglicans, and Old Catholics have similarly failed to preserve the apostolic form of baptism. It is also odd that the Old Catholics are classified along with the Anglicans, Lutherans, and Reformed Protestants as not needing to be received by baptism, while the Latins are not mentioned at all and the Old Believers are required to be baptized! Such contradictions are unavoidable when attempting to reconcile the ecclesiology of the Fathers and Ecumenical Councils with instructions on the reception of heterodox developed in the 17th century under the influence of Latin Scholasticism.

PATRISTIC ECCLESIOLOGY AND CENSORSHIP IN RUSSIA

Following the 1667 Moscow Council, opponents of the council's decisions were violently oppressed, a tremendous effort was made to prohibit independent publishing of spiritual and theological texts and approval from the Holy Synod was required for all such publications. Under Peter I, the Russian Synod was also required to seek State approval for the publication of texts. Peter I ordered the publication of Roman Catholic and Lutheran catechisms in Russian,[614] but if saints or elders after 1667 spoke against the new teachings adopted by the Russian Church at that council, such statements would not have been approved for publication.

> The very emergence of spiritual censorship was caused by the same reason as in the reign of the immediate predecessors of the first Russian tsar: by a Senate Decree it was forbidden to print church books without prior

---

613 Cyprian of Carthage, *Epistle LXXII to Pompey*. op. cit.
614 Barsov, *On Spiritual Censorship in Russia*, pp. 691-719 (In Russian).

censorship of the hierarchy. At the time of the issuance of the decree, the latter meant the Theological College, which was later transformed into the Synod. In fact, the document defining the powers of this new body of higher church administration also sanctioned censorship rules.

The text of the Spiritual Regulations unequivocally speaks of strict preliminary censorship: "If someone writes a theological letter about something, they should not print it, but first present it to the Collegium. And the Collegium should consider whether there is any error in his letter, contrary to the teaching of the Orthodox" (Spiritual Reg. Part 3, Position 3).

Throughout the 18th century, state power sought to provide the Orthodox Church with a kind of monopoly on the publication of the text of Holy Scripture, liturgical books and, in general, spiritual literature. This aspiration was carried out in two ways: a ban on the publication of spiritual literature without synodal sanction and a restriction on the import of theological literature from abroad (as an example, one can point to the 1743 ban on importing theological books into Russia without the permission of the Synod). These measures were especially intensified towards the end of Catherine's reign: for example, in April 1786, a personal decree appeared on the transfer to the spiritual authorities for approval of books "concerning the Orthodox faith."

The second measure went in parallel with the institutionalization of secular censorship: after the abolition in September 1796 of private printing houses in the two capitals, as well as the ports of Riga and Odessa, special censorships were introduced.[615]

---

615 Zadornov, *Church Censorship: Past and Prospects* (In Russian).

These special censorships were soon abolished and the Holy Synod of the Russian Orthodox Church took over all censorship responsibilities.[616]

Censorship can be justified on the grounds that it could help prevent the spread of heretical teachings. But, if State approval is needed for the Church to publish texts, if fifty years go by without any Orthodox books being published as a result,[617] and if publications are censored because they disagree with positions of the Holy Synod that are contrary to patristic teachings, such censorship becomes very problematic. This problem can be seen in the deliberation of the Holy Synod on Oct. 28, 1771 (Case No. 26) over whether to allow the publication of the writings of St. Cyprian of Carthage specifically because he taught that all heretics should be baptized.[618]

Since the Optina Hermitage labored to publish patristic books, the lives of the Optina Elders contain several references to challenges encountered with censorship. For example, the Holy Synod removed text from the writings of St. Symeon the New Theologian referring to his elder as a saint because they did not like that he spoke this way prior to the formal glorification of his elder. Also, the Holy Synod also decided against publishing the *Hymns* of St. Symeon the New Theologian and the Life of St. Gregory of Sinai.[619]

Regardless of official opposition in Russia to the apostolic teaching that heretics should be received by baptism, the affirmation that the Orthodox Church's ecclesiology is that of St. Cyprian has been met with less official opposition. For instance, St. Hilarion (Troitsky) (+1929) stated:

> Very often Church historians and patrologists express the thought, as it were, that the Bishop of Rome [St. Stephen] turned out to be right, and not St. Cyprian. I think that in history the exactitude[620] of St. Cyprian in respect to

---

616 Ibid.

617 Optina Pustyn, op. cit.

618 Case Holy Synod of 1771 October 28, No. 26. Quoted in Barsov, op. cit.

619 Kavelin, *Elder Macarius of Optina*, pp. 184-185.

620 "Exactitude" is used here as a better translation than "rigorism."

Church practice was only somewhat softened, but that his dogmatic teaching of the unity of the Church was not at all changed.[621]

Metropolitan Hilarion, formerly of Volokolamsk and now Metropolitan of Budapest and Hungary, the former head of the Department of External Church Relations for the Russian Orthodox Church, states quite emphatically:

> The Augustinian understanding of the "efficacy" of the sacraments was never fully accepted in the Orthodox Church. Such an understanding of the sacraments is unacceptable for Orthodox tradition, for it is an understanding in which the grace inherent within them is considered autonomous, independent of the Church. The sacraments can be performed only within the Church, and it is the Church that bestows efficacy, reality, and salvation on them.[622]

This same understanding is shared by the Greek Orthodox scholar Metropolitan Kallistos (Ware):

> The position of the Orthodox Church has been Cyprianic and non-Augustinian. The Cyprianic view was taken for granted by most Greek writers of the 18th century... and the Cyprianic view is still followed by the standard Greek manuals of theology in use today.[623]

While what is referred to as the "Augustinian" view here may be considered unfair to St. Augustine as it pertains mostly to his writings *Against the Donatists* as interpreted through the Latin Scholastics, what is significant is the affirmation that St. Cyprian's ecclesiology is the ecclesiology of the Orthodox Church.

The hesychastic and patristic renewal that has taken place in Russia and in the rest of the Orthodox world especially since the time of St. Paisius (Velichkovsky), St. Nikodemos the Hagiorite,

---

621 Troitsky, op. cit.

622 Metropolitan Hilarion, *Orthodox Christianity, Vol. II*, p. 405.

623 Ware, *Eustratios Argenti*, pp. 80-82.

and the Kollyvades Fathers has led to a return to the Fathers and Ecumenical Councils and an effort to remove the influences of Post-Schism Latin Scholasticism from theology. This return to the Fathers has led to a return to the ecclesiology of St. Cyprian that is the ecclesiology of the Ecumenical Councils, though a return to the ancient practice of baptizing all converts has not yet been restored.

When faced with heterodox Latin Scholastic teachings in the writings of Orthodox saints, again remembering the words of St. Barsanuphius is essential, that is, such errors can occur when holy people simply pass on what they have learned without seeking enlightenment from God. Also important to recall are the words of St. Photios when St. Augustine and other Fathers from the West were used to promote the *Filioque* teaching:

> Have there not been complicated conditions which have forced many Fathers in part to express themselves imprecisely, in part to speak with adaptation to circumstances under the attacks of enemies, and at times out of human ignorance to which they also were subject?... If some have spoken imprecisely, or for some reason not known to us, even deviated from the right path, but no question was put to them nor did anyone challenge them to learn the truth – we admit them to the list of Fathers, just as if they had not said it, because of their righteousness of life and distinguished virtue and their faith, faultless in other respects. We do not, however, follow their teaching in which they stray from the path of truth... We, though, who know that some of our Holy Fathers and teachers strayed from the faith of true dogmas, do not take as doctrine those areas in which they strayed, but we embrace the men.[624]

This patristic approach is how Orthodox Christians must embrace the holy saints of Russia and elsewhere who inadvertently adopted heterodox teachings from the Latin Scholastics. When saints in and beyond Russia, starting in the 17th century, express such views that are contrary to the consensus of the Fathers and

---

624 Rose, op. cit..

the Ecumenical Councils, we should humbly overlook these mistakes with understanding about the theological climate in which they lived, neither denouncing them as heretics nor considering their errors to represent the "best of Orthodoxy." While the study of Latin by some Orthodox was partially motivated by the desire to understand Latin teachings to better defend the Orthodox faith against incursion by the Latins, the study of heretical texts is fraught with danger and can result in lines being blurred between truth and falsehood. The words of St. Gregory Palamas on the dangers of studying philosophy are applicable here:

St. Gregory Palamas (+1359)
Feast Days: November 14 and
Second Sunday in Lent

> But is there anything useful in such knowledge for us? Most certainly there is! Even the substances which are extracted from serpents have much useful and therapeutic value for the physicians who use them as excellent antidotes. It is also customary in preparing certain poisons to add to them the sweetest of food substances that conceal the crafty concoction. There is, therefore, something useful in them, and perhaps even a great deal, such as honey in poison. But there is also a great fear perchance, when the useful substance is being extracted not to include by mistake some fatal remnants. And if one examines matters carefully one will see that all or most of the fearful heresies have received their start from here...[625]

---

625 St. Gregory Palamas, *The Triads*, p. 55.

If studying philosophy is fraught with such danger, how much more so is the study of heretical books! Having understood the errors of the Latin Scholastics, the departure of the Latin Scholastics from the teachings of the Fathers and the Ecumenical Councils, and how the suppression and loss of hesychasm led to vulnerability to heterodox influences, we must above all look to the hesychastic Fathers who have acquired the spiritual experience and phronema of the ancient Fathers for guidance regarding such matters as ecclesiology and the reception of converts.

OTHER SAINTS AFTER THE 17TH CENTURY WHO UPHELD THE PATRISTIC ECCLESIOLOGY

Additional saints and elders after the 17th century who have upheld the patristic ecclesiology of the Ecumenical Councils include Russians like St. John of Kronstadt and St. John the Wonderworker of San Francisco; Serbians such as St. Justin (Popovich); Romanians including Elder Cleopa; and many Greeks including St. Nektarios of Aegina, St. Porphyrios of Kafsokalyvia, and St. Paisios the Athonite.

St. Ambrose of Optina (+1891) taught that the Latins fell into heresy and innovation and do not at all belong to the Church.

> The Orthodox Eastern Church from the time of the Apostles and hitherto observes unchanged and intact from innovations both the teaching of the Gospel and the Apostles, as well as the tradition of the Holy Fathers and the decrees of the Ecumenical Councils... The Roman Church has long deviated into heresy and innovation... since it does not keep holy the Catholic and Apostolic decrees, but has strayed into innovations and wrong philosophies, it does not at all belong to the One, Holy and Apostolic Church.[626]

---

626 Ambrose of Optina, *Collected Letters of Blessed Memory of the Optina Elder Hieroschemamonk Ambrose to Lay Persons* (In Russian), pp. 231,232, 235.

St. John of Kronstadt (+1909) taught that only in the Orthodox Church can man attain spiritual regeneration and salvation:

> The Holy Church is the greatest, the most holy, most merciful, most wise, essential institution of God "which the Lord pitched and not man" (Heb 8:2) - not Luther, not Calvin, nor Mohammed, or Buddha, or Confucius, and suchlike sinful, passionate men. The Church is the divinely instituted union of men, united among themselves by faith, doctrine, the hierarchy, and the Mysteries...
>
> With the Protestants - the Germans and the English - the understanding of the Church is utterly distorted, for they have not the grace of lawful priesthood, no Mysteries other than Baptism and, the most important, communion of the Body and Blood of Christ[627] ... Glory to the Orthodox Church! Glory to Christ God - the most holy Head, the one Head of God's Church on earth! ...
>
> Only in the Church is this power of renewal contained; outside the Church it is not, and it cannot be...
>
> The Roman Catholics have devised a new head, having degraded the one true Head of the Church - Christ. The Lutherans have fallen away and remain without the Head, likewise the Anglicans - the Church is not to be found among them, their union with the Head has been severed, they do not have almighty help, but Belial battles with all his might and intrigues and holds everyone in his deception and destruction. Many are they that perish in godlessness and depravity.
>
> The Son of God has planted one Church on earth under His headship and under the guidance of the Holy Spirit, and in

---

627 From the entire chapter on St. John of Kronstadt's teachings concerning the Church that are cited in the following footnote, he is clearly stating simply those mysteries which the Protestants believe they possess. He is not stating that their mysteries are true or that the Holy Spirit works through their mysteries.

the Church He has given every means for the restoration of the severed union with God...

I am deeply grieved that this holy union [of those who believe in Christ] has been severed in the West and by the West, by infamous Roman Catholicism, and within it, by Lutheranism and the Reformation, and within us, by schisms and sects. The True Church remains and will be one, indivisible, and soul saving, namely, the Eastern Orthodox Church...[628]

St. Nektarios of Aegina (+1920) taught also that spiritual rebirth only occurs in the one Church and outside of the Orthodox Church there can be neither a visible nor invisible church.

Those that are not reborn by the divine grace in the only One, Holy, Catholic and Apostolic Church, they do not consist of (comprise) any church, neither visible nor invisible.[629]

St. John of San Francisco (+1966) said regarding the meaning of "anathema" which has been declared by the Ecumenical Councils against various heresies and heretics:

In the acts of the Councils and the further course of the New Testament Church of Christ, the word, 'anathema' came to mean complete separation from the Church... a complete tearing away from the Church.[630]

St. Justin (Popovich) (+1979) taught that there cannot be any Mysteries outside of the one Church:

The Church, the Body of the God-man Christ... she is the only source and the content of all divine Sacraments. Outside of this theanthropic and inclusive Mystery of the Church, the Pan Mystery itself, there are no and cannot be any

---

628 Sursky, *Saint John of Kronstadt*, pp. 244-263.

629 Grassos, *The Church Fathers on Love in Truth*, p. 21.

630 John Archbishop of Shanghai and San Francisco, *Sermons & Writings of Saint John*, Book 3, p. 44.

"mysteries"; therefore, there can be no inter-communion of Mysteries. Consequently, we can only speak about Mysteries within the context of this unique Pan-Mystery which is the Church. This is because the Orthodox Church, as the Body of Christ, is the source and the foundation of the Sacraments and not the other way around. The Mysteries, or Sacraments, cannot be elevated above the Church, or examined outside the Body of the Church. Because of this... the Orthodox Church does not recognize the existence of other mysteries or sacraments outside of itself, neither does it recognize them as mysteries, and one cannot receive the sacraments until one comes away from the heretical "churches," that is to say the pseudo-Churches, through repentance to the Orthodox Church of Christ. Until then one remains outside the Church... [and] a heretic and consequently outside of the saving communion.[631]

St. Porphyrios of Kafsokalyvia (+1991) taught that the Church is Christ, there is no life outside of the Church, and outside of the Orthodox Church are religions which are "human, hollow."

The three Persons of the Holy Trinity constitute the eternal Church. The angels and human beings existed in the thought and love of the Triune God from the beginning. We human beings were not born now, we existed before the ages in God's omniscience... The love of God created us in His image and likeness... [but] we made poor use of our freedom and lost our original beauty, our original righteousness and cut ourselves off from the Church. Outside the Church, far from the Holy Trinity, we lost Paradise, everything. But outside the Church there is no salvation, there is no life... When we live in the Church we live in Christ...The head of the Church is Christ and we humans, we Christians, are the body... The Church and Christ are one... Without Christ the Church does not exist. Christ is the Bridegroom; each individual soul is the Bride... In the Church which possesses

---

631 Popovich, *Orthodox Faith and Life in Christ*, pp. 173-176.

the saving sacraments there is no despair... We need to take care also to observe the formal aspects: to participate in the sacraments, especially the sacrament of Holy Communion. It is in these things that Orthodoxy is to be found. Christ offers Himself to the Church in the sacraments and above all in Holy Communion... Our religion is the religion of religions. It is from revelation, the authentic and true religion. The other religions are human, hollow.[632]

St. Paisios the Athonite (+1994) spiritually discerned that a Latin priest who was dressed as an Orthodox priest did not have the priesthood, testifying to the fact that priesthood does not exist outside of the Orthodox Church or among the Latins. St. Paisios said:

> Once a priest came to the skete. When I first saw him I was not "told" anything about him [by God]. As we talked, I realized that he was a Catholic. I told him sternly, "Put your biretta on first, and then go and visit monasteries."
>
> I found out later that he was a Catholic priest named Bonaventure, and wherever he went he dressed to fit in, to fool people: with Greek Orthodox clergy he dressed like a Greek Orthodox priest, with Russian Orthodox clergy, like a Russian Orthodox priest, and so on."
>
> [His disciple, Hieromonk Isaac comments:] The Elder saw before him a man with long hair, beard, and a cassock; but he wasn't fooled by appearances. Divine Grace gave witness within him that this apparent priest did not really have the priesthood. In the words of scripture, he "needed not that any should testify of man: for he knew what was in man."[633, 634]

St. Paisios also said:

---

632 Porphyrios, *Wounded by Love: The Life and the Wisdom of Saint Porphyrios*, pp. 87-94.
633 John 2:2
634 Hieromonk Isaac, *Saint Paisos of Mount Athos*, pp. 158-159.

The baptism that heretics perform only passes over their skin.[635]

Elder Cleopa of Sihastria in Romania (+1998), in reply to questions about whether the grace of the Holy Spirit is found among heretics, said:

> Question: Do all people such as idolaters, bad Christians, heretics, schismatics and Christians with mortal sins have the Grace of the Holy Spirit?
>
> Answer: ...Heretics and Schismatics do not have the Divine Grace because they sinned against the Holy Spirit and their malice of unbelief has been made evident being that it opposes the true faith of Christ...
>
> Question: What other Christian church possesses the grace of salvation except the Orthodox Church?
>
> Answer: The grace of salvation can only be received in the Orthodox Church because this is an energy of Christ which remains always the same in the Church yesterday today and forever...
>
> Question: Do the Protestant Anglican and neo-protestant confessions which do not have apostolic hierarchy maintain some grace of the Holy Spirit?
>
> Answer: Salvation in the Protestant formats of faith is terribly impossible being that it lacks the union in Christ through the True Faith in Him... it lacks the Divine Mysteries through which Christ Himself works out His salvation in the hearts of men. Therefore, the faithful do not have the ability to reach holiness or the communion in Christ among them. The man of Protestantism knows something about Christ but with words only and even these lack the fullness of the Apostolic knowledge and the sanctifying energy of Christ...[636]

---

635 Aslanidis, *Apostle to Zaire*, p. 22.
636 Grassos, *The Church Fathers on Love in Truth*, pp. 28-29.

Summary

Among the Greek saints and elders after the 17th century, the patristic ecclesiology of the Ecumenical Councils often finds clearer expression compared to the writings of Russian saints of the same time due to the influence of the 1755 Encyclical of the Three Patriarchs, the *Rudder* of St. Nikodemos the Hagiorite, and the Kollyvades Fathers among the Greeks. However, the Greeks of this period express the same teaching as the Russian Orthodox Church prior to the 1666-1667 Moscow Council and the Russian St. Paisius (Velichkovsky). The efforts in Russia since the 19th century to remove the influence of heterodox Latin Scholastic teachings is evident in the ecclesiology of many Russian saints of this period, though sometimes saints of this period expressed themselves in an unclear or seemingly contradictory manner regarding ecclesiology and the reception of the heterodox likely due to the lasting influence of Latin Scholastic teaching in the theological institutions and in the official policies adopted by the Holy Synod in Russia starting in 1667. Efforts to return to the pre-1667 understanding of Orthodox ecclesiology and the reception of converts in Russia have unfortunately been hindered by misinformation about the tradition of the reception of the heterodox in Russia prior to 1667, and by the official efforts to censor the publication of teachings that are contrary to the position of the Holy Synod.

Synaxis of the Kollyvades Fathers
Feast Day: Saturday of Bright Week

RIGHT EOUS JOSEPH THE HESYCHAST

St. Joseph the Hesychast (+1959)
Feast Day: August 16

CHAPTER 17

Hesychasm and the Reception of Converts

An Orthodox understanding of theology and ecclesiology must be connected with the hesychastic and therapeutic method of the Church—man's healing through purification, illumination, and theosis. A theology and ecclesiology separated from the therapeutic and salvific purpose of the Faith becomes speculative, academic, and useless. As Metropolitan Hierotheos of Nafpaktos explains,

> Any theology that is just a matter of fine words, which contents itself with elegant phrases and clever speculations and operates outside the context of the hesychastic tradition, is really a secularized theology. This sort of secularized theology, which goes no further than conjectural, emotional and even academic analyses, does not lead people to existential freedom or personal knowledge of God. In spite of the respect that worldly people might have for this kind of worldly theology, it is, nevertheless, a wound in the life of the Church.[637]

St. Nikodemos of the Holy Mountain, as has been said, was not simply an educated man and the producer of influential theological works. Even Ecumenists who see in his ecclesiology and commentary on the Holy Canons a chief obstacle to their goals of

---

637 Vlachos, *Hesychia and Theology,* p. 402.

forging a union with the heterodox without dogmatic agreement, nevertheless are obliged to admit that "the Orthodox world owes an immense debt to this Athonite monk, who edited and published *The Philokalia* (1783), as well as numerous other works of a patristic, pastoral, and liturgical nature."[638] While academics may see and value only his literary accomplishments, which were indeed vast, more important than his tremendous publication work was his embodiment of the teachings of the Fathers, his acquisition of noetic prayer, and his transmission of the living tradition of genuine eldership. St. Nikodemos became a temple of the Holy Spirit, was gifted in healing the passions of those who came to him and became a guide capable of leading others to dispassion* and theosis.

While the tradition of noetic prayer leading to the purification of the heart and theosis is foundational to Orthodox tradition, as St. Gregory Palamas demonstrated, at various times the practice of noetic prayer and genuine eldership became a rarity. Where noetic prayer was neglected, the Church became vulnerable to the influx of heterodox ideas and the dogmatization of external ritual forms. This played out most clearly in the tragic conflict and schism that occurred in the Russian Orthodox Church in the 17th century over liturgical rites, and the influx at the same time of Latin Scholastic teachings. As Metropolitan Kallistos (Ware) said, had both sides of the controversy over liturgical rubrics "attended more to mystical prayer, they might have argued less bitterly about ritual."[639]

The teachings of St. Nikodemos in *The Rudder* on the reception of heretics into the Church, while criticized by some out of ignorance, are nevertheless fully embraced by the clairvoyant saints and elders who were and are his spiritual brothers and successors. *The Rudder* was reviewed and authorized by St. Makarios of Corinth and St. Athanasios Parios before being approved and authorized by the Holy Synod of the Ecumenical Patriarchate,[640] and the Ecumenical Patriarch endorsed its distribution throughout the Orthodox world.

---

638 Baptism and "Sacramental Economy": An Agreed Statement of the North American Orthodox-Catholic Theological Consultation.

639 Ware, *The Orthodox Church*, p. 113.

640 *The Great Synaxaristes of the Orthodox Church, July*, p. 630.

The Russian St. Paisius (Velichkovsky), who had studied theology in Kiev before coming to the Holy Mountain, in his correspondence with Fr. Dorotheos Voulismas and the Kollyvades Fathers expressed full agreement with St. Nikodemos' teaching that all heretics should be received into the Church by baptism in three full immersions.[641, 642] The hesychastic saints and elders who came after St. Nikodemos followed his teachings on the reception of heretics into the Church, not merely because of his authority as a defender and exemplar of hesychastic Athonite monasticism; but being filled with the Holy Spirit and with spiritual discernment, they understood experientially the need for converts to be received by baptism. St. Nikodemos understood and interpreted the writings of the Fathers correctly because he shared the same experience of illumination and theosis as the Fathers of the Ecumenical Councils. The saints and elders who are the spiritual successors of St. Nikodemos and St. Paisius (Velichkovsky), who were filled with the same Spirit, understood that St. Nikodemos and St. Paisius wrote under the inspiration of the Holy Spirit.

While on Mt. Athos a period of decline was observed in the early part of the 20th century, a profound renewal took place through spiritual successors of St. Nikodemos the Hagiorite, particularly through St. Joseph the Hesychast and his disciples. Other clairvoyant elders also helped contribute to this hesychastic and patristic renewal including Elder Aimilianos of Simonopetra and St. Paisios the Athonite. These elders all agreed with St. Paisius (Velichkovsky) and St. Nikodemos the Hagiorite that all heterodox should be received into the Orthodox Church by baptism in three immersions.

---

641 Οι Κολλυβάδες και ο Δωρόθεος Βουλησμάς. Το ζήτημα της "ανακρίσεως" του Πηδαλίου και του Κανονικού (Ιερά Μονή Παναγίας Χρυσοποδαριτίσσης Νεζερών). In Greek. *The Kollyvades and Dorotheos Voulismas. The Case of the Examination of the Pedalion and the Canonikon (Holy Monastery of Panagia Chrysopodaritissa of Nezeron).* An English translation of this text will be published in the future by Uncut Mountain Press.

642 See also Heers, "St. Nikodemos, the Rudder and the Reception of Converts into the Orthodox Church: A Look at the Correspondence Between the Kollyvades Fathers & Dorotheos Voulismas."

St. Joseph the Hesychast (+1959) and His Disciples, including Geronda Ephraim of Arizona (+2019)

St. Joseph the Hesychast and the choir of holy elders and saints who succeeded him, including St. Ephraim of Katounakia and the "Apostle to America" Geronda* Ephraim of Arizona, upheld the teachings of St. Nikodemos and of the Ecumenical Councils that the heterodox should be received by baptism. Metropolitan Neophytos of Morphou—who was personally acquainted with many contemporary saints including St. Porphyrios, St. Paisios, St. Evmenios, St. Iakovos of Evia, and others—related a vision received by a holy elder he knew following the repose of Geronda Ephraim of Arizona. In this vision, Geronda Ephraim was given three crowns in Paradise. The Elder first received the crown of "saint" due to his inner purity, inner virginity, and zeal for noetic prayer; next the crown of "martyr" due to the persecution he endured during his labors on Mt. Athos and in America; and then the crown of "equal-to-the-Apostles" for his apostolic labors in America which brought authentic patristic Orthodoxy and traditional monasticism to a land where the Orthodox had become very secularized and far from the patristic understanding and practice of the Faith.[643]

As has been stated, St. Barsanuphius explained how saints can fall into error when they merely follow what they have been taught and do not seek enlightenment from God in prayer about a subject. On Mt. Athos, it was taken for granted that all converts should be received by baptism, but when Geronda Ephraim came to America he found great opposition to this practice. Turning to God in prayer, God enlightened him not only to uphold the teaching that all converts should be received by baptism despite opposition from priests and bishops who had been influenced by Latin Scholastic teachings, but he also received the gift to see in the Spirit whether or not a person had been baptized in the Orthodox Church, and

---

643 Neophytos of Morphou, "The 3 crowns of Elder Ephraim and how the U.S. will lose its superpower status."

whether their baptism was performed with three full immersions as the Apostolic Canons require.[644]

That God might grant the gift of spiritually discerning whether a person has been baptized should come as no great surprise for those who are familiar with the lives of the saints. John Moschos relates a similar story concerning Abba Sergios in the early 7th century:

St. Joseph the Hesychast

> When Abba Sergios was an anchorite at Rouba, after he had withdrawn from Sinai, he sent a young monk from there to the monastery to be baptized. When we asked why he had not been baptized, the attendant of Abba Sergios said: "When this man came wanting to stay with us in the wilderness, I, as attendant, received him and greatly exhorted him not to commit himself to this way of life without a period of probation. Having perceived his determination, the next day I took him to the elder. As soon as the elder saw him, before I had said a word, he said to me privately; 'What does the brother want?' I said: 'He is asking to become one of us.' Then the elder said to me: 'Believe me, brother, he has not been baptized: But take him to the Monastery of the Eunuchs and they will have him baptized in the holy Jordan.' In my amazement at what was said, I asked the brother who he was and where he was from. He said he was from the west and that his parents

---

644 This has been confirmed to the authors from multiple testimonies including monastic fathers who were Geronda Ephraim's close disciples as well as laypeople who confessed to Geronda Ephraim and witnessed this gift.

were pagans. He did not know whether he was baptized or not. We therefore catechized him and had him baptized in the holy Jordan."[645]

St. Iakovos of Evia (+1991)
and Reception of Heretics into the Church

In the life of St. Iakovos of Evia, we have the following story of a Latin who came to St. Iakovos asking to be received into the Church:

> The entire wondrous life of Elder Iakovos, with his spiritual and bodily struggles, was based on his Orthodox faith. Particular events and practices of the wise and discerning Elder confirm the precise observance of the dogmatic teaching of the Church. The Elder taught in practice. Let's refer to one of the many such examples.
>
> When an adherent of Catholicism expressed a desire to become Orthodox, he told him, "What prevents you to be baptized."[646] Out of respect to the ecclesiastical hierarchy he counseled us to go to the bishop of the area and to announce the man's decision. "You will go to the bishop who, immediately upon hearing of your decision, will rise from his throne and embrace you, my child, out of joy that you want to become Orthodox." In saying this, he was actually describing his own spiritual state and desire.
>
> To our great surprise we were not able to even see the face of the Bishop! Through his Deacon he communicated to us that, according to a decision of the Holy Synod [of the Church of Greece], the baptism of Latins is valid and does not need to be repeated. He simply needs to sign a written confession and the Mystery of Chrismation is performed.

---

645 Moschos, *The Spiritual Meadow*, p. 113.
646 Acts 8:36

When we informed the Elder of this, he said: "I don't know what the Holy Synod decided. I know what the Gospel says: He that believeth and is baptized shall be saved."[647] He said this and went and brought a large baptismal font, appropriate for adults, from nearby Limni, Euboea. In the chapel of St. Haralambos, which was the cell of Saint David of Euboea, the Holy Elder performed the Mystery of Baptism with great splendor, and also the Mystery of

St. Iakovos of Evia (+1991)
Feast Day: November 22

Chrismation according to the Orthodox typikon, with help of the Archimandrite Father Paul Ioannou, his spiritual child, who later became the Metropolitan of Siatista. I, who write these words, was the godfather (sponsor).[648]

St. Iakovos out of great reverence for the episcopacy, sent the Latin to get the blessing of the bishop to be received, yet in his discernment he knew the difference between true and false obedience, and when obedience to a hierarch conflicted with obedience to Christ, he knew he had to obey Christ rather than the hierarch. St. Iakovos discerned and understood that it was the will of God that all converts be received by baptism.

---

647 Mark 16:16
648 Baldimtsis, pp. 66-67.

St. Paisios the Athonite (+1994), Fr. Cosmas the "Apostle to Zaire" (+1989), and "Corrective Baptism"

Fr. Cosmas of Grigoriou (+1989) was a Hieromonk from Mt. Athos who departed from Mt. Athos with the blessing of St. Paisios the Athonite as a missionary to Africa where he brought countless people into the Orthodox faith. Fr. Cosmas wrote that St. Paisios had told him that "the baptism that the heretics perform only passes over their skin."[649] Fr. Cosmas said of their practice of receiving converts in Africa:

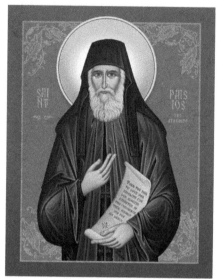

St. Paisios of Athos

When baptizing I implement the Athonite order of things. We've done 250 baptisms, and, not only with idol worshippers, but also with Catholics who become Orthodox, we baptize them in deep rivers. My actions will have consequences when news reaches the Patriarchate of Alexandria, which holds that the Protestants are only in need of chrism. Until then, however, we will only do Baptisms so as to have St. Nicodemos' blessing.[650]

Another priest who was disciplined by his bishop for baptizing those who were already received into the Orthodox Church by chrismation, asked a monk whom he knew to seek guidance on this issue from St. Paisios on Mt. Athos. When the monk went to see St. Paisios, before he had a chance to raise the question, the saint said:

---

649 Aslanidis, op. cit., p. 22.
650 Ibid., p. 129

> I know Father X is in trouble with his Bishop Y. Tell Father X to continue to do what he is doing, but to be very discreet.[651]

At the time of ordination, priests vow to uphold the canons and teachings of the Orthodox Church and do not need a special blessing from their bishop to fulfill their priestly vows. Bishops likewise vow to uphold the canons and teachings of the Orthodox Church and are not above the canons, which, as demonstrated previously, declare that the heterodox need to be baptized in the Orthodox Church especially if the canonical presuppositions for the application of economy are not met.

ELDER AIMILIANOS OF SIMONOPETRA (+2019) AND THE UNIATE ABBOT PLACIDE (DESEILLE)

One of the most remarkable conversion stories of the 20th century is that of Fr. Placide (Deseille). Fr. Placide was an Eastern Rite (Uniate) abbot, priestmonk, and well-known French patristic scholar under the Pope of Rome. As a patristic scholar, there is no surprise that Fr. Placide felt drawn to the Orthodox Church and eventually decided that he must not only admire Orthodoxy from afar but must enter the Orthodox Church. When he sought the guidance of Elder Aimilianos on Mt. Athos, Fr. Placide relates:

Elder Aimilianos of Simonopetra (+2019)

---

651 Anonymous, "Reception of Heretic Laity and Clergy into the Orthodox Church."

[Elder Aimilianos]… had not concealed from us that, in his eyes, the customary and most appropriate form of entry into the Orthodox Church was through baptism. I had never thought about this aspect of Orthodox ecclesiology and, at the time, was quite surprised by it. I made a careful study of the problem, beginning with the canonical and patristic sources. I also found several articles, written by Catholic and Orthodox theologians and canonists, to be quite helpful. After a thorough examination of the question, and with the full agreement of our new abbot, it was decided that, when the time came, we would be received into the Orthodox Church by baptism.[652]

Fr. Placide then gives a historical overview of the relevant issues, including the following:

In the East… thanks especially to the influence of Saint Basil, the ecclesiology and sacramental theology of Saint Cyprian never ceased to be considered as more in conformity with the tradition and spirit of the Church than the doctrine of Saint Augustine. Baptism remained the absolute norm, *akriveia* [lit., exactness]…

The principal canonical basis for the non-recognition of heterodox sacraments is the 46th Apostolic Canon which declares: "We ordain that a bishop, priest, or deacon who has admitted the baptism or sacrifice of heretics be deposed." These Apostolic Canons, confirmed by the 6th Ecumenical Council[653] (in Trullo) in 692, comprise the foundations of Orthodox canon law. The practice of economy in certain cases is authorized by Canon I of Saint Basil the Great.

At a later time, in the seventeenth century, the Russian Orthodox Church came under a very strong Latin influence, and was partially won over to the position of Saint Augustine.

---

652 Golitzin, *The Living Witness of the Holy Mountain*, pp. 63-93.
653 Referred in this text to the Fifth-Sixth Ecumenical Council.

She then decided to receive Catholics into Orthodoxy by confession and a profession of faith alone...

So far as present practice is concerned, the reception of Catholics by baptism is very clearly prescribe in the *Pedalion* [or *The Rudder*], an official compendium of canon law for the Churches of the Greek language, in which the text of the canons is accompanied by commentaries by Saint Nicodemus of the Holy Mountain, a very great authority. For the territories under the jurisdiction of the Patriarchate of Constantinople, the decree prescribing the rebaptism of Catholics has never been abolished. As for the Church of Greece: "Those who wish to embrace Orthodoxy must be invited to rebaptism, and only in those cases where this is not possible should they be received by anointing with Holy Chrism."[654]

Here, this former Uniate and renowned patristic scholar expresses agreement with what has been stated already in this book, particularly that the Apostolic Canons regarding heretics are still applicable to heresies of our times, that the Orthodox Church follows the ecclesiology of St. Cyprian and not that of St. Augustine, that reception of heretics by baptism is the rule, and that reception of heretics historically by methods other than baptism was the result of the influence of Latin Scholastic theology in 17th century Russia.

SUMMARY

These teachings of the contemporary successors of St. Nikodemos the Hagiorite and St. Paisius (Velichkovsky) show the importance of Orthodoxy as a living tradition passed down from Christ and the Apostles through the saints and holy elders. We should not merely go to books so that we may understand Orthodoxy, but to those holy people who have received and embodied the living

---

654 Ibid.

tradition of the Church and are able to lead their disciples to purification and theosis. As Fr. Seraphim (Rose) stated:

> In our confused days, when a hundred conflicting voices claim to speak for Orthodoxy, it is essential to know whom one can trust as a spokesman for true Orthodoxy. It is not enough to claim to speak for Patristic Orthodoxy; one must be in the genuine tradition of the Holy Fathers, not merely "rediscovering" them in a modern academy or seminary, but actually receiving their tradition from one's own fathers. A merely clever explainer of Patristic doctrine is not in this tradition, but only one who, not trusting his own judgment or that of his peers, is constantly asking of his own fathers what is the proper approach to and understanding of the Holy Fathers.[655]

Orthodoxy is not merely a subject to study through books to arrive at correct beliefs and knowledge about the Faith. Rather, Orthodoxy is a school of noetic prayer leading to theosis, a living tradition whereby we learn from the saints how to overcome the passions, acquire the Holy Spirit, and attain theosis. We must not primarily go to books for answers to our questions about the Faith, but to those living among us who are themselves saints, or are the faithful disciples of saints, whose lives show the fruit of the Holy Spirit, and who live the Faith. As St. Silouan the Athonite famously stated, even if all of the writings of the Holy Fathers were lost the Athonite monks would be able to reproduce the patristic writings from their experience.[656] The understanding of the patristic writings and their proper interpretation and application is given by the Holy Spirit to those who have become vessels of the Holy Spirit.

Some would like to view the saints of today as if they are opposed to the Holy Fathers of yesterday. When the saints of today do not teach what is the "popular consensus" among the professors, priests, and bishops of our day, they are often dismissed as "fringe" and irrelevant. The saints of today are connected to the Holy Fathers

---

655 Damascene, *Father Seraphim Rose: His Life and Works*, p. 482.
656 Sakharov, *St. Silouan the Athonite*, p. 72.

of the Ecumenical Councils and to the Holy Apostles, however, not simply because they share the same dogmatic faith, but because they also have the same way of life as the Holy Fathers and the same experience of the Holy Spirit that inspired the Councils. If we set aside the teachings of the charismatic holy saints and elders of our time, we deceive ourselves if we think we are following the saints and Fathers of the Ecumenical Councils, to whom they are spiritually linked. Again, as St. Symeon the New Theologian said:

> A man who does not express a desire to link himself to the latest of the saints (in time) in all love and humility owing to a certain distrust in himself, will never be linked to the preceding saints and will not be admitted to their succession, even though he thinks he possesses all possible faith and love for God and for all His saints. He will be cast out of their midst, as one who refused to take humbly the place allotted to him by God before all time, and to link himself to that latest saint (in time) as God had disposed.[657]

---

657 Kadloubowsky, op. cit., p. 135.

Fathers of the First Ecumenical Council in Nicea, AD 325

CHAPTER 18

The Misuse of Economy Leads to a Heretical Ecclesiology

In the Nicene Creed, the Orthodox Church confesses belief in "One, Holy, Catholic and Apostolic Church" and "one baptism for the remission of sins." There is "one Lord, one faith, one baptism,"[658] the Lord Jesus Christ has "one body"[659] united by a common faith,[660] and the Holy Spirit works only through the Mysteries of the "one body" of the Orthodox Church for the purification, illumination, and salvation (theosis) of man. For those received into the Church by economy, that they would be confused when confessing "one baptism for the remission of sins" in the Creed is understandable, since the only baptismal rite they have had was a heretical rite — and this rite in most cases was not done with three immersions in the name of the Holy Trinity. If there is only one baptism for the remission of sins, and a convert's only baptism was in heresy, doesn't this imply that remission of sins and the grace of the Holy Spirit was given through the heretical baptism? The confusion on this matter demonstrated by some critics is also shared by many of the faithful and even clergy.

Aside from the ecclesiological confusion that results in the minds of converts who aren't received by baptism, there are

---

658 Eph. 4:5-6
659 1 Cor 12:12
660 Eph. 4:5-6

unfortunately some who use the fact that some heretics have been received into the Church by methods other than baptism to imply that the charismatic boundaries of the Church are more broad than the canonical boundaries of the Orthodox Church. The "Roman" view, as taught by St. Augustine, said that the rite of baptism among heretics in the name of the Holy Trinity has grace, though heretics do not receive this grace unto remission of sins until they are united with the one Church. Nevertheless, this view implies that baptisms performed by heretics have a sacred character and are not merely "empty forms" or "a pollution" as other Fathers taught. The Latin terminology of "valid" baptism referring to the baptism of heretics gradually became understood in the West after the Great Schism as indicating "valid" as in a true Mystery that grants remission of sins. Commenting on the development of the heterodox Latin Scholastic ecclesiology in the West from Aquinas to the Second Vatican Council, Fr. Peter Heers states:

> As with Augustine, whose "new theology" of the Church was intended as a guarded development of the patristic consensus expressed before him, but who nevertheless laid the first foundation stone for much greater innovations, Aquinas can also be said to have laid the groundwork for later theological development...
>
> Aquinas writes that anyone who receives the sacraments from one excommunicated or defrocked "does not receive the reality of the sacrament, unless ignorance excuses him."[661] Thus, for Aquinas, the obstacle to efficaciousness and the reality of grace in the mystery is not necessarily the lack of unity, as Augustine would have it, but knowingly participating in the sin of disobedience and rebellion. "The power of conferring sacraments" remains with the schismatic or heretical cleric, such that one ignorantly receiving Baptism from him has not only received a true sacrament, but has also received the spiritual reality of

---

661 Aquinas. Op. cit., Part 3, Question 64, Article 9.

Baptism, which includes initiation and incorporation into Christ...

Thomas Aquinas
(+1274)

It is precisely on this point of efficaciousness by way of ignorance and in seeing "character" as the sign of ecclesiastical membership that the fashioners of the new [Vatican II] ecclesiology will form their new view of schism, heresy, and the Church. Aquinas provided, as it were, the building blocks with which to shape the new vision of the Church. The most important of these is that which would have every valid sacrament producing spiritual effects for all but those who knowingly commune with schism and heresy.[662]

St. Cyprian was rightly concerned that if the Church taught that heretics have a "valid" baptism, then heretics would conclude that they must also be part of the Church and have the rest of the Mysteries as well. As quoted previously, St. Cyprian said:

> For if [the heretics] shall see that it is determined and decreed by our judgment and sentence, that the baptism wherewith they are there baptized is considered just and legitimate, they will think that they are justly and legitimately in possession of the Church also, and the other gifts of the Church; nor will there be any reason for their coming to us, when, as they have baptism, they seem also to have the rest. But further, when they know that there is no baptism without, and that no remission of sins can be given outside the Church, they more eagerly and readily hasten to us, and implore the gifts and benefits of the Church our Mother, assured that they can in no wise attain to the true promise of divine grace unless they first come to the truth of the Church.[663]

---

662 Heers, *The Ecclesiological Renovation of Vatican II*. pp. 77-79.
663 Cyprian of Carthage, *Epistle LXXII* to Jubaianus, op. cit.

The claim that the Holy Spirit is present in the mysteries of heretics lays the foundation for the ecumenistic ecclesiology found in the text "Baptism, Eucharist, and Ministry" from the World Council of Churches, which states:

> Baptism is an unrepeatable act. Any practice which might be interpreted as "re-baptism" must be avoided.

COMMENTARY

> Churches which have insisted on a particular form of baptism or which have had serious questions about the authenticity of other churches' sacraments and ministries have at times required persons coming from other church traditions to be baptized before being received into full communicant membership. As the churches come to fuller mutual understanding and acceptance of one another and enter into closer relationships in witness and service, they will want to refrain from any practice which might call into question the sacramental integrity of other churches or which might diminish the unrepeatability of the sacrament of baptism...[664]

> Churches are increasingly recognizing one another's baptism as the one baptism into Christ when Jesus Christ has been confessed as Lord by the candidate or, in the case of infant baptism, when confession has been made by the church (parents, guardians, godparents and congregation) and affirmed later by personal faith and commitment. Mutual recognition of baptism is acknowledged as an important sign and means of expressing the baptismal unity given in Christ. Wherever possible, mutual recognition should be expressed explicitly by the churches.[665]

According to this ecumenistic ecclesiology, the unity of the Church is to be formed not by heretics renouncing their heresies and

---

664 World Council of Churches, *Baptism, Eucharist, and Ministry.*
665 Ibid.

being received by baptism into the Orthodox Church, but rather by heterodox affirming that all other heretics have true and saving Mysteries despite historical schisms between them and heretical teachings among them. Such a view sees all "baptisms" as equal and unrepeatable where "Jesus Christ has been confessed as Lord."

A similarly problematic ecclesiology is expressed in *Baptism and 'Sacramental Economy': An Agreed Statement of the North American Orthodox-Catholic Theological Consultation*,[666] released in 1999. In this document, which misrepresents many of the canons and councils covered in the present book, the following statement is made:

> The Orthodox and Catholic members of our Consultation acknowledge, in both of our traditions, a common teaching and a common faith in one baptism, despite some variations in practice which, we believe, do not affect the substance of the mystery. We are therefore moved to declare that we also recognize each other's baptism as one and the same. This recognition has obvious ecclesiological consequences. The Church is itself both the milieu and the effect of baptism, and is not of our making. This recognition requires each side of our dialogue to acknowledge an ecclesial reality in the other, however much we may regard their way of living the Church's reality as flawed or incomplete.[667]

Among the conclusions of this ecumenistic statement, we find:

> 1. The Orthodox and Catholic churches both teach the same understanding of baptism...

> 2. A central element in this single teaching is the conviction that baptism comes to us as God's gift in Christ, through the Holy Spirit. It is therefore not "of us," but from above. The Church does not simply require the practice of baptism; rather, baptism is the Church's foundation. It establishes the Church, which is also not "of us" but, as the body of Christ

---

666 North American Orthodox-Catholic Theological Consultation, *Baptism and 'Sacramental Economy': An Agreed Statement of the North American Orthodox-Catholic Theological Consultation.*

667 Ibid.

quickened by the Spirit, is the presence in this world of the world to come.

This implies that if heretics and schismatics share "the same understanding of baptism" as each other, then their baptisms are true and grace-filled, contrary to St. Basil's first canon which says those who break off from the Church lose the grace of the Holy Spirit and cannot bestow the Holy Spirit on others. This also contradicts all of the saints and Fathers of the Church who clearly taught that the baptism of heretics is without grace and a "pollution."

> 3. The fact that our churches share and practice this same faith and teaching requires that we recognize in each other the same baptism and thus also recognize in each other, however "imperfectly," the present reality of the same Church. By God's gift we are each, in St. Basil's words, "of the Church."[668]

As noted previously, this is based on a mistranslation of St. Basil's first canon where he refers to schismatics as "ὥς ἔτι ἐκ τῆς Ἐκκλησίας ὄντων" which is more accurately translated within its context as "with the understanding that they formerly belonged to the Church." As addressed in the treatment of his Canon 1 in Chapter 5, St. Basil distinguishes between unlawful assemblies or parasynagogues, schismatics, and heretics but taught that even those who gather in unlawful assemblies are outside of the Church and those who depart in schism lose the grace of the Holy Spirit and cannot bestow the Spirit on others through baptism.

> 4. We find that this mutual recognition of the ecclesial reality of baptism, in spite of our divisions, is fully consistent with the perennial teaching of both churches...[669]

This reiterates the belief that despite schisms and heresies, all who have the same belief about baptism are somehow part of the

---

668 Ibid.
669 Ibid.

same Church, rather than the grace of baptism belonging only to the one Church and not outside of the unity of the Church.

> 5. The influential theory of "sacramental economy" propounded in the *Pedalion* commentaries does not represent the tradition and perennial teaching of the Orthodox Church; it is rather an eighteenth-century innovation motivated by the particular historical circumstances operative in those times. It is not the teaching of scripture, of most of the Fathers, or of later Byzantine canonists, nor is it the majority position of the Orthodox churches today.[670]

This contradicts Apostolic Canons 46 and 47 and the Canon of Carthage under St. Cyprian which requires heretics to be received by baptism without narrowly defining the word "heretics." It also ignores the principle of "sacramental economy" which St. Basil upheld in Canons 1 and 47 and ignores how the Church has understood and applied economy historically.

> 6. Catholics in the present day who tax the Orthodox with sins against charity, and even with sacrilege, because of the practice of rebaptism should bear in mind that, while the rebaptism of Orthodox Christians was officially repudiated by Rome five hundred years ago, it nonetheless continued in some places well into the following century and occasionally was done, under the guise of "conditional baptism," up to our own times.[671]

Interestingly, here the Latin and Orthodox ecumenists point out that both Orthodox and Latins have baptized each other over the centuries, even "up to our own times," rightly pointing out the problem of claiming that it is "sacrilege" for Orthodox to receive Latins by baptism, while also showing that St. Augustine's ecclesiology in *Against the Donatists* was not normative historically for either the Orthodox or the Latins.

---

670 Ibid.
671 Ibid.

The "Agreed Statement" concludes with several recommendations including that "the Patriarchate of Constantinople formally withdraw its decree on rebaptism of 1755" and that the "Orthodox churches declare that the Orthodox reception of Catholics by chrismation does not constitute a repetition of any part of their sacramental initiation."[672] As the 1620 Council of Moscow and 1755 Encyclical which required Latins and other heterodox to be received by baptism were critical in protecting the Orthodox Church from being made subservient to the Pope, formally rejecting these decisions which upheld the Patristic ecclesiology of the Ecumenical Councils is critical for the adoption of a syncretistic and heterodox ecclesiology which separates Christ and the Mysteries from the Church.

In his brief review of this "Agreed Statement," Metropolitan Hierotheos of Nafpaktos states:

> [I]t is obvious how much confusion prevails in ecumenist circles regarding these issues. It is also obvious that [Orthodox] ecumenists understand the acceptance of the baptism of heretics (Catholics and Protestants, who have altered the dogma of the Holy Trinity and other dogmas) to mean accepting the ecclesial status of heretical bodies and, worse still, that the two "Churches," Latin and Orthodox, are united in spite of "small" differences, or that we derive from the same Church and should seek to return to it, thereby forming the one and only Church. This is a blatant expression of the branch theory...

> [B]aptismal theology creates immense problems for the Orthodox. From the standpoint of ecclesiology, the text under consideration is riddled with errors. The Patristic Orthodox teaching on this subject is that the Church is the Theanthropic Body of Christ, in which revealed truth—the Orthodox Faith—is preserved and the mystery of deification is accomplished through the Mysteries of the Church (Baptism, Chrismation, and the Divine Eucharist).

---

672 Ibid.

The essential precondition for this is that we participate in the purifying, illuminating, and deifying energy of God. Baptism is the initiatory Mystery of the Church. The Church does not rest upon the Mystery of Baptism; rather, the Baptism of water, in conjunction with the Baptism of the Spirit, operates within the Church and makes one a member of the Body of Christ. There are no Mysteries outside the Church, the living Body of Christ, just as there are no senses outside the human body."[673]

Metropolitan Hierotheos (Vlachos) of Nafpaktos and Agios Vlasios

Metropolitan Hierotheos shows that the Orthodox and Latins do not have the same teaching about baptism and that the ecumenist ecclesiology found in this statement is not Orthodox. He further states that since ecumenists use the application of economy to spread such ecclesiological confusion, greater strictness (or canonical exactitude) should be applied in receiving heretics into the Church to avoid the spread of such confusion.

> When there is such confusion, it is necessary to adopt an attitude of strictness, which preserves the truth: that all who fall into heresy are outside the Church and that the Holy Spirit does not work to bring about their deification.[674]

In his book *I Confess One Baptism*, Fr. George Metallinos says regarding the dangers of false and ecumenistic ecclesiology:

> What might be stated as a final conclusion based on the teaching of the Ecumenical Councils and the holy Fathers, which teaching our writers so lucidly and thoroughly present, is that for

Fr. George Metallinos (+ 2019)

673 Vlachos, "Baptismal Theology," pp. 40-43.
674 Ibid.

the conversion (i.e. entrance) to Orthodoxy of Latins and Western Christians in general, *economia* may be exercised only in such cases when a Christian Confession administered baptism with trine immersion and emersion according to its Apostolic and patristic form. When, on the other hand, this is not the case, but rather, despite knowing the truth, the innovation of aspersion or affusion was employed in a non-Orthodox manner, then *acrivia* is judged mandatory.

Especially in our day when everything is considered relative, even in the ecclesiastical domain, persistence in the tradition of the Saints is the most substantial counteraction against the general decline, even if such a position is ridiculed as lacking love. True love is the love for the truth in Christ.[675]

That in our times, due to ecclesiological relativism and the heresy of syncretistic Ecumenism, converts should be received by baptism, was also expressed by the Synod of the Russian Orthodox Church Outside of Russia in its 1971 decision on the reception of converts:

Metropolitan Philaret of New York (+ 1985)

Having in mind this circumstance and the growth today of the heresy of ecumenism, which attempts to eradicate completely the distinction between Orthodoxy and all the heresies... the Council of Bishops recognizes the necessity of introducing a stricter practice, i.e. that baptism be performed on all heretics who come to the Church, excepting only as the necessity arises and with the permission of the bishop, for reasons of economy or pastoral condescension...[676]

A similar comment is made by Fr. Alexey (Young) in a footnote to a letter written to him by his spiritual father, Fr. Seraphim (Rose).

---

675 Metallinos, op. cit., p. 115.
676 Council of Bishops of the Russian Orthodox Church Outside of Russia (1971).

While Fr. Seraphim himself baptized those converts who came to him from various heresies, in this particular letter he did not express objection to a Latin convert being received into the Orthodox Church by chrismation. In the published letters, Fr. Alexey says the following in a footnote:

Fr. Seraphim Rose
of Platina (+1982)

> It should be noted that in the twenty-three years since Fr. Seraphim wrote this, the situation of the heterodox Churches and the modernist Orthodox jurisdictions has deteriorated to a degree that Fr. Seraphim could not have predicted and which would have horrified him. In general, the Russian Church Abroad now finds it necessary as well as appropriate to insist on the use of less "economy" and more pastoral strictness in order to avoid unfortunate cases of scruples later on.[677, 678]

St. Cyprian of Carthage's ecclesiology is the ecclesiology of the Apostolic Canons and of the Orthodox Church, which recognizes the grace of the Holy Spirit only in the Mysteries of the Orthodox Church. This ecclesiology has become increasingly threatened in our time by dogmatic relativists who seek to utilize the Ecumenical

---

677 Fr. Seraphim Rose, *Letters from Fr. Seraphim*, p. 154.

678 Fr. Seraphim's writings on this topic do not provide an extensive examination of the relevant canons and historical material addressed in the present book. While he baptized all converts who came to him, he sometimes expressed himself in a less than clear and consistent manner on the topic. The subject of the reception of converts in his time became a major cause of debate when the teachings of St. Nikodemos the Hagiorite and the Kollyvades Fathers that were promoted by Holy Transfiguration Monastery in Boston came up against the Latin Scholastic teachings that influenced the later Russian tradition. Fr. Seraphim was very concerned about this monastery and its "super-correct" mentality and predicted that the monastery would eventually go into schism from ROCOR, which indeed happened in 1986 after Fr. Seraphim's repose. The opposition Fr. Seraphim expressed towards certain teachings promoted by the monastery appear to have been mostly driven by his concern over their sectarian mentality and their tremendous influence in ROCOR at that time. Fr. Seraphim did not know Greek and there is no evidence that he thoroughly evaluated the teachings of St. Nikodemos and the Kollyvades Fathers on this topic.

Movement to achieve a false unity with the heterodox without repentance from heresy and without unity of faith. In such an age of ecclesiological confusion, discerning spiritual fathers and bishops have insisted on receiving all converts into the Church by baptism with three immersions except in cases of emergency (in which case baptism by pouring may be done out of economy). The use of the Church's practice of economy to claim that the Orthodox Church recognizes "ecclesiality" and "the presence of the Holy Spirit" in the mysteries of heretics illustrates why converts should be received by baptism according to the exactitude of the Holy Canons: in order to both safeguard the Orthodox Dogma of the Church and protect the faithful from falling into the heretical ecclesiology of syncretistic ecumenism.

St. Cyprian
of Carthage

Hieromonk Seraphim Rose

St. Diodochos of Photiki (+500)
Feast Day: March 29

CHAPTER 19
Activity of Grace Outside of the Church

In the daily prayers found in all Orthodox Prayer books, Orthodox Christians pray to the Holy Spirit "Who art everywhere present and fillest all things" asking the Holy Spirit to "come and abide in us and cleanse us of all impurity and save our souls O Good One." The patristic teaching of St. Cyprian of Carthage and the Ecumenical Councils which declares the mysteries of heretics to be devoid of the Holy Spirit does not imply that the Holy Spirit is not present in the world, nor in the lives of the heterodox, in a general sense.

In the tradition of the Church a distinction is made between God's essence and His energies. And, although the two are often contrasted, it is understood that the energy is the natural energy of the essence, or an essential energy. This natural energy is utterly simple, even as God's essence is utterly simple. Nevertheless, one finds in the works of the Holy Fathers… [the teaching that this energy] is one and yet has many consequences, many resultant energies, and this energy of God is present throughout creation. This one energy exists in each thing as one energy, and within each of these energies, all of God is present.

In spite of this energy being simple, differences can be perceived between God's creative or providential energies and His purifying, illuminating, and deifying energies.[679]

When we acknowledge that the Holy Spirit is "everywhere present and fillest all things" and then pray that the Holy Spirit will "come and abide in us and cleanse us of all impurity and save our souls," we acknowledge that the presence of the Holy Spirit in creation does not automatically purify and deify all those who are in the world.

> If [the Holy Spirit] was already present in creation in the same way that He makes His abode in us, to cleanse, illumine, and deify us, there would be no reason to call on Him to come and dwell in us. Hence, there is a great difference between His creative and providential energies, which pervade all creation, and His illuminating and deifying energies, which only dwell in those who have been purified and illumined in Baptism and chrismation and persevere in the unity of the Body, exchanging the kiss of peace and communing of the Immaculate Body and Blood of Christ.[680]

St. Diadochos of Photiki (+500) explains how the Holy Spirit works in a person prior to baptism compared to after baptism:

> Before holy Baptism, grace encourages the soul from the outside, while Satan lurks in its depths, trying to block all the noetic faculty's ways of approaching the Divine. But from the moment that we are reborn through Baptism, the demon is outside, grace is within. Thus whereas before Baptism error ruled the soul, after Baptism truth rules it. Nevertheless, even after Baptism Satan (can) still act upon the soul. . .[681]

---

679 Heers, op. cit., pp. 168-168.
680 Ibid. p. 170.
681 Palmer et al., *The Philokalia: The Complete Text, Vol. 1*, p. 279.

The divine energies work in the Orthodox Christian through the Mysteries of the Orthodox Church, but the extent to which each person is purified, illumined, and deified depends on the extent to which they struggle to overcome the passions and acquire noetic prayer. On the distinctions between the divine energies, how the divine energies work in the Orthodox Christian through the Mysteries, and how the divine energies work in the world outside of the Mysteries, Fr. John Romanides explains:

> Purification is the first stage in the spiritual life, a stage that is also the work of the Holy Spirit. It is the Holy Spirit Who purifies, illumines, and grants *theosis*. It is God Who purifies, illumines, and glorifies. The teaching about purification and illumination not only defines the central task set before the catechumen, but it is also the chief duty of his spiritual father who is to open the eyes of the catechumen's soul to prepare him for Baptism. Naturally, a spiritual father should already be in a state of illumination in order to be able to lead others to that state and to guide them to baptism of water (unto remission of sins) and of the Spirit, which takes place when the Holy Spirit visits the heart of the baptized and illumines it.

> So in the early Church once the catechumens become newly illumined through baptism, their spiritual father continues to instruct them and guide them through their ascetic course of treatment. And when the spiritual father says that someone is ready for full illumination, then that person is brought to church and illumined (that is, he is chrismated or anointed with holy chrism).[682] In the next stage, the Holy Spirit comes and dwells permanently in that person, because he has acquired love, keeps the commandments, and so forth...

---

682 Fr. John Romanides is not advocating here for a separation between baptism and chrismation. In the Orthodox Church, chrismation is performed immediately after baptism. Here he is explaining how baptism and chrismation are distinct Mysteries and how they are related to purification and illumination.

All Christians are not in a position to participate in the energies of *theosis*, illumination, and purification. You have to be an Orthodox Christian in order to participate in these energies, and every Orthodox Christian does not do so, but only those who are properly prepared, spiritually speaking.

Now in addition to these three divine energies, we can speak about the creative energy of God in which all creation participates, as well as the cohesive and preserving energy of God in which all creation also participates. Everything within the universe partakes of the cohesive and preserving energy of God, because God is the One Who preserves the cosmos. Besides these energies, there is also the providential energy of God (Divine Providence), the loving energy of God, the chastising energy of God, and so forth.[683]

While the mysteries of the heterodox are empty of the Holy Spirit and do not purify, illumine, or deify (as St. Augustine and the saints and Fathers of the West also acknowledged), the Holy Spirit nevertheless can work in the non-Orthodox in a general way to lead them to faith and ultimately to the Orthodox Church where purification, illumination, and theosis take place.

St. Seraphim of Sarov also differentiates how the Holy Spirit works "externally" in the world while working "internally" in Orthodox Christians through the Holy Mysteries of the Church:

However, that [i.e., "the Spirit of God was not yet in the world"—St. John 7:39] does not mean that the Spirit of God was not in the world at all, but His presence was not so apparent as in Adam or in us Orthodox Christians. It was manifested only externally; yet the signs of His presence in the world were known to mankind... The grace of the Holy Spirit acting externally was also reflected in all the Old Testament prophets and Saints of Israel. The Hebrews afterwards established special prophetic schools where the sons of the prophets were taught to discern the signs

---

683 Romanides, *Patristic Theology*, pp. 172-175.

of the manifestation of God or of Angels, and to distinguish the operations of the Holy Spirit from the ordinary natural phenomena of our graceless earthly life. Simeon who held God in his arms, Christ's grandparents Joakim and Anna, and countless other servants of God continually had quite openly various divine apparitions, voices and revelations which were justified by evident miraculous events. Though not with

St. Seraphim of Sarov (+ 1833)
Feast Day: January 2

the same power as in the people of God, nevertheless, the presence of the Spirit of God also acted in the pagans who did not know the true God, because even among them God found for Himself chosen people. . . Though the pagan philosophers also wandered in the darkness of ignorance of God, yet they sought the truth which is beloved by God, and on account of this God-pleasing seeking, they could partake of the Spirit of God, for it is said that the nations who do not know God practice by nature the demands of the law and do what is pleasing to God...[684, 685]

When St. Maximos the Confessor was asked how it can be said that the Holy Spirit is present in all things while not entering into the heart that is enslaved by sin, St. Maximos answered:

684 cf. Rom. 2:14

685 Moore, "A Wonderful Revelation to the World," pp. 123-124.

The Holy Spirit is absent from no being, and especially not from those that in any way partake of reason. For the Spirit contains the knowledge of each being, inasmuch as He is God and the Spirit of God, providentially permeating all things with His power. The Spirit stirs into motion the natural inner principle of each, through which He leads a man of sense to consciousness of whatever he has done contrary to the law of nature, a man who at the same time also keeps his free choice pliant to the reception of right thoughts arising from nature. And thus we find even some of the most barbarous and uncivilized men exhibiting nobility of conduct and rejecting the savage laws that had prevailed among them from time immemorial.

St. Maximos the Confessor (+662)
Feast Day: January 21

This, then, is how the Spirit is unconditionally "present in all things." But He is present more specifically and according to another sense in all those who live according to the law. To these He gives laws and proclaims in advance mysteries to come, imbuing them with the awareness of where they have broken the commandments, as well as with true understanding of the proclaimed perfection in Christ. Consequently, and for the same reasons, we find that many abandon the old religion of shadows and types in order eagerly to embrace the new and mystical worship.

In addition to these modes of the Spirit's presence, there is another, which is found in all those who through faith have inherited the divine and truly divinizing name of Christ. In this mode, the Spirit is not present simply as one guarding and providentially setting in motion the principle of nature, nor as one pointing out the keeping and breaking of the commandments and announcing the coming of Christ, but rather as one creating the adoption given by grace through faith. For the Spirit is productive of wisdom only in those who have been purified in soul and body through the strict keeping of the commandments. With them He communicates intimately through simple and immaterial knowledge, and, by means of pure thoughts of ineffable mysteries, He configures their intellect for divinization.

Consequently, the Spirit is present unconditionally in all things, insofar as he contains all things, providentially cares for all things, and stirs into motion their natural seeds. He is present more specifically in all who are under the law, for He shows them where they have failed to keep this law, and enlightens them regarding the promise of Christ. In all Christians, however, He is present in another way, namely, as the power of their adoption as children of God. But as the author of wisdom He is unconditionally present only in those who have understanding, and who by their godly way of life have made themselves fit to receive His divinizing indwelling. For everyone who does not carry out the divine will, even though he is a believer, has a "heart lacking in understanding," because it has become a workshop of evil thoughts, and a body deeply in debt to sin because it perpetually subjects itself to the defilements of the passions.[686]

As St. Maximos explains, the Holy Spirit is present everywhere but only adopts as children of God and leads to theosis those who

---

686 Maximos the Confessor, *On Difficulties in Sacred Scripture: The Responses to Thalassios*, pp. 127-129.

are baptized in the Church and who struggle to purify their hearts of the sinful passions.

These distinctions are essential for the avoidance of confusion about the presence and activity of grace among the non-Orthodox. Such distinctions need to be kept in mind when reading statements from the saints and elders, like Elder Cleopa of Romania, that "Heretics and Schismatics do not have the Divine Grace" because they lack "the Divine Mysteries through which Christ Himself works out His salvation in the hearts of men,"[687] or like St. Paisios the Athonite who said "All people are [God's] children, but He gives His Grace only to the Orthodox";[688] while on the other hand St. Sophrony of Essex states:

> ...only the one and unique Church can have the fulness of grace. All the other churches, however, do have grace because of their faith in Christ, but not in its fulness.[689]

Since this particular quote from St. Sophrony has led to considerable confusion among the Orthodox, it is worth discussing in greater detail. Earlier in the same letter, St. Sophrony stated,

> At this point, though, I would like to say a little about the fact that at the present time a significant part of the Christian world tends to accept one of the most dangerous heresies. What it consists of is people saying that in our days there is not one Church which has kept fully the true teaching of Christ; or which possesses complete knowledge of the mystery of the holy, grace-filled Christian life on the ethical and ascetical level. Supposedly, many of the Churches which are nominally Christian have equal grace, and because of that we should proceed towards the union of the Churches on the basis of some common programme. One of the most frequent questions which one comes across is the question of who will be saved and who will not be saved. These people

---

687 Grassos, op. cit., pp. 28-29.
688 Holy Hesychasterion "Evangelist John the Theologian," op. cit., p. 477.
689 Sakharov, *Striving for Knowledge of God*, p. 146.

usually think that it is not only the Orthodox who will be saved (according to Orthodox teaching), not only the Catholics (according to Catholic teaching), but all virtuous people in general who believe in Christ. This viewpoint has passed from the Protestants to the faithful of other Churches. There are many among the Orthodox who hold this opinion. Some people think that no single one of the existing Churches can receive the fulness

St. Sophrony (Sakharov)
of Essex (+1993)

of knowledge and grace, because each one of them in one or another degree has deviated from the truth. They think that only now "at the end of the ages" they (these sages) have fully grasped the spirit of the teaching of Christ, and that the entire Christian world has been led astray for many centuries until now. That now the time has come when we must unite all the separated parts into one universal and apostolic Church, which will have the fulness of truth in all its aspects, even though this union will only embrace what is common to all the Churches... I very much want you (and I pray to God for this) not to be deceived by all that, but to be convinced firmly in your heart and mind that on this earth there is one unique and true Church which Christ founded; that this Church maintains unspoiled the teaching of Christ, that she in her totality (and not in her individual members) possesses the fulness of knowledge and grace and infallibility.[690]

These statements are from St. Sophrony's letters to David Balfour, a former Roman Catholic who was received into the Orthodox Church just a couple of months prior. St. Sophrony warns Balfour about the ecumenical movement which is based on the belief that there is not one visible Church which is the body of Christ and contains the fullness of grace and truth. St. Sophrony refers to this ecumenist ecclesiology as "one of the most dangerous heresies" and affirms that the Orthodox Church alone possesses "the fulness of knowledge and grace and infallibility." In another letter to Balfour, St. Sophrony states:

> Whoever makes a mistake in dogma will inevitably make a mistake in his inner, moral life too. So without fail we must adopt the view that the true Church must be true in both the one and the other, because if it is in error somewhere in the one, it will inevitably be in error also in the other.
>
> Of course here I am referring to the Church as a whole. Individual members of the Church may, while they live in the Church, be ignorant of many things, and even be mistaken in something, without however losing their salvation because of their incomplete knowledge. And in fact, knowledge is not accessible to any one man in its fullness; it belongs to the whole Church.
>
> What I mean by this is that for salvation it is necessary to be a member of the true Church. Outside of her it is not possible for men to receive either true grace or true knowledge.[691]

In stating that "other churches...do have grace," then, he is speaking of "churches" not in a dogmatic and ecclesiological sense, as if there is not one true Church which is the Orthodox Church; but he is speaking informally and personally to a non-Orthodox

690 Ibid., pp. 144-145.
691 Ibid., p. 304.

person using the term "churches" to acknowledge how they refer to themselves and not as an assertion that the Holy Spirit is present in the mysteries of the heterodox. When he says there is "grace" among the heterodox, then, he is speaking of the general activity of the Holy Spirit and is not implying that the mysteries of the heterodox have purifying, illuminating, and deifying grace. Clearly, St. Sophrony does not believe that grace works through the mysteries of the heterodox since he says that "for salvation it is necessary to be a member of the true Church" and outside of the true Church "it is not possible for men to receive either true grace or true knowledge."[692]

Due to the confusion that can result from terminology such as "fullness of grace," it is more precise to distinguish between the general activity of the Holy Spirit in the world (including among the heterodox) and the purifying, illuminating, and deifying energies of the Holy Spirit which work only through the Mysteries of the Orthodox Church and which benefit those who partake of the Mysteries to the extent to which they have struggled to purify their hearts from sinful passions and have acquired noetic prayer.

---

692 Ibid.

The 8th Ecumenical Council
St. Stephen's Monastery in Meteora, Greece

CHAPTER 20

True and False Councils

The history of the Orthodox Church includes numerous councils of bishops, some of which were accepted as true and some of which were rejected as false (or Robber) councils. The false council of Ferrara-Florence, for example, was rejected by St. Mark of Ephesus despite the fact that he was the only Orthodox bishop present at the council who refused to submit to the Pope of Rome. This council was formally rejected later by the 1484 Council of Constantinople. Earlier, after the Third Ecumenical Council in AD 431, Emperor Theodosius II gathered bishops together in Ephesus in AD 449 with the intent of holding an Ecumenical Council to adopt a heretical Monophysite Christology, but this council was also rejected by the Orthodox Church as a false council. Likewise, the Council of Hieria in AD 754 was called as an Ecumenical Council to condemn the veneration of icons, yet this council was also rejected as false by the Seventh Ecumenical Council in AD 787. Just as individual bishops are not infallible, neither are councils of bishops. True councils express the mind of the Church and are led by bishops who have the mind of the Church. The decrees of such councils are guided by the Holy Spirit because the bishops who lead the Council are purified of the sinful passions and are themselves filled with the Holy Spirit.

On true and false councils, Metropolitan Hierotheos of Nafpaktos states:

The glorified[693] who participate in the glory of God... are the foundation and basis of ecclesiastical life... The glorified have authority in the Church because they have acquired true and unerring knowledge of God. The people who follow the glorified have true faith. Knowledge of God is not the same as faith in God... Since the glorified are authoritative teachers, when they assemble in Local and Ecumenical Councils they formulate the teaching of the Church unerringly and with divine inspiration...

As the glorified are the basic criterion in the Church for determining the truthfulness of its members, in the early Church we observe the fact that bishops and priests were chosen from among the glorified and the Prophets... Also, the clergy needed to be glorified, because only then were they genuine physicians who knew how to cure people and to lead them from darkness of the nous* to illumination of the nous and glorification. The aim and mission of the Church is to make people glorified. The Church, as we have said many times already, is like a hospital and the clergy are like doctors.

This is the perspective from which we should view the virtue of obedience. We do not obey every teaching that comes along. We obey the glorified, who have experience of God, because in this way obedience will lead to glorification and participation in the uncreated glory of God.[694]

Similarly, Fr. John Romanides says:

...[The] decisions of the Ecumenical Councils are infallible. During the Ecumenical Councils the Fathers were divinely inspired and made divinely inspired decisions about the dogmas of the Church.

---

693 The "glorified" are those who have been purified of the passions, have received illumination from the Holy Spirit, and are deified. They are filled with the Holy Spirit, clothed with the virtues, have noetic prayer, and are led by the Holy Spirit.

694 Vlachos, *Empirical Dogmatics of the Orthodox Catholic Church, Vol. 2*, pp. 326-328.

[The Local and Ecumenical Councils were made up] of bishops who knew the therapeutic method of the Church. The Council was convened with the aim of preserving, not simply the dogma and the order of worship of the Church, as happens today, but also the therapeutic method of the Church. A true bishop is an expert on the therapeutic method of the Church.

Fr. John Romanides (+2001)

Today, however, when noetic prayer is rare among bishops, if a Council of bishops meets and they stand up at the beginning to sing together, "Heavenly King and Comforter, Spirit of truth, everywhere present and filling all things…," will the Holy Spirit come without fail and enlighten them? Simply because they are canonical bishops and assemble at a Council and pray?

However, the Holy Spirit does not act in that way, with only these preconditions. Other conditions need to be met. The one who prays must have noetic prayer already activated within him when he comes to the Council, in order for the grace of God to enlighten him. Those who attended the pseudo-Councils were not in this state of prayer.

The bishops of old, however, had this sort of spiritual experience and when they came together as a body, they knew what the Holy Spirit was assuring them of within their hearts on a specific subject. And when they reached decisions, they knew that their decisions were correct. Because they were in the state of illumination, and some of them had even reached glorification, *theosis*.[695]

St. Theodore the Studite likewise taught that a gathering of bishops does not make a true council, but a true council is one that follows the "righteous," that upholds the truth, and follows the canons.

> [A] council is not just a meeting of bishops and priests, even if there were many of them, - for it is said: "better is one" righteous, "doing the will of the Lord, than a thousand sinners" (Sir.16:3), - but an assembly in the name of the Lord, for the sake of peace and the following of the canons, and in order to bind and loose, not as it happens, but as it should be, according to truth, according to rule, and according to true judgment.[696]

Fr. George Florovsky noted that Ecumenical Councils were not called such because they met specific canonical criteria (there were many false councils called that met the same canonical criteria), but rather for their charismatic character, as being recognized as guided by the Holy Spirit.

> Indeed, those Councils which were actually recognized as "Ecumenical," in the sense of their binding and infallible authority, were recognized, immediately or after a delay, not because of their formal canonical competence, but because of their charismatic character: under the guidance of the Holy Spirit they have witnessed to the Truth, in conformity with the Scripture as handed down in Apostolic Tradition.[697]

In the Orthodox Church, while most commonly refer to Seven Ecumenical Councils, there are in fact at least nine councils that

---

695 Ibid., pp. 400-402.

696 Theodore the Studite. *Epistle 24* (In Russian), Bk. 1, p. 474, Bk. 2, p. 503.

697 Florovsky, *Theological Articles of Fr. George Florovsky*, 4, On the Church, "The Authority of the ancient councils and the tradition of the Fathers."

have Ecumenical authority. The Council of Constantinople (AD 879-880) was accepted by the entire Church, including Rome. The Council was accepted by Rome for approximately 200 years.[698] By the time of the Council, the Franks in the West had introduced the *Filioque* (that the Holy Spirit proceeds from the Father *and the Son*) into the Nicene Creed but the *Filioque* was at that time not accepted by Rome. The Council defended St. Photios and also declared anathema against any who would add to or subtract from the Creed, an act clearly directed against the *Filioque*. In the *Horos*, or Rule, of the Council, the canons and decrees of the previous Seven Ecumenical Councils were accepted as inspired by the Holy Spirit. The Council then recites the entire Creed and states:

> We enroll as brothers and fathers and coheirs of the heavenly city those who think thus. If anyone, however, dares to rewrite and call Rule of Faith some other exposition besides that of the sacred Symbol which has been spread abroad from above by our blessed and holy Fathers even as far as ourselves, and to snatch the authority of the confession of those divine men and impose on it his own invented phrases (ἰδίαις εὑρεσιολογίαις) and put this forth as a common lesson to the faithful or to those who return from some kind of heresy, and display the audacity to falsify completely (κατακιβδηλεῦσαι ἀποθρασυνθείη) the antiquity of this sacred and venerable Horos (Rule) with illegitimate words, or additions, or subtractions, such a person should, according to the vote of the holy and Ecumenical Synods, which has been already acclaimed before us, be subjected to complete defrocking if he happens to be one of the clergymen, or be sent away with an anathema if he happens to be one of the lay people.[699]

After reading the *Horos*, the bishops of the Council declared:

---

698 Ford, "St. Photios the Great, the Photian Council, and Relations with the Roman Church."

699 Dragas, "The 8th Ecumenical Council: Constantinople IV (879/880) and the Condemnation of the Filioque Addition and Doctrine."

Thus we think, thus we believe, into this confession were we baptized and became worthy to enter the priestly orders. We regard, therefore, as enemies of God and of the truth those who think differently as compared to this. If one dares to rewrite another Symbol besides this one, or add to it, or subtract from it, or to remove anything from it, and to display the audacity to call it a Rule, he will be condemned and thrown out of the Christian Confession. For to subtract from, or to add to, the holy and consubstantial and undivided Trinity shows that the confession we have always had to this day is imperfect. It condemns the Apostolic Tradition and the doctrine of the Fathers. If one, then having come to such a point of mindlessness as to dare do what we have said above, and set forth another Symbol and call it a Rule, or to add to or subtract from the one which has been handed down to us by the first great, holy and Ecumenical Synod of Nicaea, let him be Anathema.[700]

These decrees were accepted by Pope John VIII, the Eastern patriarchates, and the Emperor:

In the Name of the Father and the Son and the Holy Spirit, Basil Emperor in Christ, faithful king of the Romans, agreeing in every way with this holy and ecumenical Synod in confirmation and sealing of the holy and ecumenical Seventh Synod, in confirmation and sealing of Photios the most holy Patriarch of Constantinople and spiritual father of mine, and in rejection of all that was written or spoken against him, I have duly signed with my own hand.[701]

While the Council does not explicitly denounce the addition of the *Filioque*, the Council's anathema against additions to, or subtractions from, the Creed was specifically motivated by the addition of the *Filioque* to the Creed by Frankish missionaries in Bulgaria which St. Photios had written against in his famous encyclical to the Eastern

---

700 Ibid.
701 Ibid.

Patriarchs.[702] The Third Ecumenical Council in AD 431 confirmed the Nicene Creed that was finalized at the Second Ecumenical Council and declared "anathema" against any who would change the Creed. The purpose of the Eighth Ecumenical Council was to renew, or reaffirm, this anathema specifically in the context of the addition of the *Filioque.* When Rome finally rejected the 879-880 Council as the Eighth Ecumenical Council and formally adopted the *Filioque* addition to the Creed, the Orthodox saints and Fathers understood that the Pope of Rome had fallen into heresy and had become "anathema."

In the 1848 Encyclical of the Eastern Patriarchs to Pope Pius IX, which was signed by the patriarchs of Constantinople, Alexandria, Antioch, and Jerusalem along with many other bishops, the Council of 879-880 is referred to specifically as the "Eighth Ecumenical Council." The Patriarchs state in this Encyclical that the *Filioque* was "subjected to anathema, as a novelty and augmentation of the Creed" at the Council, and refers to the *Filioque* as one of a number of heresies and innovations that the Latins had adopted by that time, including departure from "the apostolic pattern of holy Baptism."[703]

The Ninth Ecumenical Council refers to the councils held in Constantinople between 1341-1351 which upheld the hesychastic teachings of St. Gregory Palamas and condemned the rationalistic and anti-hesychastic teachings of Barlaam and Akindynos. The dispute between St. Gregory Palamas and his opponents concerned the experience and teaching of the Athonite hesychasts. St. Gregory Palamas defended the patristic teaching that God is unknowable in His Essence but is known through His Uncreated and divine Energies. While Barlaam and Akindynos claimed that the study of philosophy was necessary for one to know God and avoid error, St. Gregory taught that such study was unnecessary and that God is known empirically by those who overcome the passions, acquire noetic prayer, and participate in the purifying, illumining, and

702 Ibid.
703 "Encyclical of the Eastern Patriarchs, 1848. A Reply to the Epistle of Pope Pius IX, 'to the Easterns.'"

deifying divine energies. Study does not lead one to arrive at experiential knowledge of God, but prayer and hesychia are necessary.

St. Gregory Palamas

St. Gregory Palamas was himself an Athonite and a hesychast. His defense of the distinction between the essence and energies of God, and of the hesychasts as true empirical theologians, shined a light on the Athonite hesychastic way of life as the foundation of Orthodox spiritual experience and dogma. While many Orthodox are unfamiliar with the councils that defended St. Gregory Palamas as being the "Ninth Ecumenical Council," the authority and centrality of St. Gregory's teachings are undisputed in the Orthodox Church. Just as all Orthodox churches on the first Sunday of Great Lent celebrate the defense of the Holy Icons at the Seventh Ecumenical Council as "The Sunday of Holy Orthodoxy," the following Sunday in Great Lent is dedicated to St. Gregory Palamas. In the canon of Orthros in his honor, the entire Church praises him:

> O wise Gregory, thou has burnt up the error of the heretics, and hast revealed in its true beauty the faith of the Orthodox, bringing light to all the world. Thou art triumphantly victorious, a pillar of the Church and a true bishop.[704]

> O blessed saint, by the grace of God thou hast become the great glory and strong support of the Orthodox, a good shepherd, a second Gregory the Theologian, and the ever-watchful guardian of thy flock.[705]

---

704 Mother Mary and Kallistos Ware, *The Lenten Triodion*, p. 320.
705 Ibid. Canticle Four, p. 321.

Earth and sea acknowledge thee as their common teacher, as the holy pillar of Orthodoxy and the sacred armoury of divine dogmas, as a wise and saintly theologian, as the comrade and companion of the apostles.[706]

The vindication of St. Gregory Palamas and his teaching at the Ninth Ecumenical Council, and his universal veneration following the Sunday of Orthodoxy, proclaims hesychasm as the basis of true theology. As St. Gregory Palamas was an Athonite, and Mt. Athos has been the spiritual center of the Orthodox Church, the main preserver of the hesychastic life, and the producer of enumerable hesychastic saints over the centuries, Metropolitan Hierotheos concludes regarding this significance:

> All these things show the great value of St. Gregory, but also the value of the Holy Mountain, with its hesychastic tradition, which is preserved to this day by the Hagiorite Fathers. This tradition of hesychasm is the greatest treasure of the Holy Mountain, a hope for the World and a true life for the Christians.
>
> Rejection of the Holy Mountain and the hesychastic tradition is in reality a denial of the Orthodox Tradition and a departure from the "One, Holy, Catholic and Apostolic Church."[707]

The Eighth and Ninth Ecumenical Councils are important for understanding the distinction between true and false councils, why Latins and Protestants who added the *Filioque* to the Creed were considered heretics by the Orthodox (aside from the other Latin and Protestant heresies), and that the essence-energy distinction and hesychasm are the foundation of Orthodox theology which is empirical and not merely academic. The non-Orthodox cannot know God empirically as they are cut off from the purifying, illumining, and deifying energies of God which man can participate in only through the Mysteries of the Orthodox Church. As the Non-Orthodox do not understand the Mysteries from the

---

706 Ibid. Canticle Five, p. 322.
707 Vlachos, *Saint Gregory Palamas as Hagiorite*, p. 391.

standpoint of the essence-energy distinction, nor understand the role of hesychasm in leading to empirical knowledge of God and theosis, to claim that the Orthodox and heterodox have the "same understanding of baptism" as Ecumenists assert is impossible. The Ninth Ecumenical Council in particular, and the universal honor given to St. Gregory Palamas on the Second Sunday of Lent, show the true significance and authority of the hesychasts in the life of the Church.

If bishops of the Church gather in council and issue decrees contrary to the God-inspired Holy Canons and Ecumenical Councils of the Church, such a council must be rejected as a false council. The "most recent council" does not have authority by virtue of being recent nor is a council authoritative solely because it is comprised of a certain number of bishops or patriarchs. A true and authoritative council is one that is led by God-bearing Fathers and is in agreement with the teachings of the Fathers of the Ecumenical Councils. Regarding the 1666-1667 Council in Moscow, which was led by bishops of dubious Orthodoxy and not by God-bearing Fathers, which contradicts and undermines the Apostolic Canons and the ecclesiology of the Ecumenical Councils, which misrepresented the teachings of St. Mark of Ephesus and the canons of the Ecumenical Councils regarding the reception of heretics, and which is understood by the Russian Church to have made decisions based on falsehood (in the case of the Old Rite): such can hardly be considered a true council of the Church even if it has not yet been completely and officially rejected by the entire Church.

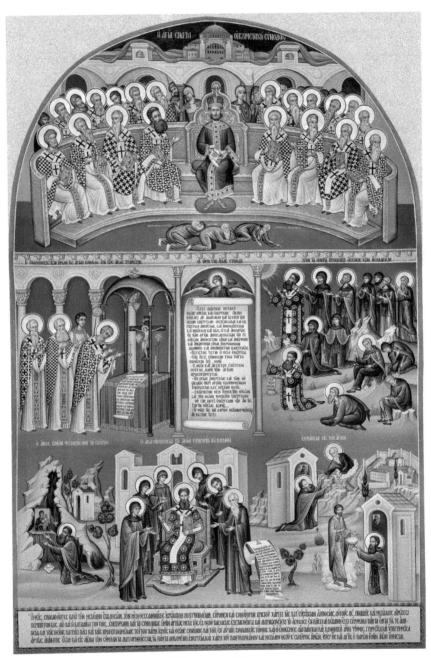

9th Ecumenical Council
St. Stephen's Monastery in Meteora, Greece

Baptism of Christ
Celebrated January 6

CONCLUSION

The Orthodox Church confesses belief in "One, Holy, Catholic and Apostolic Church" which is the Orthodox Church; and "one baptism for the remission of sins" which is baptism performed by three immersions in the name of the Holy Trinity in the Orthodox Church. The Lord instructed the Apostles to make disciples of all nations and to baptize them. Only those who received authority from the Apostles to baptize others were able to bestow the Holy Spirit on others through baptism. Priests and bishops who have departed from the Orthodox Church through schism and heresy ceased to be priests and bishops and became laymen, unable to bestow the Holy Spirit on others through baptism or ordination (Canon 1 of St. Basil the Great). Those heterodox clergy who were never ordained in the Orthodox Church never received the power and authority to bestow the Holy Spirit on others through baptism or ordination. Since baptism unites a person to the Church, to suggest that heretics outside of the Church can unite their followers to the Church is impossible since they themselves do not belong to the Church.

The instruction of the Lord to the Apostles to make disciples of all nations and to baptize them applies to the reception of the heterodox into the Orthodox Church. Apostolic Canons 46 and 47, the Council of Carthage under St. Cyprian, the canons of St. Basil the Great and the Ecumenical Councils affirm that the rule (*akriveia*) for receiving the heterodox into the Orthodox Church is by baptism. Canons of Ecumenical Councils which allowed for specifically named heretics to be received by chrismation "by economy" were based on the needs of the times and presupposed that the heterodox person had already received the apostolic form of baptism in three immersions in the name of the Holy Trinity. The canons which have permitted the use of economy in specific cases nevertheless affirmed that the reception of heretics by baptism is the rule (*akriveia*). The application of economy is a temporary deviation from the rule due to necessity on the basis of certain presuppositions and does not replace the rule established by the Lord and His Apostles to baptize all nations. While our Tradition forbids knowingly baptizing an individual in the apostolic form twice in the Orthodox Church, in cases where it cannot be verified whether someone has been previously baptized correctly in the Orthodox Church, the canons state that to baptize such an individual is better than for one to risk remaining unpurified and unsanctified.

The reception of heterodox into the Orthodox Church by baptism was the rule throughout history prior to the 17th century. The Church in Russia departed from the ancient practice of receiving all heterodox by baptism at the 1666-1667 Council due to the influence of Patriarch Macarius III of Antioch who was loyal to the Pope of Rome, and other participants in the Council who held to a Latin Scholastic ecclesiology that was incompatible with the teachings of the Ecumenical Councils. This departure from the historical practice of the Church was based also on a misrepresentation of the teachings of St. Mark of Ephesus and an effort to align Russian practice with that of Constantinople. Yet, when the Patriarchates of Constantinople, Alexandria, and Jerusalem decreed in 1755 that all heterodox must be received by baptism, based firmly on the canons and councils of the Church, Russia unfortunately did not adopt this decision but departed even further from the 1667 decision by deciding to receive Latin faithful by confession of faith alone, and Latin clergy by vesting.

The 1755 Council of the Three Patriarchs upheld the patristic teaching regarding the reception of the heterodox into the Church and insisted that all heterodox must be received by baptism in all cases except dire emergency where a person may repose before the possibility of baptizing them in three full immersions (in which case baptism by pouring may be done out of economy). This was the last formal declaration on the reception of the heterodox into the Church signed by multiple Patriarchates and was the same teaching formally adopted by the 1620 Moscow Council as representing the ancient practice of the Russian Church. The 1755 Encyclical decreed that economy could no longer be applied in the reception of the heterodox because economy presupposes the heterodox had already received the apostolic form of baptism (three immersions in the name of the Trinity); and by 1755 the Latins and Protestants had abandoned the apostolic form of baptism in favor of pouring, sprinkling, or baptism by single immersion under the influence of the 16th century Latin Council of Trent.

Despite the extensive efforts to propagate heterodox Latin Scholastic ecclesiology among the Orthodox during the time of the Ottoman Empire, with the ultimate goal of forcing the Orthodox into submission to the Pope of Rome, the Orthodox churches were able to overcome this Latin captivity primarily through the patristic and hesychastic renewal that took place in Greece, Russia, and throughout the Orthodox world from Mount Athos. This renewal took place primarily through the influence of St. Paisius (Velichkovsky) among the Russians and Slavs, and St. Nikodemos the Hagiorite and the Kollyvades Fathers among the Greeks. St. Paisius, St. Nikodemos, and the Kollyvades Fathers revived the importance of the writings of the Holy Fathers, the Holy Canons and teachings of the Ecumenical Councils, along with the centrality of hesychasm and spiritual fatherhood. These hesychastic Fathers all insisted that economy is no longer applicable to the reception of heterodox into the Church (except, again, in emergencies where full immersion baptism is not possible, in which case baptism by pouring may be done out of economy), that all heterodox must be received into the Orthodox Church by baptism, and that baptism must be done in three full immersions in the name of the Holy Trinity. These teachings on the reception of heterodox into the Church have been faithfully kept and maintained by the saints and elders in Greece, on Mt. Athos, and throughout the world by the spiritual successors of St. Paisius (Velichkovsky) and St. Nikodemos the Hagiorite.

These saints lived that struggle described in the words of St. John Cassian in regards to the responsibility, which is upon all of us, for preserving the patristic consensus:

> [W]e ought in every respect to bestow an unshakable faith and an unquestioning obedience not on those institutes and rules that were introduced at the wish of a few but on those that were long ago passed on to later ages by innumerable holy fathers acting in accord.[708]

However, many take issue with the patristic consensus regarding the reception of the heterodox; and following that, many assert the heterodox should be received by a method other than baptism on account of recent customs. This is a development in the Church to redefine things and propose alternate theories. Such attempts raise the question that when a faulty theory leads to a faulty practice, then what happens to the victim of erroneous practices? Much heed should be given to the following words of St. Cyprian regarding those received into the Church in an incorrect manner:

> But someone says, "What, then, shall become of those who in past times, coming from heresy to the Church, were received without baptism?" The Lord is able by His mercy to give indulgence, and not to separate from the gifts of His Church those who by simplicity were admitted into the Church, and in the Church have fallen asleep. Nevertheless it does not follow that, because there was error at one time, there must always be error; since it is more fitting for wise and God-fearing men, gladly and without delay to obey the truth when laid open and perceived, than pertinaciously and obstinately to struggle against brethren and fellow-priests on behalf of heretics.[709]

We live in a time of ecclesiological confusion largely due to the misrepresentation of Orthodox teaching by those members

---

708 John Cassian, *The Institutes*, p. 23.
709 Cyprian of Carthage, *Epistle LXXII* to Jubaianus, op. cit.

of the Orthodox Church who are committed to the Ecumenical Movement, and due to the abuses of economy in the reception of the heterodox. This confusion has led some to assert that the Orthodox Church believes that the rites of the heterodox have the presence of the Holy Spirit and that heterodox communities are somehow invisibly connected to the Orthodox Church by "degrees of ecclesiality." Such teachings are used to oppose the reception of heterodox into the Orthodox Church by baptism. To arrive at their assertions, such propagators of heterodox ecclesiology ignore or misrepresent the teachings of the Holy Fathers and the God-inspired Holy Canons and Ecumenical Councils. Such confusion is further propagated by the use of quotes from Orthodox saints and councils who had been influenced by Latin Scholastic teaching during and after the 17th century. This confusion about Orthodox ecclesiology and the reception of converts has necessitated the present response.

As this is a complex topic involving the authority of the Ecumenical Councils, the interpretation of the teachings of the saints, and Church history, necessity demanded this text address the many broad but overlapping issues. Our hope is that this book helps to provide clarification and dispel confusion about this all-important subject. We also hope that these clarifications will help the clergy and the faithful see that St. Nikodemos the Hagiorite, St. Paisius (Velichkovsky), and the many saints and holy elders of our Church who have insisted on receiving all converts by baptism should not be criticized for this, but rather praised and faithfully followed, recognizing in their writings the same Holy Spirit that inspired the Ecumenical Councils and the Holy Fathers before them. The insistence of these saints to receive all converts by baptism was motivated not by any hatred of the heterodox, but by a love that desires the salvation of all who are outside of the Church, and a love for the Lord and eagerness to obey His command to baptize the nations. A further hope is that readers will look with understanding upon those saints who may have unintentionally deviated from the ecclesiology of the Ecumenical Councils and continue to venerate them and follow their teachings where they do clearly align with the teachings of the Holy Fathers. Thus, may we be "of one mind"[710] maintaining "the unity of the Spirit in the bond of peace"[711] within the One, Holy, Catholic and Apostolic Church.

710 1 Peter 3:8
711 Ephesians 4:3

GLOSSARY

Definitions are derived from the following texts (unless reference is blank, then definitions are original compositions):

- CHM: Counsels from the Holy Mountain: Selected from the Letters and Homilies of Elder Ephraim
- OFWL: The Orthodox Faith, Worship, and Life: Orthodox Catechism by Hieromonk Gregorios

+ + +

ANATHEMA: The most severe ecclesiastical penalty consisting of the expulsion and complete separation of a Christian from the body of the Church. (OFWL)

CANON: Rule or standard against which to measure. The Ecumenical and Local Councils established canons for the preservation of Church order in accordance with the Holy Scriptures and the teachings of the God-inspired Holy Fathers.

DISPASSION: Dispassion is achieved when all three aspects of the soul (i.e. the intelligent, appetitive, and incensive aspects) are directed towards God. It is the transfiguration of the passionate aspect of the soul rather than its mortification. Dispassion, then, does not signify stoic indifference, but rather, a transfiguration and sanctification of the powers of the soul and eventually of the body also. (CHM)

ECCLESIOLOGY: The teaching concerning the Church.

ELDER: See GERONDA

GERONDA: A geronda (pronounced "yeh'-ron-da") is a hieromonk, priest, or monk who, ideally, has reached dispassion by the grace of God. Thus, because of his own experience he is able to lead his spiritual children to dispassion as well. In a broader sense, though, it is used as a respectful title for any spiritual father and any elderly hieromonk, priest, or monk. Also called "Elder" in English or "Starets" in Russian. (CHM)

GRACE, DIVINE: God's uncreated energy offered to man for his salvation, through the Mysteries of Holy Baptism, Holy Unction and Holy Communion. It constitutes a divine gift, as is reflected in the Greek word for grace, *charis*, which also means "gift." Man must subsequently endeavor to safeguard this gift. Divine Grace gives a foretaste of the heavenly good things to come, its manifestations are manifold, and it is only truly known by those who have tasted of it. (OFWL)

HERESY: A belief contrary to the teachings of the Orthodox Church.

HESYCHAST: A hesychast is someone who lives a life of hesychia in seclusion from the world and is wholly dedicated to God. His chief struggle is to bring his nous into his heart. (CHM)

HESYCHASM: Hesychia is the ascetical practice of noetic stillness linked with watchfulness and deepened by the unceasing Jesus prayer. Hesychia is an undisturbed nous and heart with peace, freed from thoughts, passions, and from influences of the environment. It is dwelling in God. The only way for man to achieve theosis is through hesychia. External stillness can help one achieve hesychia. Hesychia can also mean noetic stillness itself. (CHM)

JESUS PRAYER: The Jesus prayer is a short prayer which is continually repeated, usually consisting of the words: "Lord Jesus Christ, have mercy on me." (CHM)

KOLLYVADES FATHERS: The Kollyvades Fathers in the eighteenth century on Mt. Athos defended the teachings and way of life of the Holy Fathers in the face of Westernizing influences and departures from Holy Tradition. They are named Kollyvades after the boiled wheat, or kollyva, used at memorial services due to their involvement in the dispute on the Holy Mountain over praying memorial services on Sundays, the day of the Resurrection. The Kollyvades Fathers spoke out against the praying of memorial prayers on Sundays instead of Saturdays when memorial prayers are appointed to be prayed. The Kollyvades Fathers were known for their emphasis on hesychasm, noetic prayer, the importance of frequent communion, and the reception of heterodox by baptism. Among the Kollyvades Fathers are many Athonite saints including St. Nikodemos the Hagiorite, St. Makarios of Corinth, St. Athanasios Parios, St. Kosmas Aitolos, St. Nektarios of Aegina, St. Sabbas of Kalymnos, St. Paisius (Velichkovsky), and St. Nicholas Planas. Their teachings and writings had a tremendous influence on patristic and spiritual renewal throughout the Orthodox Church, including Romania and Russia through the influence of St. Paisius (Velichkovsky). Contemporary saints who have faithfully inherited and embodied the living tradition passed down by the Kollyvades Fathers have also been referred to as "Kollyvades."

NOETIC PRAYER: Noetic prayer is prayer done with the nous without distraction within the heart. Another name for it is "prayer of the heart." (CHM)

NOUS: The nous is the energy of the soul, the eye of the soul, and the innermost aspect of the heart. (CHM)

PASSIONS: Passions are spiritual diseases that dominate the soul. When one repeatedly falls into a certain sin, it becomes second nature – a passion – for him to keep falling into this sin. It is primarily through obedience to an experienced elder that one is cleansed of the passions and reaches dispassion. (CHM)

PATRISTIC: This adjective is used to describe something of, or relating to, the Holy Fathers of the Church. (CHM)

PURIFICATION: In Patristic Theology, purification refers to three states: 1) the rejection of all thoughts from the heart, 2) the ascetical effort by which the three powers of the soul are turned towards God, thereby moving in accordance with and above nature, and 3) the ascetical method by which man overcomes selfish love and achieves unselfish love. (CHM)

STARETS: See GERONDA

THEOSIS: Theosis, or divinization, is a participation in the uncreated grace of God. At this stage of perfection, one has reached dispassion. Through the cooperation of God with man, theosis is attained through the action of the transfigurative grace of God. (CHM)

RECOMMENDED READING

The following works are essential to read and/or study for a basic level of understanding regarding the history of patristic ecclesiology and the Church's struggle to defend Her boundaries from eradication or blurring:

- *Pedalion (The Rudder)* by Hieromonk Agapios and St. Nikodemos the Hagiorite (upcoming from SAGOM Press)
- *I Confess One Baptism...* by Fr. George D. Metallinos, translated by Priestmonk Seraphim
- *The Unity of the Church and the World Conference of Christian Communities* by St. Hilarion (Troitsky)
- *Eustratios Argenti: A Study of the Greek Church under Turkish Rule* by Metropolitan Kallistos Ware
- "Orthodox Ecclesiology: The One, Holy, Catholic and Apostolic Church – A Ten Week Course" by Fr. Peter Heers: youtube.com/playlist?list=PLCFiE3qfVkDggL0YGWAfbQdUayK1221Gg
- *The Ecclesiological Renovation of Vatican II* by Fr. Peter Heers
- "Fr. George Florovsky on The Boundaries of the Church" by Athanasius Yevtich (bishop of Zahumlje and Herzegovina)
- *Blessed Paisius Velichkovsky: The Man Behind the Philokalia* by Schema-Monk Metrophanes
- "Reception of Heretic Laity and Clergy Into the Orthodox Church" http://orthodoxinfo.com/ecumenism/tikhon_response.aspx

- *Rock and Sand: An Orthodox Appraisal of the Protestant Reformers and Their Teachings* by Fr. Josiah Trenham
- *On Common Prayer with the Heterodox* by Fr. Anastasios Gotsopoulos
- *The Science of Spiritual Medicine* by Metropolitan Hierotheos (Vlachos) of Nafpaktos and Agios Vlasios
- *Noetic Prayer as the Basis of Mission and Struggle Against Heresy* by Archimandrite Ephraim Triandaphillopoulos
- *On the Dogma of the Church: An Historical Overview of the Sources of Ecclesiology* by St. Hilarion (Troitsky)

BIBLIOGRAPHY

Acts of the Ecumenical Councils (In Russian) vol. 7. Kazan, 1873.

Agapios, Hieromonk, and Monk Nicodemus. *The Rudder (Pedalion) of the Metaphorical Ship of the One Holy Catholic and Apostolic Church of Orthodox Christians.* Edited by Ralph J. Masterjohn, The Orthodox Christian Educational Society, 2005.

Ambrose of Milan, St. *On the Mysteries.* Nicene and Post-Nicene Fathers, Second Series. Vol. 10, Hendrickson Publishers, 2004.

Ambrose of Optina, St. *Collected Letters of Blessed Memory of the Optina Elder Hieroschemamonk Ambrose to Lay Persons.* Sergiev Posad, 1913.

Andrew of Ufa, St. "St. Andrew of Ufa: On Bishops and Catascops (1928)." Archive of the FSB of the Russian Federation for the Republic of Tatarstan (In Russian). D. 2-2527. T. 1. L. 236-243 vol. Handwritten original on notebook sheets. Translation: *Catacomb History,* 4 Jan. 2022. Accessed 23 Jan. 2023. https://catacombhistory.blogspot.com/2022/01/st-andrew-of-ufa-on-bishops-and.html.

Anonymous, "Reception of Heretic Laity and Clergy Into the Orthodox Church." Orthodox Russia, vol. 1144, no. 22, 1978, pp. 1-3. Accessed 10 Feb. 2023. http://orthodoxinfo.com/ecumenism/tikhon_response.aspx.

Aquinas, Thomas. *The Summa Theologiae*. 2nd ed., Burns, Oates & Washbourne Ltd., 1920. Accessed 23 Jan. 2023. https://www.newadvent.org/summa/.

Armentrout, Don and Slocum, Robert (editors). "Gardiner, Robert Hallowell". *An Episcopal Dictionary of the Church*. Church Publishing, 2000. Accessed 1 April 2023. https://www.episcopalchurch.org/glossary/gardiner-robert-hallowell/.

Aslanidis, Demetrios, and Grigoriatis, Monk Damascene. *Apostle to Zaire: The Life and Legacy of Blessed Father Cosmas of Grigoriou*. Uncut Mountain Press, 2001.

Athanasios the Great, St. *Against the Arians*. Nicene and Post-Nicene Fathers, Second Series. Vol. 4, Hendrickson Publishers, 2004.

Augustine, St. *Letters of St. Augustine*, New Advent. Accessed 15 Mar. 2023. https://www.newadvent.org/fathers/1102185.htm.

Augustine, St. *On Christian Doctrine, In Four Books*. Christian Classics Ethereal Library. Accessed 23 Jan. 2023. https://ccel.org/ccel/augustine/doctrine/doctrine.i.html.

Augustine, St. *On Baptism: Against the Donatists;* Nicene and Post-Nicene Fathers, First Series. Vol. 4, Hendrickson Publishers, 2004.

Augustine, St. "Sermon XXI," Nicene and Post-Nicene Fathers, First Series. Vol. 6, Hendrickson Publishers, 2004.

Axarloglou, Kostas, et al. "A Cartel That Lasts for Centuries: The Case of the Eastern Orthodox Church Indulgences." Yale International Center for Finance, no. 06-13, 2012.

Baldimtsis, Nicholas, Dr. *Life and Witness of St. Iakovos of Evia*. Uncut Mountain Press, 2023.

Balsamon, Theodoros. *Guide for a Church Under Islam: The Sixty-Six Canonical Questions Attributed to Theodoros Balsamon*. Translated by Patrick Viscuso. Holy Cross Orthodox Press, 2014.

Barsanuphius and John, Sts. *Letters*. Translated by John Chryssavgis. Vol. 2, Catholic University Press, 2007.

Barsov, T.V. *On Spiritual Censorship in Russia* (In Russian). Christian Reading, 1901. pp. 691-719. Accessed 23 Jan. 2023. https://azbyka. ru/otechnik/Timofej_Barsov/o-duhovnoj-tsenzure-v-rossii/.

Basil, St. *On the Spirit.* Nicene and Post-Nicene Fathers, Second Series. Vol. 8, Hendrickson Publishers, 2004.

Bede, The Venerable. *The Venerable Bede: Commentary on the Acts of the Apostles.* Translated by Lawrence Martin. Cistercian Publications, 1989.

Beek, A. van de. "Heretical Baptism in Debate." *In Die Skriflig*, vol. 43, no. 3, 2009, pp. 537-561.

Bernatsky, M.M. *Dositheus II Notar, The Encyclopedia of the Russian Orthodox Church*. Vol. 16, 2013. pp. 71-79. Accessed 23 Jan. 2023. https://www. pravenc.ru/text/180353.html.

Birchall, Christopher. *Embassy, Emigrants, and Englishmen: The Three Hundred Year History of a Russian Orthodox Church in London.* Holy Trinity Publications, 2013.

Brent, Allen, *On the Church, Select Letters of St. Cyprian of Carthage.* SVS Press, 2006.

Brianchaninov, Ignatius, St. *The Arena.* 4th ed., Holy Trinity Monastery, 1997.

Brianchaninov, Ignatius, St. *Collected Works, Vol. IV* (In Russian). Palomnik, 2002. Accessed 23 Jan. 2023. https://predanie.ru/ book/71590-asketicheskaya-propoved/.

Britannica, The Editors of Encyclopaedia. "Demetrius Cydones." *Encyclopedia Britannica*, July 28, 2020. Accessed 23 Jan. 2023. https:// www.britannica.com/biography/Demetrius-Cydones.

Britannica, The Editors of Encyclopaedia. "Maximus Planudes." *Encyclopedia Britannica*, 1 Jan. 2023. Accessed 23 Jan. 2023. https://www.britannica.com/biography/Maximus-Planudes.

Bulgakov, Macarius, Metropolitan of Moscow. *History of the Russian Church.* (In Russian) *Publishing House of the Spaso-Preobrazhen*, 1996. Accessed 23 Jan. 2023. https://azbyka.ru/otechnik/Makarij_Bulgakov/istorija-russkoj-tserkvi/.

Cabe, Benjamin. "Rebaptism: Patristic Consensus or Innovation?" *Theoria: Orthodox Christian Faith and Culture*, 27 Dec. 2022. Accessed 10 Feb. 2023. http://theoriatv.substack.com/p/rebaptism-patristic-consensus-or.

Cassian, John, St. *The Institutes*, Newman Press, 1997.

Catechism of the Council of Trent. "The Catechism of the Council of Trent On: The Sacrament of Baptism." *My Catholic Source*. Accessed 10 Feb. 2023. www.mycatholicsource.com/mcs/pc/sacraments/catechism_of_the_council_of_trent_baptism.htm.

Cavarnos, Constantine. *St. Nicodemus the Hagiorite.* 2nd ed., The Institute for Byzantine and Modern Greek Studies, Inc., 1994.

Clement of Alexandria. *Stromata*. Ante-Nicene Fathers. Vol. 2, Hendrickson Publishers, 2004.

Constitutions of the Holy Apostles. Ante-Nicene Fathers. Vol. 7, Hendrickson Publishers, 2004.

Council of Bishops of the Russian Orthodox Church Outside of Russia. "Resolution of the Council of Bishops of the Russian Orthodox Church Outside of Russia (1971)." *Orthodox Life*, vol. 29, no. 2, 1979, pp. 35-43. Accessed 10 Feb. 2023. https://www.rocorstudies.org/2017/04/04/ukaz-of-the-russian-orthodox-church-outside-of-russia-on-the-baptism-of-converts-from-the-west-1528-september-1971/.

Council of Trent. "The Council of Trent." Accessed 10 Feb. 2023. www.thecounciloftrent.com/ch7.htm.

Cowdrey, H.E.J. "The Dissemination of St. Augustine's Doctrine of Holy Orders During the Later Patristic Age." *The Journal of Theological Studies*, vol. 20, no. 2, 1969, pp. 448-481. Accessed 10 Feb. 2023. https://www.jstor.org/stable/23960143.

Cracraft, James. *The Church Reform of Peter the Great*. Stanford University Press, 1971.

Crystal, James Rev. *A History of the Modes of Christian Baptism: From Holy Scripture, the Councils Ecumenical and Provincial, the Fathers...* Philadelphia, Lindsay and Blakiston, 1861.

Cyprian of Carthage, St. *Letters*. Ante-Nicene Fathers. Vol. 5, Hendrickson Publishers, 2004.

Cyprian of Carthage, St. *Treatises*. Ante-Nicene Fathers. Vol. 5, Hendrickson Publishers, 2004.

Cyril of Jerusalem, St. *Catechetical Homilies*. SAGOM Press, 2019.

Cyril of Jerusalem, St. *Lectures on the Christian Sacraments*. St. Vladimir's Seminary Press, 1986.

Dabovich, Sebastian, St. "The True Church of Christ." *The Orthodox Word*, vol. 1, no. 5, 1965, pp. 182-187.

Damascene, Hieromonk. *Father Seraphim Rose: His Life and Works*. St. Herman of Alaska Brotherhood, *2003*.

Dragas, George. "The 8th Ecumenical Council: Constantinople IV (879/880) and the Condemnation of the Filioque Addition and Doctrine." *Orthodox Outlet for Dogmatic Enquiries (OODEGR)*, 28 Dec. 2009. Accessed 10 Feb. 2023. www.oodegr.com/english/dogma/synodoi/8th_Synod_Dragas.htm.

Dragas, George. "The Manner of Reception of Roman Catholic Converts into the Orthodox Church." *Greek Orthodox Theological Review*, vol. 44, No.1-4, 1999, pp. 235-271. Accessed 10 Feb. 2023.

http://orthodoxinfo.com/ecumenism/The-Manner-of-Reception-of-Roman-Catholic-Converts-into-the-Orthodox-Church-Fr-George-Dragas.pdf.

Drozdov, Philaret, St. *The Longer Catechism of the Eastern Orthodox Church: The Catechism of St. Philaret of Moscow*. Translated by R.W. Blackwell. Independently Published, 2000.

Elder Ephraim. *Counsels from the Holy Mountain*. St. Anthony's Greek Orthodox Monastery, 1999.

Elder Paisios of Mount Athos. *With Pain and Love for Contemporary Man*. 3rd ed., Holy Monastery "Evangelist John the Theologian," 2011.

"Encyclical of the Eastern Patriarchs, 1848." *Orthodox Christian Information Center*, orthodoxinfo.com/ecumenism/encyc_1848.aspx. Accessed 10 Feb. 2023.

Epiphanios of Salamis, St. *The Panarion of Epiphanius of Salamis, Books II and III; De FIde*. Translated by Frank Williams. 2nd ed., SBL Press, 2013.

Erickson, John H. "The Reception of Non-Orthodox into the Orthodox Church: Contemporary Practice." *St. Vladimir's Theological Quarterly*, vol. 41, 1997, pp. 1-17.

Eusebius. *The Church History of Eusebius*. Nicene and Post-Nicene Fathers, Second Series. Vol. 1, Hendrickson Publishers, 2004.

Evans, Ernest. Introduction to *De Baptismo* of Tertullian, S.P.C.K.,1964.

Ferguson, Everett. *Baptism in the Early Church: History, Theology, and Liturgy in the First Five Centuries*. Eerdmans, 2013.

Firmilian, St. "Epistle LXXIV." Ante-Nicene Fathers. Vol. 5, Hendrickson Publishers, 2004.

Florovsky, George. "The House of the Father". *Orthodox Info*. 20 Dec. 2013. Accessed 10 Feb. 2023. http://orthodoxinfo.com/general/the-house-of-the-father-florovsky.aspx.

Florovsky, Georges. "The Limits of the Church." *Ancient Faith*, 28 Jun. 2012. Accessed 10 Feb. 2023. https://blogs. ancientfaith.com/orthodoxyandheterodoxy/2012/06/28/ the-limits-of-the-church-by-fr-georges-florovsky/.

Florovsky, George. "On the Church, Theological Articles of Fr. George Florovsky, Vol. 4." *Holy Trinity Mission*. Accessed 10 Feb. 2023. www. holytrinitymission.org/books/english/theology_church_florovsky_e. htm.

Florovsky, Georges. *Ways of Russian Theology*. Nordland Pub Intl, 1978. Accessed 10 Feb. 2023. http://www.holytrinitymission.org/books/ english/ways_russian_theology_florovsky.htm.

Ford, David. "St. Photios the Great, the Photian Council, and Relations with the Roman Church." *Orthodox Christianity*, 18 Oct. 2016. Accessed 10 Feb. 2023. https://orthochristian.com/97929.html.

Frend, W.H.C. *Saints and Sinners in the Early Church*. Darton, Longman and Todd, 1985.

Golitzin, Alexander. *The Living Witness of the Holy Mountain: Contemporary Voices from Mount Athos*. 2nd ed., St. Tikhon's Seminary Press, 1999.

Gotsopoulos, Anastasios, Protopresbyter. *On Common Prayer with the Heterodox*. Uncut Mountain Press, 2022.

Grabbe, Bishop Gregory. *Canons of the Orthodox Church* (In Russian). Holy Trinity Orthodox Mission, 2001. Accessed 10 Feb. 2023. https:// azbyka.ru/otechnik/pravila/kanony-pravoslavnoj-tserkvi-grabbe/.

Grabbe, George, Protopresbyter. "Strictness and Economy: Resolution of the ROCA Synod of Bishops on the Reception of Converts." *Orthodox Life*, vol. 29, No. 2, 1979, pp. 35-43. Accessed 10 Feb. 2023. http:// orthodoxinfo.com/ecumenism/strictness.aspx.

Grassos, Alexandra M. *The Church Fathers on Love in Truth*. Translated by Constantine Zalalas. Orthodox Kypseli Publications, 2000.

Gregory the Great, St. "Letter from Pope St. Gregory I to Catholicos Kirion I," translated from Russian. *VK.com*, 23 May 2020. Accessed 10 Feb. 2023. https://vk.com/@12581929-pismo-papy-grigoriya-i-katolikosu-kirionu-i.

Gregory the Theologian, St. "Orations." Nicene and Post-Nicene Fathers, Second Series. Vol. 7, Hendrickson Publishers, 2004.

Gregorios, Hieromonk. *The Orthodox Faith, Worship, and Life: Orthodox Catechism an Outline*, Newrome Press. 2020.

Heers, Peter, Protopresbyter. *The Ecclesiological Renovation of Vatican II: An Orthodox Examination of Rome's Ecumenical Theology Regarding Baptism and the Church*. 1st ed., Uncut Mountain Press, 2015.

Heers, Protopresbyter Peter. "St. Nikodemos, the Rudder and the Reception of Converts into the Orthodox Church: A Look at the Correspondence Between the Kollyvades Fathers & Dorotheos Voulismas." The Orthodox Ethos. Accessed 9 May 2023. https://www.orthodoxethos.com/post/st-nikodemos-the-rudder-and-the-receptionof-converts-into-the-orthodox-church.

Heppell, Muriel (translator). *The Paterik of the Kievan Caves Monastery*. Vol. 1, Harvard University, 1989.

Holy Apostles Convent and Dormition Skete. *The Great Synaxaristes of the Orthodox Church (July, August)*. Holy Apostles Convent, 2008.

Holy Hesychasterion "Evangelist John the Theologian." *Saint Paisios the Athonite*. Translated by Peter Chamberas. 1st ed., Holy Hesychasterion "Evangelist John the Theologian," 2015.

Holy Monastery of Panagia Chrysopodaritissa of Nezeron. *The Kollyvades and Dorotheos Voulismas: The Case of the Examination of the Pedalion and the Canonikon*. Holy Monastery of Panagia Chrysopodaritissa of Nezeron, 2020.

Ignatius of Antioch, St. "Epistle to the Philadelphians." Ante-Nicene Fathers. Vol. 1, Hendrickson Publishers, 2004.

Irenaeus of Lyons, St. *Against Heresies.* Ante-Nicene Fathers. Vol. 1, Hendrickson Publishers, 2004.

Isaac, Hieromonk. *Elder Paisios of Mount Athos.* Translated by Hieromonk Alexis (Trader) and Fr. Peter Heers. Holy Monastery "Saint Arsenios the Cappadocian," 2012.

Jerome, St. *The Dialogue Against the Luciferians.* Nicene and Post-Nicene Fathers, Second Series. Vol. 6, Hendrickson Publishers, 2004.

John Chrysostom, St. *Homilies on Ephesians.* Nicene and Post-Nicene Fathers, First Series. Vol. 13, Hendrickson Publishers, 2004.

John of Damascus, St. *An Exact Exposition of the Orthodox Faith.* Nicene and Post-Nicene Fathers, Second Series. Vol. 9, Hendrickson Publishers, 2004.

John of Shanghai and San Francisco, St. "A Discourse in Iconography by St. John of Shanghai and San Francisco." *The Catalogue of Good Deeds*, 25 Mar. 2017. Accessed 10 Feb. 2023. http://catalog.obitel-minsk.com/blog/2017/03/a-discourse-in-iconography-by-st-john.

John of Shanghai and San Francisco, St. *Sermons & Writings of Saint John Archbishop of Shanghai and San Francisco, Book 3.* Holy Dormition Sisterhood, 2004.

Justinianeus, Codex. "Why I Don't Support Re-Baptism." *Ancient Insights*, 4 Feb. 2021, ancientinsights.wordpress.com/2021/02/04/why-i-dont-support-re-baptism/. Accessed 10 Feb. 2023.

Kadloubowsky, E., and G. E. H. Palmer. *Writings from the Philokalia: On Prayer of the Heart.* Vol. 2, Faber & Faber, 1992.

Kavelin, Leonid. *Elder Macarius of Optina.* Translated by Valentina V. Lyovina. St. Herman of Alaska Brotherhood, 1996.

Kazhdan, Alexander P (editor). *The Oxford Dictionary of Byzantium.* Vol. 3, Oxford University Press, 1991.

King, J.R. *Writings in Connection with the Donatist Controversy*. Nicene and Post-Nicene Fathers, First Series. Vol. 4, Hendrickson Publishers, 2004.

Kohanik, Peter G. *The Most Useful Knowledge for the Orthodox Russian-American Young People*. Orthodox Life. Vol. 43, No. 6, 1993.

Krestiankin, John, Elder. "'One Faith, One Baptism, One God and Father of All': Archimandrite John Krestyankin on the Heresy of Catholicism." *Inform-Religion*. Accessed 10 Feb. 2023. www.inform-relig.ru/news/detail.php?ID=13989&sphrase_id=16013493.

Krivoshein, Vasily, Archbishop. *Symbolic Texts in the Orthodox Church* (In Russian). Christian Library, 2011. Accessed 10 Feb. 2023. https://azbyka.ru/otechnik/Vasilij_Krivoshein/simvolicheskie-teksty-v-pravoslavnoj-tserkvi/.

Leo the Great, St. "Letter XVI"; "Letter CLIX." Nicene and Post-Nicene Fathers, Second Series. Vol. 12, Hendrickson Publishers, 2004.

Local Council of 1620. "Local Council of 1620" (In Russian). *Dishupravoslaviem*. Accessed 10 Feb. 2023. http://dishupravoslaviem.ru/pomestnyj-sobor-1620-g-moskovskij/.

Luke, Archbishop of Simferopol and Crimea, St. "Decrees of St. Luke Voyno-Yasenetsky" (In Russian). Pravmir. Accessed 8 May 2023. https://lib.pravmir.ru/library/readbook/2279.

Makarios, Hieromonk. "The Life of Our Holy Monastic Father Maximus the Confessor and Martyr." *The Synaxarion: The Lives of the Saints of the Orthodox Church*, vol. 3. Sebastian Press, 1999.

Mansi. Vol. XII, *Proceedings of the Holy Œcumenical Synods* [in Greek], ed. Spyridon Melias, vol. I Holy Mountain: Kalyve of the Venerable Forerunner Publications, 1981.

Mark of Ephesus, St. "Address of St. Mark of Ephesus on the Day of His Death." *The Orthodox Word*, vol. 3, no. 3, 1966, pp. 103-106.

Mark of Ephesus, St. "The Encyclical of St. Mark of Ephesus." *The Orthodox Word*, vol. 3, no. 2, 1967, pp. 53-59. Accessed

10 Feb. 2023. https://www.orthodoxethos.com/post/ the-encyclical-letter-of-saint-mark-of-ephesus.

Marushchak, Vasiliy, Archdeacon. *The Blessed Surgeon: The Life of Saint Luke Archbishop of Simferopol.* 2nd ed. Divine Ascent Press, 2008.

Mary, Mother, and Ware, Kallistos, Archimandrite. *The Lenten Triodion*, St. Tikhon's Seminary Press, 2001.

Maximos the Confessor, St. *On Difficulties in Sacred Scripture: The Responses to Thalassios.* Translated by Fr. Maximos Constas. The Catholic University of America Press, 2018.

McGuckin, J.A. *Illumined in the Spirit: Studies in Orthodox Spirituality.* St. Vladimir's Seminary Press, 2014.

Medieval Sourcebook, "Twelfth Ecumenical Council: Lateran IV 1215." Fordham University. Accessed 16 May 2023. https://sourcebooks. fordham.edu/basis/lateran4.asp.

Metallinos, George. *I Confess One Baptism...* 1st ed., St. Paul's Monastery, Holy Mountain, Athos, 1994. Accessed 10 Feb. 2023. https://www. oodegr.com/english/biblia/baptisma1/perieh.htm.

Metrophanes, Schema-monk. *Blessed Paisius Velichkovsky: The Man Behind the Philokalia.* Translated by Fr. Seraphim Rose. Saint Paisius Abbey, 1994.

Meyendorff, Paul. *Russia, Ritual, and Reform.* St. Vladimir's Seminary Press, 1991.

Meyendorf, Paul. "Toward Mutual Recognition of Baptism," *in Baptism Today: Understanding, Practice, Ecumenical Implications*, Thomas Best, Editor, WCC-Liturgical Press, 2008.

Milas, Nikodim. *Rules of the Holy Apostles and Ecumenical Councils with Interpretations* (In Russian). Otchiy Dom Publishing House, 2001. Accessed 10 Feb. 2023. https://azbyka.ru/otechnik/Nikodim_Milash/ pravila-svjatyh-apostolov-i-vselenskih-soborov-s-tolkovanijami/.

Milas, Nikodim, Bishop. *Rules of the Orthodox Church with Interpretations of Bishop Nicodemus of Dalmatia-Istria* (In Russian). St. Petersburg Spiritual Academy, 1912. Accessed 10 Feb. 2023. https://azbyka.ru/otechnik/Nikodim_Milash/pravila-svjatyh-ottsov-pravoslavnoj-tserkvi-s-tolkovanijami/.

Minnich, Nelson H. *The Decrees of the Fifth Lateran Council (1512–17): Their Legitimacy, Origins, Contents, and Implementation.* Routledge, 2016.

Moore, Lazarus, Fr. *An Extraordinary Peace: St. Seraphim, Flame of Sarov.* Anaphora Press, 2009

Moschos, John. *The Spiritual Meadow.* Translated by John Wortley. Cistercian Publications, 1992.

Munier, Charles. *Concilia Galliae a.314-a.506. Turnholti, Typographi Brepols Editores* Pontificii, 1963. Accessed 10 Feb. 2023. https://archive.org/details/conciliagalliaea0000muni, https://www.fourthcentury.com/arles-314-canons/.

Neophytos of Morphou, "The 3 crowns of Elder Ephraim and how the U.S. will lose its superpower status" YouTube. Accessed 10 Feb. 2023. https://www.youtube.com/watch?v=Wk19mMAx9vU.

"Nikodemos, the Rudder and the Reception of Converts into the Orthodox Church: A Look at the Correspondence Between the Kollyvades Fathers & Dorotheos Voulismas." *YouTube,* uploaded by Orthodox Ethos, 1 Feb. 2022, youtu.be/7CkYHymiSgU.

"Nikodim Milas - Bishop." *Serb National Council,* 2 Feb. 2022, snv.hr/en/znameniti-srbi/nikodim-milas-episkop/. Accessed 10 Feb. 2023.

North American Orthodox-Catholic Theological Consultation. "Baptism and 'Sacramental Economy' An Agreed Statement of the North American Orthodox-Catholic Theological Consultation, St. Vladimir's Seminar, June 3, 1999." *Assembly of Canonical Orthodox Bishops of the United States of America.* Accessed 10 Feb. 2023. www.assemblyofbishops.org/ministries/ecumenical-and-interfaith-dialogues/orthodox-catholic/baptism-and-sacramental-economy-an-agreed-statement-of-the-north-american-orthodox-catholictheological-consultation-saint-vladimirs-orthodox-seminary-june-3-1999 .

Novoselov, St. Mikhail Alexandrovich Novoselov. "Understanding the Important Distinction between Church-Organism vs. Church Organization." The Orthodox Ethos. Accessed 9 May 2023. https://www.orthodoxethos.com/post/understanding-the-important-distinction-between-church-organism-vs-church-organization.

Ogorodnik, Elena. "Perfect Baptism of 'Imperfect in the Faith': What Is the 'Epistle of the Eastern Patriarchs' Really Talking About?" (In Russian) Pravoslavie, 3 Apr. 2019. Accessed 10 Feb. 2023. http://pravoslavie.ru/120312.html .

"On the Abolition of Oaths to Old Rites" *Report of Metropolitan of Leningrad and Novgorod Nicodemus at the Local Council on May 31, 1971.* Accessed 10 May 2023. https://azbyka.ru/otechnik/dokumenty/ob-otmene-kljatv-na-starye-obrjady/.

Optatus of Milevis. *Against the Donatists*. 1917. Accessed 10 Feb. 2023. https://www.tertullian.org/fathers/optatus_05_book5.htm. Accessed 15 Mar. 2023.

Optina Pustyn. "Blessed Optina" (In Russian). Optina Pustyn. Accessed 10 Feb. 2023. https://www.optina.ru/history/optina/.

Optina Pustyn. "Correspondence of St. Ignatius (Brianchaninov) with the Optina Elders and Other Fathers and Brothers of the Optina Hermitage" (In Russian). Optina Pustyn. Accessed 10 Feb. 2023. www.optina.ru/starets/ignatiy_letters/.

Optina Pustyn. "History of the Monastery" (In Russian). Optina Pustyn. Accessed 10 Feb. 2023. www.optina.ru/history/optina/2#3.

Ostroumoff, Ivan. *The History of the Council of Florence*. Translated by Basil Popoff. Holy Transfiguration Monastery, 1970.

Palamas, Gregory, St. *Saint Gregory Palamas: The Homilies*. Translated by Christopher Veniamin. 2nd ed., Mount Thabor Publishing, 2016.

Palamas, Gregory, St. *The Triads: In Defense of Those Who Practice Sacred Quietude.* Translated by Fr. Peter A. Chamberas. Newfound Publishing, 2021.

Palmer, G.E.H., et al. *The Philokalia: The Complete Text.* Vol. 1, Faber & Faber, 1979.

Pelikan, Jaroslav. *The Emergence of the Catholic Tradition (100-600),* in the series *The Christian Tradition, A History of the Development of Doctrine.* The University of Chicago Press, 1971.

Photios, St. *The Mystagogy of the Holy Spirit.* Translated by Joseph P. Farrell. Holy Cross Orthodox Press, 1987.

Pogodin, Ambrosius, Archimandrite. "On the Question of the Order of Reception of Persons into the Orthodox Church, Coming to Her from Other Christian Churches." Vestnik Russkogo Khristianskogo Dvizheniya, no. 173-174, 1996. Accessed 10 Feb. 2023. https://holy-trinity.org/ecclesiology/pogodin-reception/reception-ch0.html.

Popovic, Justin, St. *The Orthodox Church and Ecumenism.* Translated by Benjamin Stanley. Lazarica Press, 2000.

Popovich, Justin, St. *Orthodox Faith & Life in Christ.* Translated by Asterios Gerostergios. Institute for Byzantine & Modern Greek Studies, 1994.

Porphyrios, Elder. *Wounded by Love.* Translated by John Raffan. Denise Harvey, 2005.

Raheb, Abdallah, Archimandrite. *Conception of the Union in the Orthodox Patriarchate of Antioch.* Abdallah Raheb, 1981. Accessed 10 Feb. 2023. https://phoenicia.org/orthodox-antioch-union.html.

Ramsey, John (Patrick). "Canon 95 - Council of Trullo." Academia. Accessed 10 Feb. 2023. www.academia.edu/36579829/Canon_95_Council_of_Trullo.

Robertson, J.N.W.B. *The Acts and Decrees of The Synod of Jerusalem: Sometimes Called The Council of Bethlehem Holden Under Dositheus, Patriarch of Jerusalem in 1672.* Thomas Baker, 1899.

ROCOR Synod of Bishops. "Decision of the Council of Bishops of the ROCOR Concerning the Old Ritual." ROCOR Studies. Accessed 10 Feb. 2023. www.rocorstudies.org/2015/02/27/the-decision-of-the-council-of-bishops-of-the-rocor-concerning-the-old-ritual/.

Romanides, John S., Protopresbyter. *The Cure of the Neurobiological Sickness of Religion*. Romanity. Accessed 9 May 2023. http://romanity.org/htm/rom.02.en.the_cure_of_the_neurobiological_sickness_of_rel.01.htm#s5

Romanides, John S., Protopresbyter. *Franks, Romans, Feudalism, and Doctrine*. Romanity. Accessed 10 Feb. 2023. http://romanity.org/htm/rom.03.en.franks_romans_feudalism_and_doctrine.02.htm.

Romanides, John S., Protopresbyter. *Patristic Theology*. Uncut Mountain Press, 2008.

Rose, Seraphim, Fr. *Letters from Father Seraphim*. Nikodemos Orthodox Publication Society, 2008.

Rose, Seraphim, Fr. *The Place of Blessed Augustine in the Orthodox Church*. Saint Herman of Alaska Brotherhood, 1996.

Runciman, Steven. *The Great Church in Captivity: A Study of The Patriarchate of Constantinople from the Eve of the Turkish Conquest to the Greek War of Independence*. 1st ed., Cambridge University Press, 1968.

Russian Faith. "Acts of the Consecrated Council of the Russian Old Orthodox Church, Held on April 10-13 (23-26) N.St. 2015" (In Russian). Russian Faith, 29 Apr. 2015. Accessed 10 Feb. 2023. http://ruvera.ru/articles/deyaniya_rdc_23_26_aprelya.

Russian Faith. "Was the Great Moscow Cathedral of 1666-67 Heretical? Part 1." Russian Faith, 24 Jun. 2015, http://ruvera.ru/articles/bolshoiy_moskovskiy_sobor_disput_1. Accessed 13 Feb. 2023.

"Saint Auxentios the Ascetic in Kartilio." Saint.Gr. Accessed 10 Feb. 2023. www.saint.gr/3708/saint.aspx.

Sakharov, Sophrony, St. *Saint Silouan the Athonite*. Translated by Rosemary Edmonds. 1st ed., St. Vladimir's Seminary Press, 1999.

Sakharov, Sophrony, St. *Striving for Knowledge of God: Correspondence with David Balfour*. Translated by Sister Magdalen. Stavropegic Monastery of St. John the Baptist, 2016.

"Second Council of Lyons – 1274." Papal Encyclicals Online. Accessed 10 Feb. 2023. www.papalencyclicals.net/councils/ecum14.htm.

Sederholm, Clement. *Elder Leonid of Optina*. 2nd ed., St. Herman of Alaska Brotherhood, 2002.

Seraphim, Archbishop of Sofia, St. *Orthodox Teaching About Grace* (In Russian). Sviato-Troitskiĭ Novo-Goluvtin Monastyr', 1951. Accessed 10 Feb. 2023. https://azbyka.ru/otechnik/Serafim_Sobolev/pravoslavnoe-uchenie-o-blagodati/.

"Service to Holy Hieromartyr Hilarion (Troitsky) of Verey". Translated by Isaac E. Lambertsen. Orthodox Christianity, 9 May 2012. Accessed 30 March 2023. https://orthochristian.com/53416.html.

Snychev, John, Metropolitan. "The Life of Hieromartyr Hilarion (Troitsky), Archbishop of Verey". Orthodox Christianity, 20 May 2012. Accessed 1 April 2023. https://orthochristian.com/33316.html.

"St. Theophan the Recluse Adopted an Ecumenistic Ecclesiology?". The Orthodox Ethos. Accessed 10 May 2023. https://orthodoxethos.com/post/st-theophan-the-recluse-adopted-an-ecumenistic-ecclesiology.

Stavitskaya, Nina. "St. Ignatius (Brianchaninov) and Optina Hermitage." Optina Pustyn. Accessed 10 Feb. 2023. www.optina.ru/19_svjatitel_ignatij_lect/.

Sozomen. *Ecclesiastical History*. Nicene and Post-Nicene Fathers, Second Series. Vol. 2, Hendrickson Publishers, 2004.

Sursky, I.K. *Saint John of Kronstadt*. Translated by Holy Transfiguration Monastery. Holy Transfiguration Monastery, 2018.

Sysoev, Daniel. *Catechetical Talks*. Translated by Nathan Williams. The Rev. Daniel Sysoev Missionary Center Benevolent Fund, 2014.

Sysoev, Daniel. *Letters*. Translated by Nathan Williams. Daniel Sysoev Inc., 2022.

Teaching of the Twelve Apostles. Ante-Nicene Fathers. Vol. 7, Hendrickson Publishers, 2004.

Tertullian. *The Chaplet, or De Corona*. Ante-Nicene Fathers. Vol. 3, Hendrickson Publishers, 2004.

Tertullian. *On Baptism*. Ante-Nicene Fathers. Vol. 3, Hendrickson Publishers, 2004.

"The 3 Crowns of Elder Ephraim and How the U.S. Will Lose Its Superpower Status." *YouTube*, uploaded by Orthodox Teaching of the Elders, 5 Nov. 2021, www.youtube.com/watch?v=Wk19mMAx9vU.

Theodore the Studite, St. *Epistles* (In Russian). Accessed 9 May 2023. https://azbyka.ru/otechnik/Feodor_Studit/poslania/40.

Theodore the Studite, St. *The Works of Saint Theodore the Studite*, Vol. II. (In Russian). St. Petersburg, 1908.

Theophan the Recluse, St. *Collection of Letters of St. Theophan* (In Russian). Athos Russian St. Panteleimon Monastery, 1899. pp. 201-202. Accessed 10 Feb. 2023. http://pagez.ru/olb/feofan1/1181.php.

Theophan the Recluse, St. *Preaching Another Christ: An Orthodox View of Evangelicalism*. Translated by Dr. Dimitri Kagaris. Orthodox Witness, 2011.

Theophan the Recluse, St. *Thoughts for Each Day of the Year*. St. Herman of Alaska Brotherhood, 2010.

Theophylact, Blessed, *The Explanation of the Epistle of Saint Paul to the Galatians*. Chrysostom Press, 2011.

Theophylact, Blessed. *The Explanation by Blessed Theophylact of the Holy Gospel According to St. Matthew*. Translated by Fr. Christopher Stade. Chrysostom Press, 2000.

Thornton, James. *The OEcumenical Synods of the Orthodox Church: A Concise History*. Center for Traditionalist Orthodox Studies, 2007.

Touloumtsis, Basil I. *The Ecclesiological Framework and Presuppositions of Reception of Heretics According to the Minutes of the Seventh Ecumenical Council*. Kypris Publications, 2020.

Townsend, John. *The Holy and Righteous King David the Restorer of Georgia & The Holy and Righteous Queen Tamar of Georgia: Lives, Akathist, Canons, Works*. Creative Angel Publishing, 2021.

Trenham, Josiah, Protopresbyter. *Rock and Sand: An Orthodox Appraisal of the Protestant Reformers and Their Teachings*. New Rome Press, 2015.

Triandaphillopoulos, Ephraim, Archimandrite. *Noetic Prayer as the Basis of Mission and the Struggle Against Ecumenism*. Uncut Mountain Press, 2022.

Troitsky, Hilarion, St. *On the Dogma of the Church: An Historical Overview of the Sources of Ecclesiology*. Uncut Mountain Press, 2022.

Troitsky, Hilarion, St. "The Unity of the Church and the World Council of Churches." ROCOR Studies, 13 Apr. 2020. Accessed 10 Feb. 2023. www.rocorstudies.org/2020/04/13/the-unity-of-the-church-and-the-world-conference-of-christian-communities/.

Vaporis, Nomikos M. *Father Kosmas The Apostle of the Poor*. Holy Cross Orthodox Press, 1977.

Vincent of Lerins, St. *The Commonitory*. Nicene and Post-Nicene Fathers, Second Series. Vol. 11, Hendrickson Publishers, 2004.

Vlachos, "Baptismal Theology" *Ekklesiastike Parembase*, No. 71 (December 2001), 12. Reprinted from Orthodox Tradition, Vol XX, No 2. Accessed 10 May 2023. http://orthodoxinfo.com/ecumenism/methierotheos_baptism.aspx.

Vlachos, Hierotheos, Metropolitan of Nafpaktos and Agios Vlasios. *Empirical Dogmatics of the Orthodox Catholic Church: According to the Spoken Teaching of Father John Romanides*. Translated by Sister Pelagia Selfe. 2nd ed., Vol. 2, Birth of the Theotokos Monastery, 2011.

Vlachos, Hierotheos, Metropolitan of Nafpaktos and Agios Vlasios. *Hesychia and Theology: The Context for Man's Healing in the Orthodox Church*. Translated by Sister Pelagia Selfe. 1st ed., Birth of the Theotokos Monastery, 2007.

Vlachos, Hierotheos, Metropolitan of Nafpaktos and Agios Vlasios. *Orthodox Monasticism As the Way of Life of Prophets, Apostles and Martyrs*. Translated by Sister Pelagia Selfe. 1st ed., Birth of the Theotokos Monastery, 2011.

Vlachos, Hierotheos, Metropolitan of Nafpaktos and Agios Vlasios. *Saint Gregory Palamas As A Hagiorite*. Translated by Esther Williams. 1st ed., Birth of the Theotokos Monastery, 1997.

Vlachos, Hierotheos, Metropolitan of Nafpaktos and Agios Vlasios. *Science of Spiritual Medicine: Orthodox Psychotherapy in Action*. Translated by Sister Pelagia Selfe. 1st ed., Birth of the Theotokos Monastery, 2010.

Ware, Kallistos, Metropolitan. *Eustratios Argenti: A Study of the Greek Church under Turkish Rule*. 2014 ed., Wipf & Stock, 1964.

Ware, Timothy. *The Orthodox Church*. Penguin Books, 1997.

Will, C. "A Brief or Succinct Account of What the Ambassadors of the Holy Roman and Apostolic See Did in the Royal City attributed to Cardinal Bishop Humbert of Silva Candida." Translated from the Latin by W. L. North from the edition of C. Will, Acta et Scripta Quae de Controversiis Ecclesiae Graecae et Latinae Saeculo Undecimo Composita Extant, Leipzig & Marburg 1861, Documents VIII-X, pp. 150-4. Accessed 10 May 2023. https://acad.carleton.edu/curricular/MARS/Schism.pdf.

Willis, Geoffrey Grimshaw. *Saint Augustine and the Donatist Controversy*. Wipf and Stock, 2005, reprint of 1950 edition by SPCK, London.

Women's Monastery of the Protection of the Most-Holy Theotokos. "Archbishop Seraphim of Bulgaria." Russian Orthodox Cathedral of St. John the Baptist. Accessed 10 Feb. 2023. https://stjohndc.org/en/orthodoxy-foundation/saints/archbishop-seraphim-bulgaria.

World Council of Churches. *Baptism, Eucharist and Ministry.* World Council of Churches, 1982. Accessed 10 Feb. 2023. https://www.oikoumene.org/sites/default/files/Document/FO1982_111_en.pdf.

Yakovlev, Vladislav. "Sacramental Rigourism: Tradition or Modern Phenomenon?" Arche-Athanatos, 22 Nov. 2021. Accessed 10 Feb. 2023.   https://arche-athanatos.com/2021/11/22/sacramental-rigourism-tradition-or-modern-phenomenon/ .

Yevtich, Athanasius, Bishop of Zahumlje and Herzegovina. "Fr. George Florovsky on The Boundaries of the Church." THEOLOGIA («Θεολογία), vol. 4, 2010. Accessed 10 Feb. 2023.   https://www.orthodoxethos.com/post/fr-george-florovsky-on-the-boundaries-of-the-church.

Zadornov, Alexander. "Church Censorship: Past and Prospects" (In Russian). Bogoslov, 29 Jun. 2008. Accessed 10 Feb. 2023. https://bogoslov.ru/article/305703.

Zernov, Nicolas. *The Russians and Their Church.* St. Vladimir's Seminary Press, 1978. Accessed 10 Feb. 2023. http://www.holytrinitymission.org/books/english/russians_and_church_n_zernov.htm.

Zizioulas, John D., *Being as Communion, Studies in Personhood and the Church.* Crestwood: St. Vladimir's Seminary Press, 1993.

Zizioulas, John, Metropolitan of Pergamus. *Eucharist, Bishop, Church: The Unity of the Church in the Divine Eucharist and the Bishop During the First Three Centuries.* Holy Cross Orthodox Press, 2001. Accessed 10 Feb. 2023.   https://www.oodegr.com/english/biblia/episkopos1/perieh.htm.

INDEX OF NAMES

A

B

V

Z

UNCUT MOUNTAIN PRESS TITLES

Books by Archpriest Peter Heers

Fr. Peter Heers, *The Ecclesiological Renovation of Vatican II: An Orthodox Examination of Rome's Ecumenical Theology Regarding Baptism and the Church*, 2015

Fr. Peter Heers, *The Missionary Origins of Modern Ecumenism: Milestones Leading up to 1920*, 2007

The Works of our Father Among the Saints, Nikodemos the Hagiorite

Vol. 1: *Exomologetarion: A Manual of Confession*

Vol. 2: *Concerning Frequent Communion of the Immaculate Mysteries of Christ*

Vol. 3: *Confession of Faith*

Other Available Titles

Elder Cleopa of Romania, *The Truth of Our Faith*

Elder Cleopa of Romania, *The Truth of Our Faith, Vol. II*

Fr. John Romanides, *Patristic Theology: The University Lectures of Fr. John Romanides*

Demetrios Aslanidis and Monk Damascene Grigoriatis, *Apostle to Zaire: The Life and Legacy of Blessed Father Cosmas of Grigoriou*

Robert Spencer, *The Church and the Pope*

G. M. Davis, *Antichrist: The Fulfillment of Globalization*

Athonite Fathers of the 20th Century, Vol. I

St. Gregory Palamas, *Apodictic Treatises on the Procession of the Holy Spirit*

St. Hilarion Troitsky, *On the Dogma of the Church: An Historical Overview of the Sources of Ecclesiology*

Fr. Alexander Webster and Fr. Peter Heers, Editors, *Let No One Fear Death*

Subdeacon Nektarios Harrison, *Metropolitan Philaret of New York*

Elder George of Grigoriou, *Catholicism in the Light of Orthodoxy*

Protopresbyter Anastasios K. Gotsopoulos, *On Common Prayer with the Heterodox According to the Canons of the Church*

Archimandrite Ephraim Triandaphillopoulos, *Noetic Prayer as the Basis of Mission and the Struggle Against Heresy*

Dr. Nicholas Baldimtsis, *Life and Witness of St. Iakovos of Evia*

Select Forthcoming Titles

The Orthodox Patristic Witness Concerning Catholicism

Georgio, *Errors of the Latins*

Fr. Peter Heers, *Going Deeper in the Spiritual Life*

Abbe Guette, *The Papacy*

Athonite Fathers of the 20th Century, Vol. II

Patrick (Craig) Truglia, *The Rise and Fall of the Papacy: An Orthodox Perspective*

Dn. Matthew Keil, *St Ephraim the Syrian: The Complete Greek Texts*

St. Hilarion Troitsky, Collected Works, Vol. II

This 1ˢᵗ Edition of

ON THE RECEPTION OF THE HETERODOX INTO THE ORTHODOX CHURCH:
The Patristic Consensus and Criteria

an Orthodox Ethos publication, with a cover design by George Weis, typeset in Baskerville printed in this two thousand and twenty third year of our Lord's Holy Incarnation, is one of the many fine titles available from Uncut Mountain Press, translators and publishers of Orthodox Christian theological and spiritual literature. Find the book you are looking for at

uncutmountainpress.com

**GLORY BE TO GOD
FOR ALL THINGS**

AMEN.

Printed in the USA
CPSIA information can be obtained
at www.ICGtesting.com
LVHW050026260823
756256LV00014B/329/J

9 781639 410279